T0214853

Communications in Computer and Information Science 886

Commenced Publication in 2007
Founding and Former Series Editors:
Phoebe Chen, Alfredo Cuzzocrea, Xiaoyong Du, Orhun Kara, Ting Liu,
Dominik Ślęzak, and Xiaokang Yang

More information about this series at http://www.springer.com/series/7899

Natrah Abdullah · Wan Adilah Wan Adnan
Marcus Foth (Eds.)

User Science and Engineering

5th International Conference, i-USEr 2018
Puchong, Malaysia, August 28–30, 2018
Proceedings

 Springer

Editors
Natrah Abdullah
Universiti Teknologi MARA
Shah Alam
Malaysia

Wan Adilah Wan Adnan
Universiti Teknologi MARA
Shah Alam
Malaysia

Marcus Foth
Queensland University of Technology
Brisbane, QLD
Australia

ISSN 1865-0929   ISSN 1865-0937 (electronic)
Communications in Computer and Information Science
ISBN 978-981-13-1627-2   ISBN 978-981-13-1628-9 (eBook)
https://doi.org/10.1007/978-981-13-1628-9

Library of Congress Control Number: 2018948811

This Springer imprint is published by the registered company Springer Nature Singapore Pte Ltd.
The registered company address is: 152 Beach Road, #21-01/04 Gateway East, Singapore 189721, Singapore

Preface

i-USEr 2018 (International Conference on User Science and Engineering) is a biennial conference that began its journey as a brainchild of a group of HCI enthusiasts and researchers from the Universiti Teknologi MARA Malaysia. It serves as a platform for practitioners and researchers from academia, industry, and government agencies to share their research insights and innovations within the field of human–computer interaction (HCI) and user experience (UX).

This year's conference celebrated the growth of the HCI field, which traversed across disciplines and technological aspects encompassing both tangible and intangible elements. The papers this year illustrate how HCI is inclusive and omnipresent within the domains of informatics, Internet of Everywhere, quality of life and others, more so with a diverse range of users and possibilities. The discussions brought forth by the papers further prove that the marriage between HCI and various application domains has resulted in a variety of user requirements, needs, and experiences, converting to ever-changing symbiotic conditions. Hence, it is only fitting that this year's theme was "Traverse for Diverse."

This year, i-USEr received a high number of submissions. With a thorough double-blind review process, 32 papers of high quality were selected for presentation as full papers. This volume contains 32 full papers presented at i-USEr 2018.

To further celebrate i-USEr 2018, we invited globally recognized keynote speakers and organized workshops to give opportunities for participants to put traverse to diverse as a form of practice. We believe i-USEr 2018 could further position HCI as a humane-technological-experience design and development strategy discipline but this would not be possible without the trust and participation of the authors who chose i-USEr 2018 as a venue for their publications. Some of the authors have been with us since our infancy – thank you all for the support. Also, my utmost gratitude to the committee members for their unwavering commitment in ensuring i-USEr 2018 was a success.

We hope you find the proceedings compelling and thought-provoking, further inspiring ever more revolutionary research at the future. We hope to have your participation again at the next i-USEr 2020. Here's to the future of human-centered experience. Let's make it happen!

July 2018   Natrah Abdullah

Organization

i-USEr 2018 was organized by the Technical Committee of the Faculty of Computer and Mathematical Sciences, Universiti Teknologi MARA, Shah Alam, Selangor, Malaysia, and co-organized by the International Islamic University, Malaysia, Universiti Teknologi Malaysia, Universiti Utara Malaysia, and Malaysian Global Innovation and Creative Centre (MAGIC).

Organizing Committee

Patron

Hassan Said   Universiti Teknologi MARA, Malaysia

Advisors

Azlinah Hj Mohamed   Universiti Teknologi MARA, Malaysia
Abdul Wahab Abdul   International Islamic University, Malaysia
  Rahman
Wan Adilah Wan Adnan   Universiti Teknologi MARA, Malaysia

Founding Chair

Nor Laila Md Noor   Universiti Teknologi MARA, Malaysia

General Chair

Natrah Abdullah   Universiti Teknologi MARA, Malaysia

Co-chairs

Murni Mahmud   International Islamic University, Malaysia
Masitah Ghazali   Universiti Teknologi Malaysia, Malaysia
Torkil Clemenson   Copenhegan Business School, Denmark

Co-chair (Finance)

Fariza Hanis Abdul Razak   Universiti Teknologi MARA, Malaysia

Co-chair (Operations)

Nurulhuda Noordin   Universiti Teknologi MARA, Malaysia

Program Chairs

Wan Adilah Wan Adnan   Universiti Teknologi MARA, Malaysia
Afdallyna Fathiyah Harun   Universiti Teknologi MARA, Malaysia

Program Committee

Abdul Rahman Ahmad Dahlan	International Islamic University Malaysia, Malaysia
Afdallyna Fathiyah Harun	Universiti Teknologi MARA, Malaysia
Ahmad Iqbal Hakim Suhaimi	Universiti Teknologi MARA, Malaysia
Aliimran Nordin	Universiti Kebangsaan Malaysia, Malaysia
Alipta Ballav	Cerner Healthcare Solutions Private Ltd., India
Amitkumar Manekar	Shri Sant Gajanan Maharaj College of Engineering, India
Anitawati Mohd Lokman	Universiti Teknologi MARA, Malaysia
Ariffin Abdul Mutalib	Universiti Utara Malaysia, Malaysia
Ashutosh Kumar Dubey	Jk Lakshmipat University, India
Azhar Abd Aziz	Universiti Teknologi MARA, Malaysia
Azlan Ismail	Universiti Teknologi MARA, Malaysia
Azrina Kamaruddin	Universiti Putra Malaysia, Malaysia
Carina Gonzalez-González	Universidad de La Laguna, Spain
Carsten Röcker	Fraunhofer IOSB-INA, Germany
Chui Yin Wong	Universiti Multimedia Malaysia, Malaysia
Cristian Rusu	Pontificia Universidad Catolica de Valparaiso, Chile
Daniela Quiñones	Pontificia Universidad Catolica de Valparaiso, Chile
Dipti Theng	H. Raisoni College of Engineering, India
Dusan Simsik	Technical University of Kosice, Slovakia
Ellya Zulaikha	Institute of Technology of Sepuluh Nopember, Indonesia
Emma Nuraihan Mior Ibrahim	Universiti Teknologi MARA, Malaysia
Fariza Hanis Abdul Razak	Universiti Teknologi MARA, Malaysia
Fatma Meawad	University of Glasgow, UK
Fauzi Mohd Saman	Universiti Teknologi MARA, Malaysia
Fauziah Redzuan	Universiti Teknologi MARA, Malaysia
Hanif Baharin	Universiti Kebangsaan Malaysia, Malaysia
Harry B. Santoso	Universitas Indonesia, Indonesia
Hazwani Mohd Mohadis	International Islamic University Malaysia, Malaysia
Jasber Kaur	Universiti Teknologi MARA, Malaysia
Javed Anjum Sheikh	The University of Lahore, Pakistan
Jim Ang	University of Kent, UK
João Manuel R. S. Tavares	Universidade do Porto, Portugal
Juliana Aida Abu Bakar	Universiti Utara Malaysia, Malaysia
Kannadhasan S.	Tamilnadu Polytechnic College, India
Krzysztof Walczak	Poznań University of Economics and Business, Poland
Lili Nurliyana Abdullah	Universiti Putra Malaysia, Malaysia
Madihah S. Abd. Aziz	International Islamic University Malaysia, Malaysia
Mark Apperley	University of Waikato, New Zealand
Masitah Ghazali	Universiti Teknologi Malaysia, Malaysia

Organizers

Organized by:

Universiti Teknologi MARA   Faculty of Computer and Mathematical Sciences

Co-organized by:

International Islamic University Malaysia

Universiti Teknologi Malaysia   Universiti Utara Malaysia

Malaysian Global Innovation and Creativity Centre (MAGIC)

Co-sponsored by:

Kuala Lumpur ACM SIGCHI Chapter

Contents

Human Centered Computing

HCI and IT Infrastructure

HCI and Analytics

Design, UX and Usability

Evaluating Construction Defect Mobile App Using Think Aloud

Zan Azma Nasruddin[✉], Azleen Markom[✉], and Maslina Abdul Aziz[✉]

Faculty of Computer and Mathematical Sciences, Universiti Teknologi MARA,
40450 Shah Alam, Selangor Darul Ehsan, Malaysia
{zanaz,maslina}@tmsk.uitm.edu.my, azleen@engineer.com

Abstract. Construction Defect mobile app is used by Ministry of Defense's Construction Defect Inspection Team to ease the team to record construction defect. However, the mobile app has never been evaluated formally to identify any usability problems. The objectives of this study are to identify usability problems of Construction Defect mobile app using Think Aloud and to recommend design improvement of Construction Defect mobile app based on the identified usability problem. The Think Aloud study involve with 15 participants. During the evaluation, every participant carries out the given tasks on and he gives his impressions as he goes along the tasks. There are three usability problems were identified. Some recommendations have been proposed to improve the design of Construction Defect mobile app based on the identified usability problem. As for the future work, the study may be conducted using different usability evaluation technique.

Keywords: Usability · Human computer interaction · Think aloud · Mobile app
Defect inspection

1 Introduction

Construction defects are among the major concerns in the construction industry. Defect inspection process is performed to assess the physical condition of building components such as structural works, architectural works, mechanical and electrical works and external work. The process includes building site inspections, identifying defects, recording defective information using paper, entering information into the database online, and hand over such information to designers and builders to repair such defects [1].

The implementation of defect inspection using mobile device can be considered in the early stages of the construction industry. It is a typical information that the construction industry personnel require them to be at the construction site where the working conditions and the environment at the construction site are very different from the work in the office. The use of mobile device is an ideal choice for construction industry personnel as they are presented to natural variables, for example, terrible climate and lack of information technology infrastructure.

© Springer Nature Singapore Pte Ltd. 2018
N. Abdullah et al. (Eds.): i-USEr 2018, CCIS 886, pp. 3–11, 2018.
https://doi.org/10.1007/978-981-13-1628-9_1

A mandatory step in developing mobile applications is to conduct usability evaluation [2]. The evaluation is to evaluate the design and the characteristics of the product based on the selected user feedback [3]. The evaluation is also an important requirement but often neglected in evaluating the design and efficiency of software applications [4, 5]. The evaluation results will save resources while reducing the overall system error [5, 6].

Currently, Ministry of Defense's Construction Defect Inspection Team who is responsible to record construction defect is having problems that lead to mistakes were often made. The head of Defect Inspection Team wants the team to make less mistakes which often indicate less productivity, also the feedback and response from the team will be important to the developer to improve the mobile application design.

This study is evaluating the usability of the mobile application. The evaluation is important for a mobile application to highlight usability problems from user side. An interview session was conducted with Lt Kol Ahmad Sallahuddin Ibrahim, the head of Defect Inspection Team, and based on the interview he said that the mobile application has never been evaluated formally to identify any usability problems to know either this mobile application is facing usability problems, for instance navigation and orientation error. Currently, only verbal complain such as having lag time when recording construction defects into the mobile application. The team might have other difficulties but they do not give formal feedback about the performance of the mobile application in terms of effectiveness, efficiency and error while using the mobile applications.

The scope of this study focuses on the Defect Inspection Team and the participants are from engineering discipline which include Architectural, Structural, Mechanical and Electrical at Ministry of Defense's construction projects. This study uses mobile application as data entry tools for the defect reporting. This study is about investigating the usability problem of the Construction Defect mobile application's main modules, which are user login and logout, projects reporting, defect reporting and photographs (evidence) attachment. Also, provides suggestion for improvements.

This study helps to identify the mobile application usability problems in which the identification of the usability problems will help to rectify the current design problems and to view the mistake that developer is not aware of from user's perspectives. Also, helps to improve the mobile application design in which the design improvement of Construction Defect mobile application will help to provide a better user experience among the Defect Inspection Team and help to accomplish the task in a more structured manner. The design improvement of Construction Defect mobile application will be beneficial in reducing mistakes and error in recording construction defect thus increasing efficiency and productivity of Ministry of Defense's Construction Defect Inspection Team.

2   Literature Review

2.1   Think Aloud

This study uses the Think Aloud method which is an instrument that involves particular participants who will interact with the interface. The fundamental part of the think aloud method strongly urge the participants to give verbally depictions what they are proposing to do and what is going on their screen [7].

This method is often used in human computer interface evaluation, though traditionally it is used as a psychological research method. Think Aloud usability evaluation method is one of the most basic evaluation methods where testing is performed with real participants [4]. This evaluation process requires the participants to verbalize their thoughts and comments while using a system or prototype to complete a set of pre-defined tasks. All observations and comments will be recorded, and then analyzed. The purpose of the analysis is to determine the problem in the system or the prototype that can prevent the user experience.

Think Aloud is a direct observation method of user testing that involves asking users to think out loud as they are performing a task. Users are asked to say whatever they are looking at, thinking, doing, and feeling at each moment. This method is especially helpful for determining users' expectations and identifying what aspects of a system are confusing. There is a vast amount of literature which critically discusses the method of Think Aloud. Below, the benefits and drawbacks of this evaluation method are discussed and referred to determine how Think Aloud may be best applied to website evaluation to gain further insight into user experience. Think Aloud plays an important role in educational research, as a tool for studying both teacher and student thought processes [8].

In the usability lab worldwide, Think Aloud is the main method. Moreover, this method is also a popular method in the scientific community of psychology and computer science. According to some researchers, this method is often expected as the most widely used evaluation method in the computer industry [9].

2.2 Benefits of Think Aloud

Think Aloud is the most important method in the toolkit of usability evaluators because it uncovers more problems than any other measure [10]. Perhaps due to this, Think Aloud is one of the most popular and frequently applied techniques in testing [11].

The most vital benefit of Think Aloud is that it provides input to designs from actual users, who are representative of the user population. By verbalizing their thoughts, participants give practitioners an understanding of how they view the computer system, enabling evaluators to identify users' major misconceptions [4]. The process of Think Aloud allows practitioners to gain thorough examination of users" behavior, which can be analyzed to reveal the causes of usability problems.

Additionally, think aloud data provides insight into users' affective reactions including; sighs, frowns and scowls which speak of users' dissatisfaction and frustrations [12]. Flexibility of the Think Aloud approach is also beneficial for usability practitioners. Some facilitators of the method realize that changing conduct during Think Aloud can affect the kind and amount of data collected. They may therefore manipulate the session to ensure user exploration of certain areas to match the objectives of the test [10]. This is a great benefit of the approach when concentrating on certain aspects of an interface which may be suspected to be problematic and to uncover reasoning for the problems.

3   Methodology

This study uses the Think Aloud evaluation technique, which used task scenario that have been created to evaluate the Construction Defect using mobile application. The reception of think aloud method permits straightforwardly and effectively accumulate the issue emerging from mobile application design. This incorporated the actual tasks for the particular data entry which represented the real purpose of the defect inspection.

The participant were given a brief explanation about think aloud and the concept of usability. During the evaluation, every participant carries out the given tasks using mobile application. The participants were advised to think out loud while they do each task. They permitted to speak uninhibitedly on any blunder they confront or the great aspect about the mobile application while playing out the tasks scenario. The usability evaluation of mobile application concentrates further on the accumulation of qualitative data, for example, participants' considerations, feelings and responses. All information and actions are scribed on a notebook and recorded by Advanced Digital Video (ADV) Screen Recorder software from ByteRev Mobile Solutions with built-in Smartphone camera.

During the evaluation sessions, smartphone screen activities were recorded for detailed analysis. Then, transcripts were coded using both predetermined codes and analyzed using Microsoft Excel.

4   Analysis and Findings

4.1   Task Scenario and Interview

The task scenario usability evaluation sessions and debriefing session was written in English and Malay to ensure all participants understand the questions. The participants were given the task scenario prior to the evaluation session. It gives information to the participants ahead of time in regards to the interview. The open-ended questions were used throughout the debriefing session.

4.2   Research Result

The result showed overall satisfaction with the mobile application but some usability problems were identified. The usability problems will be helpful to improve the design of Construction Defect mobile application. During the evaluation, each participant provided comments regarding the user interface during the evaluation.

Tasks. All participants were able to complete all the tasks. The screens of the Construction Defect mobile application appear as shown in Figs. 1 and 2. Table 1 list findings from the think aloud.

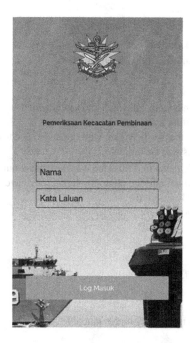

Fig. 1. (a) Login; (b) Defects list ("Senarai kecacatan")

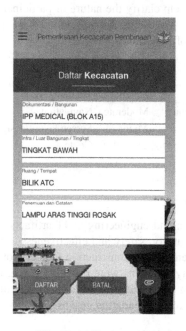
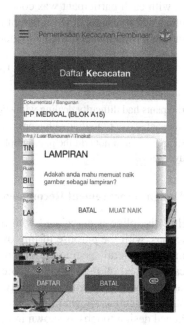

Fig. 2. (a) Register defect ("Daftar kecacatan"); (b) Attach photograph

Table 1. Summary of think aloud

Tasks	Think Aloud
1. Please open the Construction Defect Inspection mobile application and enter the username and password that have been given to you	Login is easily understandable
2. You are now in the Commanding Officer's Toilet located at Level One, IPP Training (Block A14) building and found that the stopcock is not working. Please register the defect	• Some icons are small and options for adjusting the font size is needed • All the text fields are well organized and text boxes size are suitable
3. Update the defect report as in Task 2 by uploading and attaching the photograph to the report	Participants find this step was the easiest but could not edit the photograph that they have already inserted
4. You are now in the ATC Room located at Ground Floor, IPP Medical (Block A15) building and found that the high bay light fitting malfunction. Please register the defect	See #2
5. Update the defect report as in Task 4 by uploading and attaching the photograph to the report	See #3
6. End of Tasks and logout	Logout is easily understandable

Usability Problems. After the participant completed doing the tasks, a debriefing session with each participant was conducted to help clarify the nature of participant's difficulties and to assess how important the interface to him. Table 2 provides a list of the usability problems identified and their level of importance.

Table 2. Usability problems.

Usability problem	Severity	Theme
1. Participants had difficulty dealing with slide in menu	Moderate	Navigation
2. Participants do not familiar with icons used	Minor	Screen layout/design
3. Participants could not edit the photograph that they have already inserted	Critical	Content

4.3   Design Improvement Recommendations

The HCI discipline is associated with the design and engineering of IT artifacts and interactions, with the purpose of improving the utility, safety and effectiveness of the system [13]. Several specific design improvement of the Construction Defect mobile application based on the identified three usability problems were provided during the evaluation. The first identified usability problem is participants had difficulty dealing with slide in menu as shown in Fig. 3(a) and the recommendation design improvement is switched design to tabs as shown in Fig. 3(b).

The next identified usability problem is participants not familiar with icons used as shown in Fig. 4(a) and the recommendation design improvement is to add tooltip next to icon as shown in Fig. 4(b).

Fig. 3. (a) Slide in menu; (b) Tabs menu

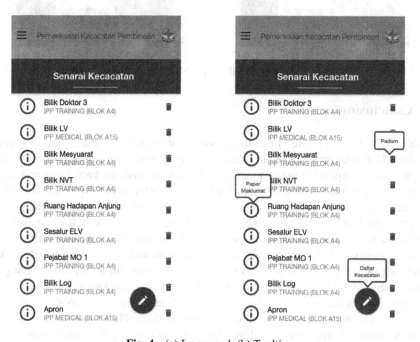

Fig. 4. (a) Icons used; (b) Tooltip

The next identified usability problem is participants could not edit the photograph that he/she has already inserted as shown in Fig. 5(a) and the recommendation design improvement is participants is able to edit the photograph under Update Photograph ("Kemaskini gambar") button as shown in Fig. 5(b).

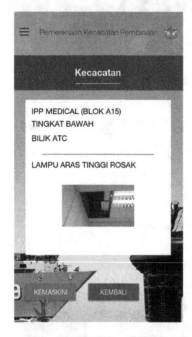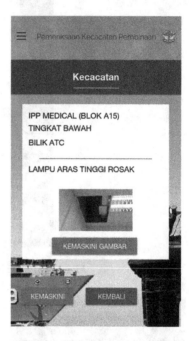

Fig. 5. (a) Inserted photograph; (b) Update photograph ("Kemaskini gambar") button

5 Conclusion

In this study, there are three limitations associated with the sample. First, this study involved 15 participants. The contribution of a bigger participants may prompt diverse outcomes or an expansion in the quantity of themes. Second, the knowledge and experience of the participants in construction defect and the use of smartphones. Results of this study only apply to the populace under scrutiny and ought not be exchanged to someone else that has no involvement at all. Third, the study focused exclusively on Construction Defect mobile application that has been introduced to participants.

The Construction Defect mobile application is an android version, which means people who are Apple or iPhone users will not be able to use the application. Having an iPhone/Apple version of Construction Defect mobile application would be beneficial in the future because there is some chance that this target group may respond differently. This study is about identifying usability problems by using Think Aloud usability evaluation technique. Future work could be using different usability evaluation technique to identify the usability problems.

Acknowledgements. We would like to express our deepest appreciation to Universiti Teknologi MARA (UiTM) Malaysia for the financial support for both research and publications through the internal funding of LESTARI Grant Scheme (600-IRMI/DANA 5/3/LESTARI (0112/2016). A great thanks to all staffs and members of Research Management Institute (RMI), UiTM Shah Alam, Selangor, MALAYSIA.

References

1. Dong, A., Maher, M.L., Kim, M.J., Gu, N., Wang, X.: Construction defect management using a telematic digital workbench. Autom. Constr. **18**(6), 814–824 (2009)
2. Zhang, D., Adipat, B.: Challenges, methodologies, and issues in the usability testing of mobile applications. Int. J. Hum.-Comput. Interact. **18**(3), 293–308 (2005)
3. Rebelo, F., Soares, M.M.: Advances in Usability Evaluation. CRC Press, Boca Raton (2012)
4. Nielsen, J.: Usability Engineering. Morgan, Fremont (1993)
5. Hamborg, K.-C., Vehse, B., Bludau, H.B.: Questionnaire based usability evaluation of hospital information systems. Electron. J. Inf. Syst. Eval. **7**(1), 21–30 (2004)
6. Dumas, J.S., Redish, J.: A Practical Guide to Usability Testing. Intellect Books, Washington D.C. (1999)
7. Rubin, J.H., Jeffrey, H.: Log analysis pays off. Netw. Comput. **15**, 76–78 (2004)
8. Rikard, G.L., Langley, D.J.: The think aloud procedure: a research technique for gaining insight into the student perspective. Phys. Educ. **52**(2), 92 (1995)
9. Jacob, R.J., Schmolze, J.G.: A human-computer interaction framework for media-independent knowledge, pp. 26–30 (1998)
10. Ramey, J., Boren, T., Cuddihy, E., Dumas, J., Guan, Z., Van den Haak, M.J., De Jong, M.D.: Does think aloud work? How do we know?, pp. 45–48. ACM (2006)
11. Nielsen, J., Clemmensen, T., Yssing, C.: Getting access to what goes on in people's heads?: reflections on the think-aloud technique, pp. 101–110. ACM (2002)
12. Preece, J., Rogers, Y., Sharp, H.: Interaction Design, Beyond Human-Computer Interaction. Wiley, Hoboken (2002)
13. Majid, R.A., Noor, N.L.M., Adnan, W.A.W.: Strengthening the HCI approaches in the software development process. In: Proceedings of World Academy of Science Engineering and Technology (2012)

Emotional Response Towards Cultural-Based E-Government Portal Design Using Card Sorting Method

Farez Mahmood[✉], Wan Adilah Wan Adnan, Nor Laila Md Noor, and Fauzi Mohd Saman

Faculty of Computer and Mathematical Sciences, Universiti Teknologi MARA (UiTM), Shah Alam, Selangor, Malaysia
farez97@yahoo.com, {adilah,norlaila,fauzi}@tmsk.uitm.edu.my

Abstract. This paper aims to identify emotional responses towards the culture-based e-government portal design focusing on Power Distance (PD) dimension of Hofstede cultural model. We employ a card sorting method where a set of twenty eight pre-written cards with emotional words taken from the Russell Affect Model. Twenty four participants who were divided into eight groups were asked to choose the cards that best describe the look and feel of given e-government portals homepage representing high PD and low PD designs. Analysis based on frequency was calculated for each of the emotional response. Findings indicate that the e-government portal design that is characterized as high PD is more likely to evoke a negative emotional experience. Whereas for the e-government portal design characterized as low PD has tendency to evoke positive emotional response. This finding provides valuable insights into citizen's emotional experience of culture-based portal design of Power Distance culture values.

Keywords: E-government portal design · Cultural design Power distance dimension and card sorting

1 Introduction

The governments all over the world today are reaching the alternative in delivering information online by utilizing e-government portals that are believed to provide wider range of information to their citizens without borders. Usually e-government portals are developed according to their own specifications and standards reflecting their national life style and culture. Literature has recognized the influence of culture in the design of a website [1], particularly in the design of e-government portal [1–3]. Cultural consideration is critical in the design of e-government portal as it influences its adoption.

Majority of cultural studies in Human Computer Interaction emphasize on exploring and examining design elements or features that match with a particular cultural factor. Subsequently, many guidelines on cultural-based design have been proposed to help designers produce usable design. However, there is little emphasize in prior studies that aimed to determine the differences in user emotional response on different cultural-based website design, particularly in the context of e-government portal. This paper attempts

© Springer Nature Singapore Pte Ltd. 2018
N. Abdullah et al. (Eds.): i-USEr 2018, CCIS 886, pp. 12–22, 2018.
https://doi.org/10.1007/978-981-13-1628-9_2

to determine the emotional response that evoke from the culture-based website design, focusing on Power Distance cultural values of e-government portal. Card sorting method is employed and emotional responses based on Russell Affect Model are used for the cards.

2 Literature Review

2.1 Hofstede Model

Hofstede's cultural model is well acknowledged and known as the most widely used in studies examining the culture differences in various context [4, 5] including in e-government [5, 6]. Therefore, Hofstede's cultural model is employed in this research as the foundation to examine the influence of culture on e-government development and homepage design.

Literature has recognized that Power Distance is one of the strongest influential cultural dimension and strongly recommends to include Power Distance in any cross-cultural studies [7, 8]. For this reason, in this study, Power Distance is chosen to be explored in determining the emotional response that could evoke from a cultural-based e-government portal design.

Hofstede defines Power Distance as "the extent to which the less powerful members of institutions and organizations within a country expect and accept that power is distributed unequally" [9]. In other words, it relates to the degree of equality among the society in the country. Thus, countries that rank high in the Power Distance Index, tend to accept that inequality in power is a norm. A high power distance society believes in strict authority and hierarchy whereas a low power distance society emphasizes equality.

Key components of web design that reveal the cultural values in a government portal design include language, page layout, symbols, color, visual images and sound/music [10]. Prior studies have shown that Power Distance cultural dimension is one of the national cultures that have been recognized to affect the web design, particularly the e-government portal [11, 12].

Daniel et al. [1] proposed a framework and guidelines for designing a cultural-based website. They identified key characteristics of culture-based usable website and established the key features that help cultural understanding of a website. Their study merely focused on the design features to promote a particular cultural value. For instance, they have outlined as shown in Table 1 the design features that can be incorporated in website design that portray the high and low values of Power Distance dimension. However, their study did not provide a deeper insight into differences in emotional response that evoke from these design features.

Table 1. Key design feature of power distance

High power distance	Low power distance
Prominence given to leaders	Prominence given to citizens
Vision statement	No vision statement
Quality assurance and awards	No quality assurance and awards
Formal layout	Informal layout
More flashy outlook	Less flashy outlook

2.2 Russell Model

Human computer interaction researchers emphasize on the importance of addressing emotion in ensuring a pleasurable user experience [13]. Emotions are recognized as a multi-component phenomenon consisting of cognitive, physiological, motivational, behavior and subjective feelings that form one's emotional experience.

A number of emotion theories and models are widely available in the literature. One of the prominent emotion related models is proposed by Russell. Russell's Model of Affect focuses on subjective emotional experience that maps into a two bipolar dimensional form where the y-axis represents the degree of arousal and x-axis measures the valence representing the degree of pleasantness [14] as illustrated in Fig. 1. The model covers twenty eight set of comprehensive emotion as shown in Table 2.

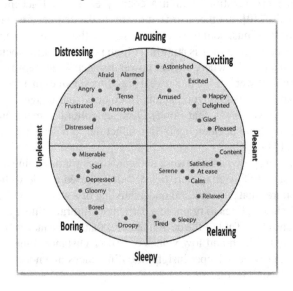

Fig. 1. Emotional types on Russell model

This study uses all twenty eight words of emotion recommended in the Russell Model of Affect to identify citizen's emotional response towards cultural-based e-government portal website.

Table 2. List of twenty eight emotions suggested in Russell's model of affect

No.	Emotional word	No.	Emotional word
1.	Astonished	15.	Tense
2.	Satisfied	16.	Gloomy
3.	Afraid	17.	Delighted
4.	Miserable	18.	Relaxed
5.	Excited	19.	Frustrated
6.	At ease	20.	Bored
7.	Alarmed	21.	Glad
8.	Sad	22.	Sleepy
9.	Happy	23.	Annoyed
10.	Serene	24.	Droopy
11.	Angry	25.	Pleased
12.	Depressed	26.	Tired
13.	Amused	27.	Distressed
14.	Calm	28.	Content

2.3   Card Sorting

Card sorting is an empirical method that helps to obtain better understanding of an individual mental model of a domain of a concept [15, 16]. It is a standard research tool that is popular among the usability expert and information architects [16–18] as an effective means of data collection. Card sorting has been recognized as an influential user research method and has been employed in major area of research including information architecture, cognitive, developmental, perceptual, and social psychology [18–20]. Moreover, card sorting is deployed for user testing to help articulate user's emotional response to an IT artefact including websites, systems and applications, products as well as IT services. Subsequently, it helps to gain valuable insights into the needs and terminology expectations as well as emotional experience of users [21, 22]. This is very crucial particularly in the context of e-government portal that is aimed to effectively deliver information and services to citizen from all walks of life.

In cards sorting method, participants are presented with a set of random pre-written cards where they are required to sort or prioritize the cards into a particular label or categories [23]. There are two common approaches of performing card sorting, namely open card sorting and close card sorting. For close card sorting approach, participants are required to select and classify cards into a predefined categories or groups. They need to sort the cards between these defined categories or groups. On the other hand, for open card sorting, the categories are not predefined. The participants are required to sort out the given cards into groups or categories where they need to name the categories by themselves. The purpose of open card sorting is exploratory and the close card sorting is for validation or confirmation [24].

3   Research Method

In this research, we conducted card sorting study with aim to identify emotion responses towards the culture-based e-government portal design which focuses on Power Distance (PD) dimension of Hofstede cultural model.

Two e-government portals were selected, named as E-govt1 representing high PD which was labelled as formal-type portal, and E-govt2 representing low PD which was labelled as informal-type portal. These classifications of low and high PD were based on the design guideline by Danial et al. [1]. In this study, five cultural markers were used to differentiate the formal and informal portal design which were text style (formal text/ informal text), picture (formal picture - minister, logo, building, coat of arm/informal picture – people, NGO logo, public space), and colour (formal color - same with flag colour/informal color – appropriate colour). Based on the classification of PD design guidelines for these cultural markers, a sample screen shot from the e-government portal of Indonesia was chosen as high PD labelled as formal-typed portal as shown in Fig. 2. Meanwhile a sample of screen shot from e-government portal of Singapore ((https:// www.ecitizen.gov.sg) was chosen as low PD labelled as informal-typed portal as shown in Fig. 3.

Fig. 2. Formal-typed portal

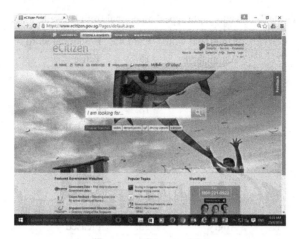

Fig. 3. Informal-typed portal

3.1 Participants

Two card sorting sessions were conducted. The first session involved twelve participants who were post-graduate students from Master of Science in Information Technology programme at Universiti Teknologi MARA Shah Alam, with age ranging from 25 to 30 years old. In the second session, there were twelve participants who were teachers with age 40 years old and above. For both sessions, we divided participants into groups, with three members in a group. Therefore, we had a total of 8 groups, with four groups for each session, who participated in this card sorting study.

3.2 Preparation of Cards

The cards used in this study were written with emotional words which were proposed in the Russel Affect Model. In this study we selected all the twenty eight emotional words suggested by Russel as shown in Table 3. Thus, a total of twenty eight cards representing emotional response were prepared to be selected and sorted by participants into the given culture-based portal design. The participants were asked to choose the cards that best described their emotion towards each of the given portal design. With this study, we were able to obtain a sense of how culture-based design were perceived through the use of emotional words.

Table 3. Twenty eight types' emotional from Russell model

Card no.	Emotional word	Card no.	Emotional word
1.	Astonished	15.	Tense
2.	Satisfied	16.	Gloomy
3.	Afraid	17.	Delighted
4.	Miserable	18.	Relaxed
5.	Excited	19.	Frustrated
6.	At ease	20.	Bored
7.	Alarmed	21.	Glad
8.	Sad	22.	Sleepy
9.	Happy	23.	Annoyed
10.	Serene	24.	Droopy
11.	Angry	25.	Pleased
12.	Depressed	26.	Tired
13.	Amused	27.	Distressed
14.	Calm	28.	Content

In both studies, we employed close card sorting methods. The procedure of these studies are presented below:

3.3 Procedure for Close Card Sorting Session

The purpose of this study was to gather emotional responses from participants' first impression by looking at the design of a e-government portal. In addition, we hoped to examine if there was any differences in emotional response between the high and low PD e-government portal design. Thus, the result was expected to provide insights in determining the emotional words that best described each of the culture-based portal designs based on PD cultural values.

The session started with a brief introduction on the purpose of the study and a detail explanation on the procedure of the close card sorting method. After the briefing, the participants were separated into groups of three members. Each group was given a set of 28 pre-written cards with emotional words. Then both informal and formal e-government portal design were displayed on the screen.

We instructed the participants to choose the cards that best described their first impression of the given portals. They were asked at the end of the session to provide names that best described both categories of e-government portal design.

4 Analysis and Results

The cards representing emotional response, from a total of eight groups were gathered and analyzed. The analysis based on frequency was calculated on each of the emotional words for both e-government portals. Since there were eight groups which participated and conducted the card sorting, therefore the maximum frequency for these emotional words was 8. These emotional words with frequency of five or more were considered as emotional response of majority. These emotional responses of majority were identified as the words best described and reflected the portal design. The results showed that there were ten words out of 28 that best described about the formal portal design. These emotional words are calm, sleepy, tired, afraid, alarmed, bored, satisfied, tense, annoyed and content. Meanwhile, the results showed that there were eight words best described and reflected informal portal design, which are astonished, excited, at ease, happy, serene, amused, relaxed and pleased. Table 4 shows the list of emotional words best described and reflected about both the formal and informal portal design.

Table 4. List of emotional words with frequency ≥5

E-govt1 (formal-high PD)		E-govt2 portal (informal-low PD)	
Calm	7	Astonished	6
Sleepy	7	Excited	6
Tired	7	At ease	6
Afraid	6	Happy	5
Alarmed	6	Serene	5
Bored	6	Amused	5
Satisfied	5	Relaxed	5
Tense	5	Pleased	5
Annoyed	5		
Content	5		

These eighteen words were then mapped to Russell Model of Affect (as shown in Fig. 1) to determines its pleasantness (pleasure/unpleasant) and arousal (arousing/sleepy) dimensions. According to Russell Model of Affect, the pleasantness reflects the positive or negative feelings. Positive feelings lead to pleasure and negative feelings lead to unpleasantness whereas, for arousal dimension, it reflects the high or low user attention or engagement. High arousal associates to feeling of alertness and low arousal is feeling of sleepy. From this mapping, results show very clearly that all ten emotional words that best described the informal portal design fall under the positive feelings of pleasantness. Meanwhile for the informal portal design, majority of the words, which was six out of eight, fall under low arousal.

On a general comment by the participants, three groups had suggested names to classify the given portal design. Group 1 commented that the formal-typed e-government portal has a very *official* look and the informal-typed portal looked more *citizens friendly*. For Group 2, they suggested that the portal can be categorized as *formal* and *relax* design. In addition, Group 3 described the portals as very *authoritative* and the other one as *citizen-centred*. Table 5 summarizes the suggested classification names from the participants for both formal and informal portal designs.

Table 5. Suggested category names from participants

Formal-typed portal design (high PD value)	Informal-typed portal design (low PD value)
Official	Citizen friendly
Formal	Relax
Authoritative	Citizen-centred

4.1 Discussion

The result from the frequency analysis shows that the formal category, representing the high power distance design, is described by words that more incline towards negative feelings. The informal category on the other hand, is described by words that are incline towards positive feelings. Therefore it indicates that the high PD design is likely to evoke a negative emotional experience and the low PD design has tendency to evoke positive emotional experience.

The findings from the mapping of the emotional responses to the Russell Model of Affect indicate that portal design with low PD values is associated with positive feelings of pleasantness. On the other hand, the portal design with high PD values is associated with low arousal which would lead to low user attention and engagement.

We can conclude that the findings from this card sorting study provide insights on emotional experience of culture-centered portal design based on Power Distance culture values. Thus, the findings indicate that the low PD portal design is likely to provide a positive emotional experience compared to high PD portal design.

5   Conclusion and Further Research

Card sorting method is employed in this study to determine any differences in emotional response towards cultural-based e-government portal design. Analysis based on frequency for each of the emotional response were conducted. Results showed that the e-government portal design that is characterized as high PD has tendency to evoke a emotional response with low arousal whereas, for e-government portal design with low PD is more inclined towards positive emotional response of pleasantness. The findings from the card sorting study provide insights on emotional experience of culture-based portal design based on Power Distance culture values. The next step would be to conduct experimental studies that examine the effect of different culture-based design for different user groups particularly the digital immigrant and native differences on their emotional user experience. This kind of study is hoped to provide a good empirical evidence to justify the importance of cultural consideration in e-government portal design for citizen engagement and adoption.

Acknowledgment. The authors would like to record sincere thanks to the Research Management Institute (RMI) and Ministry of Higher Education Malaysia for the financial support. This research was conducted under the support and funding of Fundamental Research Grant Scheme (FRGS) no.: FRGS/2/2014/ICT01/UITM/01/1.

References

1. Daniel, A.O., Yinka, A., Frank, I., Adesina, S.: Culture-based adaptive web design: an approach for designing culturally customized websites. Int. J. Sci. Eng. Res. **4**(2) (2013)
2. Wan Adnan, W.A., Noor, N.L.M., Mohd Saman, F., Mahmood, F.: Web content analysis on power distance cultural presence in e-government portal design. In: Rau, P.-L.P. (ed.) CCD 2017. LNCS, vol. 10281, pp. 441–450. Springer, Cham (2017). https://doi.org/ 10.1007/978-3-319-57931-3_35
3. Noor, N.L., Harun, A.F., Adnan, W.A., Saman, F.M., Noh, M.A.: Towards the conceptualization of citizen user experience: citizens' preference for emotional design in e-government portal. In: 2016 4th International Conference on User Science and Engineering, i-USEr, pp. 69–74 (2016)
4. Nguyen, A.: A cross-cultural study on e-government services delivery. Electron. J. Inf. Syst. Eval. **19**(2), 121–134 (2016). http://www.ejise.com
5. Allaya, A., Mellouli, M.: National culture and e-government services adoption Tunisian case. In: Recent Advances in Communications, pp. 287–290 (2015)
6. Zhao, F., Shen, K.N., Collier, A.: Effects of national culture on e-government diffusion: a global study of 55 countries. Inf. Manag. **51**, 1005–1016 (2014)
7. Thomas, D.: The moderating effects of power distance and collectivism on empowering leadership and psychological empowerment and self-leadership in international development organizations, vol. 80. Ph.D. Dissertation. Faculty Publications - School of Business (2015). http://digitalcommons.georgefox.edu/gfsb/80
8. Lee, K., Scandura, T.A., Sharif, M.M.: Cultures have consequences: a configural approach to leadership across two cultures. Leadersh. Q. **25**(4), 692–710 (2014). https://doi.org/ 10.1016/j.leaqua.2014.03.003
9. Hofstede, G.: www.geert-hofstede.com
10. Goyal, N., Miner, W., Nawathe, N.: Cultural differences across governmental website design. In: Proceedings of the 4th International Conference on Intercultural Collaboration, pp. 49–152 (2012)
11. Al-Hujran, O., Al-dalahmeh, M., Aloudat, A.: The role of national culture on citizen adoption of e-government services: an empirical study. Electron. J. E-Gov. **9**(2), 93–106 (2011)
12. Moura, T., Singh, N., Chun, W.: The influence of culture in website design and users' perceptions. J. Electron. Commer. Res. **17**(4), 312–339 (2016)
13. Basri, N.H., Noor, N.L.M., Adnan, W.A.W., Saman, F.M., Baharin, A.H.A.: Conceptualizing and understanding user experience. In: Proceedings of 2016 4th International Conference on User Science and Engineering, i-USEr 2016, pp. 81–84. Institute of Electrical and Electronics Engineers Inc. (2017). https://doi.org/10.1109/iuser.2016.7857938
14. Russell, J.A.: Affective space is bipolar. J. Pers. Soc. Psychol. **37**(3), 345–356 (1979). https:// doi.org/10.1037/0022-3514.37.3.345
15. Schmettow, M., Sommer, J.: Linking card sorting to browsing performance – are congruent municipal websites more efficient to use? Behav. Inf. Technol. **35**, 1 (2016). ISSN 0144-929X
16. Zimmerman, D.E., Akerelrea, C.: A group card sorting methodology for developing informational web sites. In: The Proceedings of International Professional Communication Conference, IPCC (2002)
17. Baum, C.M., Edwards, D.F.: Activity Card Sort (ACS): Test manual, 2nd edn. AOTA Press, Bethesda (2008)
18. Mozyrko, B.: Card Sorting: A Quick and Dirty Guide for Beginners. Usability Tools, 24 February 2015

19. Nawaz, A., Clemmensen, T., Hertzum, M.: Information classification on university websites: a cross-country card sort study. In: Information Systems Research Seminar in Scandinavia, IRIS, Turku (2011)
20. Nawaz, A.: A comparison of card-sorting analysis methods. In: The 10th Asia Pacific Conference on Computer Human Interaction, APCHI 2012, Matsue, Japan, August 2012
21. Petrie, H., Power, C., Cairns, P., Seneler, C.: Using card sorts for understanding website information architectures: technological, methodological and cultural issues. In: Campos, P., et al. (eds.) INTERACT 2011. LNCS, vol. 6949, pp. 309–322. Springer, Heidelberg (2011). https://doi.org/10.1007/978-3-642-23768-3_26
22. Sakai, R., Aerts, J.: Card sorting techniques for domain characterization in problem-driven visualization research. In: Eurographics Conference on Visualization, EuroVis (2015)
23. Blanchard, S.J., Banerji, I.: Evidence-based recommendations for designing free-sorting experiments. Behav. Res. Methods **48**, 1318–1336 (2016). https://doi.org/10.3758/s13428-015-0644-6
24. Yoon, J., Pohlmeyer, A.E., Desmet, P.M.A.: Positive Emotional Granularity Cards. Delft University of Technology, Delft (2015). ISBN 978-94-6186-440-6

Informing Technological Enhancements Through Art: Practitioners' Perspectives and Reflection

Afdallyna Fathiyah Harun[1(✉)], Noris Mohd Norowi[2(✉)], Hanif Baharin[3(✉)], Khairul Anuar Mt Nawi[4], and Adam Salehuddin[2]

[1] Universiti Teknologi MARA, 40450 Shah Alam, Selangor, Malaysia
afdallyna@tmsk.uitm.edu.my
[2] Universiti Putra Malaysia (UPM), 43400 Serdang, Malaysia
noris@upm.edu.my, adamsalehuddin@hotmail.com
[3] Universiti Kebangsaan Malaysia (UKM), 43600 Bangi, Selangor, Malaysia
hbaharin@ukm.edu.my
[4] IACT College, VSQ@PJ Centre, 46300 Petaling Jaya, Selangor, Malaysia
alternaanuar@gmail.com

Abstract. In this paper, we reflect on our experience, and outline our design process in using an app, which is freely available on mobile app stores, called Artcodes that reads custom-made markers in an artwork, and with markers made using temporary tattoos. Artcodes was used previously with permanent markers drawn on objects. However, our application of Artcodes is different from previous work because we used moveable markers and used markers on human skin. By appropriating Artcodes for our artwork and temporary tattoos, we suggest that, in the future, Artcodes algorithm may be improved to differentiate between shadows, wrinkles and lines if it were to be used in other settings involving human skins as to create a more embedded experience.

Keywords: Digital installation · Interactive artwork · Spectator experience
Tangible interface · Performance · D-touch · Artcodes

1 Introduction

Visual markers such as QRcodes or AR markers have grown exponentially from simply being used as tagging objects, to interactivity with virtual content and now as decorative interactive patterns. The underlying technicality of such technology involves the use of hyperlinks connecting the reality to virtual world with some form of pattern to attract user attention.

However, the typical markings of one QRcode may be dismissed entirely by users as its pattern is not far different from another QRcode. Seeing the missed opportunity, [1] has developed a visual marker technology called d-touch that allows users to design their own markers while being efficiently identifiable by a recognition algorithm. The technology is significantly attractive as it embodies a bottom-up, drawing based approach making marker design as natural as a drawing on a paper [2]. This in turn opens an opportunity for everyday users to design their own markers within various settings

© Springer Nature Singapore Pte Ltd. 2018
N. Abdullah et al. (Eds.): i-USEr 2018, CCIS 886, pp. 23–34, 2018.
https://doi.org/10.1007/978-981-13-1628-9_3

such as personalised announcements, educational posters [3], ceramic designs as well as dining placemats and menus [4] and also on guitars [5].

To enable an interactive experience between users and the visual markers, [6] have expanded the d-touch technology and created an app called Artcodes, which is readily available from the PlayStore. Artcodes is a mobile app that reads custom-made machine-readable markers working on the technology created by [1]. It allows users to create drawings by following certain rules which can then be read by the app and linked to virtual content. It is with this apps that [4] has explored the potentiality of visual markers as decorative patterns on ceramics, placemats and menus.

As excited as we were with the availability of the apps (as this makes the process of scanning and interacting with d-touch markers easier), we noticed that the use of markers is still within the boundaries set by designers. This means, users simply consume the embedded content by scanning the markers. We were motivated to explore how everyday users could embed the markers within everyday or novel interactions, appropriating the designs itself as form of personalised interactions.

This paper reports our experience of using Artcodes in a novel way. We demonstrate the use of Artcodes to read moveable markers, and markers made for human skin. The moveable markers were used in an interactive artwork, while temporary tattoos were used as markers on the skin. Through the discussions of our experience, the main contribution of this paper will be the demonstration of how the appropriation of technology in an art may inspire the improvement of said technology, which may then be applied in new contexts. The focus of this paper is on how art can improve aspects of Human-Computer Interaction (HCI) [7] and not on evaluating artworks from the perspectives of HCI [8].

2   Related Work

Digital art brings up the best on the abstract nature of art and the bytes of technology setup. Quite often we can find digital art installations that are exhibited for public spaces where the very nature of its setup is to 'perform' to enticing spectators and participants (from herein referred to S/P for brevity) to interact with the installations. Some examples include manipulation of visuals and sound in real time while creating organic fluid connections between music pieces and visual forms [9]. There is also the multi-user environments concept where users collaboratively create soundscapes through tangible instruments such as mobile phones [10].

Digital art installations can be found in museums, art galleries and public places such as clubs and city streets. For the benefit of understanding, consider the use of exhibit artefacts where visitors can press buttons or adjust the dial for information demonstration. Such exhibits form a digital installation enabling user manipulation either individually or collaboratively with other visitors. A digital installation when carefully designed would allow visitors to craft personalised interactions, which at times call for the observations and participation of other S/P.

The interpretation of these digital artistic exhibition hosts many HCI challenges but as it moves into the form of public affair, the challenges multiplies. Digital installation involving S/P calls for the consideration on (i) the technology to be employed, (ii) experience flow and (iii) S/P roles and state of mind [11, 12] as the combination of these elements would frame S/P experiences, establishing that an artefact engagement is taking place as well as making them aware of the role they play.

Our work is also motivated with the perception that art can be perceived as amplifications of humanity, bringing forth human experience into realisms through narrative presentation of stories, songs and poems as well as through visual illustration of paintings, drawings, films and animations. These amplifications are brought forth not only for a more lifelike and relevant representation of nature, but also involve a mixture of distortions, fragmentation or even combining the patterns of human experience that is repeated throughout humanity. Human *is* a part of nature. Perhaps it is human tendency to separate ourselves from the natural world, because our hunter gatherer ancestors were always fighting and trying to command nature to ensure human's survival, thus nature is a beast that must be reigned. Separating ourselves from the brutality of nature had ensured our survival. But nature is counter-intuitive. Systematic observation of nature through science has enable humanity to reveal the reality of nature.

We explored the use of Artcodes to bring forth an aspect of human nature that remains largely a mystery to humanity – the human consciousness. Consider the experiment with a split-brain patient; when the patient's right brain received a written instruction to stand up, the patient would stand up. However, when enquired why he stood, the patient's left side of the brain (which control speech) would make up a story that only seems logical to the patient, such as, "I'm standing up to get some water." This shows the patient's left side of the brain receives information from the right side unconsciously. Much evidence in neuroscience shows that consciousness and free will are only illusions [8]. We explore the notion that consciousness is only a story that the brain creates to justify human actions which are triggered by the unconscious.

3   An Introduction to 'Free Will Is an Illusion'

'Free Will is an Illusion' is an interactive artwork which attempts to provide a digital experience comprising visual art and installation. The visual art are compositions of human figures with nuances of Greek mythology while the installation is simply the hanging of the artwork in a gallery serving as an 'exhibit face' where S/P arrange magnets to set their personalised experience. The digital interaction setup is enabled by Artcodes [6] which will be further explained in the later sections.

'Free Will is an Illusion' takes the form of rationalization of human consciousness where users would receive appropriate information presented to them as they see fit regardless of the information presented to them were true or false.

We purposely designed the interaction where users feel they are in control of the interaction outcome. These users who play the role of S/P need to decide the placement of magnets on the visual artwork where the 'placed magnets' *supposedly maps* onto their user profiling – in short S/P would be under the impression that their very action influence the installation output when at the very fact, all elements of the interaction have been pre-composed.

The idea to create an artwork that makes use of Artcodes came into being when the authors met during an Artcodes workshop in 2016. The idea was then discussed with a curator to be exhibited in a yearly science and art exhibition at a gallery. The theme for 2016 exhibition was 'Brain.' The curator requested our work to be interactive, catalysing the audience to think more about topics surrounding the theme of the exhibition. After several brainstorming sessions, we came out with the theme of human consciousness. We wanted the audience to be able to interact with our artwork and bring something with them after the exhibition. Therefore, we proposed a wall exhibit in which the audience can interact with the work publicly and a more private interaction where the audiences' skin would be stamped with Artcodes marker linked to a website that provides interactive explanation about our artwork and human consciousness.

However, the experience concept underwent several iterations to ensure it is approachable by the audience and feasible for execution. This is largely due to the limitations of the Artcodes apps which were originally designed for static markers. Moreover, Artcodes markers have never been conceptualized for use on human skin before.

3.1   Artcodes as Technology Enabler

Artcodes is a mobile app which can be downloaded from the iPhone Apps Store or Google Play Store. It makes use of d-touch technology where users can design their own markers while still being efficiently identifiable by a recognition algorithm.

To appreciate how Artcodes function, one must acknowledge the technical build-up of d-touch technology. As summarized in [2], d-touch utilizes region adjacency tree where for a marker to be valid, its associated tree must satisfy three key constraints: (i) there must be at least three levels of nesting (root, branch and leaf); (ii) there must be at least 3 branches present; and (iii) at least half of the branches must have at least one leaf each. These rules are intended to achieve a balance between flexibility of design and reliability of recognition [1] where the resulting markers can take the various design such as a flower, words, animals and many more. Examples and in-depth description of the technology can be seen in [1].

Each Artcode markers has a numerical code which corresponds to d-touch region adjacency tree diagram. This numerical code can be keyed in into the apps which then link specific markers to specific website pages. Users simply need to run the Artcodes apps to scan the markers of which the interface will generate the webpage link for users to click and engage with.

3.2   Experience Flow in the Interactive Artwork

The form of artwork for the exhibit underwent a series of iterations. We first decided to use blocks of wood with Artcodes markers carved or printed on them. The audience could choose and combine the blocks to make their own artwork which could then be scanned using Artcodes apps to reveal the hidden meaning of their unconscious behaviour. We tested the ideas by drawing markers on papers. We cut the markers and arranged them to be scanned by Artcodes. It however proved highly unreadable because the edges of each piece of markers cast shadows making it difficult for the app to recognise the lines drawn on the edges of the paper (Fig. 1, left). This is especially challenging when the cut-out markers were scanned at an angle, as would most likely be done by the audience since the markers were to be arranged on a flat surface.

Fig. 1. (Left) Each marker is enclosed by lines. (Right) Each marker is combined using lines

We refined our marker design by highlighting the use of line connectors by assuming that users would attempt to join the lines together to form a unique marker (see Fig. 1, right). However, during testing, we observed that the placement of the papers itself could overlap the line connectors causing the overall marker composition to be unrecognized by the apps. Thus, we concluded that printing the markers on wooden blocks to be scanned from a horizontal surface would not be suitable for the exhibition.

We then decided to make the lines permanent and the dots moveable. This way, the artwork would still be interactive but in a more controlled manner, as there would be less room for mistakes which would made the markers unreadable. We tested the idea by using magnets as dots placed on lines drawn on paper. As shown in Fig. 2, the rounded magnets used cast shadows making the dots unintentionally merged with lines. To avoid the shadows, we used very small pieces of magnets with the lines of the marker drawn directly on a white board. However, as shown on Fig. 2 (right), direct lights on the whiteboard caused reflections which made the marker unreadable. Therefore, instead of drawing on the whiteboard, we printed our markers on papers and pasted them on the whiteboard.

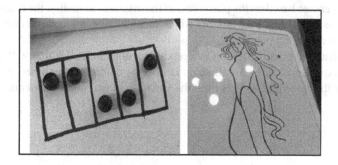

Fig. 2. (Left) Rounded magnets used as markers nodes. (Right) Reflections on the whiteboard made the markers unreadable

Having addressed the recognition and stability issue, we decided to produce Artcodes markers that take the form of human figures with nuance of Greek mythology. The reason for this choice was mainly random as we opine that drawings for Greek mythology present a sense of metaphor, story and romanticism. For interaction control, we have pre-set five Artcodes markers baselines. Despite the markers taking different figure composition, the region adjacency diagram will have at most 5 branches with different numbering nodes depending on magnet placements. Figure 3 shows the figure composition used in the interactive artwork.

Fig. 3. Artcodes markers in 'Free Will is an Illusion'

S/P can arrange magnets on any of the five human figures on the wall. Each human figure has five regions enclosed by unbroken lines where S/P is required to place the magnets only within the hands, body and legs of the figures. This means, based on d-touch region adjacency diagram, there will be 5 branch nodes, with the first two nodes pre-set within the artwork and the next three nodes dependent on the number of placed magnet within the artwork. The nodes will take the composition of 1:1:n:n:n with n being the value between 0 to 3.

They can place the magnets however they like provided (i) it does not touch the line of the placement area, (ii) at least one magnet is placed in any of the placement area and (iii) there are at most three magnets within one placement area. S/P would then scan the artwork using Artcodes apps through a phone provided at the exhibit which will then generate a hyperlink to a webpage with specific narratives that supposedly describe their personal tendencies based on the placement of the magnets. In reality, the interpretations are only made up by one of the authors which include combinations of horoscopes and online personality quizzes results.

Table 1 lists the possible region adjacency tree diagram nodes that will trigger the interactive experience. The overall setup is done to control the number of narratives produced by the system as well as limit the variation of magnet placements.

Table 1. Region adjacency tree diagram nodes for 'Free Will is an Illusion'

Face - pre-set by artwork design			Body (Hands, Legs, Torso) – set by users through magnet placement					
1	:	1	:	0	:	0	:	1
1	:	1	:	0	:	1	:	0
1	:	1	:	1	:	0	:	0
1	:	1	:	1	:	0	:	1
1	:	1	:	1	:	1	:	0
1	:	1	:	1	:	1	:	1

3.3 S/P Roles

The gallery visitors were our targeted audience. We expected them to play the role of spectator where they initially observe how to engage with the artwork. We believe that the interaction with an artwork is a novelty and would attract them to experience it henceforth becoming a participant.

To prove our theory that "*the notion that consciousness is only a story that the brain creates to justify human actions which are triggered by the unconscious*" we invited the S/P to answer a brief questionnaire to capture their agreement on the narratives provided in the webpage.

4   Art Exhibition as a Place of Testing in the Wild

Our work was displayed in an art gallery from 24 October to 31 December 2016 for an exhibition titled 'Brain' (Fig. 4). During the exhibition, an assistant curator gave guidance to some audience to interact with the work.

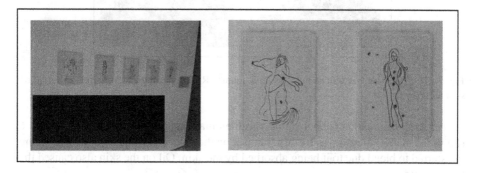

Fig. 4. Our interactive artwork at the gallery

We recorded 65 responses from our webpage. The ways the audience interacted with the work were akin to three levels of Peirce's semiosis – the ways people make meanings out of signs and symbols [13]: Firstness - the audience observes the artwork as it is, without interacting with it. Secondness - the audience views the artwork as an interactive object which can be manipulated to achieve certain goals (the audience downloaded the app and arranged the magnets on the images). Thirdness - the audience interpretation of the artwork, in relation to their previous experience (the audience clicked 'Agree' or 'Disagree' buttons on the webpage that provides interpretations of their magnets arrangements).

The assistant curator noticed that there were audiences who only interacted on the firstness level because they were facing technological problems such as the inability of the app to read the images. This was due to the wrong arrangements of magnets or the app simply failed to work. Many people could not relate the images with the message that consciousness could be an illusion. Our intent was to use images of human bodies as something that people can relate to, but the style and content of the images were perhaps too alien to the culture of the audience hence their inability to relate to them.

5   Artcodes Markers as Second Skin

In addition to the interactive artwork exhibition, we also explored the use of Artcodes markers on human skin. We made prototypes using potatoes and stamp pad ink to test our markers design. Figure 5 shows a simple Artcodes marker carved on a potato. The marker was then stamped on a piece of paper, and on the skin to test its visibility and stability for image recognition.

Fig. 5. (Left) Carving Artcodes markers on a potato. (Right) Testing Artcodes potato stamp on skin and paper

An Artcodes marker rubber stamp was then made and tested on the skin. Figure 6 shows the marker after it was freshly stamped on the skin. After about 10 min the stamp ink started to bleed due to it being absorbed by the skin. Oil on the skin also caused the ink to smudge.

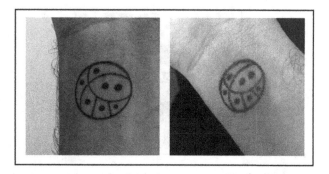

Fig. 6. (Left) Artcodes marker freshly stamped on the skin. (Right) The ink bled after about 10 min

Figure 7 shows Artcodes app reading the potato stamp marker on a piece of paper, displaying the word 'baby'. This implies that the marker is recognised by the apps where when the word 'baby' is clicked, user will be brought to a specific webpage. Unfortunately, similar observation was not achieved on markers stamped on the skin (see Fig. 7, right). This is because body hair on the skin was registered as lines by the app, implying additional nodes in the design disabling any valid recognition from the apps. The bled ink was also read by the app as extra lines and the criss-cross pattern created by the ink on the marker lines registered as extra regions by Artcodes.

Fig. 7. (Left) Artcodes successfully reading the stamped marker on paper. (Right) Undetected stamped Artcodes marker on the skin

We also explored the use of henna tattoo to make Artcodes marker on the skin. Henna-based marker seems promising as it appears more stable and more readable compared to rubber stamp marker. However, it took a henna tattoo artist to draw the marker due to its delicate process. Moreover, the drying process took a longer time compared to rubber stamp marker. If during the drying process, the henna was smudged, the lines would also be unreadable by Artcodes. The henna tattoo seen in Fig. 8 was initially easily readable, but after the first wash the tattoo could not be detected by Artcodes anymore.

Fig. 8. Henna-tattoo based Artcodes marker

Figure 9 shows an Artcodes marker on the skin made with a temporary tattoo. The tattoo was made by printing the marker on temporary tattoo sticker using a laser printer. To apply the tattoo, the plastic side of the temporary sticker was applied on the skin and the paper side was dampened using water. After 10 min, the paper was removed and the tattoo sticked to the skin. Compared to stamped-based markers and henna tattoo-based markers, temporary tattoo Artcodes marker has the most reliable readability. Applied on hairless skin, it is readable by Artcodes apps in various lighting conditions. However, to make the tattoo easily readable, it needs to be applied without causing creases on the skin by damping it adequately before removing the back paper of the temporary tattoo sticker.

Fig. 9. Tattoo-based Artcodes marker

5.1 Observation

We did not manage to make temporary tattoos for the 'Brain' exhibition; however, we did test the concept during a one-day research exhibition in September 2016. The visitors to our booth were given an envelope that contains Artcodes temporary tattoos and an instruction to apply the tattoo and read it using Artcodes. The tattoo was linked to a Facebook page, and visitors were encouraged to like the page and post the image of their tattoo on the page. Only one booth visitor tried it at the booth. We did not get any likes or post on the Facebook page. Another visitor remarked that tattoos are considered as forbidden in his culture and our choice of using temporary tattoos was disrespectful. We also applied the tattoo on our arms and demonstrated to the visitors how it worked with Artcodes. It was difficult for ArtCodes to read the tattoo and as the day went by, the tattoo become more wrinkled on our skin. As the lighting in the hall where the exhibition took place was very bright, the wrinkles were registered as extra regions by the app making it unreadable.

6 Lesson Learned and Future Work

Our experience of using Artcodes app to read moveable markers and markers used on human skin reveals technological aspects to be improved if the app were to be used in similar contexts in the future. In the art gallery, the audience were perhaps much readier to face ambiguity, thus were more tolerable with the process using the app and exploring ways to make it work with the artwork. This is in contrast with the visitors of our science exhibition booth. We argue that moveable markers can be used in the future, especially in educational settings. Meanwhile, the skin marker may be used in medical settings or at events such as festivals or concerts. However, for it to be applied in a more practical context where accuracy is important, the pattern recognition algorithm of Artcodes app needs to be improved in the following manner:

- It needs to be able to differentiate between shadows created by three-dimensional objects and the lines on the moveable markers.
- It needs to recognise the creases on temporary tattoos as noise and filter it out from the patterns on the tattoos.

Despite the many hiccups faced in the use of Artcodes as interactive artwork, these are mainly technicality issues that perhaps could be addressed with better camera specifications and improving the sensitivity of the algorithm recognition. The engagement observed by visitors of our exhibit indicates that such interaction has potential and can be very exciting for some. Artwork if just paint and paper may be too abstract but the application of Artcodes markers may make passive objects interactive and be a talking point for years to come. As we move on to the realm of Internet of Things, the use of Artcodes could offer control over virtual environments as well as the aesthetic appearance of tangibles used to initiate the interaction.

References

1. Costanza, E., Huang, J.: Designable visual markers. In: Proceedings of the 27th International Conference on Human Factors in Computing Systems, pp. 1879–1888. ACM (2009)
2. Harun, A.F., Benford, S., O'Malley, C., Md Noor, N.L.: Playing with rules: structuring written rules for visual marker design. In: 3rd International Conference on Computer and Communication Systems (2018, to be Published)
3. Harun, A.F.: The design and use of visual markers in school. Ph.D. thesis. University of Nottingham (2014)
4. Benford, S., Boriana, K., Quinn, A., Thorn, E.-C., Glover, K., Preston, W., Hazzard, A., Rennick-Egglestone, S., Greenhalgh, C., Mortier, R.: Crafting interactive decorations. ACM Trans. Comput.-Hum. Interact. **24**, 26 (2017)

5. Glover, K., Boriana, K., Benford, S., Thorn, E.-C.: The Artcodes App. UK Research and Innovation Homepage. http://gtr.ukri.org/project/B594DAA0-6C02-4CC2-AF1F-6F287B7 CED8F. Accessed 20 Feb 2018

6. Benford, S., Hazzard, A., Chamberlain, A., Xu, L.: Augmenting a guitar with its digital footprint. In: 15th International Conference on New Interfaces for Musical Expression, Baton Rouge, Louisiana, USA (2015)

7. Edmonds, E.A.: Human computer interaction, art and experience. In: Candy, L., Ferguson, S. (eds.) Interactive Experience in the Digital Age. SSCC, pp. 11–23. Springer, Cham (2014). https://doi.org/10.1007/978-3-319-04510-8_2

8. Höök, K., Sengers, P., Andersson, G.: Sense and sensibility: evaluation and interactive art. In: Proceedings of the SIGCHI Conference on Human Factors in Computing Systems, pp. 241–248 (2003)

9. Levin, G.: A personal chronology of audiovisual systems research. In: Proceedings of the 2005 Conference on New Interfaces for Musical Expression, pp. 2–3. National University of Singapore (2005)

10. Levin, G., Shakar, G., Gibbons, S., Sohrawardy, Y., Gruber, J., Semlak, E., Schmidl, G., Lehner, J., Feinberg, J.: Dialtones (A Telesymphony) (2001)

11. Benford, S., Crabtree, A., Flintham, M., Greenhalgh, C., Koleva, B., Adams, M., Tandavanitj, N., Farr, J.R., Giannachi, G., Lindt, I.: Creating the spectacle: designing interactional trajectories through spectator interfaces. ACM Trans. Comput.-Hum. Interact. (TOCHI) **18**, 11 (2011)

12. Benford, S., Crabtree, A., Reeves, S., Sheridan, J., Dix, A., Flintham, M., Drozd, A.: The frame of the game: blurring the boundary between fiction and reality in mobile experiences. In: Proceedings of the SIGCHI Conference on Human Factors in Computing Systems, pp. 427–436 (2006)

13. Peirce, C.S.: Peirce on Signs: Writings on Semiotic. UNC Press Books (1991)

A Systematic Review on Digital Technology for Enhancing User Experience in Museums

Nurul Fathihin Mohd Noor Shah[1(✉)] and Masitah Ghazali[2]

[1] Faculty of Science and Technology, Universiti Sains Islam Malaysia (USIM), Nilai, Negeri Sembilan, Malaysia
fathinshah@usim.edu.my

[2] ViCubeLab, Faculty of Computing, Universiti Teknologi Malaysia, Skudai, Johor, Malaysia
masitah@utm.my

Abstract. This paper presents a review on using digital technology (DT) for enhancing visitors' user experiences in museums. The user experience (UX) is one of the key aspects of human-computer interaction between human and technology. Studies have found that using digital technology can enhance user experience in visiting museums, however, more research need to be conducted about what user needs and expects from the technology. The results of the study show, there are many types of digital technology for enhancing user experience in museums that had been developed, but an understanding of the user expectation will be the main key point to develop better-design digital technology applications.

Keywords: Human-computer interaction · Digital technology
User experience · Museums

1 Introduction

There has been a dramatic rise in the studies of the usage of digital technology (DT) in museums. Museum institutions start to digitizing their collection of artifact, for presentation and preservation and combined physical museum exhibitions with digital content for visitors. Allison states that the technology nowadays can bring the history closer to us because it was found that human-computer interaction can enhance users' experiences and provide more intuitive and usable systems from re-conceptualize the past and stimulate reality [1], which goes with the saying, "The more you know about your past, the better prepared you are for the future" [2].

Museum is a cultural institution which plays an important role as a reference center, particularly about the past and the history of cultural identity and the civilization of a country by exhibiting a large number of materials and artifacts. A definition of a museum by the International Council of Museums (ICOM) is, museum can be described as a non-profit, permanent institution which is developed and open to the public for the service of society, which acquires, conserves, identifies, communicates, and exhibits material evidence of people and their environment for purposes of study, education and enjoyment [3]. With the advent of digital technologies in museums, the

© Springer Nature Singapore Pte Ltd. 2018
N. Abdullah et al. (Eds.): i-USEr 2018, CCIS 886, pp. 35–46, 2018.
https://doi.org/10.1007/978-981-13-1628-9_4

visitors can enhance their on-site visiting experience by discovering and involving directly with what they see.

In general, user experience (UX) defines the people's feelings, perceptions and responses that result from the use and/or imagined use of a product, system or service. Focusing on UX enables design to focus on the user's needs. User experience has also been defined as a variety of feeling and ongoing reflection on the events that one is going through [4, 5], fulfilling the human needs [5] and consequence of user's internal state [6] while using a product, system or service in a specific context.

In this paper, we aim to identify and review the types of digital technology that have been used to enhance user experience while visiting museums. This is pertinent in order for us to understand, among others, the criteria that made it work, and the interaction styles chosen with regard to the DT. This paper will first describe the review method performed in this study, including the research questions, followed by a section which will be presenting the findings from the review. The subsequent section will discuss the findings by answering the research questions which were posed earlier. This paper will then conclude with a closing remark and future work.

2 Method

2.1 Research Questions

This paper is based on considering following research questions, which the scope of the study includes child to tertiary level, as well as disabled people.

[Q1] What types of digital technology that have been used to enhance visitor experience while visiting museums?

[Q2] How does digital technology enhance visitors' experience?

2.2 Data Collection

Considerable literature search was performed from the ACM Digital Library, Scopus, Science Direct, IEEE Digital Library and Springer Link with the keywords: (digital technology) AND (enhance user experience) AND (museums). The year of the articles published were selected in the past five years (excluding 2018), i.e. between 2013 and 2017. The total number of the articles found are 525, by using the keywords which are not limited to any subject area.

2.3 Inclusion Criteria

The selection criteria for data extraction process should be relevant to computer science and sub-disciplines under human-computer interaction. Qualitative analysis questions have been designed to gather paper related to the research questions. Table 1 shows the qualitative analysis questions that were asked while analyzing the articles to produce data findings.

Table 1. Qualitative analysis question

Question	Answer
Q1: Was the article about digital technology in museums?	Yes/No
Q2: Was user experience or HCI mentioned in the paper?	Yes/No
Q3: Did the paper mention about digital technology enhance user experience?	Yes/No/Partially
Q4: Will the paper contribute to the research conducted?	Yes/No/Partially

3   Findings

Table 2 shows the results of the selected articles from the search procedure. Articles other than the inclusion criteria and did not meet the criteria under the qualitative analysis question were eliminated. A total number of 22 articles relevant to the study were selected for the final reading. Table 2 shows the list of findings from the selected articles that answer the qualitative analysis questions.

Table 2. List of selected reviewed papers

ID	Author	Year	Title	Type	Q1	Q2	Q3	Q4
S1	Allen, K. et al.	2013	Interactive Sensory Objects for Improving Access to Heritage	Journal	Yes	Yes	Yes	Yes
S2	Clini, P. et al.	2014	Augmented Reality Experience: From High-Resolution Acquisition to Real Time Augmented Contents	Journal	Yes	Yes	Yes	Yes
S3	Fevgas, A. et al.	2014	The iMuse Virtual Museum: towards a cultural education platform	Proceeding	Yes	Yes	Yes	Yes
S4	Pagano, A. et al.	2015	Evaluation of the Educational Potentials - Interactive Technologies Applied to Cultural Heritage	Journal	Yes	Yes	Partially	Yes
S5	Graf, H. et al.	2015	A Contextualized Educational Museum Experience Connecting Objects, Places and Themes through mobile Virtual Museums	Proceeding	Yes	Yes	Yes	Yes
S6	Jean, H.C. et al.	2015	Mapping Place: Supporting Cultural Learning through a Lukasa-inspired Tangible Tabletop Museum Exhibit	Paper Demonstration	Yes	No	Partially	Partially
S7	Price, S. et al.	2015	Exploring Whole-Body Interaction and Design for Museums	Journal	Yes	Yes	Partially	Partially

(continued)

Table 2. (*continued*)

ID	Author	Year	Title	Type	Q1	Q2	Q3	Q4
S8	Yoshida, R. et al.	2015	Experience-based Learning Support System to Enhance Child Learning in Museum – Touching Real Fossils and "Experiencing" Palaentological Environment	Proceeding	Yes	No	Yes	Partially
S9	Hürst, W. et al.	2016	Using Digital Extensions to Create New VR Museum Experiences	Proceeding	Yes	No	No	Partially
S10	Jacobs, M. et al.	2016	Two Countries, Eight Museums: Aiming for Cross-Cultural Experience Blend	Proceeding	Yes	No	Yes	Yes
S11	Anagnostakis, G. et al.	2016	Accessible Museum Collections for the Visually Impaired: Combining Tactile Exploration, Audio Descriptions and Mobile Gestures	Proceeding	Yes	No	No	Partially
S12	Hürst, W. et al.	2016	Complementing Artworks to create Immersive VR Museum Experience	Proceeding	Yes	No	No	No
S13	Velho, L. and Duprat, M.	2016	Olhar 3D	Proceeding	Yes	No	Yes	Partially
S14	Pedersen, I. et al.	2016	TombSeer: Illuminating the Dead	Proceeding	Yes	No	Yes	Partially
S15	Mokatren, M. et al.	2016	Using Eye Tracking for Enhancing the Museum Visit Experience	Proceeding	Yes	No	Yes	Partially
S16	Jean, H.C. et al.	2016	Sensing History: Contextualizing Artifacts with Sensory Interactions and Narrative Design	Proceeding	Yes	No	Yes	Yes
S17	Rodrigues, J.M.F. et al.	2016	An Initial Framework for a Museum Application for Senior Citizens	Proceeding	Yes	Yes	Partially	Yes
S18	Kasomoulis, A. et al.	2016	MagicHOLO – A Collaborative 3D Experience in the Museum	Proceeding	Yes	No	Yes	Yes
S19	Koutsabasis, P. and Vosinakis, S.	2017	Kinesthetic interactions in museums: conveying cultural heritage by making use of ancient tools and (re-) constructing artworks	Journal	Yes	Yes	Partially	Yes
S20	Hayes, S. et al.	2017	Piecing Together the Past: Constructing Stories with Jigsaw Puzzles in Museums	Proceeding	Yes	Yes	Yes	Yes

(*continued*)

Table 2. (*continued*)

ID	Author	Year	Title	Type	Q1	Q2	Q3	Q4
S21	Jim, R.K. et al.	2017	Touch3D: Touchscreen Interaction on Multiscopic 3D with Electrovibration Haptics	Poster	Yes	No	Partially	Partially
S22	Pederson, I. et al.	2017	More than Meets the Eye: The Benefits OF Augmented Reality and Holographic Displays for Digital Cultural Heritage	Journal	Yes	No	Yes	Yes

Meanwhile, Fig. 1 illustrates a bar chart that shows the number of publications between the year 2013 and 2017. The year of 2016, shows the highest number of publications with 10 articles, as opposed to only 1 article in 2013. 5 articles were found from the year 2015 and 4 articles in 2017, and 2 articles from 2014. The studies of DT in museums to enhance UX is surely becoming popular and deemed to be important in integrating technology in the museums setting.

Table 3 shows the results of distribution of the papers from the electronic database. The most notable publication is from the Association for Computing Machinery (ACM) Digital Library since 16 articles came from this electronic database followed by IEEE Digital Library with 3 articles. Meanwhile, there are only 2 articles from Scopus and 1 article from Springer Link. There is no article selected or related to the topics from Science Direct database.

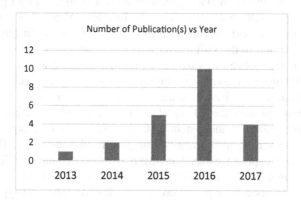

Fig. 1. Number of publication (s) vs year

Table 3. Distribution of the papers according to electronic database

Electronic database	Number
ACM Digital Library	16
IEEE Digital Library	3
Science Direct	0
Springer Link	1
Scopus	2

4   Discussion

This section will now discuss the research questions posed earlier for this study.

[Q1] What types of digital technology that have been used to enhance user experience while visiting museums?

Nowadays, museums have been using various digital technologies to improve and enhance their visitors' experience. Emerging technologies such as smart phone, tablet, Kinect, HMD (Head Mounted Display), multimedia element, touchscreen and tabletop, moving the way of visiting museums from can only see the display of artifacts from a distant, to visitors can now touch, engage, immerse and get interactive information from the exhibits. Based on the data collected, all the articles show numerous types of digital technology that have been used to enhance user experience while visiting museums. Portable devices such as smartphones and tablets are the two top of types of technology, which had been used, because most visitors bring their own devices when visiting the museums [7].

There are approximately 10 articles from 22 selected articles showing the use of mobile as the type of digital technology in the museum which is S2, S3, S5, S10, S11, S13, S15, S17, S18 and S21. From these 10 articles, mobile has been used with various types of application such as virtual reality, augmented reality, QR code, eye tracking and 3D display. S2 presents the result of using augmented reality in mobile application for museum exhibition of cultural contents, which by using augmented reality it enhances user appreciation and understanding of tangible and intangible cultural heritage. S3 is about the use of mobile application named iMuse as a tour guide to assist the visitor during a walk inside the museum. Besides, iMuse also contains virtual presenter application and virtual wing, which is based on the web platform and kiosk to give digital information to the visitor with interactive games.

While S5 is using mobile as virtual museum interconnected with 4 local museums, objects and stories under one storyline. This application uses image recognition and QR code reading technique for visitor to retrieve information about selected objects. This mobile application will show the 3D digital replicas along with digital information after the objects are recognized by the system. S10 discussed about user experience beyond the mobile museums using mixed reality with gamification elements. This project is about cross-cultural experience blend involved with two countries (Netherland and Germany) and eight museums. Meanwhile S11 described about accessibility of museum exhibits to visually impaired users using mobile. The prototype system has been created with touch sensitive audio description and touch gestures application in mobile to explain and presenting about the exhibit replicas in an exhibition room. S13 is about mobile application name Olhar 3D. This application expands the content of exhibition in advanced mathematics, Poincare' theorem and using mixed reality through mobile devices to enhance user experience with multimedia content and interaction.

In S15, the articles are discussing about the potential of using mobile eye-tracking application and vision technology to enhance museum visitor experience. This technology will combine with a mobile museum visitors' guide to identifying visitors' object of interest to generate personalized information distribution. S17 presents an initial framework about an adaptive user interface for museum application with augmented reality and gamification aiming to create an emotional experience for the user. This application which is designed for senior citizen with mobility, vision, hearing and digital-literacy restrictions, however, has the capacity to point the mobile device and capable to "touch" and slide". S18 propose MagicHOLO a collaborative digital application with personal mobile-devices for the delivery of 3D experiences. MagicHOLO will show 3D digital imaging with the help of 3d projecting pyramid and synchronized video playback. For S21, Touch3D presents an interactive mobile with realistic 3D viewing experience with touchscreen interaction. This integrates with 2 technologies, which is automultiscopic 3D display and electrovibration display.

S7, S8 and S19 are published about the use of Kinect as a digital tools technology for visitors to use in museum spaces. S7 discussed about collaboration of visitor groups (families and children) in the museum with collective interactive by using a whole-body interface using Kinect. Meanwhile S8 is about body experience in the digital paleontological environment. Kinect sensor will record the movement of learner and measure the learner location, pose, and action. The learning content will base on measurement result recorded. S19 is about using Kinect through body movement and hand gestures and interaction with 3D sculpturing application for sculpturing Cycladic figurines.

S1 is about interactive, multisensory box to represent visitor experience of Speke Hall, a heritage site in the UK. This sensory box will have a sound effect(s), visual effects and possible vibration movement and this project involved with artists, people with technology and people with learning disabilities. S4 article discussed about interactive exhibition which to enhance learnability and memorability with the support of technology using all the multimedia elements for enhancing user experience among young visitors (but also adults). During the exhibition at the museum, young visitor will learn about "History of Rome, the city of Augustus" with QR code technology, touch tables, 3D print, AR, 3D scenes, serious-game and holographic display to give best and exciting experience for visitors. S16 is about narrative design using visual, audio and projector to evoke visitor's feeling to perform interaction to relate historical content with personal experience. Olfactory has been used for sensory interaction.

S6 and S20 pointed out about to engage children to learn about history in museums with playful way with the help of technology. S6 is about tangible interactive tabletop which gives visitors experience to learn and understand about symbol and nonlinguistic mapping history of African notions. Concurrently, the S20 is about interactive computer mediated jigsaw puzzle, PuzzleBeo. PuzzleBeo is designed for stimulating child's curiosity to play about maritime museum. PuzzleBeo is one of the analog games with digital technology that allows children to construct stories about maritime museum.

In S14 and S22, the studies are using HMD as a hardware platform for 3D Interactive holographic images. Both articles discussed about an augmented reality application that immerse the visitors in a museum space appealing, seeing and gesturing, using holographic that makes the artifacts "backs to life" through gesture activity. S9 and S12 are about recreating existing museum experiences in VR museums and giving visitor experience in how painting can be extended, modified or enhanced to be explored. Table 4 shows a list of digital technologies from the selected articles.

Table 4. List of types and criteria of digital technology from selected reviewed papers

Type of DT	Criteria of DT	ID
Multimedia elements: camera, videos, audio recorder, simple electric circuits, Arduino technology, LEDs and Buzzer	Sensory box	S1
Mobile application: mobile, desktop, social application, mobile software and AR	Augmented reality painting	S2
iMuse- mobile tour guide system. Mobile, mobile UHF RFID reader, handheld integrated pistol grip	Virtual museum tour guide and virtual presenter	S3
Multimedia elements: audio, video, text, images. QR code and holographic	Interactive exhibition with serious games and digital storytelling	S4
Mobile app. for virtual museums. Web technologies, 3D interactive graphic. Image recognition, QR codes	Virtual museum connects with venues, objects and stories	S5
Tangible tabletop	Interactive tangible tabletop	S6
X-box Kinect, projection	Body interaction Kinect	S7
Kinect sensor and RFID tag/sensor, projector, laptop, screen. Video content tour	Digital real book system and immersive learning system	S8
3D, Unity 3d game engine, Oculus rift (headset), Samsung gear VR	Digitization painting extension use to VR museums	S9
IBeacons and persuasive technology (computers, mobile phones, websites, wireless technologies, mobile applications, video games, etc.)	Mix reality blended experience with gamification elements	S10
Mobile device, 3d printed exhibits, touch sensors, Arduino board and mobile app	Touch-sensitive audio descriptions and touch gestures	S11
VR Museum. 3d representation on painting. Photographic images, headset	Digital painting in virtual museum setting	S12
Mobile micro location, 3D, wireless communication and interactive multimedia, Bluetooth low energy (BLE) Beacon	Interactive multimedia content and information with mix reality	S13
TombSeer- immerse (sight and touch) Wearablle technology, holographic, AR, HMD, handheld devices	Gestural and visual augmented reality experience	S14
Mobile eye tracking, mobile guide, vision technology	A smart context-aware mobile guide	S15
Projector, multimedia elements	Narrative design and sensory interactions	S16
Mobile AR: unity 3d and AR toolkit	Augmented reality and gamification relate to an adaptive user interface	S17

(continued)

Table 4. (*continued*)

Type of DT	Criteria of DT	ID
3D digital imaging, video and mobile	Collaborative digital application with personal mobile-devices for the delivery of enchanting 3D experiences	S18
3D environment, Kinect, leap motion sensor, unity game engine	Kinesthetic interactions with 3D applications through body movements and hand gestures	S19
Multisensory tangible user interface, thermal node, audio haptic and RFID, digital projector	An interactive installation that allows children to construct stories using computer mediated jigsaw puzzle and multimodal display	S20
Mobile Touch 3D: automultiscopic 3D display, Electrovibration display, multimodal interface, glasses-free 3d illusion and tactile sensation with real time touch interaction	An interactive touchscreen that delivers realistic viewing and touching experiences through glasses-free 3D	S21
Immerse two sense (visual n gesture): 3D holographic, AR and HMD with gesture	Gestural and visual augmented reality experience	S22

Figure 2 shows 6 types of digital technology used to enhance user experience while visiting the museum, based from data collected. Overall, 46% of articles have used mobile in their research as their digital technology to enhance user experience in museums. From the pie-chart, it clearly shows that 18% of the articles used headset as their digital technology tools, meanwhile multimedia elements and Kinect display 14% respectively. There were only 4% each for touch screen and tabletop used as a digital technology to enhance user experience in museum from the 22 articles selected.

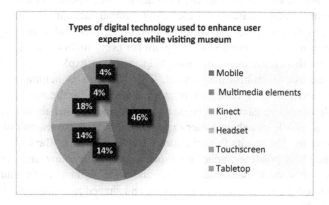

Fig. 2. Types of digital technology used to enhance user experience while visiting museums

[Q2] How *does digital technology enhance visitors' experience?*

User experience is something that ensures user to find valuable and meaningful involvement besides evoking user emotion while using the digital product, system or services provided [8]. User experience includes a user attitude, behavior and feelings [9] to respond towards the context. It is undeniable that the use of technologies can enhance visitor experience and give visitor valuable experience, to engage and connect with artifact and exhibits [10].

Nowadays, having sophisticated smartphones and tablets is a trend. From the articles collected, mobile has been used extensively and merged with other technologies such as augmented reality, virtual reality, eye tracking and many more new technologies to enhance visitors' experience. An example of S15, mobile eye tracking is used to encourage visitors to use devices that provide multimedia content rather than using a guide book. Multimedia content includes text, video, audio, animation, photo which gives the user some experience while exploring the museum. Mobile devices also can enhance accessibility of museum exhibits to visually impaired users in S11. The approach supports navigation in exhibition halls and tactile exploration of exhibit replicas. Olhar3D in S13 is a mobile which integrates with micro location, wireless communication and interactive multimedia. This allows visitor to personalize interaction with information and media content. Olhar3D, gives visitor experience by extending the traditional exhibit beyond the physical collection.

MagicHOLO in S18 also gives user experience to have social interaction with other visitor, while using personal mobile application and collocated experience with 3D presentation of artifacts. Through 3D digital imaging, visitor can enhance their understanding about cultural artifacts and learning in engaging way. Not being left behind, interactive mobile application Touch3D in S21 gives visitor experience in human sensory system (see and touch) [11] for realistic 3D viewing and touching experience.

S2 has stated that using augmented reality (AR) mobile application, able to enhance the museum visit experience by capturing the attention of visitor. By using interactive tool, visitor can do active vision and identify important facts at museums. Museums will become an enjoying place for visitor to spend their time and visiting the museum with a new perception. A virtual museum platform using mobile was discussed in S3 which aims to enhance the museum visits, help visitor to explore inside the museum and provide access to multimedia content. This platform is helping the visitor to improve their understanding about information and artifact at the museum using presentation with interactive games and guide tour. S5 also discussed about ongoing result of using virtual mobile to enhance user experience and increase learnability of visitor inside the museum. The results from this study shows that, using the technology gives new experience and positive impact on aspects indirect learning such as enhanced memorability and gain deeper understanding about the artifacts at the museum. The mobile app helped the visitor to memorize color and shaped associated with the objects at museum exhibition.

Besides, to increase experience of visitor, some project is being developed using Kinect sensor, RFID tag/sensor, video, projector and laptop to give immersion for the user. In S8, the article is about immersion learning which visitor can watch and touch the real fossil. This technology gives new experience and interest of the visitor can be enhanced by touching the real artifact. Furthermore, S19 pointed out that kinesthetic interaction (body movement and hand gesture) used in a 3D environment for sculpturing gives visitor fun and immerse experience because the user acts in the role of ancient craftsman who construct the figurine. This activity can enhance visitor's experience while visiting the museum.

HMD also can enhance user experience by making visitor immerse in visual and gesture interaction in museum spaces. S14 and S22 projects allow users to simply choose what they want to discover about the artifact without having to read through screens of unnecessary information. Both projects can give user experience to grab an artifact, and turn it around in order to review it.

Tangible user interface and tabletop can give visitor fun and learning experience in museum since the practice is interaction between the real world and virtual world [12], wherein the physical dimensions were enriched by digital elements which are discussed in articles S6 and S20. The role of digital technology also can help people with disabilities to have better access to cultural heritage. In S1, people with learning disabilities are working together with researcher to create interactive sensory objects which can give them better experience and understanding about museums and heritage by exploring, handling and responding to artifacts.

5 Conclusion and Future Work

Using digital technology for visiting and exploring museums will surely help the visitors to enhance their museum experience. Visitor can immerse and engage during the visit as well as explore more about artefact information using digital technology. Furthermore, using digital technology it can attract especially young visitor to have interest to visit the museum since the way of learning and exploring around the museum is fun and excitement. This paper aims to review the current types of digital technology that have been used to enhance user experiences at museum settings. The systematic literature review has been used in order to achieve the objective. There is a clear evidence that digital technology really helps enhancing the user experience in museums. We learned that the right combinations of types and criteria of DT, with the suitable types of users, bring out the best of experience at museums. For future research, we aim to identify what is the user expectation from digital technology to visit museums for better-designed application. Hopefully, this paper can be a reference for research in the field to develop better digital tools for enhancing the user experience while visiting museums.

Acknowledgement. This work is supported by the Malaysia Ministry of Higher Education (MOHE) and Research Management Centre (RMC) at the Universiti Teknologi Malaysia (UTM) under the Research University Grant Category (VOT Q.J130000.2528.13H45).

References

1. Allison, J.J.: History educators and the challenge of immersive pasts: a critical review of virtual reality tools and history pedagogy. Learn. Media Technol. **33**(4), 343–352 (2008)
2. Roosevelt, T.: History quote of the day (2015). http://discoverhistorictravel.com/history-quote-of-the-day-teddy-roosevelt/. Accessed 30 Oct 2017
3. Museum definition 24 August 2007. http://icom.museum/the-vision/museum-definition/. Accessed 30 Oct 2017
4. Hancock, P.A., Pepe, A.A., Murphy, L.L.: Hedonomics: the power of positive and pleasurable ergonomics. Ergon. Des. **13**(1), 8–14 (2005)
5. Hassenzhal, M.: User experience (UX): towards an experiential perspective on product quality. In: Proceedings of the 20th Conference on Interaction Homme-Machine, pp. 11–15 (2008)
6. Hassenzhal, M., Tranctinsky, N.: User experience – a research agenda. Behav. Inf. Technol. **25**(2), 91–97 (2006)
7. Vaz, R., Fernandes, P.O., Veiga, A.C.N.R.: Interactive technologies in museums: how digital installations and media are enhancing the visitors, chapter 2. Experience, Handbook of Research on Technological Developments for Cultural Heritage and e-Tourism Applications (2017). https://doi.org/10.4018/978-1-5225-2927-9.ch002
8. Pagano A., Armone G., De Sanctis E.: Virtual museums and audience studies. the case of keys to Rome exhibition. In: Proceedings Digital Heritage 2015, International Congress, 28 ottobre – 2 ottobre 2015, Granada, Spagna, IEEE Press (2015)
9. Konstantakis, M., Aliprantis, J., Caridakis, G., Michalakis, K., Kalatha, E.: Formalising and evaluating cultural user experience. In: Conference 2017 12th International Workshop on Semantic and Social Media Adaptation and Personalization (SMAP) (2017)
10. Othman, M.K., Petrie, H., Power, C.: Engaging visitors in museums with technology: scales for the measurement of visitor and multimedia guide experience. In: Campos, P., Graham, N., Jorge, J., Nunes, N., Palanque, P., Winckler, M. (eds.) INTERACT 2011. LNCS, vol. 6949, pp. 92–99. Springer, Heidelberg (2011). https://doi.org/10.1007/978-3-642-23768-3_8
11. Meyer, K., Kaplan, T.J., Essex, R., Damasio, H., Damasio, A.: Seeing touch is correlated with content-specific activity in primary somatosensory cortex. Cereb. Cortex **21**(9), 2113–2121 (2011)
12. Shaer, O., Hornecker, E.: Tangible user interfaces: fast, present and future directions. Found. Trends Hum. Comput. Interaction **3**(1–2), 1–137 (2010)

Design and Development of Mobile Augmented Reality for Physics Experiment

Juliana Aida Abu Bakar[1]([✉]), Valarmathie Gopalan[2],
Abdul Nasir Zulkifli[1], and Asmidah Alwi[1]

[1] Institute of Creative Humanities, Multimedia and Innovation,
School of Creative Industry Management & Performing Arts,
University Utara Malaysia, Sintok, Malaysia
liana@uum.edu.my
[2] School of Multimedia Technology and Communication,
College of Arts and Sciences, University Utara Malaysia, Sintok, Malaysia

Abstract. Augmented Reality (AR) provides an authentic and realistic learning experience. It is obvious that younger generation prefers technology intervened learning rather than conventional learning. Although previous work on AR have shed some lights on the use of such technology on learning, studies focusing on science experiment practices are still lacking. Experiments are crucial for students to enhance critical understanding of science phenomena. This article discusses the process of designing and developing a mobile app for physics experiment using AR technology. This is an auxiliary learning tool for upper secondary school students. The aim of this Mobile AR app for Physics experiment (MARPEX) is to provide rigorous information beyond conventional experiment practices and additional learning materials. Several experiments have been selected to be included in MARPEX. An expert review is conducted to gauge feedback and recommendations. Future work includes user evaluation of MARPEX on real classroom settings.

Keywords: Augmented Reality · Mobile app · Physics experiment

1 Introduction

Science experiments enhances the critical thinking and understanding. It is essential that the formation of deep-rooted minds and the installment of curiosity in science must surface in the process of building a science talent chain as early as possible. Subsequently, the inculcation of talent at higher education institutions with the application of scientific and technical knowledge and skills may continue to develop prior to specialization. As the fourth industrial revolution (4IR) comes in, the needs of producing science talents are significantly critical. However, current statistics indicate that the trend is shrinking due to the number of students choosing science specializations and the number of female students are less than male to opt for science [1]. This situation may impede the development of science talent chain. Hence, drastic solution may include the use of technology intervened learning to motivate these students to love learning science.

N. Abdullah et al. (Eds.): i-USEr 2018, CCIS 886, pp. 47–58, 2018.
https://doi.org/10.1007/978-981-13-1628-9_5

Mobile device in the practice of learning is widely welcomed among young generation. As the generation changes, their way of life and thinking also transformed. The teaching and learning techniques and the learning materials must also be parallel. If not, students will easily become uninterested which leads to lack of motivation [2, 3] states that technology and education are correlated and have a positive relationship, but there is a lack of representation medium or force that may make it more dynamic and energized. Currently, there are plenty of digital initiatives such as the Frog Virtual Learning Environment (Frog VLE) in order to make the learning process more interesting. However, these facilities can only be used within schools because the internet connection is required to participate in the online classroom learning and/or to login to Frog VLE. Therefore, there is a need for an auxiliary learning tool that temporary guides students outside their classrooms. This study proposes an augmented learning environment for science experiment using AR technology.

2   Background

2.1   Mobile Augmented Reality

Mobile learning grows in formal and informal educational landscape whereby Mobile Augmented Reality (MAR) merges both learning environments. It is forecasted that mobile device would be fully adopted in less than one year where global market for mobile learning is predicted to grow by 36% annually, increasing from $7.98 billion in 2015 to $37.6 billion by 2020 [4]. A survey of Mobile IT in higher education revealed that 67% of surveyed students in foreign countries utilize their mobile devices for academic activities [5]. AR technology provides the opportunity to witness the hidden part of learning that we should know to master the science concept. Mobile AR provides the opportunity to construct independent learner experiences based on their prior knowledge in the respective subject matter. These types of learning may develop active participation during indoor and outdoor learning activities. Mobile AR is developed to provide a flexible learning beyond time and location with less guidance from teachers and parents.

Mobile AR concepts are superimposing digital information on real environment and enhances the interaction between virtual environment and real environment [6]. Besides that, MAR provides opportunity for students to practice 21st century pedagogy skills such as of: (i) constructing own learning, (ii) student-centered learning, (iii) ubiquitous, (iv) cultivating critical, creative and higher-order thinking, (v) meaningful use of technology, and (vi) gaining wide knowledge. Previous studies have proven that only 30% of teaching influences students and the other 70% depends on the factors beyond teachers' control such as students' ability, prior preparation, value systems and personal considerations [7, 8]. On the other hand, [9] suggests that teachers can only filter, highlight, provide guidance, and always encourage students, but at the end, it is up to the learner's representation that determines the learning performance.

2.2 Challenges in Physics Experiments

Currently, there are several challenges in physics experiments. These challenges may hinder students to master the respective subject matter. In general, the challenges include the abstract nature of science learning content which may contribute to the difficulties in visualization. The accumulated difficulties would result in decreasing level of motivation. The conventional physics experiment may not able to extract the inner process of certain phenomenon and students could hardly visualize the content correctly because it is not visible or tangible. Mobile AR experiments may then extract the inner phenomenon and make it visible. Besides, there are other practical challenges of conventional experiments compared to Mobile AR experiments as listed in Table 1.

Table 1. Challenges of conventional experiment compared to mobile AR experiment.

Challenges	Conventional experiment	Mobile AR experiment
Time	Limited	Unlimited
Location/venue	School lab	Anywhere
Cost	High	Low
Availability of materials and apparatus	Not complete	Complete and mimic the real apparatus
View of content	90°	360°
Availability of content	Limited	Unlimited
Experiment type	Non-hazardous	All types of experiment

Table 1 attempts to compare conventional experiment and Mobile AR experiment. Conventional experiment takes place in school laboratory within allocated time and may suffer high expenditure in cost to provide complete materials as well as apparatus. The cost is probably higher due to the maintenance of lab materials under time limitation. Meanwhile, mobile AR experiments may take place anywhere and anytime. There is also lesser need to upgrade lab materials and apparatus and under no time frame. Conventional experiment provides 90° to content viewing while mobile AR experiment may provide 360° view. Besides that, the availability of conventional experiment is only available during school hours and it is only allowed to practice non-hazardous experiments. Whereas, mobile AR experiment provides the opportunity to repeat the same experiment as much as one wants until one really understands it and practice may resume over either hazardous or non-hazardous experiments.

3 Design and Development of MARPEX

Science consists of Pure Science, Physics, Chemistry and Biology. This study concentrates on Physics discipline because the contents are abstract and deal with non-living things. Physics is "the study of matter, momentum, and the collaboration between them" yet what really matter is that Physics is about querying and trying to seek answers to fundamental questions by observing and experimenting [10]. The difficulty in Physics is students fail to visualize and understand the scientific process correctly during experiments. Eventually, students find Physics as difficult and start to lose interest in learning.

Literature review reveals gaps in science experiment related research. It is observed that the learning impact on student flow experience and educational effectiveness related to electromagnetism topic which was compared between the web-based approach and AR based approach [11]. The result from pretest and posttest depicts that AR approach provides a highly effective learning experience and critical knowledge; and AR approach allows the students to reach a higher level of flow experience compared to those using the web-based application [11]. Then, an interactive Physics AR book is developed in a pilot study which revealed that AR approach has potentials to be effective in teaching complex 3D concepts [12]. Therefore, this study proposes MARPEX which is developed based on the hypothesized conceptual model of Mobile AR in science experiments towards learning motivation as discussed in [13].

3.1 Requirement Analysis

Prior to requirement analysis, it is a must for researchers to seek permission and approval from the Ministry of Education before conducting any research in schools. Hence, we did obtain the approval from these authorities prior to submitting the required documents.

For requirement analysis, teachers were appointed as content experts for this study. There were several characteristics followed in selecting the content experts. The criteria are as follows: should have at least 10 to 12 years of teaching experience, particularly in Physics and who are interested in technology intervention in teaching and learning. Those who were interested to be the expert in this study were approached which then led to further discussion.

The selected teachers became a part of this project from as early as possible. The selection of experiments and its content were reviewed by the experts. The mobile app was then developed based on their guidance and instruction. The focus of MARPEX was experiment activities and the core content adapted from the Physics textbook. In consensus, it is agreed that the topic of electromagnetic, among others, is considered the toughest to explain its concepts in classrooms and even after completing its experiment. It is probably due to the abstract concept of electromagnets which students hardly see with their naked eyes hence making understanding of such concepts rather unsuccessful.

The objectives of the selected experiments are as follows: to determine the strength of an electromagnet (Experiment 1); to determine the magnitude of the catapult force on a current-carrying conductor in a permanent magnetic field (Experiment 2); and to determine the magnitude of an induced current (Experiment 3). In addition, a quiz section with several multiple-choice questions related to the experiments were provided to access their self-knowledge. The students could hear either a round of applause audio for the correct answers, or a buzzer audio for wrong answers. Table 2 illustrates the aim and hypothesis of these selected experiments.

Table 2. The aim and hypothesis of experiments included in MARPEX

Aim of experiment	Hypothesis
Experiment 1: to determine the strength of an electromagnet	The strength of an electromagnet (indicated by the number of iron clips attached to the electromagnet) increases as the current increases
Experiment 2: to determine the magnitude of the catapult force on a current-carrying conductor in a permanent magnetic field	The magnitude of the force on a current-carrying conductor in a magnetic field (indicated by the distance of movement of the short copper wire) increases as the magnitude of the current increases (indicated by magnitude of potential difference)
Experiment 3: to determine the magnitude of an induced current	As the speed of the relative motion between the conductor and magnet increases (indicated by the height of the magnet above the solenoid), the magnitude of the induced current also increases

A real demonstration was conducted by the teachers with the presence of the researcher. The hypothesized result was also available in MARPEX app. There are plenty of features like zoom in and zoom out, take apart (break the apparatus parts apart and disassemble), label, highlight and hide the touched part, snap the image and glassy view in the existing mobile app that are related to Physics. All these features are attracting user's attention but the effectiveness of the features in terms of academic is yet to be discovered. Therefore, a content analysis was conducted to determine the most preferred interactive multimedia element. Based on the analysis, animated 3D model is the most common and preferred element utilized by the researchers in their previous work. Thus, this study utilized only animated 3D models to determine the impact on learning experience.

3.2   MARPEX Architecture

The MARPEX architecture includes development tools, database storage, sensors to trigger AR marker, and multimedia objects and/or scenes as illustrated in Fig. 1. MARPEX is packaged as an Android application package (apk) which is compatible with Android Operating System 4.1 and above. This mobile AR app consists of two main procedures of Java Software Development Kit (SDK) and Android SDK before publishing it to an Android compatible file.

The Java SDK illustrates the objects/scenes utilized at the development phase and stored them in the database. The Android SDK encrypts these objects with the target manager from database storage. Then, it helps to publish the apk file to be compatible with that of Android devices. The published apk file can instantly be transferred to various compatible Android phones to launch the MARPEX app.

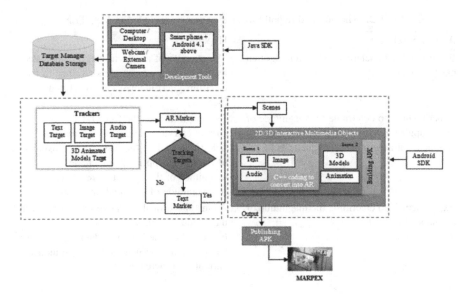

Fig. 1. The architecture of MARPEX.

3.3   Development of MARPEX

As we established user requirements, it is easier to iteratively executing develop – test – develop techniques of prototyping. As for triggering the MARPEX, it is decided to use a bookmark size for the AR marker. This bookmark is certainly handy for students to hold. Figure 2 illustrates the AR marker customized for MARPEX that is designed for 21 cm in height and five centimeters width.

Fig. 2. AR marker

The main interface of this app includes Help, Back, Info, Play plus a hidden sidebar. The Help button is to guide first time users. It is important as Mobile AR is considered a new concept and students need to be directed on how to use this app. The Back button is to go back to the main menu of this app. Students may choose which experiments they want to practice at the main menu. The Play button is to perform the animation of each 3D model. Lastly, the side bar button consists of several selection sub-buttons to manipulate the experiments. This sidebar will only appear if the student clicks the provided button at the bottom left of the app.

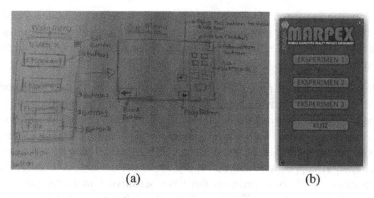

(a)   (b)

Fig. 3. The MARPEX in (a) initial sketch to visualize the idea of buttons and sidebar; and (b) its implementation.

The splash screen of MARPEX is displayed prior to the main menu display as shown in Fig. 3(b) where students can choose the experiment. The sub-menu consists of several buttons like Back button, Play button, sidebar button shown in Fig. 3(a).

Apparatus Definitions. There are several apparatus and materials included. The real experiment apparatus is as listed in Table 3. The simulated 3D models are Ammeter, connection wires, rheostat, retort stand, switch direct current (dc) supply, soft iron core, solenoid, small iron clips, and iron container for Experiment 1 as shown in Fig. 4.

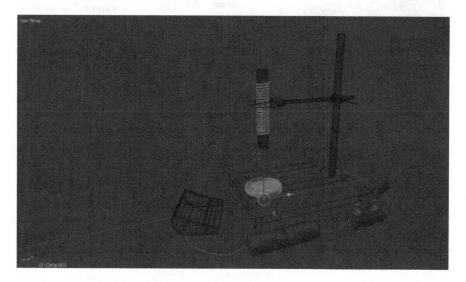

Fig. 4. Apparatus simulation includes 3D models with similar representation of real objects.

After determining the apparatus and material, they were modeled and animated in 3D modeling software. Biped files attached to this apparatus to animate them. Skin modifier is utilized to attach biped files to apparatus. The apparatus is developed using polygon functions and the process of transforming into a new shape requires more polygons onto an object. The 3D models were animated according to its pre-determined movement.

3D Modelling. The real experiment apparatus is as shown in Table 3. 3D modelling performed to transform the real apparatus into virtual form. The simulated 3D models are Ammeter, connection wires, rheostat, retort stand, switch dc supply, soft iron core, solenoid, small iron clips, and iron container for Experiment 1 and followed by apparatus for Experiment 2 inclusive of magnadur magnets, U-shaped iron yoke, thick copper wire, short copper wire and dc supply as shown in Table 3. Finally, the simulated apparatus of 3D for experiment three are Sensitive zero-center galvanometer, solenoid, and bar magnets (see Table 3). These items were modeled in the 3D modeling software and exported to file formats compatible to those of game engines.

Table 3. Simulated apparatus and materials of experiments.

Real experiment in laboratory	Simulated 3D Experiment	Apparatus and materials
Experiment 1		Ammeter, connection wires, rheostat, retort stand, switch dc supply, soft iron core, solenoid, small iron clips, and iron container
Experiment 2		Magnadur magnets, U-shaped iron yoke, thick copper wire and short copper wire
Experiment 3		Sensitive zero-centered galvanometer, solenoid, bar magnets

Then, the file of 3D models was imported into a game engine, so that they can be used multiple time. This is because they are accessible from the software library and developer can "drag and drop" these 3D models into the main scene. This ability makes the development of prototype faster and the 3D models can be stored in the software library for future projects.

MARPEX Scripting. Scripting is an inside act to set up cameras and adding in collision detection onto objects. This is performed after integrating all 3D models and other materials. The camera is set up to detect the movement of 3D models. Virtual buttons were added to manipulate and control the movements of 3D models.

User Testing. User testing was conducted iteratively during the development phase to ensure the usability of MARPEX is guaranteed and its functional requirements are all met. User testing is mainly conducted in the lab setting and in science exhibition.

3.4 Expert Evaluation

In the final stage of the development, an expert review was conducted using two content experts. The content expert should have the following criteria; experience of teaching Physics for more than 10 years. The experts who fulfill the criteria has been identified and approached to discuss the purpose of the study and their role as content experts. The expert consent and evaluation forms were distributed among those willing to be the content expert. The content expert who became part of this evaluation phase was different from those involved in the development phase. They were given a week to analyze the MARPEX app in terms of content. After one week, the expert evaluation forms were collected and analyzed.

4 Results and Discussions

The main objective of the MARPEX app is to provide students an auxiliary learning tool for Physics experiments using mobile Augmented Reality. MARPEX app is a unique path for students to discover the fun of science experiments. The implementation of Mobile AR in Physics experiment among upper secondary school students is still in infancy.

Figure 5 depicts a screenshot of the MARPEX app in action. The MARPEX app provides an opportunity to control the manipulating, responding, and constant variables in the respective experiment.

Students can experience the zoom in and zoom out function by pointing the mobile closer or move it further from the AR bookmark respectively. They can visualize it in 3D environment, allowing them to pan and rotate the 3D models. User testing of MARPEX is conducted iteratively and includes those by school students in a science exhibition and Physics teachers as shown in Fig. 6.

During expert evaluation, both experts unanimously agreed to have Mobile app using AR technology in Physics experiment to assist their students. Based on the expert review, there are additional suggestions to make the app more usable. The following are their recommendations:

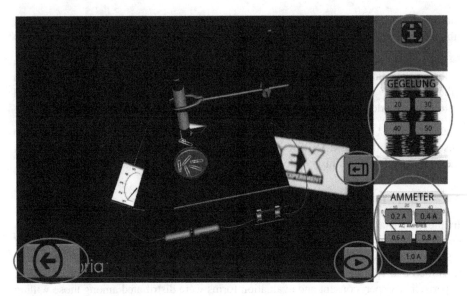

Fig. 5. Screenshot of MARPEX shows its interface layout as well as the content of experiment 1 with the ability to visualize the strength of current (Ammeter) and electromagnet (number of solenoid) which also indicated by the number of iron clips attached to the solenoid.

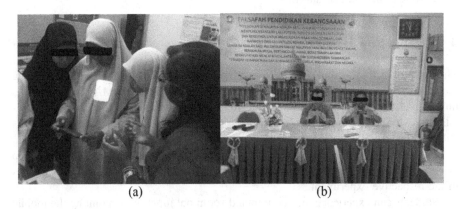

(a)   (b)

Fig. 6. Rigorous user testing of MARPEX (a) by students in science exhibition, and (b) by physics teachers.

i. They suggested to expand the concept in other experiments of Physics such as the heat topic and recommend simplifying the instructions that provided in the help button.

ii. Recommended to add a stop or pause button. This button is to provide additional time for students to observe and critically understand the phenomena occurs.

iii. Recommended to magnify the selection button displayed in sidebar.

5   Conclusion and Future Work

We have elaborated on the design and development of the MARPEX app which is targeted to physics experiments using Mobile AR. The MARPEX app is able to provide students interesting information which is not possible to experience through conventional experiment practices.

The future directions of this study are to focus on the interface and functionality evaluation by experts as well as to gather user evaluation. Intrinsic and extrinsic motivation will be taken into consideration to determine the learning experience using the proposed Mobile app. The MAR and design and development of the MARPEX app have been discussed in this paper. This paper can provide guidance for the AR developers and academicians who are interested to pursue research related to this background.

Acknowledgement.   Our deepest gratitude goes to the Ministry of Higher Education for granting the Fundamental Research Grant Scheme (FRGS) and Research and Innovation Management Center, Universiti Utara Malaysia for administrative support and facilities provided. Our heartfelt appreciation also goes to all school teachers and students who are directly and indirectly involved in this study.

References

1. Chin, C.: Fewer women opt for STEM. The Star. https://www.thestar.com.my/news/nation/2017/07/23/fewer-women-opt-for-stem-malaysia-records-low-female-enrolment-in-science-stream/. Accessed 05 May 2018
2. Oh, E., Reeves, T.C.: Generational differences and the integration of technology in learning, instruction, and performance. In: Spector, J., Merrill, M., Elen, J., Bishop, M. (eds.) Handbook of Research on Educational Communications and Technology, pp. 819–828. Springer, New York (2014). https://doi.org/10.1007/978-1-4614-3185-5_66
3. Muller, A., Muller, D.A., Eklund, J., Sharma, M.D.: The future of multimedia learning: essential issues for research (2006)
4. New Media Consortium: The NMC Horizon Report: 2017 Higher Education Edition. http://cdn.nmc.org/media/2017-nmc-horizon-report-he-EN.pdf. Accessed 05 May 2018
5. Gikas, J., Grant, M.M.: Mobile computing devices in higher education: student perspectives on learning with cellphones, smartphones & social media. Internet High. Educ. **19**, 18–26 (2013)
6. Weimer, M.: Getting students to take responsibility for learning. https://www.facultyfocus.com/articles/teaching-professor-blog/getting-students-take-responsibility-learning/. Accessed 05 May 2018
7. Hattie, J.: Teachers make a difference, what is the research evidence? (2003)
8. Chiu, S., Wardrop, J.L., Ryan, K.E.: Use of the unbalanced nested ANOVA to examine the relationship of class size to student ratings of instructional quality (1999)
9. Svinicki, M.D.: New directions in learning and motivation. New Dir. Teach. Learn. **1999** (80), 5–27 (1999)
10. Baruah, R.K.: Career prospects in physics. http://www.thesangaiexpress.com/career-prospect-physics/. Accessed 05 May 2018

11. Ibáñez, M.B., Di Serio, Á., Villarán, D., Kloos, C.D.: Experimenting with electromagnetism using augmented reality: impact on flow student experience and educational effectiveness. Comput. Educ. **71**, 1–13 (2014)
12. Dunser, A., Walker, L., Horner, H., Bentall, D.: Creating interactive physics education books with augmented reality. In: Proceedings of the 24th Australian Computer-Human Interaction Conference, pp. 107–114 (2012)
13. Gopalan, V., Abubakar, J.A., Zulkifli, A.N.: A brief review of augmented reality science learning. In: AIP Conference Proceedings, vol. 1891, p. 020044 (2017). https://doi.org/10.1063/1.5005377

Towards Understanding the Concept of Tourism Experience Sharing

Noor Durani Binti Jamaluddin[✉], Wan Adilah Wan Adnan, Nurulhuda Noordin,
Nor Laila Md Noor, and Ahmad Iqbal Hakim Suhaimi

Faculty of Computer and Mathematical Sciences, Universiti Teknologi MARA (UiTM),
Shah Alam, Selangor, Malaysia
`duranijamaluddin@gmail.com`,
`{adilah,hudanoordin,aiqbal}@tmsk.uitm.edu.my`,
`norlaila@tmsk.edu.my`

Abstract. Tourism embraces nearly all aspects of our society. As tourists travel from different places to another, a lot of experiences and memories can be captured during the journey of the vacation. Despite the exciting experience that one can get from traveling, experience sharing among tourists used to be private and undisclosed that was only shared within trusted acquaintances or circles among them. This paper reviews and explores various existing approaches to understand the concept of experience sharing in tourism. It covers views of the relationship of tourism with the main motivation concept which is pull and push factor that were derived from Maslow's basic needs hierarchy. The role of ICT and experience sharing in tourism are also discussed. Thus, this paper provides a better understanding of experience sharing in tourism by covering aspects related to it and highlights the important role of information technology in enhancing tourists' experience sharing.

Keywords: Tourism · User experience · Tourism experience sharing
Technology-enabled experience sharing

1 Introduction

Tourism undoubtedly has become one of the most important and promising industries in the world. The term "tourism" can be simply put as a tourist who travels to either international or domestic destination to which the activity includes economic activities that are organized around the needs of the travelers themselves. Figure 1 shows the basic fundamental of tourism that starts with a tourist who travels either to the international or domestic destination. According to Metelka [1], tourism is not only defined as travel for pleasure and fun but also plays important role as an umbrella term for a variety of product or services offered and desired by other people while being away from home. On the other hand, United Nation (UN) has seen the marked growth in the attention paid by policymakers, development experts, and industry leaders to the contributions made by the tourism sectors in many countries, especially in the developing world [2]. Tourism in Malaysia plays a prominent factor in contributing to the economic development.

© Springer Nature Singapore Pte Ltd. 2018
N. Abdullah et al. (Eds.): i-USEr 2018, CCIS 886, pp. 59–68, 2018.
https://doi.org/10.1007/978-981-13-1628-9_6

Tourism is a sector that has been recognized by Malaysian government as an economic catalyst for the country. Due to this in 2015, Malaysia's travel and tourism were expected to grow to MYR 169.5 billion through the economic activity and it was forecasted to rise further to MYR 262.2 billion by the year 2025 [3]. According to Salleh et al. [4], the main factors that make Malaysia as a favorite destination for tourists is because of the beautiful scenery, quality of services provided, customs and culture, quality of food and the friendliness of the local people.

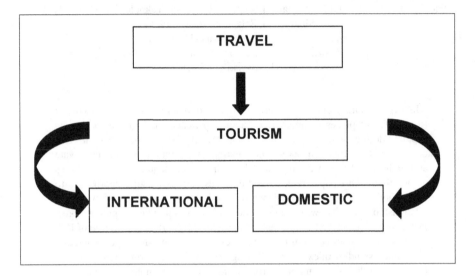

Fig. 1. Fundamental tourism

This paper discusses the existing examples of the concept in tourism experience sharing by reviewing the main motivation that makes a person travel, which is known as pull and push factor. The great exploration to look on too about the tourism experience background and the flow of the evolution throughout the process. Experience sharing in tourism mainly includes the tourist's experiences from all angles and situation, along with the technology that can enhance the process throughout the tour is also highlighted in this paper.

2   Theoretical Overview of Tourist Motivation

Despite the growing impact of tourism on country's economy, the main contribution that one must look in depth is the motivation that leads a person to decide on the vacation or holiday. The most applied motivation in tourism literature was Maslow's [5] hierarchical theory of motivation which is shown in Fig. 2. The hierarchical theory was modeled as an extend to Growth Needs (G-Needs) and Deficiency Needs (D-Needs) pyramid that divides the growth of self-actualization and add on the lower-level growth that is cognitive and aesthetic. The idea of D-Needs happens due to deprivation which deals to influence and motivate people when the needs are unmet. It describes that the motivation to meet the needs will become stronger when they are denied. Maslow [5] also mentioned that individuals must satisfy the lower level deficit before moving on to the higher level G-Needs. When the D-Needs are met, G-Needs will continue to be felt and may become stronger and then reach the highest level of the pyramid. Maslow [5] believed that the top level that is the self-actualization can be measured by having a peak experience. This can occur when a person experiences the feeling of joy, euphoria, serenity, and wonder. According to Backman [6], motivation can be explained as "a state of need, a condition that serves as a driving force to display different kinds of behavior toward certain types of activities, and arriving at some expected satisfactory outcome". While Yoon and Uysal [7] in their writing mentioned that motivation is referred as psychological and biological needs and wants that initially affect the integral forces that arouse, direct and combine a person's behavior and activity. It is important to look at the pattern of the tourist before they go for their vacations [8].

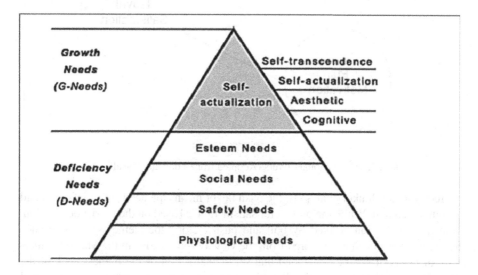

Fig. 2. Maslow's hierarchy of needs extended with G-Needs and D-Needs (Adopted from Maslow [5]).

According to Yoon and Uysal [7] the motivations that lead tourist to choose their vacation are mainly driven by two aspects which are push factors and pull factors. The concept of pull and push factor is the fundamental way to know the feature and the type of person who goes traveling to their chosen tourist destination. The idea behind push and pull dimension factor is that people travel because they are pushed by their own internal forces and pulled by the external forces of destination's attributes [9]. The push factors refer to the internal forces that might affect one's emotions, such as desire to escape from the routine and search for authentic experience or sometimes refer to spiritual needs. Push factors are factors that contribute to a person's need to escape from the normal routine or to explore a new environment at other places [10]. Tourists may travel to find something new in their lives and perhaps to get fresh ideas from something new. Whereas for pull factors, they include the external forces from the destination's attributes. Pull factors can be influenced and inspired by a destination's attractiveness, for instance, tourist get the idea of a vacation to look at the beautiful sceneries, beaches, recreations facilities, other culture, shopping malls or parks [7]. Yoon and Uysal [7] summarized that the push and pull factors have impacts towards tourists decision and satisfaction on traveling as shown in Fig. 3.

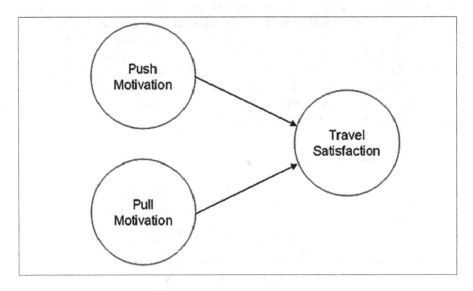

Fig. 3. Motivational drivers (Adopted from Yoon and Uysal [7]).

According to Shukor et al. [11], the push factor means the needs of satisfaction and the tourist demand. While the pull factor satisfaction is based on the tourist destination. From the satisfaction derived by pull and push factors, the elements of experience sharing in tourism can be explored from the view of tourists. From the Maslow's hierarchy of needs, it can be concluded that self-actualization or the highest peak of the hierarchy can relate to push and pull motivations that motivates a person to go for travel where these motivations can presumably be the factor that brings someone to the highest level of needs and experience.

3 Tourism Experience

In the broad sense of tourism, the tourist is the main actor and the main essence of tourism scope after the sustainable development factors for the industry. Without tourist, the tourism concept will be useless and void. The definition of tourist can be as simple as mentioned by UNWTO [12] that a visitor to either domestic, inbound or outbound, can be called as a tourist if the trip includes an overnight stay, or as a same-day visitor. In general, a tourist is a person that travels and stays in places outside their usual environment for not more than one consecutive year for leisure, business and other purposes [13].

Ritchie et al. [14] mentioned that understanding the nature of tourism experience is valuable information to academician and practitioners. The study also highlighted that providing tourists with high-quality memorable experiences becomes the essence of tourism and tourism management. Ritchie and Hudson [15] provided useful insights into the major research challenges faced by many tourism experience researchers as shown in Fig. 4. Pine and Gilmore [16] who mentioned about "the experience economy" argued that actions should be taken in account for supplier and provider to fully understand the tourism experience in all forms and levels in order to meet their customer's satisfaction. Decroly [17] highlighted two main trends of today's world of tourism, which are; 1. the process-oriented which focusses on learning and transformation of the world's resources into knowledge, and 2. which considers the tourist experience as "a moment to be lived" towards pleasure and hedonism, to make it as a successful and memorable experience.

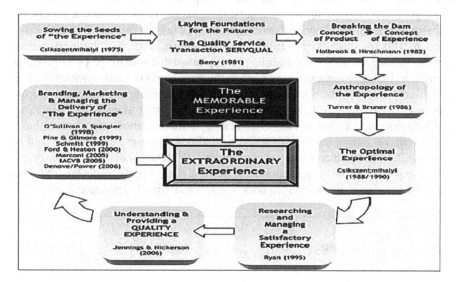

Fig. 4. The evolution of the extraordinary/memorable travel/tourism experience (Adopted from Ritchie and Hudson [15]).

Tourists travel from different places to other places, interact with people from different cultural backgrounds, adapt to the environments and come home to bring back all the travel memories. These are part of activities that tourists will encounter. As cited in Jacobsen and Munar [18], the sharing of experiences includes not only knowledge-related aspects such as facts about holiday attributes (e.g. prices, weather conditions, beaches and other attractions) but may additionally include communicating emotions, imaginations, and fantasies about features of a holiday, for example through photo-graphs, emoticons and other linguistic markers online. Research has also shown that advice on practical matters and embodied feelings of comfort or discomfort are relevant in online reviews of tourism attractions (Jacobsen and Munar [18]). Argued by Ying et al. [19], the environment of tourism service is hedonic and experiential in nature where the tourist might stress more on the tourism experience themselves rather than focusing on the service quality level. Therefore, during the holiday visits, the tourists might seek for the unique and different experience during their tour at the specific destinations, which could vary from their daily norms. "Experience is a blend of many individual elements that come together which may involve the consumer emotionally, physically and intellectually" [20]. However, Cetin [21] in his paper described that to provide a pleasing tourist experience is crucial for destinations' "long-term success". Therefore tourism experience can be beneficial for tourists to expect and predict their vacations as well as to perceive and enjoy their holidays.

4 Role of ICT and Experience Sharing in Tourism Perspectives

Despite having many examples and literature on experience sharing, Ritchie and Hudson [15] argued that there is still no substantial increase in experience-related papers and they also found that experience-related research is still under-represented in the tourism literature. This argument has proven that the exploration of experience sharing in tourism is still in infancy. Neuhofer and Buhalis [22] explained that with the ICTs supports, the experience sharing in tourism can be used on the three levels of tourism which are; pre-travel, during travel and post-travel as shown in Fig. 5. During these processes, numerous activities from the pre-travel, during travel and post-travel such as inspiration to preliminary information, decision making and booking, communication, engagement, information retrieval during travel to experience sharing for post-travel can be created by using the ICTs to enhance the traveler's journeys. With the available technology, the tourism experience is no longer restricted to a closed circle or only particular groups but also can be extended dynamically in both physical and virtual experience [22].

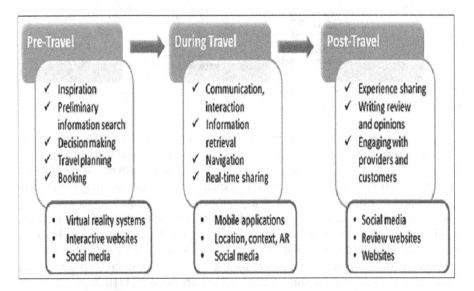

Fig. 5. Level of tourism in the context of tourist user experience sharing. (Adopted from Neuhofer and Buhalis [22]).

Experience sharing in tourism can also be applied to many aspects of tourism. One of them is through the currently available technology. Information and communication technology (ICTs) have changed the tourist experience drastically and developed the technology that enhanced the tourist experience [23]. In Le [23] studies, he comprised that tourism experience can be shared by having many technologies such as interactive and cross-platform website, social media, mobile applications, virtual reality and augmented reality, games, and recommender systems. ICTs have changed the efficiency and effectiveness in many tourism businesses and organizations. It also changed the way businesses see their business models, and enable them to understand how their consumers respond with the organizations [24]. According to [24], ICTs encompass technologies that include hardware, software, groupware, netware and humanware that enable users to manage their information, functions, and processes as well as to communicate to their stakeholders to achieve their goals.

One of the emergences of ICTs is the revolutionary of the internet. The internet has changed many travelers' behaviors [25]. From the internet, comes the evolution of Web 2.0 or Travel 2.0 that initially bring the concepts of social networking including virtual communities that encourage all travelers to participate in the tourism industry. Among the popular social networking/virtual community according to Buhalis and Law [25], is TripAdvisor. It allows travelers to search for the hotels around the world including the recommended places of interests, do's and don'ts and brings together individuals in discussion forums provided for them to make reviews. According to Wang and Fesenmaier [26], the travel communities such as TripAdvisor, give many benefits to the user to obtain information, gain ideas from the comments, reviews from independent travelers, reviews from TripAdvisor members and experts advisors using their platforms.

The other popular application that enables travelers to share their experiences and review with others is Airbnb. It can be accessed by websites or mobile apps and offers users hospitality services that incorporate ideas of home, travel experiences such as tours and make reservations at the restaurants [27]. They also recalled that Airbnb is a phenomenal platform because of their individualized and tailor-made travel experiences to unknown places. This is another factor why this application is a good experience sharing for other travelers.

Experts Neuhofer and Buhalis [28] summarized that the technology-enabled XXX enhanced the tourism experience in a conceptual model as shown in Fig. 6. Communicating by sharing words, pictures, videos and other types of media has increased tremendously, that leads to better support in tourist information searches and decision-making behavior [29]. Besides having ICT as the main driver of experience sharing in tourism, the aspects through activities, emotions, and outcomes can contribute to experience sharing [30]. Leisure activities done by travelers can enhance their willingness to share the experience with others. Emotions of sharing can lead to many useful experiences about the destinations. The outcome refers to the consequences of travel leisure in tourist. As cited in Luo [30], the emotional experience can create an effective relationship between consumers and tourism company. In tourism, designing for tourism experience is not only a matter of creating a tour for the tourists but to design even more important experiences where all elements associated with senses, cognition, emotions, affect, and other values [31]. Other key aspects of experience sharing in tourism can be highlighted from the Memorable Tourism Experiences (MTEs). Based from the studies of antecedents of MTEs, where the elements such as memorable experiences for instance, iconic tourist attractions, perceived outcomes of the trip, perceived opportunities for social interactions and feelings of pleasure and arousal can be taken into account [32]. Chandralal and Valenzuela [32] also highlighted that the significance of MTEs derived from the influencing power of past memories on tourist decision-making and also can give a positive impact of attracting new visitors to the recommended destinations. Thus, the importance of experience sharing in tourism is undeniable. The experience from the tourist is a major player in the tourism industry. Understanding the tourist experience can lead to many great opportunities in the tourism industry and tourism experience itself.

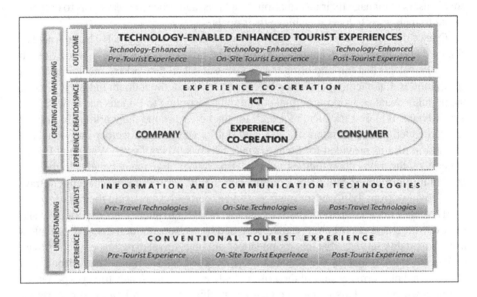

Fig. 6. Conceptual model technology-enabled enhanced tourist experience (Adopted from Neuhofer and Buhalis [28]).

5   Conclusion and Further Direction of Research

This paper provides the valuable insight of tourism experience concept and highlights the importance of experience sharing for the success of tourism industry. Based on the literature, it can be concluded that the experience sharing in tourism requires a holistic approach to be used in many aspects of tourism itself. It can also be put as the tourist experience which includes everything that happens in a tourist situation. A ground study of tourism and the motivation that lead people to go travel was discussed whereby it has shown that the dependencies of the top of Maslow's hierarchy of needs which is self-actualization can be achieved from the pull and push motivations. With the support from the ICTs, the experience sharing in tourism can be used and expand on the three levels of tourism on tourist which are: pre-travel, during travel and post-travel. In addition to that, the tourist experience can also be shared by many mediums such as; by/from the technology of ICTs which includes hardware, software, groupware, netware and humanware. The most common ICTs usage is the internet, which enables travelers to gain information of places where they want to go to. Besides the technology of ICTs, experience sharing can also be obtained from the activities, emotions, outcomes and also from MTEs. All of these elements that enable experience sharing can be applied to the stages of levels in tourism mentioned before.

Further research is needed to expand on the theoretical consideration of tourist-centered user experience sharing in the context of technology use. In relation to that, investigating the pattern and motivations of local and international travelers in all stages including pre-tourist, during and post-tourist, is required to provide good inputs in recommending the right technology for a better tourist centered experience sharing. In addition to that, the future research on tourist-centered experience sharing in the halal tourism perspective would provide good insight for tourism industry.

Acknowledgments. The authors would like to record our sincere thanks to the Universiti Teknologi MARA, Shah Alam Selangor for the financial support. This publication is supported by the funding of 600-IRMI/DANA 5/3/LESTARI (0137/2016).

References

1. Metelka, C.J.: The Dictionary of Hospitality, Travel and Tourism, 3rd edn. Butterworth-Heinemann, Burlington (2003)
2. Ashley, C., De Briene, P., Lehr, A., Wilde, H.: The Role of the Tourism Sector in Expanding Economic Opportunity. The Fellow of Havard college, Oversea Development Institute, International Business Leaders Forum, Harvard University, pp. 6–8 (2007)
3. WTTC: Travel & Tourism Economic Impact 2015 Malaysia, pp. 1–3. World Travel and Tourism Council, London, UK (2015)
4. Salleh, M., et al.: Tourist satisfaction in Malaysia. Int. J. Bus. Soc. Sci. 4(5), 221–225 (2013)
5. Maslow, A.H.: Motivation and Personality, 3rd edn. Harper & Row, New York (1970)
6. Backman, K., Backman, S., Uysal, M., Sunshine, K.: Event tourism: an examination of motivations and activities. Festiv. Manage. Event Tour. 3(1), 15–24 (1995)
7. Yoon, Y., Uysal, M.: An examination of the effects of motivation and satisfaction on destination loyalty: a structural model. Tour. Manage. 26, 45–56 (2005). https://doi.org/10.1016/j.tourman.2003.08.016
8. Khuong, M.N., Ha, H.T.T.: The influences of push and pull factors on the international leisure tourists' return intention to Ho Chi Minh City, Vietnam–A mediation analysis of destination satisfaction. Int. J. Trade Econ. Finan. 5(6), 490 (2014)
9. Mohammad, B., Som, A.: An analysis of push and pull travel motivations of foreign tourists to Jordan. Int. J. Bus. Manage. 5(12), 41–50 (2010)
10. Crompton, J.L.: Motivations for pleasure vacation. Annals Tour. Res. 6(4), 408–424 (1979)
11. Syukor, M.S., Salleh, N.H.M., Idris, S.H.M.: An evaluation of the effects of motivation, satisfaction on destination loyalty: case study tourism Malaysia. Int. J. Soc. Sci. Manage. 4(2), 137–147 (2017). https://doi.org/10.3126/ijssm.v4i2.16577
12. United Nations World Tourism Organization: International recommendations for tourism statistics (2008). http://www.unwto.org/
13. World Tourism Organization/UNWTO. http://www2.unwto.org/

14. Ritchie, J.R.B., Tung, V.W.S., Ritchie, R.J.B.: Tourism experience management research: emergence, evolution and future directions. Int. J. Contemp. Hosp. Manage. **23**(4), 419–438 (2011)
15. Ritchie, J.R.B., Hudson, S.: Understanding and meeting the challenges of consumer/tourist experience research. Int. J. Tour. Res. **11**(2), 111–126 (2009)
16. Pine II, B.J., Gilmore, J.H.: The Experience Economy: Work is Theatre & Every Business a Stage. Harvard Business School Press, Boston (1999)
17. Decroly, J.M.: The tourist experience: an experience of the frameworks of the tourist experience? Tour. Rev. **10**, 3–16 (2016)
18. Jacobsen, J.Kr.S., Munar, A.M.: Motivations for sharing tourism experiences through social media. Tour. Manage. (2014). http://dx.doi.org/10.1016/j.tourman.2014.01.012
19. Ying, K.S., Jusoh, A., Khalifah, Z., Said, H.: An empirical study of tourist satisfaction in Malaysia. Mediter. J. Soc. Sci. **6**(6 S4), 360–369 (2015)
20. Dettori, A., Giudici, E., Aledda, L.: Sharing experience in tourism: what role can social media play? In: XXVIII Sinergie Annual Conference Referred Electronic Conference Proceeding Management in a Digital World. Decisions, Production, Communication, pp. 47–58 (2016)
21. Cetin, G., Bilgihan, A.: Components of cultural tourists' experiences in destinations. Curr. Issues Tour. **19**, 137–154 (2014). https://doi.org/10.1080/13683500.2014.994595
22. Neuhofer, B., Buhalis, D.: The technology enhanced tourist experience (2014). https://www.researchgate.net/publication/272566581_Technology_enhanced_tourism_experience
23. Le, N., Vi, T.: Technology enhanced tourist experience: insights from tourism companies in Rovaniemi (2014)
24. Buhalis, D.: eTourism: Information Technology for Strategic Tourism Management. Pearson Harlow, Prentice Hall (2003)
25. Buhalis, D., Law, R.: Twenty years on and 10 years after the internet: the state of eTourism research. Tour. Manage. **29**(4), 609–623 (2008)
26. Wang, Y., Fesenmaier, D.R.: Towards understanding members' general participation in and active contribution to an online travel community. Tour. Manage. **25**(6), 709–722 (2004)
27. Roelofsen, M., Minca, C.: The superhost. biopolitics, home and community in the *Airbnb* dream-world of global hospitality. Geoforum **91**, 170–181 (2018). https://doi.org/10.1016/j.geoforum.2018.02.021
28. Neuhofer, B., Buhalis, D.: Understanding and managing technology-enabled enhanced tourist experiences. In: 2nd Conference on Hospitality and Tourism Marketing & Management Conference, Greece (2012)
29. Fotis, J.: Discussion on the impacts of social media in leisure tourism: the impact of social media on consumer behavior: focus on leisure travel (2012). http://johnfotis.bologspot.com.au/p/projects.html
30. Luo, W.: Shared tourism experience of individuals with disabilities and their caregivers. Master thesis. Purdue University (2014)
31. Tussyadiah, I.P.: Toward a theoretical foundation for experience design in tourism. J. Travel Res. **53**, 543–564 (2014). https://doi.org/10.1177/0047287513513172
32. Chandralal, L., Valenzuela, F.-R.: Exploring memorable tourism experience: antecedents and behavioral outcomes. J. Econ. Bus. Manage. **1**(2), 117–181 (2013). https://doi.org/10.7763/JOEBM.2013.V1.38

A Comparative Study on E-Government Website Design Between Malaysia and United Kingdom

Nasrah Hassan Basri[1(✉)], Wan Adilah Wan Adnan[2], and Hanif Baharin[3]

[1] Kolej Poly-Tech MARA, Ipoh, Malaysia
nasrah@gapps.kptm.edu.my
[2] Universiti Teknologi MARA, Shah Alam, Malaysia
adilah@tmsk.uitm.edu.my
[3] Universiti Kebangsaan Malaysia, Bangi, Malaysia
hbaharin@ukm.edu.my

Abstract. Over the years, many countries are optimizing the technology as an opportunity to enhance the quality of public service delivery. The electronic service or better known as e-government has a significant impact on the growth of performance of public sector. This paper investigates the website design of Malaysia e-government and compares it with the website design of United Kingdom e-government. A content analysis of the websites highlights considerable differences in representation of the e-government in both Malaysia and United Kingdom. From the content analysis, it also gave us more critical remarks related to Malaysia e-government website design and thus enable this study to provide more suggestions in improving the website design.

Keywords: E-government · Website design
E-government development index

1 Introduction

Advancements in information and communication technologies have brought significant transformations in the way governments deliver information and services to their citizens. In making sure user really enjoy their experience while navigating the website in particular e-government, proper design of the website is indeed a critical element [10]. Website design is crucial in engaging users as an innovative website designs could create positive experiences to the user [2, 18].

Reference [14] stated that e-government websites can benefit from a high level of usability by acting as a first impression of a government and improves users' performance as well as their satisfaction with e-government. For citizens, web based services offer empowerment, freedom and convenience while for government it can be viewed as a mean to deliver as much information as possible while maintaining the financial efficiencies.

A good website design should characterize informational, navigational and graphical aspects [15]. Furthermore, it is possible to note the relevance of presenting high quality information, good contents and attractive navigation as the important advantages of the online activity [3].

© Springer Nature Singapore Pte Ltd. 2018
N. Abdullah et al. (Eds.): i-USEr 2018, CCIS 886, pp. 69–78, 2018.
https://doi.org/10.1007/978-981-13-1628-9_7

This paper examines some aspects of informational, navigational and graphical of Malaysia and United Kingdom e-government home page. In addition, a comparative study is conducted between Malaysia with United Kingdom which had been ranked as number one in E-Government Development Index (EGDI) 2016 as shown in Table 1. The same report also ranked Malaysia in number 60 with the index of 0.6175.

Table 1. Top 10 performers in E-Government Development Index (EGDI) in 2016

Rank	Country	Index
1	United Kingdom	0.9193
2	Australia	0.9143
3	Republic of Korea	0.8915
4	Singapore	0.8828
5	Finland	0.8817
6	Sweden	0.8704
7	Netherlands	0.8659
8	New Zealand	0.8653
9	Denmark	0.8510
10	France	0.8456

2　Literature Review

This section is divided into five parts consisting of the definition of e-government and followed with the development of e-government in Malaysia itself. The third part discusses about the E-Government Development Index (EGDI); next is the relevancy of website design in accordance with e-government and the last part is on web site design measures.

2.1　E-Government

E-government is often viewed as the use of Information Communication Technologies (ICTs) and World Wide Web (WWW) to provide governmental services to citizens, businesses and other organizations online [1]. It can also be defined as the use of ICTs to improve and enable the efficiency of services provided to citizens, employees, businesses and agencies [4]. In the E-Government Act of 2002, the 107th Congress referred e-government as "using internet-based information technology to enhance citizen access to government information and services" [23]. According to [28], e-government describes the electronic handling of administrative and governance process in the context of governmental activities by using information and communication technologies to support public duties.

The implementation of e-government would bring benefits to the public administration and Malaysian society in several ways [21]. First, e-government improves efficiency by utilizing the use of information technology to operate mass processing tasks and public administration operations. Next, e-government improves services as it adopts a customer-focused approach and thus improves conventional government services.

2.2 E-Government in Malaysia

The implementation of electronic government started with the initiation of Multimedia Super Corridor (MSC) by the Malaysian government in 1996. The initial objective was to reinvent itself to lead the country into the Information Age by transforming the way it operated, modernizing and enhancing its service delivery. It was hoped to improve information flow and processes within the government and enhanced the accessibility of information to the public [27].

E-government is one of the seven flagship applications introduced in MSC and under the e-government flagship, seven main projects were identified to be the core of the e-government applications. The e-government projects are Electronic Procurement (eP), Project Monitoring System (PMS), Electronic Services Delivery (eServices), Human Resource Management Information System (HRMIS), Generic Office Environment (GOE), E-Syariah and Electronic Labour Exchange (ELX).

2.3 E-Government Development Index (EGDI)

World e-government rankings are increasing under the limelight as they act to guide countries' focus of their efforts. Furthermore, the e-government rankings are in a process of maturation in that direction, moving from genuinely measuring web sites to accessing the use and government qualities [20].

E-Government Development Index or known as EGDI, which assesses e-government development at national level, is a composite index based on the weighted average of three important dimensions of e-government. One third is derived from a Telecommunications Infrastructure Index (TII), one third from Human Capital Index (HCI) and one third from the Online Service Index (OSI). EGDI aims to give performance rating of national governments relative to one another [23] (see Table 1).

2.4 The Relevance of Website Design to E-Government

According to [5], designing is *"the process of creating an artifact with structure of form which is planned, artistic, coherent, purposeful and useful"*. Over the years, the design of websites has been rigorously studied from multiple points of view and most of them identified the factors that could lead to the acceptance of the websites [6, 16, 19]. A good design does not only look beautiful and appealing but also has high level of usability because it influences the affective state of the user [8]. Meanwhile, a poor interface design has been found as one of the key elements in a number of high profile sites failures [9].

Usability of a website as defined by [25] is the ease of use of the artifact, the efficiency of the design, error avoidance and satisfaction of the user in using the artifact. [25] also defines the quality attributes of usability as learnability, efficiency, memorability, errors and satisfaction. Another widely accepted definition of usability comes from ISO 9241 which is *"the extent to which a product (or website) can be used by specified users to achieve specified goals with effectiveness, efficiency and satisfaction in a specified context of use"*.

Usability also can be a form of tool for measuring the quality of a website [26] and thus a good usability could improve a more complex learning and better understanding of the content. In fact, a good level of usability could lead to higher level of satisfaction, trust and loyalty towards certain website [12].

2.5   Web Site Design Measures

Many elements exist to form the interface of a web page. The website interface is a complex mixture of text, links and graphics. The overall quality of a website can be determined by all the elements and the formatting associated with those elements [15]. Study conducted by [24] found that there are three main dimensions of concern within the web design focus; information design, navigation design and graphic design (see Fig. 1). These web site elements are also being suggested by [7, 11] to represent key elements of web site usability.

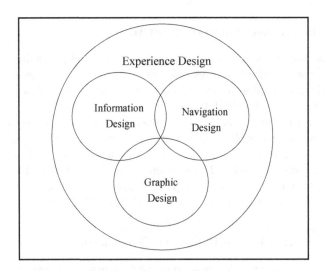

Fig. 1. Overview of website design, derived from [24].

They referred *information design* as identifying groups of related content and structuring information into a coherent whole. *Navigation design* on the other hand is defined as the design of methods of finding ways around the information structure and lastly graphic design refers to the visual communication by using color, images and others.

3   Methods

In this study, web content analysis is being used as a method to conduct the comparative study. The selection of website content analysis is because this method allows researcher to perform and prepare data at any given time and to avoid lengthy ethics approval procedures. The primary unit of analysis for this study was the "home page" of the e-government website as it can effectively compares websites of varying sizes. The "home page" also acts like a front door to any website and the first impression is crucial in determining whether user will continue browsing the website [13].

The Malaysia e-government website or MyGovernment (www.malaysia.gov.my) was compared to the United Kingdom (www.gov.uk) (see Figs. 2 and 3). The dimensions of good website elements derived from [24] were used as a base of the discussion between those two websites.

Fig. 2. Home page of Malaysia e-government portal (www.malaysia.gov.my)

Fig. 3. Home page of United Kingdom e-government portal (www.gov.uk)

All the three dimensions used in this study were evaluated by reviewing the e-government's home page. For the information design, there are four indicators which are timely information, relevant information, organization scheme and language. As for navigation design, only one indicator was used which is link but divided into four checklists. Lastly, the third dimension which is graphical design discussed about three indicators; image, banner and font.

3.1 Data Collection

Researcher collected e-government website data from Malaysia and United Kingdom before conducted web content analysis for this study. Basically, the analysis focuses on the three main aspects; information design, navigation design and graphic design. Apart from that, the researcher also reviewed United Nations E-Government Survey reports and previous work or research papers.

3.2 Data Analysis and Discussion

To achieve research objectives, the three dimensions that are being analyzed are as follow; (1) Information Design, (2) Navigation Design and (3) Graphic Design. Every dimension is accessed through their indicators and check elements to compare and contrast the e-government websites design between Malaysia and United Kingdom.

Information Design. Information design is about identifying groups of related content and structuring information into a coherent whole. All the e-government websites contain information about government and services offered to their citizens. The information design is agreed to be the major source of value to customers as it deals with the websites' content [22] (see Table 2).

Table 2. Comparison of information dimension between Malaysia and United Kingdom e-government websites.

Indicator	Check list	Malaysia	United Kingdom
Timely	Updated information	Yes	Yes
Relevant	Government's policies and announcement	Yes	Yes
Organization scheme	Categorization of content	Topical scheme	Alphabetical scheme
Language	Number of language(s) used	Multilanguage English and Malay	English only
		Misleading information between English and Malay version	NA

Despite the dual language used in Malaysia e-government portal, still there are errors when users are browsing for the same information. As depicted in Figs. 4 and 5 below, both pages are supposed give the same information but when translated into English language, the information differed from each other and misleading.

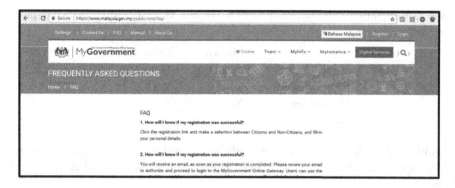

Fig. 4. "Frequently asked questions" page

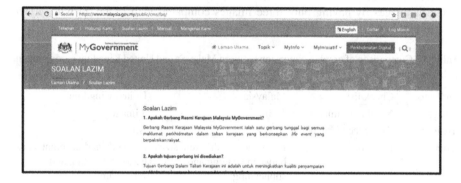

Fig. 5. "Soalan Lazim" page

Navigation Design. Navigation is an important design element as it allows users to access to more information and help them to find what information they are looking for. Navigation plays an important role in prolonging the site stay, increasing engagement and creating a great user experience. This dimension discussed the aspect of moving around the web site and accessing information.

Basically, this measure whether there are text links that are not underlined and colors used for links. It can improve access and navigation within websites and avoid user from getting lost in the hyperspace because a poorly designed navigation can cause the user to be lost in hyperspace [17]. According to Forrester Research, 50% of potential sales are lost because users can't find the related information. In addition, 40% of users never return to a site when they have negative experience during their first visit.

As depicted in Table 3, both e-government websites use hypertext as the main linking medium and United Kingdom website uses an underlined text as an additional cue for the navigational text. In addition, Malaysia e-government website use image as a link to external agencies and ministries. The navigational texts for both e-government websites also are in different colors and stand out from the informational texts.

Table 3. Comparison of navigation dimension between Malaysia and United Kingdom e-government websites.

Indicator	Check list	Malaysia	United Kingdom
Links	Links formatting	Text, image	Text and underlined
	Color changed	Yes	Yes
	Provide feedback	Yes	Yes
	Working links	Yes	Yes

Graphic Design. The look and feel of a website is important as it brings the authenticity to the experience. This dimension focuses on any graphical and visual elements that belong to both.

Overall, both websites use light colors as the background and only 3 font colors within the same page. The e-government website of the United Kingdom minimizes the usage of images by having only three images compared with Malaysia with fifteen images (Table 4).

Table 4. Comparison of graphic dimension between Malaysia and United Kingdom e-government websites.

Indicator	Check list	Malaysia	United Kingdom
Image	Number of images	15 images	3 images
Banner	Existence of banner	Yes	No
Font	Font size	Readable and different sizes between heading and subheading	Readable and different sizes between heading and subheading
	Number of font colors	3 colors	3 colors

4 Discussions and Conclusions

E-government offers new opportunity to government to reach to their citizen and deliver the best services online. This brief study is designed to merely understand the differences of e-government websites design between Malaysia and United Kingdom. Awareness of website designs has affected every government in recent years, since this online service is now becoming the first point of contact between public and government. Therefore, it is important for e-government to access the quality of its website design in order to improve its services over time and also to benchmark against any best practices.

The findings from this study show that there are significant differences between United Kingdom and Malaysia websites. Future improvement can be made to Malaysia e-government website by following the best practices shown in the United Kingdom website. As for future research, more dimensions need to be examined to uncover the mechanisms of design elements that determined the e-government website development. In addition, the findings can be extended to e-participation as another context to be studied as e-participation is one of the criteria being covered under the United Nations survey.

Acknowledgment. The authors would like to record our sincere thanks to the Ministry of Higher Education Malaysia and Universiti Teknologi MARA for the financial support. The research is conducted under the support and funding of Fundamental Research Grant Scheme (FRGS) no: FRGS/2/2014/ICT01/UiTM/01/1).

References

1. Bank, T. W.: The E-Government Handbook for Developing Countries (2002)
2. Bilgihan, A.: Computers in human behavior Gen Y customer loyalty in online shopping: an integrated model of trust, user experience and branding. Comput. Hum. Behav. **61**, 103–113 (2016)
3. Cappel, J.J., Huang, Z.: A usability analysis of company websites. J. Comput. Inf. Syst. **48**(1), 117–123 (2016)
4. Carter, L., Bélanger, F.: The utilization of e-government services: citizen trust, innovation and acceptance factors. Inf. Syst. J. **15**, 5–25 (2005)
5. Cato, J.: User-Centered Web Design, 1st edn. Addison-Wesley, London (2001)
6. Crowder, R.M., Wills, G.B.: An exploratory study of proposed factors to adopt e- government services: Saudi Arabia as a case study. Int. J. Adv. Comput. Sci. Appl. **4**(11), 57–66 (2013)
7. Cyr, D.: Modeling web site design across cultures: relationships to trust, satisfaction, and e-loyalty, 37–41 (2008)
8. Desmet, P., Hekkert, P.: Framework of product experience. Int. J. Des. **1**(1), 57–66 (2007)
9. Flavian, C., Gurrea, R., Oru, C.: Web design : a key factor for the website success. J. Syst. Inf. Technol. **11**, 168–184 (2008)
10. Garett, R., Chiu, J., Zhang, L., Young, S.D.: A literature review: website design and user engagement, 1–11 (2017)
11. Garrett, J.J.: The Elements of User Experience: User-Centered Design for the Web and Beyond, 2nd edn. New Riders Publishing, San Francisco (2011)
12. Guinalı, M., Gurrea, R., Flavia, C.: The role played by perceived usability, satisfaction and consumer trust on website loyalty. Inf. manage. **43**, 1–14 (2006)
13. Ha, L., James, E.L.: Interactivity reexamined: a baseline analysis of early business web sites. J. Broadcast. Electron. Media **42**(4), 457–474 (1998)
14. Huang, Z., Benyoucef, M.: Usability and credibility of e-government websites. Govern. Inf. Q. **31**, 584–595 (2014)
15. Ivory, M.Y., Hearst, M.A.: Towards quality checkers for web site designs (2001)
16. Kim, S., Stoel, L.: Apparel retailers : website quality dimensions and satisfaction. J. Retail. Consum. Serv. **11**, 109–117 (2004)
17. Lazar, J., Bessiere, K., Ceaparu, I., Robinson, J., Shneiderman, B.: Help! I'm lost: user frustration in web navigation. IT Soc. **1**, 18–26 (2003)
18. Lee, Y., Kozar, K.A.: Understanding of website usability: specifying and measuring constructs and their relationships. Decis. supp. syst. **52**, 450–463 (2012)
19. Liang, T., Lai, H.: Effect of store design on consumer purchases : an empirical study of on-line bookstores. Inf. Manage. **39**, 431–444 (2002)
20. Martin, L.: E-government development index and its comparison in the EU member states (2016)
21. Mohsin, H.A., Raha, O.: Public sector ICT management review implementation of electronic government in Malaysia: the status and potential for better service to the public (2007)
22. Molla, A., Licker, P.S.: E-commerce systems success : an attempt to extend and respecify the delone and maclean model of IS success. J. Electron. Commer. Res. **2**, 131–141 (2001)

23. United Nations: United Nations e-Government Survey 2016: E-Government in Support of Sustainable Development, p. 263. UN Publishing Section, New York (2016). ISBN 978-92-1-123205-9
24. Newman, M.W., Landay, J.A.: Sitemaps, storyboards, and specifications: a sketch of web site design practice as manifested through artifacts (2001)
25. Nielsen, J.: Designing Web Usability: The Practise of Simplicity. New Riders Publishing, San Francisco (1999)
26. Ranganathan, C., Ganapathy, S.: Key dimensions of business-to-consumer web sites. Inf. Manage. **39**, 457–465 (2002)
27. Shafie, S.: E-government initiatives in Malaysia and the role of the national archives of Malaysia in digital records management, pp. 1–15 (2007)
28. Wirtz, B.W., Daiser, P.: E-Government Strategy, Process, Intruments, 1st edn. Imprint, Riga (2015)

Evaluating Students' Emotional Response in Augmented Reality-Based Mobile Learning Using Kansei Engineering

An-Nur Atiqah Khairuddin[✉], Fauziah Redzuan[✉], and Nor Aziah Daud

Faculty of Computer and Mathematical Sciences, Universiti Teknologi MARA (UiTM), Shah Alam, Selangor, Malaysia
atiqah@ict.upsi.edu.my, fauziahr@tmsk.uitm.edu.my

Abstract. Augmented reality (AR) is believed to be the next wave of online learning. New user experiences become possible to afford AR capabilities with the advent of powerful smartphones. Most studies related to the use of augmented reality in education focused on cognition with little consideration given to emotions which is important in learning. Therefore, this research aims to identify salient connections between emotions and design elements of augmented reality-based mobile learning material by applying Kansei Engineering (KE) approach. In this research, mobile augmented reality application related to the human heart was prepared to be used as a case study. Seven specimens of the mobile augmented reality application were evaluated with 55 emotions of Kansei Words (KW). 28 students from one of the public universities performed the evaluation experiment. The gathered data were then analyzed using Factor Analysis and Principal Component Analysis. The results revealed the important pillars of emotions or *kansei* semantic space emotions for augmented reality-based mobile learning materials. Based on Factor Analysis, it revealed four main pillars; *professional-motivated, confused, wandering-thrilled* and one additional pillar; *trustable*. Besides that, this research described design elements of augmented reality-based mobile learning material that might evoke specific emotions based on five identified pillars. Ultimately, this research is an attempt to guide the design with affective elements during preparation of augmented reality learning materials in the future.

Keywords: E-learning · Mobile learning · Augmented reality · Emotion · Design
Kansei Engineering

1   Introduction

Currently, internet penetration in Malaysia stands at 67%, thus making it reliable to harness the power of e-learning, in order to globalize online learning [1]. Despite the increase of online course enrolment, online courses continue to display serious issues of low retention rates [2]. Among the factors that contribute to dropout in online course are educational level, failure in understanding the content, student's satisfaction and student's motivation [2–4]. Based on the preliminary study, students have difficulty to

© Springer Nature Singapore Pte Ltd. 2018
N. Abdullah et al. (Eds.): i-USEr 2018, CCIS 886, pp. 79–89, 2018.
https://doi.org/10.1007/978-981-13-1628-9_8

learn complex course with abstract concept. Moreover, they are less satisfied with current online learning material.

Significantly, augmented reality is the future of e-learning [5, 6]. A comprehensive survey by [7] presented that augmented reality (AR) can be utilized with online learning, thus provide effective learning. Current trend for AR applications is the rapid development and adoption of mobile computing devices such as smartphones and tablets [8, 9]. The aids of multimedia elements and interaction in the design of AR can facilitate learning including abstract concept [10, 11]. However, education oriented AR applications have not been so deeply explored [12]. Mostly, previous research related to augmented reality focused on cognition while the focus on effective value in learning is still lacking [13].

Undoubtedly, the delivery of the right content to the learners with good design results in an effective learning including in e-learning [14, 15]. Moreover, researchers believed the emotions of a student during course engagement play a vital role in any learning environment including e-learning [16, 17]. Recently, researchers explored progressively on student's emotion in e-learning especially in higher education. However, researches that capture student's emotion in e-learning are still lacking, even though the understanding of learner's emotion is important in order to design the learning material [18].

Therefore, the focus of this research is to engineer emotional experience in order to achieve affective formula during preparation of augmented reality mobile learning materials. This research is intended to provide answer for two questions which are; "what are the emotions of students in the experience with augmented reality-based mobile learning materials?" and "how specific emotions associate with the design elements?"

2 Literature Review

2.1 Student's Emotion

There are various definitions of emotions and by way of summary, emotion can be defined as the inner feelings, desires and psychological responses that drives one's action tendencies which can be measured [19, 20]. Generally, there are lack of adequate empirically proven strategies to address the presence of emotions in learning [21, 22]. Mostly, positive activating emotions (enjoyment) is known to improve academic achievement, while negative activating (anxiety) and deactivating emotions (boredom) in contrast, can impair motivation and interest [23, 24]. According to [25], students play a more demanding role in online learning and take more responsibility for their learning. In this kind of learning, it is important to design emotionally engaging experiences [26]. A study by [27] conveyed that experiencing enjoyment foster self-regulated learning, while confusion, frustration and boredom are often related with negative emotions in online learning [28].

2.2 Augmented Reality-Based Mobile Learning

Generally, AR can be described as a multidisciplinary field that encompass computer graphics, computer vision and multimedia, which deals with the real-time combination of digital (computer-generated data) and physical information (real world) through different technological devices [29]. Meanwhile, Mobile Augmented Reality (MAR) extends the scope and prospective functionality of AR, thus presenting a dynamic way for people to interact with computers and digital information [30].

Most studies have indicated the effectiveness of AR in learning such as enhancing learning performance by making abstract concept as mentioned in [31], promoting learning motivation and increasing learning engagement [32]. Despite these benefits, until now education oriented AR applications have not been so deeply explored [12]. Moreover, AR can be integrated with e-learning and is believed to be the next wave of online learning [7, 33].

Recently, AR has been introduced in new application areas using mobile device such as historical education [34], tourism [35], human anatomy [36], computer sciences [37] and engineering education [38].

One characteristic of AR is the integration and interaction between the real and the virtual world which allows a huge versatility and creativity in learning [39]. Learners can actually see, listen to supplementary digital information and can intuitively manipulate the virtual information, allowing them to repeat a specific part of the augmentation which can benefit in learning [40]. According to [41] there are two types of contents deployed in an augmented reality application; static (texts, 3D model) and dynamic (animation). Commonly, the interaction is made by the mean buttons or gestures in which students can move the 3D object with buttons, scale the size of the video, image or object, or to play a video [36, 42]. A study by [43] classified five usability principles for smartphone AR applications which are; user-information, user-cognitive, user-support, user-interaction and user-usage.

2.3 Augmented Reality-Based Learning and Student's Emotion

There is lack of empirical work that explores the role of emotions in supporting learning with AR technology. A few examples can be found in [36, 44]. Both studies revealed that most of the students enjoyed learning complex or difficult course (abstract or technical course) by using AR. Reference [35] suggested that designers may manipulate the properties of the artefact to trigger the desired emotional state, thus should not neglect the importance of reinforcing positive emotions. This is supported by [45] as they stated that the most remarkable experiences seem to originate from the product itself in which empowerment, surprise, amazement and fascination are satisfying experiences, while frustration and disappointment are dissatisfying experiences.

2.4 Kansei and Kansei Engineering

Among methods, KE is identified as a proven method that is able to capture emotion, thus to connect emotion to specific design elements. Kansei is originated from Japanese term that is used to express one's impression towards artefact, situation and surrounding [46]. As described by [47], Kansei refers to the state of mind where knowledge and emotion as well as passion are harmonized.

Kansei Engineering (KE) is defined as a technique which is an ergonomic and consumer-oriented technology to translate user's Kansei (emotions, feelings, and demands) for a product into design elements [48, 49]. In other words, KE is a technology which unites Kansei into engineering realms by providing a systematic way of understanding the insight of user perceptions about the artefacts in order to produce concrete design characteristics that match consumer's need and desire via several physiological and psychological measurement methods [46].

KE has been applied in various field which aims at assisting designers to understand consumers emotions and impressions that contribute to design solutions and concrete design parameters [50]. Implementations of KE that focus on design of physical product, particularly IT artefact are online clothing website [51], virtual reality [52], online learning [53] and video-based learning [54]. Therefore, KE is the chosen method, since KE is the most suitable approach in order to meet the objective of this research.

3   Methodology

KE methodology with quantitative approach using psychological measurement is applied in this research. Overall, this research follows KE Type II procedure which is adapted from [55] and is divided into two phases; phase 1 and phase 2. As initiation of this research, literature review has been performed in order to identify issues and problem occurred in an e-learning environment. In order to support issues and obtain information as well as opinion regarding e-learning, a preliminary study was conducted on 32 students from a local public university through an online survey. Then, problem statement, research questions and research objectives were defined based on findings from both literature review and preliminary study. Next is phase 1 which identifies important emotions in e-learning environment. 55 emotions are selected which was adopted from a research carried out by [53]. Moreover, these emotions are used for phase 2 of the research. Meanwhile, phase 2 aims at identifying the design elements for specific emotions which is the main focus in this research.

Phase 2 begins with selecting a survey target. The first step is purposely to determine the focus domain which has been derived from the initial phase. The next step is preparation of evaluation target which consist of three important things. is the first one is the specimen or augmented reality mobile learning material. In this research, seven specimens are prepared which focus on the human anatomy course, particularly the human heart topic. The decision is based on earlier preliminary study and the observation activity of existing application in current market. Results from the preliminary study revealed that majority of students have an Android smartphones. This topic (the heart) is among the highest topic that needs support for mobile learning and has more options of augmented reality mobile learning materials. Therefore, four specimens are mobile-based obtained from Google Play Store, while the remaining three are generated through the development of The Human Heart Mobile Augmented Reality application (HeMAR). The HeMARs was developed in Android platform which used camera-based tracking method in visualizing the AR scene via marker. The functional requirement is identified from the observational activity, while user requirement is obtained from the preliminary study. Unity and Vuforia platform were used to develop HeMARs, while user experience (UX) which encompasses human factor and usability as mentioned in [8, 56] is taken as basis. All seven specimens have differences and similarities in design which was found to fit with selection criteria based on the rules in KE method.

Secondly, the subjects to participate in evaluation experiment are selected. The selection of subjects are based on purposive sampling in one of the public universities in Malaysia. The subjects or participants are undergraduate students who currently enrol or had taken the human anatomy course. Moreover, the criteria for the participants are that they are familiar with e-learning and able to express emotions accordingly. As stated by Nagamachi in [57], a number of 20 or 30 people are sufficient to be employed as subjects in KE research. Therefore, 35 students were invited for the evaluation. However, only 32 students came and joined for the evaluation. Thirdly, Semantic Differential (SD) scale for the experiment was configured and 55 emotions as mentioned in phase 1 were used in 5-level SD scale for evaluation. Next step was extracting item/ category to investigate the design of the specimen (e.g. color, size and layout). The item refers to specific characteristics in product design, while the category refers to the small groupings in each item. The evaluation experiment was conducted in a library room to provide a controlled environment. Data gathered from the evaluation experiment were analyzed through three categories of analysis; descriptive analysis (demographic profile) while the second category is a combination of Factor Analysis (FA) and Principal Component Analysis (PCA) (Kansei semantic space) and finally Partial Least Square (PLS) (design elements or guidelines).

4 Result and Discussions

There are two expected findings of this research which are (1) Kansei semantic space of augmented reality-based mobile learning specifically for Human Anatomy learning materials for higher education, (2) the design elements in association with a specific emotion. These findings was obtained from FA, PCA and PLS by using the average evaluation data. FA and PCA with a varimax rotation was performed to identify the semantic space for augmented reality-based mobile learning material. From FA, variance analysis result can be obtained to determine the most significant factors of emotion as shown in the following Table 1.

Table 1. Variance analysis.

Factor	Variance	Percentage (%)	Cumulative percentage (%)
Factor 1	22.96	41.75	41.75
Factor 2	8.66	15.75	57.49
Factor 3	7.09	12.89	70.39
Factor 4	6.28	11.42	81.81
Factor 5	6.01	10.92	92.73
Factor 6	4.00	7.27	100

The result shows that the first factor has the highest variance thus value which is 22.96 representing 41.75% of the data. The second, third and fourth factors indicate 15.75%, 12.89% and 11.42% of the data respectively. The total contribution of the first four factors is 81.81% of the variability. Therefore, these four factors might significantly influence on the semantic space of the emotions in the domain under investigation. The fifth factor explains 10.92% which contribute to 92.73% that could be expanding the representation of the data. The sixth factor with value less than 10% to represent data could be considered as insignificant factor. The selection factors are consistent with the results derived from the Eigenvalue. Figure 1 shows the result of FA which has been sorted in descending order to enable the observation of the semantic space and the value of approximately 0.6 is considered as the reference value. The identified semantic space for augmented reality-based mobile learning materials is structured based on five factors or pillars. The four main pillars are the *professional-motivated, confused, wandering-thrilled* and *challenging*. The additional pillar is identified as *trustable*.

Emotions	Factor 1	Emotions	Factor 2	Emotions	Factor 3	Emotions	Factor 4
Astonished	0.984747835	Questionable	0.84945234	Wandering	0.92441715	Challenging	0.8473554
Professional	0.974920211	Disappointed	0.83632879	Ambiguous	0.82674638	Neutral	0.727589
Ebullient	0.968916194	Dull	0.7560434	Thrilled	0.73404356	Discouraged	0.6374256
Pleased	0.955713524	Confused	0.7325043	Inspired	0.63325324	Integrated	0.50941
Fun	0.949451735	Bored	0.73232482	Unexpected	0.61162171	Tranquil	0.4869004
User Friendly	0.930119615	Deceptive	0.67277394	Deceptive	0.57193943	Fully Controlled	0.4679173
Optimistic	0.91845722	Furious	0.42639401	Confused	0.50588771	Time Consuming	0.4467904
Interested	0.900522003	Failed	0.36107388	Touched	0.49227239	Convinced	0.4385413
Learnable	0.883717834	Inspired	0.29851039	Soothing	0.48323721	Comprehensible	0.4368345
Motivated	0.877646342	Wandering	0.26090633	Furious	0.45786918	Easy to read	0.3959714
Engaged	0.872886301	Motivated	0.22929678	Surprised	0.44854871	Conscious	0.369321

Fig. 1. Partial view of the factor analysis result of the Kansei words

The first pillar, known as "professional-motivated" includes the Kansei words such as fun, user friendly, interested, pleased, learnable, harmonious and others. The second pillar, which is "confused", includes the Kansei words such as questionable, deceptive, dull and others. The third pillar, known as "wandering-thrilled" includes Kansei words such as inspired, unexpected, ambiguous and others. The fourth pillar includes Kansei words such as neutral and the fifth additional pillar consists of time consuming, joking and integrated. The obtained result has similarity with other related work. The common important factor that is professional-motivated in this research is in line with the first factor in [54]. This first factor consist of two emotions that are important as engaged-motivated, the first factor in [53] and motivated-confident, the first factor in [52]. This three are identified as important factors in respective work. Based on that, the emotion motivation is revealed to be an important emotion in e-learning environment. This is supported by [36], as augmented reality helps to visualize in motivating students in learning. Besides that, there are similar members of first factor which have high value of FA such as "pleased" and "interested" with previous work. Another factor which is fourth factor known as "challenging" is similar to second factor in [53]. While the rest of the factors are quite different with previous work as it might be due to the different domain under investigation.

Figure 2 illustrates the PCA of the Kansei words which shows mostly the positive words on the right of x-axis, while negative words are towards the left of x-axis. This demonstrates the semantic space for most of positive emotion words can be represented by "professional-motivated". The emotion words such as wandering, thrilled and inspired are located at the top part of the y-axis. This suggests the "wandering-thrilled" as the semantic space in this axis. Based on the Kansei semantic space of professional-motivated and wandering-thrilled in Fig. 3 specimens C might have the design elements best fir for these Kansei emotions, while specimen F and G can be considered a good fit in design towards positive emotions. Both Kansei semantic spaces, professional-motivated and wandering-thrilled are based on the dimension of Factor 1 and Factor 3. Specimens C, F and G are more professional-motivated, but specimens' F and G less wandering-thrilled as compared to specimen C. These three specimens have the dynamic 3D model and have two 3D models. In addition, specimen C has used an icon type of button with simple interface. Meanwhile, both specimen F and G have an audio as an additional multimedia element. This indicates that the richness of the content can evoke emotional experience which has been highlighted in [56]. Specimens C, F and G have dynamic type of 3D object (3D model), object manipulation using touch gesture (scale) and error-handling (reset function).

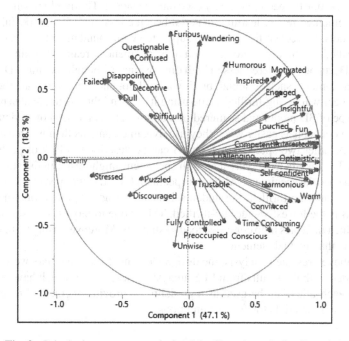

Fig. 2. Principal component analysis of the Kansei words (loading plot)

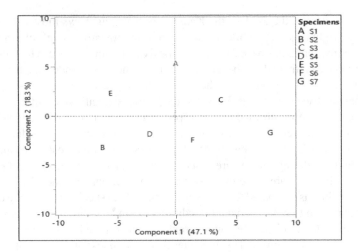

Fig. 3. Principal component analysis of the specimens based on component 1 and 2 (score plot)

In contrast, specimen A is less professional-motivated, but the highest wandering-thrilled. This is due to specimen A only used one 3D model. This might result in students who use augmented reality learning material become less motivated, especially with a few 3D models. Moreover, the content is supported with sound that might lead students to feel thrilled when they interact with this augmented reality learning material. Specimen D can be considered less in both dimensions. Although specimen D has extra multimedia elements such as sound, but it was still not enough to motivate the student and make them wandering-thrilled while using it. This might due to the absence of the dynamic type of 3D model and scattered of a button. The perception of students is that learning the concepts is easier when they use dynamic contents than when using static ones [41]. Another two specimens, E and B can be described as lack of professional-motivated. The insufficient contrast of both specimens might result in the student to be not pleased with the specimens. Although specimen E used static type of 3D model, but it still can "wandering-thrilled" the students. Instead of a lack of professional-motivated, specimen B is the lowest wandering-thrilled. This is due to more text description than pictures which indicates high cognitive load of students. Moreover, using visual element is preferable than textual element.

From above presented analysis, the design elements for these pillars were explored and supported with the results from PLS analysis. These results which have influential relation to each other can be used as a guideline to provide augmented reality-based mobile learning materials for specific emotions.

5   Conclusion

Based on the two findings, the objectives of this research have been achieved. For the first objective, there are four main factors and one are additional pillar that refers to the emotions which is the structure of semantic space for augmented reality-based mobile learning material for the Human Anatomy course. The main pillars are professional-motivated, confused, wandering-thrilled and challenging. Meanwhile, the additional pillar is trustable. Kansei emotions of professional, motivated, wandering, thrilled, challenging, trustable, pleased, learnable, interested, fun, engaged and user-friendly are among important emotions in augmented reality-based mobile learning material that are based on five factors. Therefore, these emotions are essential in e-learning specifically in augmented reality-based mobile learning. For the second objective, classification of design elements of augmented reality-based mobile learning material was derived from the first objectives. The outcome is encompassed of five sets of design elements that have the highest influence in eliciting emotions resulting from the five pillars correspondingly.

Acknowledgment. The authors would like to record our sincere thanks to the Universiti Teknologi MARA for the financial support of this publication under the funding of 600-IRMI/ DANA 5/3/LESTARI (0119/2016).

References

1. MOE, Executive Summary Malaysia Education Blueprint 2015–2025 (Higher Education), vol. 2025 (2015)
2. Bawa, P.: Retention in online courses: exploring issues and solutions—a literature review (2016)
3. Hart, C.: Factors associated with student persistence in an online program of study: a review of the literature. J. Interact. Online Learn. **11**(1), 19–42 (2012)
4. Park, J., Choi, H.J.: Factors influencing adult learners' decision to drop out or persist in online. J. Educ. Technol. Soc. **12**, 207–217 (2009)
5. EXULT, E-learning Trends (2017). Exult Corporation. www.exultcorp.com/IT/E-learning_Trends_2017_V4.pdf
6. Ira, K., Berge, Z.: Online learning's future in the workplace with augmented reality. In: Encyclopedia of Information Communication Technology. IGI Global (2009)
7. Satpute, T., Pingale, S., Chavan, V.: Augmented reality in e-learning review of prototype designs for usability evaluation, pp. 15–18 (2015)
8. Huang, W., Alem, L., Livingston, M.A. (eds.): Human Factors in Augmented Reality Environment. Springer, New York (2013). https://doi.org/10.1007/978-1-4614-4205-9
9. Nincarean, D., Phon, E., Ali, M.B.: Collaborative augmented reality in education: a review, pp. 78–83 (2014)
10. Solak, E., Cakir, R.: Exploring the effect of materials designed with augmented reality on language learners' vocabulary learning. J. Educ. Online **13**(2), 50–72 (2015)
11. Yen, J., Tsai, C., Wu, M.: Augmented reality in the higher education: students science concept learning and academic achievement in astronomy. Proc. Soc. Behav. Sci. **103**, 165–173 (2013)
12. Saidin, N.F., Halim, N.D.A., Yahaya, N.: A review of research on augmented reality in education : advantages and applications. Int. Educ. Stud. **8**(13), 1–8 (2015)
13. Radu, I., Zheng, R., Golubski, G., Guzdial, M.: Augmented reality in the future of education, pp. 1–8. ACM (2010)
14. Krishnan, P., Vanitha, V.: An integrated framework to enhance performance of online students. Asian J. Res. Soc. Sci. Human. **6**, 839–855 (2016)

15. Lim, S., Lee, J.: An immersive augmented-reality-based e-learning system based on dynamic threshold marker method. ETRI **35**(6), 1048–1057 (2013)
16. You, J.W.: The relationship among college students' psychological capital, learning empowerment, and engagement. Learn. Indiv. Differ. **49**, 17–24 (2016)
17. Barker, J., Gossman, P.: The learning impact of a virtual learning environment: students' views. Teach. Educ. Netw. Journal **5**, 19–38 (2013)
18. Krithika, L.B., Priya, L.: Student emotion recognition system (SERS) for e-learning improvement based on learner concentration metric. Proc. Comput. Sci. **85**(Cms), 767–776 (2016)
19. Scherer, K.R.: Appraisal considered as a process of multilevel sequential checking. In: Appraisal Processes in Emotion: Theory, Methods, Research. Oxford University Press, New York (2001)
20. Scherer, K.R.: What are emotions ? And how can they be measured? Soc. Sci. Inf. **44**(4), 695–729 (2005)
21. Hascher, T.: Learning and emotion: perspectives for theory and research. Eur. Educ. Res. J. **9**(1), 13–28 (2010)
22. D'Mello, S., Taylor, R., Davidson, K., Graesser, A.: Self versus teacher judgments of learner emotions during a tutoring session with AutoTutor. In: Woolf, B.P., Aïmeur, E., Nkambou, R., Lajoie, S. (eds.) ITS 2008. LNCS, vol. 5091, pp. 9–18. Springer, Heidelberg (2008). https://doi.org/10.1007/978-3-540-69132-7_6
23. Pekrun, R.: The control-value theory of achievement emotions : assumptions, corollaries, and implications for educational research and practice. Educ. Psychol. Rev. **18**(4), 315–341 (2006)
24. Pekrun, R., Stephens, E.J.: Achievement emotions: a control-value approach. Soc. Pers. Psychol. Compass **4**, 238–255 (2010)
25. Broadbent, J., Poon, W.L.: Internet and higher education self-regulated learning strategies and academic achievement in online higher education learning environments: a systematic review. Internet High. Educ. **27**, 1–13 (2015)
26. Cho, M., Kim, Y., Choi, D.: The effect of self-regulated learning on college students perceptions of community of inquiry and affective outcomes in online learning. Internet High. Educ. **34**(April), 10–17 (2017)
27. You, J.W., Kang, M.: The role of academic emotions in the relationship between perceived academic control and self-regulated learning in online learning. Comput. Educ. **77**, 125–133 (2014)
28. Graesser, C., D'Mello, S.: Emotions during the learning of difficult material, vol. 57 (2012)
29. Azuma, R., Behringer, R., Feiner, S., Julier, S., Macintyre, B.: Recent advances in augmented reality. IEEE comput. Graph. Appl. **21**, 34–47 (2001)
30. Kourouthanassis, P.E., Boletsis, C., Lekakos, G.: Demystifying the design of mobile augmented reality. Multimed. Tools Appl. **74**, 1–41 (2013)
31. Weng, N.G., Bee, O.Y., Hsia, T.E., Yew, L.H.: An augmented reality system for biology science education in Malaysia. Int. J. Innov. Comput. **6**(2), 8–13 (2016)
32. Kiourexidou, M., Antonopoulos, N., Sgantzos, M., Veglis, A.: Augmented reality for the study of human heart anatomy. Int. J. Electron. Commun. Comput. Eng. **6**(6), 658 (2015)
33. Docebo: Elearning Market Trends And Forecast 2017–2021 (2016)
34. Harley, J., Poitras, E.G., Duffy, M., Lajoie, S.P.: Comparing virtual and location-based augmented reality mobile learning : emotions and learning outcomes. Educ. Technol. Res. Dev. **64**, 359–388 (2016)
35. Kourouthanassis, P.E., Boletsis, C., Chasanidou, D., Bardaki, C. Tourists responses to mobile augmented reality travel guides: the role of emotions on adoption behavior (2014)

36. Jamali, S.S., Shiratuddin, M.F., Wong, K.W., Oskam, C.L.: Utilising mobile-augmented reality for learning human anatomy. Proc. Soc. Behav. Sci. **197**(February), 659–668 (2015)

37. Kose, U., Koc, D., Anil, S.: An augmented reality based mobile software to support learning experiences in computer science courses. Proc. Comput. Sci. **25**, 370–374 (2013)

38. Shirazi, A., Behzadan, A.H.: Design and assessment of a mobile augmented reality-based information delivery tool for construction and civil engineering curriculum. Am. Soc. Civil Eng. 1–10 (2015)

39. Kaufmann, H.: Construct3D: an augmented reality application for mathematics and geometry education, pp. 656–657. ACM (2002)

40. Liarokapis, F., Petridis, P., Lister, P.F., White, M.: Multimedia augmented reality interface for e-learning (MARIE). World Trans. Eng. Technol. Educ. **1**(2), 173–176 (2002)

41. Diaz, C., Hincapié, M., Moreno, G.: How the type of content in educative augmented reality application affects the learning experience. Proc. Comput. Sci. **75**(Vare), 205–212 (2015)

42. Cubillo, J., Martín, S., Castro, M., Díaz, G., Colmenar, A.: A learning environment for augmented reality mobile learning (n.d.)

43. Ko, S.M., Chang, W.S., Ji, Y.G.: Usability principles for augmented reality applications in a smartphone environment. Int. J. Hum. Comput. Interact. **29**(8), 501–515 (2013)

44. Majid, N.A.A., Mohammed, H., Sulaiman, R.: Students perception of mobile augmented reality applications in learning computer organization. Proc. Soc. Behav. Sci. **176**, 111–116 (2015)

45. Olsson, T., Salo, M.: Narratives of satisfying and unsatisfying experiences of current mobile augmented reality applications, pp. 2779–2788. ACM (2012)

46. Lokman, A.M.: Design & emotion: the Kansei engineering methodology. Malays. J. Comput. **1**(1), 1–11 (2010)

47. Nagamachi, M., Lokman, A.M.: Innovations of Kansei Engineering. CRC Press Taylor & Francis Group, New York (2011). Badiru, A.B. (ed.)

48. Nagamachi, M.: Kansei engineering: a new ergonomic consumer-oriented technology for product development. Int. J. Ind. Ergon. **15**, 3–11 (1995)

49. Nagamachi, M.: Kansei engineering as a powerful consumer-oriented technology for product development. Appl. ergon. **33**, 289–294 (2002)

50. Schütte, S.: Engineering emotional values in product design-Kansei engineering in development. Linkoping University Institute of Technology (2005)

51. Lokman, A.M., Noor, N.L., Nagamachi, M.: Kansei engineering: a study on perception of online clothing website (2000)

52. Chuah, K.M., Chen, C., Teh, C.S.: Designing a desktop virtual reality-based learning environment with emotional consideration. Res. Pract. Technol. Enhanc. Learn. **6**(January), 25–42 (2011)

53. Redzuan, F., Lokman, A.M., Othman, Z.A.: Kansei semantic space for emotion in online learning, pp. 168–173 (2014)

54. Adnan, H., Redzuan, F.: Evaluating students' emotional response in video-based learning using Kansei engineering, pp. 237–242 (2016)

55. Lokman, A.M., Nagamachi, M.: Kansei Engineering Procedures: Kansei Engineering Type II. In: Badiru, A.B. (ed.) Innovations of Kansei Engineering, p. 50. CRC Press Taylor & Francis Group, New York (2011)

56. Irshad, S., Rambli, D.R.A.: Preliminary user experience framework for designing mobile augmented reality technologies. In: ICIDM (2015)

57. Lokman, A.M., Nagamachi, M.: Kansei Engineering A Beginner Perspective. UiTM University Publication Centre, Shah Alam (2010)

HCI and Underserved

Usability and Design Issues of Smartphone User Interface and Mobile Apps for Older Adults

Chui Yin Wong[1,2(✉)], Rahimah Ibrahim[2], Tengku Aizan Hamid[2], and Evi Indriasari Mansor[3]

[1] Faculty of Creative Multimedia, Multimedia University, 63100 Cyberjaya, Malaysia
cywong@mmu.edu.my
[2] Malaysian Research Institute on Aging (MyAging), Universiti Putra Malaysia, Serdang, Selangor, Malaysia
{imahibrahim,aizan}@upm.edu.my
[3] Department of Computer Science, Prince Sultan University, Riyadh, Saudi Arabia
emansor@psu.edu.sa

Abstract. Smartphones have become essential communication tools for older adults to stay connected with their family and peers. The older adults are generally perceived as *techno-phobic,* and this poses challenges for them to adopt some advanced features on smartphones. Moreover, smartphones and some mobile apps are not designed to meet the needs and expectations of older adults. This hinders them from fully utilizing their functions and services. A mobile-user interaction study was conducted to examine the usability of smartphone user interface and mobile apps among 80 older adults. The 4 tasks were 'making and retrieving voice calls', 'using phone book', 'installing a mobile app from Google Play Store', and 'using WhatsApp'. The usability result revealed that the 'voice call' task had the highest success task completion rate (83.44%), followed by phonebook (70.16%), mobile app (63.13%) and using WhatsApp (60.42%). To conclude, majority faced problems downloading a mobile app from Play Store. Although WhatsApp is their favourite communication app, it reveals the usability problems of using features such as sending audio recording files. They feared of upgrading their apps as they were not familiar with the notifications. There is still some room to improve issues in smartphone user interface design especially for older adults' cohort.

Keywords: Smartphone · Mobile apps · Older adults · Usability · Design

1 Introduction

1.1 Smartphone Trend

Smartphone and mobile apps have become ubiquitous communication tools for everybody. The launch of Apple iPhone in 2007 marked a 'smartphone' era [1]. All the mobile retail shops these days are only keen to promote and sell touch-screen based smartphones. We seldom find any keypad-enabled mobile phones at the storefront unless there is a special request from customers. Thus, this phenomena leads to the situation where

© Springer Nature Singapore Pte Ltd. 2018
N. Abdullah et al. (Eds.): i-USEr 2018, CCIS 886, pp. 93–104, 2018.
https://doi.org/10.1007/978-981-13-1628-9_9

older adults are left with not many mobile phone choices. Eventually they have to gradually migrate to become *'silver'* smartphone users. However, the current mobile operators in Malaysia mainly target young adults (age 18–45) as their main consumer markets. The older adults cohort (aged 60 and above) have been sidelined in this matter.

1.2 Ageing Population

With the rising ageing population worldwide, Malaysia as a developing country cannot be spared from joining other advanced countries to become an aged nation by 2035 [2]. Due to better healthcare and improved standards of living, this implies that there will be an estimated 6.96 million or 15% of the total Malaysian population joining the older adult cohort. As stated in the National Policy and Action Plan of Older Persons (DPTWEN, 2011–2020), the Malaysian Ministry of Women, Family and Community Development [3] aims *'to create older persons who are independent, with dignity, high sense of self-worth and respected by optimizing their self-potential through a healthy, positive, active, productive and supportive ageing to lead a well-being life.'* As such, there will be an implication towards healthcare, transportation, housing, and also different demands of lifestyle for the ageing population.

As a result, it becomes essential for the older adults to use smartphones to stay in touch with their family, peers and children in terms of running their daily chores, keeping themselves updated and connected to the mainstream society as well as living independently. However, the current smartphone user interface is mainly designed for young adults cluster but not for the older adults. This is because the older adults are usually perceived as *techno-phobic* [4] and *laggards* [5] to adopt a new mobile technology such as smartphones and their mobile apps services. Older adults face challenges to switch from keypad-enabled feature phones to touch screen smartphones. That being said, this paper aims to examine the usability and design issues of smartphones as well as their mobile apps for older adults.

2 Literature Review and Related Work

2.1 Mobile Research Studies

In human-computer interaction and interaction design fields, there have been a number of research studies done on mobile phones with the elderly. Instead of using mobile phone for communication, the elderly were revealed as passive users for their mobile phones usage, where they merely considered the phone as a means for making emergency calls only for security purpose [6]. For the gender aspect, male elderly are identified as frequent mobile users than female elderly [7]. The female elderly groups generally use the mobile phones for security reasons rather than for casual talk, and seldom use for text messaging. They face the problems of interacting with some features on the mobile phones (such as display, mobile size, buttons, colour, backlighting) and functionalities (i.e. memory aid, operational complexity, layout and shortcuts). However, the likelihood of this circumstance may change with the prevalent use of WhatsApp communication app and other mobile apps on smartphones.

Hwangbo et al. [8] conducted a study to investigate the pointing performance of elderly on smartphones in Korea. It revealed that the pointing performance of elderly was significantly influenced by size, spacing and location of the target, and the performance was higher in audio tactile feedback as compared to auditory or tactile feedback. Boulos et al. [9] highlighted that touchscreen-based smartphone is suitable for older adults due to its virtual buttons as large as needed as compared to the small buttons available on feature phones. However, this statement is arguable because older adults prefer the metallic button of feature phone than typing on the virtual keyboard on smartphone. They find it difficult to type messages on the virtual keyboard and think it was their problem due to their fat fingers. This was supported by the research done by [8, 10] that pointing performance is increased with larger targets and wider spacing between them. The optimal target size is between 14 and 17.5 mm. In addition, older adults have difficulties to tap on the virtual keyboard. They experience problems of detecting which buttons or target to press, which often leads to long taps of a virtual button, or pressing the wrong button on the virtual keyboard [11, 12]. Petrovčič et al. [13] has conducted a comprehensive review of design guidelines along with checklists for feature phone and smartphone that should embrace and address usability dimensions and categories for the interest of mobile user interface designers as well as developers.

In Malaysian context, only a few studies were done on mobile phone usage. Generally, the older adults face the following problems of using mobile phones, which are (i) mobile design namely small and rubbery buttons, small screen size to view the font size and also small buttons and characters. They are prone to press the keypad numbers wrongly and are not familiar with slide or touch screen interaction mode plus the complexities of menu design. They prefer to use the Malay or Chinese language rather than English. Apart from that, they do not feel secure to use mobile banking, (ii) there is cognitive decline in terms of difficulty to recall functions, memory difficulties of remembering own mobile phone numbers, complex menu arrangement, complicated functions and unclear instructions on how to proceed to use a certain function, (iii) motivational (i.e. fear of using mobile applications, using mobile phones for emergency situations only, not familiar of other functions except calling or sending SMS, and getting help from grandchildren to use some features on mobile phones), (iv) physical impairment or decline in motor skills, vision and hearing (i.e. eyesight problems in viewing messages and saving contact numbers, the shape and size of the mobile phone is too big or too small to hold) and (v) circle of support (lack of support or training from family members, friends or any experts) [14–16].

To find out the issues, purposes and context of use for mobile device among the older people, focus group studies were conducted on 11 older adults aged 65 years old and above in Malaysia [16]. The findings summarised the mobile phone usage into four categories, which are; mobile usage purposes, mobile usage applications, mobile usage issues, and mobile usage context. In terms of mobile usage purpose, the older adults' main interest in using mobile devices was to communicate with their children, followed by friends, business and work, and emergency. It was learnt that the most frequent mobile usage was to call and send SMS. It also showed that older adults, who had higher educational background, were more conversant in adopting the latest mobile technology because they usually had experience in using computers before.

The above-mentioned studies were conducted before the smartphone era when the usage of mobile phone mainly refers to the keypad-enabled feature phones. Thus, the findings are not applicable and relevant to the current smartphone trend for the elderly. For example, rubbery or metallic button is no longer an issue for older adults as the current smartphone user interface is touch-screen based. They are also no longer constrained in using small screen size on feature phone as before. There are numerous touch-screen size for the consumers to choose in the mobile shops these days. For the font size, smartphones these days allow the users to choose different viewing options from small to large size. In the past, there were senior phones catered mainly for the senior citizens market that came with big buttons and simple shapes. However, the smartphones these days no longer differentiate the user clusters. Instead, the smartphone user interface allows 'one size fits all' concept whereby it provides users two options of standard or easy mode (with simple user interface). The issue that hinders the older adults in fully utilizing the function and features of smartphones are the complicated menus and the availability of various mobile applications.

There are limited studies of smartphone usage in Malaysian context. [17] conducted a survey with 1814 respondents on the trend of smartphones and their usage in Malaysia. However, the study mainly described the smartphone usage in general, and only 0.9% (16 out of 1814) respondents fell under the age of more than 57 years old. Thus, the study indicated that the design of the mobile device is the most important factor for choosing a mobile phone for young generation, and not for the older consumers. In addition, Wi-Fi capability is not pertinent to the older consumers (age more than 57 years old). Overall, the findings of the study was done in 2012, and most of the content is not relevant to today's smartphone era. For instance, the study also revealed that Instant Messaging acted like a complimentary to SMS (short messaging services) rather than a substitution of SMS. This is contrary to the current communication landscape where WhatsApp is the main communication tool across all age group mobile users, regardless of age. The findings also summarized that the smartphone is yet to be fully utilized by the consumers. It was suggested that user training, proper redesign of the mobile applications, prevalent user support to improve usability and user acceptance of the future smartphones.

Reference [18] conducted a study to investigate the barriers of using a smartphone among the elderly in Malaysia. The study conducted semi-structured interviews with 21 elderly respondents to understand the barriers in using smartphones among the elderly population. The barriers of adopting smartphones among non-smartphone users were; 'not affordable', 'no interest', 'no necessity', 'lack of knowledge', 'vision, cognitive, hearing and motor impairment' that deter them from using a smart phone. It is also interesting to learn that prior experience of using feature phones did not help to transfer the technology experience to using a smartphone. This is due to the difference in the interaction mechanism between a feature phone and a smartphone. The elderly are generally familiar with the 'pressing' interaction mode on hard keypad as compared to a total different interaction mode of using 'swiping', 'sliding', 'touching' on a touchscreen user interface. The change from previous alphanumerical hard key button keypad to QWERTY virtual keyboard makes it difficult for the elderly to type SMS, or any messages. The change of user interface and interaction mode somehow deters the elderly to adopt to using a smartphone. However, some findings such as being pricey and fixed standard mode of screen user interface of this study may not be applicable in the current smartphone scenario.

Since the older adults face the challenges of adopting and familiarizing with the smartphone user interface, this study aims to examine the usability issues of smartphones user interface among the older adults in Malaysian context.

3 Research Methodology

A mobile-user interaction study using mixed methods (observation, questionnaire, verbal protocols and interview) was conducted with 80 Malaysian young old adults (60–74 years old, 40 males and 40 females) from May to July 2016.

3.1 Inclusion and Exclusion Criteria for Participants

The inclusion criteria for the participants are young old adults' cohort [4], who are aged 60 to 74, and own a smartphone for at least 3 months prior to the research. The reason for choosing this cohort is because they are considered a huge potential *silver smartphone users* for the rising grey market for mobile operators.

As this research focuses on active and productive ageing, and is not so much on a health-related study, the exclusion criteria includes older adults who are severely ill from mental, physical, motor and hearing impairment.

The participants were mainly recruited from the University of the Third Age (U3A), which provides life-long learning courses for older adults. The sampling techniques are purposive sampling and snowballing method based on the above-mentioned criteria.

3.2 Task Design

Four main tasks were selected from a previous Smartphone Usage Survey study to find out the preferred smartphone features and its usage among older adults [19]. The tasks are shown in Table 1 as below.

Table 1. The four tasks for mobile-user interaction study.

Task 1: voice calls	Task 3: installing a mobile app
Sub-task 1: making a call	Sub-task1: go to Google Play store to download a torchlight mobile application
Sub-task 2: retrieving calls	Sub-task 2: start initiating the application
Task 2: Phonebook	Task 4: Using WhatsApp
Sub-task 1: adding a contact with a phonebook	Sub-task 1: sending a message using WhatsApp
Sub-task 2: making a call from phonebook contact	Sub-task 2: sending photos using WhatsApp
	Sub-task 3: sending an audio file using WhatsApp

3.3 Apparatus and Location

Based on the Smartphone survey study [19], the Android mobile phone is the most used and well accepted smartphone among the older adults. Hence, the apparatus for usability testing was the Samsung S7 Edge. It was chosen for testing purpose because it was newly launched in May 2016 and none of the participants had used it before except for those who were familiar with the previous same brand model. In addition, we needed a larger internal memory space with 32 GB to store the screen capturing video for video analysis in later stage of the research. Android 5.0 Lollipop design was the Android mobile OS software version used at the time of the user testing sessions from May-July 2016. We used Mobizen screen capture software to record the user interacting with the tasks on the smartphone. The whole process was recorded using video camera and a digital audio recorder for further data analysis.

The venue for the study was conducted at a quiet meeting room at the Institute of Gerontology (later known as the Malaysian Research Institute on Aging).

3.4 Measures

Based on ISO9241-11 [20], the usability metrics are effectiveness, efficiency and satisfaction scores. For this particular study, we only consider the performance metrics, which are effectiveness and time. To measure the effectiveness, we refer to task completion rate (in percentage) for each task, where 100% is considered successful, 50% is partially successful, and 0% means failure to complete the task. To calculate the task completion rate for each task, it is based on the total values (in percentage) of all the sub-tasks completion rate, and divide them in average.

To further investigate the user perception of older adults interacting with the testing apparatus, in this case Samsung S7 Edge, we conducted Device Attitudinal Survey, which was adopted from O'Brien's work [21]. It uses a 7-point semantic differential scale, which is categorized into 3 sections as 'enjoyment, ease of use and appearance'.

3.5 Procedures

During the usability trial, a consent form was given to the participants to highlight that participation was voluntary. They were informed that the whole process would be audio-video recorded, and that their identity would be kept anonymous for data analysis purpose. The participants were asked to fill-up a questionnaire to find out their demographic profile, and their perception of a smartphone and its icons. After that, they were given the 4 tasks to interact with the test apparatus, and this was followed by filling up a post-questionnaire with a debriefing interview. The participants were prompted to use verbal protocol to speak their thoughts and opinion throughout the process. The whole session took around 1 h to 1.5 h, depending on the individual's performance.

4 Findings and Discussions

This section illustrates a brief demographic profile and the usability results. In terms of demographic profiles, the 80 participants consisted of 40 males and 40 females. They were all Malaysian with the breakdown of Malay (n = 22, 27.5%), Chinese (n = 47, 58.8%), Indian (n = 10, 12.5%) and others (n = 1, 1.3%). The proportion of Chinese are higher than that of Malays. This does not represent the correct proportion of the Malaysian population, only that there was a higher number of Chinese memberships at the U3A during the recruitment time. For occupation, a majority of them (77.5%) was retirees, some were still working (11.3%) and some had never worked before (11.3%). In terms of educational background, a majority had upper secondary education (40%) and tertiary education (50%), followed by lower secondary (6.3%) and primary school (2.5%) while no formal education was the lowest percentage (1.3%). The reason why there were many of educated members in U3A was that these set of people are the ones interested in joining life-long learning courses for self-improvement. Many of them speak and write English and Bahasa Malaysia (national language of Malaysia) well, and only half can speak and write Mandarin, while only a number of them speak and write Tamil. Their good command of English language was not a surprise because Malaysia was a British colony before thus the old generation generally conversed well in English as compared to the younger generation.

Figure 1 shows the result of overall task completion rate for the 4 main tasks. Table 2 illustrates the breakdown of task completion rates for the main and sub-tasks. The result reveals that voice calls receive the highest task completion rate of 83.44%, followed by phonebook (70.16%), installing a mobile app (63.13%) and using WhatsApp (60.42%).

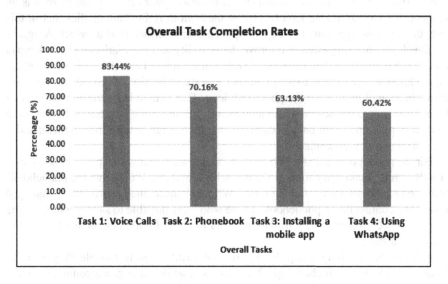

Fig. 1. Overall task completion rate.

Table 2. Task completion rates for 4 main and sub-tasks.

Tasks and sub-tasks	Percentage (%)	Tasks and sub-tasks	Percentage (%)
Task 1: voice calls	83.44	Task 3: installing a mobile app	63.13
Sub-task 1.1: making a call	80.63	Sub-task 3.1: go to Google Play Store to download a 'torch light' mobile app	64.38
Sub-task 1.2: retrieving a call	86.25	Sub-task 3.2: after downloading, open the torch light application	61.88
Task 2: Phonebook	70.16	Task 4: using WhatsApp	60.42
Sub-task 2.1: adding a contact with a phonebook	71.88	Sub-task 4.1: sending a message using WhatsApp	81.88
Sub-task 2.2: making a call from phonebook contact. Call WongCY from the phonebook	68.44	Sub-task 4.2: sending a photo using WhatsApp	63.13
		Sub-task 4.3: sending an audio record	36.25

Table 2 illustrates the details of task completion rates for all the 4 main and sub-tasks.

For the voice call sub-tasks, it was no surprise that users are generally more familiar with making phone call (80.63%). Some were not successful in making phone call because of its complexed and non-intuitive phone keypad icon on the Samsung S7 user interface. The users did not realize that after pressing the 'phone' icon, it showed the recent contact list. They had no clue as to how to make a phone call, which was not part of the existing contact list. With assistance, the users later realized that there was an unnoticeable keypad phone icon located at the bottom right. This implies that in this case, there is a design issue for the smartphone user interface (UI) to which designers and developers are suggested to improve the visibility and familiarity of phone keypad icon. Some participants had problems in retrieving a missed call (86.25%) while others did not know where to refer to the phone because the indication of missed call was only shown in a small number on the phone call icon. They had to learn the convention that the number shown on the phone call icon means 'missed call'. To return call, they were hesitant to pick up or call back because the numbers were not familiar to them, and it was not shown in their contact list.

For the phonebook task, the sub-task of 'adding a contact with a phonebook' shows 71.88%, while 'making a call from the phonebook and call WCY from the phonebook' decreased to 68.44% task completion rate. With assistance, many participants managed to save the contact into a phonebook. Those who were not able to save a contact in the phonebook were because they usually referred to their children and others to save the numbers for them.

In terms of installing a mobile app, the sub-task of 'go to Google Play Store to download a torch light mobile app' shows 64.38%, while 'after downloading, open the torch light application' is 61.88% task completion rate. Even though downloading a torch light mobile app is considered an easy task, a majority did not know how to download a mobile app from the Play Store. They mainly referred to their children or grandchildren to download the mobile apps for them. They also had no clue on which mobile apps were good and useful for them. Interesting enough, many of them only experienced exploring the Google Play Store because of this research requirement. They were lost in the navigation system of the Play Store, and the search text field was not obvious to them. To improve the user interface design, it is suggested that Play Store needs to have a 'search' text label or 'magnifier' icon shown at the search text field. We also received comments and feedback that the Google Play Store icon did not represent a 'place' for users to download mobile apps. With the current Play Store icon design, it looks more like a shopping bag or triangle shape rather than a mobile app store place for them. In addition, the label name of 'Play Store' sounds like a game place for gamers rather than mobile apps store place.

The task completion rates for the 3 sub-tasks of using WhatsApp, which are 'sending a message using WhatsApp' (81.88%), 'sending a photo using WhatsApp' (63.13%), and 'sending an audio record' (36.25%). The main reason for older adults to adopt using a smartphone is the encouragement and push from family members as well as peers to use WhatsApp for free messaging and sharing of media files. Basically, there were not many problems in sending a message using WhatsApp. However, many participants would close the WhatsApp and go to the photo gallery to select photos to send rather than sending them via WhatsApp itself. This reveals that the 'paper clip' icon is not apparent, or appropriate to meet the expectations of older adults to choose to 'attach' the photos for sending. They prefer some other icons that carry the meaning of 'sending' rather than the 'paper clip of attachment' concept. During the testing time, sending an audio record was considered quite a new concept in WhatsApp. It revealed a severe usability problem that majority of them had problems in using the audio record feature in WhatsApp. Users need to 'press and hold' the 'audio speaker' icon to speak for recording, and then release it to "send". The action is not a norm for users to 'press and hold' to speak. Instead, the users just pressed once on the icon, and then released it. They just continued to speak without recording it. Thus, the task completion rate is low as it is not a user-friendly feature, and it requires a serious design improvement. The latest WhatsApp audio version has improved a lot by providing 2 action options, which is to choose an audio record from music track, or record with WhatsApp. The latter action is more straightforward and shows a simpler UI of WhatsApp Recorder.

The device attitudinal result is as shown in Fig. 2. The mean for the respective 3 main categories of device attitudinal are (i) *Enjoyment (5.26)*, which consists of 'boring-fun', 'unpleasant-pleasant', 'negative-positive', 'painful-pleasurable', 'dull-exciting', 'foolish-wise', and 'unenjoyable-enjoyable', (ii) *Ease of use (4.73)*, which consists of 'difficult-simple', 'boring-elegant', and 'complex-easy' and (iii) *Appearance (5.75)*, which comprises of 'unattractive-attractive', 'repulsive-delightful', 'ugly-gorgeous' and 'plain-striking'. The highest scores are 'unattractive-attractive' item (5.75), 'ugly-gorgeous' (5.71) and 'plain-striking' (5.69). It looks like these 3 items are inter-related. The high score could be influenced by the Samsung S7 Edge apparatus, which was covered by a gold colour casing that appears to be an elegant look at that time for the participants.

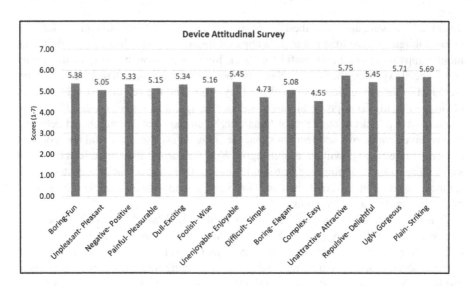

Fig. 2. Device attitudinal result.

All the scores are above 5 (from 1–7 scores) except 'difficult-simple' item (4.73) and 'complex-easy' (4.55) under 'Ease of Use' category. This implies that the participants were somehow struggling using the smartphone itself. Although the score is acceptable, it is a known fact that in Malaysian attitude, they generally do not like to give lower scores or express their honest feelings when it comes to filling up questionnaires. They also wanted to give the impression that they were able to use the smartphone. However, through observation, the score itself is much lower than what was filled up. It was obvious that many were struggling when using the smartphone, especially some advanced features like sending photos, recording audio files using WhatsApp, and adding contacts on the phonebook.

In a nutshell, the findings imply that older adults enjoy using the smartphone and find it essential to learn how to use a smartphone. Generally, they were quite keen to use WhatsApp, but they were honest that they were only familiar with the basic features of WhatsApp like receiving and sending messages or photos. They were not familiar with other more advanced features like audio-recording. They did not perceive it useful and it was also difficult to use. The participants also expressed their concern and frustration of how to transfer and save media files, especially photos and videos when their mobile phones memory was full. They had also no clue as to how to proceed and deal with the frequent hanging issue of the phone due to memory space limitation.

As they do not have the technical know-how to solve some phone issues, they always refer to their children or grandchildren to help solve the problems. However, in some cases, their children are always busy and have no time to attend to them resulting them to go to mobile shop to seek technical help. That being said, they also expressed their interest to attend mobile training courses to pick up some skills rather than refer to their children.

5   Conclusion

It is found that the main reason of problems experienced by older adults with their smartphone is due to discrepancy between the design of devices and users' needs [7, 13]. Hence, it is crucial for smartphone developers and UI designers to incorporate older adults' needs and expectations in designing and developing smartphones as they are the rising consumer market. The older adults had little difficulty making calls. However, a majority of them had difficulties in downloading application from Google Play Store and referring to their children to pre-install the apps in their smartphones. They are generally able to use the simple functions of WhatsApp. However, usability problems for advanced features were apparent, especially sending audio recording file. Usability issues reveal that the older adults were confused between WhatsApp's Voice Call with Phone's Voice Call icons. They fear and have no idea how to proceed for advanced usage of smartphones to enhance their daily life.

In this paper, we only present the usability result of smartphone user interface among the older adults, which is a part of a larger study. The future study is recommended to discuss the affordance design and icons recognition for intuitive smartphone user interface, which caters for older adults.

Acknowledgement. The authors would like to express gratitude to the participants from University of Third Age (U3A) Malaysia involved in this study. This research study was funded by Malaysia Ministry of Higher Education Fundamental Research Grant Scheme (FRGS) [FRGS/1/2015/MMUE/150036]; and Universiti Putra Malaysia (UPM) Putra Grant [UPM/700-2/1/GP-IPS/2013/9390400].

References

1. Tan, K.H.: The iPhone is 10 (2017). http://www.thestar.com.my/tech/tech-news/2017/01/09/how-the-world-haschanged-thanks-to-the-iphone/. Accessed 03 Nov 2017
2. Malaysia Healthy Ageing Society: Malaysia to be ageing nation by 2035 (2012). http://healthyageing.org/index.php/malaysia-to-be-ageing-nation-by-2035/. Accessed 06 May 2017
3. Ministry of Women, Family, and Community Development. https://www.kpwkm.gov.my/. Accessed 03 Feb 2017
4. Fisk, A.D., Rogers, W.A., Charness, N., Czaja, S.J., Sharit, J.: Designing for Older Adults: Principles and Creative Human Factors Approaches, 2nd edn. CRC Press, Florida (2009)
5. Rogers, E.M.: Diffusion of Innovations, 5th edn. Simon and Schuster, New York (2003)
6. Kurniawan, S.: An exploratory study of how older women use mobile phones. In: Dourish, P., Friday, A. (eds.) UbiComp 2006. LNCS, vol. 4206, pp. 105–122. Springer, Heidelberg (2006). https://doi.org/10.1007/11853565_7
7. Kurniawan, S.: Older people and mobile phones: a multi-method investigation. Int. J. Hum Comput Stud. **66**(12), 889–901 (2008)
8. Hwangbo, H., Yon, S.H., Jin, B.S., Han, Y.S., Ji, Y.G.: A study of pointing performance of elderly users on smartphones. Int. J. Hum. Comput. Interact. **29**(9), 604–618 (2013)
9. Boulos, M.N.K., Wheeler, S., Tavares, C., Jones, R.: How smartphones are changing the face of mobile and participatory healthcare: an overview, with example from eCAALYX. Biomed. Eng. Online **10**, 24 (2011)

10. Leitao, R., Silva, P.A. Target and spacing sizes for smartphone user interfaces for older adults: design patterns based on an evaluation with users. Presented at the Conference on Pattern Languages of Programs, Tucson, Arizona (2012). http://www.hillside.net/plop/2012/. Accessed 29 Apr 2018

11. Motti, L.G., Vigouroux, N., Gorce, P.: Interaction techniques for older adults using touchscreen devices: a literature review. In: Proceedings of the 25th IEME Conference Francophone on L'Interaction Homme-Machine, pp. 125–134. ACM, New York (2013)

12. Zhou, J., Rau, P.-L.P., Salvendy, G.: Age-related difference in the use of mobile phones. Univ. Access Inf. Soc. 13(4), 401–413 (2014)

13. Petrovčič, A., Taipale, S., Rogelj, A., Dolničar, V.: Design of mobile phones for older adults: an empirical analysis of design guidelines and checklists for feature phones and smartphones. Int. J. Hum. Comput. Interact. 34(3), 251–264 (2018)

14. Nasir, M., Hassan, H., Jomhari, N.: The use of mobile phones by elderly: a study in Malaysia perspectives. J. Soc. Sci. 4(2), 123–127 (2008)

15. Wong, C.Y.: Exploring the relationship between mobile phone and senior citizens: a Malaysian perspective. Int. J. Hum. Comput. Interact. 2(2), 65–77 (2011)

16. Azuddin, M., Malik, S.A., Abdullah, L.M., Mahmud, M.: Older people and their use of mobile devices: issues, purpose and context. In: The 5th International Conference on Information and Communication Technology for the Muslim World (ICT4 M) 2014, pp. 1–4. IEEE (2014)

17. Osman, M.A., Talib, A.Z., Sanusi, Z.A., Tan, S.-Y., Alwi, A.S.: A study of the trend of smartphone and its usage behavior in Malaysia. Int. J. New Comput. Archit. Their Appl. (INJCAA) 2(1), 275–286 (2012)

18. Mohadisdudis, H.M., Ali, N.M.: A study of smartphone usage and barriers among the elderly. In: 2014 3rd International Conference on User Science and Engineering (i-USEr), pp. 109–114. IEEE, Selangor (2014)

19. Wong, C.Y., Ibrahim, I., Hamid, T.A., Mansor, E.I.: The use of smartphone and mobile application among older adults in Malaysia. In: Kommers, P. (ed.) Proceedings of the International Conference ICT, Society and Human Beings 2017, pp. 87–94. IADIS Press, Lisbon, 20–23 July 2017

20. International Organization for Standardization (ISO), ISO 9241-11: 1998 (en): Ergonomic Requirements for Office Work with Visual Display Terminals (VDTs) – Part 11: Guidance on Usability. https://www.iso.org/obp/ui/#iso:std:iso:9241:-11:ed-1:v1:en. Access 03 Nov 2011

21. O'Brien, M.A.: Understanding human-technology interactions: the role of prior experience and age. Ph.D. dissertation, Georgia Institute of Technology (2010)

Exploring Blind Users' Experience on Website to Highlight the Importance of User's Mental Model

Suraina Sulong[(✉)] and Suziah Sulaiman[(✉)]

Department of Computer and Information Sciences,
Universiti Teknologi PETRONAS, 32160 Seri Iskandar, Perak, Malaysia
{surainasulong, suziahsulaiman}@utp.edu.my

Abstract. As website layout is often designed with sighted users in mind, a number of difficulties can be experienced by blind user. The evolution of a website from static page to dynamic page makes the website even more inaccessible to the blind user due to the different feedback they received from the system compare to the previous website. This paper serves as a preliminary study which explores blind users' experience interacting with websites with the aid of a screen reader. Semi-structured interviews and observation were carried out to find out these usability issues encountered by the blind users. The study indicates that blind user mental model plays an important role in improving the user's web usability experience. Associating with the user existing experience on the website with familiar and unfamiliar information of the website, enhances the user learning process. The study findings also highlight that understanding the mental model of blind users contributes to improving the web usability guidelines.

Keywords: Blind user · Mental model · Usability · Accessibility

1 Introduction

The Internet is being used by a wide range of users to satisfy their information seeking [1]. The internet has increasingly become as the primary source to look for and gather information, with huge collection of data and information. Today, a tremendous change happen to develop the mode website and the means information is shared through them. Latest used technologies such as AJAX, Flash and DOM, increase the richness of the web content and provide dynamic information content based. Due to this, it has made accessibility of these sites a bit difficult to the disability. The dynamic content generated on the web page cannot read by the screen reader.

Nowadays, most of the websites and assistive software used by the disabled to access the website have accessibility barriers [2]. The Web is an progressively significant source in many aspects of life such as; government, employment, commerce, education and more [3]. Due to the number of this usage, it is essential that the website is accessible to provide equal opportunity to the all types of users [4]. An accessible website will help the group of disabilities participate more actively in society.

© Springer Nature Singapore Pte Ltd. 2018
N. Abdullah et al. (Eds.): i-USEr 2018, CCIS 886, pp. 105–113, 2018.
https://doi.org/10.1007/978-981-13-1628-9_10

The website offers the possibility of unique access to information and interaction for many people with disabilities. The challenges in life and acquiring a new skill especially on IT field seem to be a matter of subject to the blind [5].

2 Background Study

2.1 Defining Web Usability

From the ISO definition of usability, web usability accordingly measured as the ability of web applications to support such tasks with effectiveness, efficiency and satisfaction. Derived from the usability principles defined by Nielsen's, web usability can be constructed as; (1) Web applications learnability: the disability users to understand from the first page and services available, in a way that the contents are easy to understand and navigational mechanisms are easy to identify, (2) Web applications efficiency; user can reach the content quickly through the available links, able to orient themselves and understand the meaning of the page with respect to their navigation starting point, (3) Memorability; implies that after a period of non-use, users are still manage to browse the website within the hypertext; (4) few errors; in case the users have erroneously followed a link, they could be able to return to their earlier location, (5) users' satisfaction; users feel that they are in control with the comprehension of available contents and navigational commands [6]. Recently, this concept of usability has been extended to cover accessibility. More precisely, Web accessibility means that people with disabilities can perceive, understand, navigate and interact with the Web. Web accessibility also benefits others, including older people with changing abilities due to aging [7]. The article [8] describes scenarios of people with disabilities using the web.

2.2 User's Mental Model

Most of the internet users have their own experience and expectation of the website. Due to this ability, the designers address the user's existing mental model as a valuable information, to formulate a usable user mental model. [9]. During the development stage of a system, applying the user's mental model as a basis is found as a great contribution to have a user's preferred system. To comprehend a user's view on system content, every designer considers a user mental model to be a essential element as it helps them to have the system [10] but the system design still not accessible to wide range of users ability. Usually, the user tend to use their existing mental model to interact with the system [11]. Familiarity can be achieved from these questions to investigate the user mental model (1) Do the user imagination of the systems look alike? Or (2) Do the user understand how system supposedly behave? or (3) How user expects a system to respond? The user mental model can be in any form, such as a diagram, an image, a theory, a set of concepts, some guideline or others [12]. This representation is said to be a great help to enhance the user understanding the functionality of any system [13]. Usually, a system is built accordingly to a designers' view. In another word, the developed system is based on a designer's mental model.

Study by Dingli and Cassar [14], highlighted the usability issues for user browsing activities which is measured through the interaction between a user and the system.

It was also addressed by Ferreira et al., the need for assistive technology when a blind computer user accesses a website. It is important for the designer to design a website or an application that is approachable for the screen readers to read the content.

3 The Study to Investigate the Blind User Interaction

There two objectives will be highlighted in this paper as a preliminary work of the whole research:

a. To examine the blind user's strategies while browsing the website
b. Determine the problems encounter by the blind user while browsing the website.

3.1 Semi – Structured Interviews

Semi-structured interview were conducted iteratively with fifteen blind users. The most experienced participant is a teacher who work at MAB and the rest are students who are taking the computer literacy class at MAB. The participants is above 20 years old and most of them came from different background of education and occupations. These are list of the initial questions that were asked before the session begin:

(a) How do you browse the internet?
(b) How did you solve unfamiliar website?
(c) How did you correct the mistake or error while browse the internet?

Due to the nature of this method, which has a very high response rate and the technique emboldens the collection of true and correct responses, semi – structured interview was conducted to address the nature of the difficulty [15]. The questions will addressed the user's usability issues while browsing the website (Table 1).

Table 1. Table show the list of questions in the interview session based on the usability principle.

Usability Principle	Explanation	Questions
Web application learnability	The hypertext front-end composed in a way so as contents are easy to understand and navigational are easy to identify	1. Web behaviour: When first accessing a new, unfamiliar website, I'm most likely to
		2. I navigate by headings to find information on a lengthy webpage
Web application efficiency	Users manage to find contents through the available links. Users are able to orient the page by themselves and understand the page with respect to their navigation starting point	3. I use site search functionality
		4. Skip links/content: I use "skip to content" or "skip navigation" links
		5. I use shortcut or access key to navigate the website
		6. If a text only version of a website is available, how often do you use it?

(continued)

Table 1. (*continued*)

Usability Principle	Explanation	Questions
Memorability	Users are able to get oriented within the hypertext, navigation bars pointing to landmark pages after a period of non -use	7. How difficult are pop - up windows to you?
		8. How often do you navigate by landmark in the website?
Few errors	In case users have erroneously followed a link, they should be able to return to their previous location	9. If a site map is available, how often do you use it?
		10. How do you usually navigate on the website when lost?
		11. What are the most problematic items you find on the website?
User's satisfaction	Users feel that they are in control with respect to the hypertext, comprehension of available contents and navigational commands	12. How accessible the Web 2.0 and dynamic Web applications to you?
		13. Describe your feeling regarding the usability of web content over the years?

The interview questions were categorized based on the usability principles to determine the participants achieved the web usability principles based on Nielsen usability definition. The sequence of actions done by the participants determined the participants thinking and mental model on strategies to browse the website.

To apply Nielsen usability definition on website usability, some refinement on the usability principles were done over the broad definitions. It is important to apprehension the specificity of the usability issues counter by the participants while giving the feedback from the interview questions. Thorough information about a person's thoughts and imagination gain from direct interview. The section below highlights two of the questions asked after the interview session:

a. In your opinions, how to improve the website layout to ease the blind user?
b. Do you any suggestion any kind of features or system to be added in the website to help the blind user browse the internet?

The participant's thoughts and expectation were very important to understand how the user interact with the website. To ensure the participants communicate their idea, these questions were asked at the end of the interview session. From the user feedback, it allows the researchers to cognitively identify the user thinking, such as the difficulties they are facing with the current website which does not satisfy their need.

3.2 Observation and Think – Aloud Methods

Then the participants were given five tasks with different scenarios to accomplish after the first session. The main objective of the tasks was to ensure the responses from the participants are consistent and direct to the main problem of this research. Below (Table 2) list of the scenarios provided to the blind participants in this study.

Table 2. Show the tasks given to the participants during the second session

Num. of task	Scenario
1	You're planning a vacation to Sabah from March 3rd – March 14. You need to buy both ticket flight and hotel. Compare the lowest price ticket
2	Send an email and attach a file to your friends and invite him to MAB events
3	You have forgotten few of the JAWS Screen Reader function and look for online reference on how to use the screen reader
4	You are looking for an archive news on online news about the latest technology for the blind
5	Share what you had experience today in our interview session on your Facebook wall. Tag your friends to alert them with the post

Hence, the participants need to set the goal they need to achieve; finding desired information by direct search or discovering new information by exploring the website, comprehending the information in the webpage, invoking and executing certain web applications, such as the ordering and downloading of products. The usability problems of the website were identified based on the usability definition and the result and analysis will be explained in next session.

User observation and think-aloud method were conducted during this session. Video recorded was done for multiple reviews and due to the ability to capture the actual user behavior. Direct observation removes the propensity of a respondent being biased or exaggerates to express their problems. The facial reactions such as eagerness or lack of interest and irritations when the participants encounters issues while working with the website were recorded. The negative emotions of the participants and the factors which cause this negative emotion during accomplished the task were detected. User emotions is out of the research scope. But the result of observation will be benefit for future research.

This observation was gained by the observers who assisted the interviewer during the observation process, since the interviewer was focusing on verbal feedback from the participants. User emotion and psychological feedback was not focused in the scope of this research, but the findings will be beneficial for future research. A quick review shows that the expert participants were more emotionally stable compared to beginner participants. Both negative and positive vibes affect the participants browsing behavior. This can be due to their success rate to complete the task. Apart from the session, the researcher joined a slot of class literary learning and internet training class at MAB to observe how the blind user action during the class compare to during the interview session. Figure 1 shows the setting during the interview session.

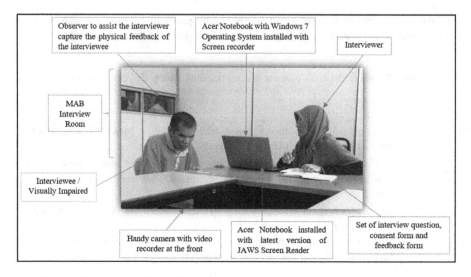

Fig. 1. Figure shows the setting during the interview session with the participants

4   Results and Findings

4.1   Interviews Result

Most of the participants use dynamic web. Based on the participant's response, they were unable to open or browse the dynamic content webpage. However, for the blind participants who rely on screen reader, dynamic websites force them to adapt to inaccessible use model. From the result of observation, most of the blind users tend to avoid dynamic web pages.

4.2   Observation Results

The analyses were done based on the observation from the session and video recorded. The results point out the nature or characteristics of the participants during the interview session. Refer Table 3.

The main factors contributes to the inaccessible elements for the blind are arranged from the most frequent encountered to the less frequently encountered by the users and also according to the most frustrating to the less emotion felt by the users;

(a)   Blocks by the pop – blocker
(b)   Inability to know the actual content of the page
(c)   Web unable to load or crash.
(d)   Having to listen repetitively the same information
(e)   Inability to login.

Table 3. The participants' feedback from the task given.

Num. of task	Participant feedback
1	Can I use another website? The website is much easier than the desktop web. The user uses mobile version web at the desktop. >https://mobile.airasia.com/index.php. I like to recommend this page to all my friends. I can effectively complete my work using the system (1)
2	The application link assists me to access the email application. I use the shortcut key to attach the file. It makes me easy to do it (1)
3	The screen reader crash, and after restart, the screen reader read the page all over again. It is quite long to wait if I skipped some link the navigation may be going somewhere else or to another page, as I had experienced it before. The advertisement automatically played in the video was confusing (1)
4	I used search function and search the news on archive. Sometime the advertisement pop windows disturb my navigation and make me lost from the landmark, but I manage to find the news using shortcut keys and available links
5	I will use Facebook for blind user. It is easier and very familiar to me >https://m.facebook.com/ (1). But I'm quite worry if I had mistakenly key in the username and password as it is my privacy (1)

4.3 The Results

Based on result of the task given to the participants, some of the participants mapped the intention directly onto a single intention; others require a sequence of operations. In other case, the selection of an action sequence requires considerable knowledge of the participants. Based on the study, there are two aspects of user actions need to be considered. First, to figure out the method that is used by the participants to accomplish the task, two, to investigate which system commands are to be appealed to the user. The selection process involves the consideration of the participants' decision; to investigate the way they know the commands. Based on the result of observation, there are four ways to consider how the user made decision in the selection process, which are:

i. The participants retrieved the decision to be made from their memory
ii. The participants were being reminded by other person, the system or system manual
iii. The participants were able to derive or construct the possibilities from the application or the system
iv. The participants used their existing knowledge from what have been taught by other person, the system, a manual or previous experience on the website.

In the first case, recall-memory is used to recognize the desired features in the website to be used by the participants. In the second case, recognition-memory cast-off to identify the preferred item from the list or description of the substitutes. In the third case, the user occupies in problem-solving either by using analogy or remove the possibilities. The fourth case, the user learns from some external source. This raises the issue of how the user knows that their first experience with a website will be different with other website, and when the assistance is needed. How that assistance is provided to access the website, becomes a major theme of the study.

5 Discussions and Future Work

The problems encounter by the blinds participants were investigate. Series of interviews, recorded observations and task browsing activities were effectively conducted to solve the issues. The challenges faced by the blinds to perform a simple task have been highlighted. The result of accessibility from the different type of web page has taken into consideration and the result shown that the complexity of the web page layout could affect the learning process and task completion of a blind person. Moreover most of the participants have their existing experience and mental model of the system.

As a future work, the formulation of a usable model representing the mental model of the blind user will be focused onto. Hence, this study learns mental model of blind users as an important contribution to improve website accessibility. It is foreseen that a developer use the model as a website development guide in future.

References

1. Ainsworth, J., Ballantine, P.W.: That's different! How consumers respond to retail website change. J. Retail. Consum. Serv. **21**(5), 765–772 (2016)
2. Babu, R., Singh, R., Ganesh, J.: Understanding blind user's web accessibility and usability problems. AIS Trans. Hum.-Comput. Interact. **2**(3), 73–94 (2016)
3. Dingli, A., Cassar, S.: An intelligent framework for website usability. Adv. Hum.-Comput. Interact. **2014**, 1–13 (2014)
4. Fakrudeen, M., Ali, M., Yousef, S., Hussein, A.H.: Analysing the mental model of blind users in mobile touch screen devices for usability. In: Proceedings of the World Congress on Engineering, pp. 837–842, July 2013
5. Ferreira, S.B.L., Nunes, R.R., Da Silveira, D.S.: Aligning usability requirements with the accessibility guidelines focusing on the visually-impaired. Procedia Comput. Sci. **14**(Dsai), 263–273 (2012)
6. Johnson-Laird, P.N.: Mental models and cognitive change. J. Cogn. Psychol. **25**, 131–138 (2013)
7. Kurniawan, S.H., Sutcliffe, A.G., Blenkhorn, P.L., Box, P.O., Manchester, M.: How blind users' mental models affect their perceived usability of an unfamiliar screen reader. In: INTERACT, vol. 3, pp. 631–638 (2003)
8. Mealin, S., Murphy-hill, E., Carolina, N.: An exploratory study of blind software developers. In: IEEE Symposium on Visual Languages and Human - Centric Computing, vol. 12, pp. 71–74 (2012)
9. Nacheva, R.: The importance of users' mental models for developing usable human-machine interfaces, July 1990, 132–135 (2015)
10. Nganji, J.T., Nggada, S.H.: Disability-aware software engineering for improved system accessibility and usability. Int. J. Softw. Eng. Appl. **5**(3), 47–62 (2011)
11. Power, C., et al.: Navigating, discovering and exploring the web: strategies used by people with print disabilities on interactive websites. In: Kotzé, P., Marsden, G., Lindgaard, G., Wesson, J., Winckler, M. (eds.) INTERACT 2013. LNCS, vol. 8117, pp. 667–684. Springer, Heidelberg (2013). https://doi.org/10.1007/978-3-642-40483-2_47
12. Saei, S.N.S.M., Sulaiman, S., Hasbullah, H.: Mental model of blind users to assist designers in system development. In: 2010 International Symposium on Information Technology, pp. 1–5 (2010)

13. Sandhya, S., Devi, K.A.S.: Accessibility evaluation of websites using screen reader. In: 7th International Conference on Next Generation Web Services Practices, pp. 338–341 (2011)

14. Semaan, B., Tekli, J., Issa, Y. B., Tekli, G., Chbeir, R.: Toward enhancing web accessibility for blind users through the semantic web. In: 2013 International Conference on Signal-Image Technology & Internet-Based Systems, vol. 50, pp. 247–256 (2013)

15. Steinfeld, E., Maisel, J.: Universal Design: Creating Inclusive Environments. John Wiley & Sons, Inc, Hoboken (2012)

A Conceptual Framework for Co-design Approach to Support Elderly Employability Website

Marlina Muhamad[✉], Fariza Hanis Abdul Razak, and Haryani Haron

Faculty of Computer and Mathematical Sciences, Universiti Teknologi MARA,
Shah Alam, Selangor, Malaysia
marlina326@kedah.uitm.edu.my, {fariza,haryani}@tmsk.uitm.edu.my

Abstract. This paper aims to understand and develop a conceptual framework of Co-Design approach to support elderly age-friendly employability website. The research focuses on literature in elderly employment, co-design approach, co-design component and the roles of elderly in co-design approach to support the design and development of elderly employability website. The results of the research suggest a conceptual framework to map the concept of co-design as an approach to support elderly employability website with eight components of co-design which are active engagement, foster creativity, ownership, sustainability, inspired ideas, saved cost, user satisfaction, and user learning. This framework considers that the roles of elderly as explorer, ideator, designer, and diffuser, co-design components and employment website components are the main key to enable elderly to find a suitable job. To help recognize and rectify particular problem areas in a website development, involving users at initial process can be very beneficial. This conceptual framework is an initial research for researchers and practitioners to further examine co-design practices in designing products or services by elderly and for elderly.

Keywords: Elderly employment website · Component of co-design ·
Roles of elderly

1 Introduction

In this digital era, the use of the Internet by many elderly people is not only to control their finances, keeping in touch with current interests and staying in touch with relatives, friends, and acquaintances [1], elderly also is very likely to search for a job [2]. Similar to other forms of aging, retirement, is a shift rather than a simple difference of opinion in which an individual who is a worker today and retired later. The glimpse of retirement is viewed as a process rather than evidently defined role transition [3], it was noted that only partly of elderly workers shift from full-time employment to retirement. The rest, some retired workers decided partial retirement in which they continue to work on part-time basis, while others retire and then return to work, typically "unretiring" [4]. For elderly people, job opportunities continue to cater for compelling financial resources to them and their family even after they pass their prime working life. Health and well-being have been rated as the most significant factors in deciding whether elderly people

© Springer Nature Singapore Pte Ltd. 2018
N. Abdullah et al. (Eds.): i-USEr 2018, CCIS 886, pp. 114–124, 2018.
https://doi.org/10.1007/978-981-13-1628-9_11

can contribute in working life and are some of the most essential factors in people's choice to prolong their working life [5]. Work also has been explained as being very important in maintaining mentally and emotionally sharp. [5] demonstrated some of those who were working past 65 years of age considered their social interaction and participation in working life as extremely inspiring and somewhat that elderly people did not want to refrain. [5] described elderly people enjoy social contact with patrons, colleagues, etc., and it was one of the very important things in their life and something they could not live without. [5] continued that social connectivity is a very important part of work that most people cannot live without. Being an important part of the surrounding community, promises to deliberate one's independence, and being part of a social group provided status and gratification, creating this as one of the important thought for the elderly people pertaining working after retirement.

References [6, 7] acknowledged ICTs originally have been considered as an enriching component for the enhancement of socio-economic situations in growing countries. However, what kind of technologies, with what elements and how these should be constructed to exploit effective usage is a point to ponder. The methods to technology design for developing contexts evolved in relation to considerations and beliefs in the nature of development and the effective means to pursue it. In considering that the elders are much likely to develop age related deteriorations such as visual or mobility related disabilities, age friendly website to search for a job turn out to be an important matter. If web designers do not comprehend the ground rules, then the problem of poor accessibility will unavoidably remain. Co-design approach defined as the practice on user to facilitate user participation, requesting them to deliberate their feel and information precisely in the design process [8]. It is claim that co-design includes the user more closely in the process, and to not favor the expertise of the designer over that of the user. Reference [9] added co-design approach assists users to use or reconfigure their capability thus creating input more effectively, thus facilitating their capability in use.

2 Literature Review

2.1 Ageism in Malaysia

In Malaysia, Institute of Gerontology located in Universiti Putra Malaysia (UPM) addressed that the pace of increment in the amount of the aged people in growing countries is alarming trends in which innovative critical thinking at all levels is needed to combat the issues to avert a crisis. Director from Institute of Gerontology, UPM [10], said in an interview with The Star that "Malaysia has a rather short time to prepare for the transition into an aged nation". She continues, becoming an aging nation is a silent epidemic. It is therefore crucial to prepare the nation for this eventuality as it takes more than a decade for social institutions to change. As the study also points out, an important sanity to be worried about the rising aged population is that by the year 2050 and 2055, the figure of senior persons aged 60 years or over will match the number of young people under the age of 15 years in Malaysia. Thus, all of these changes will have important implications for Malaysia's economy and society. In relation to population ageing, Asian countries including Malaysia face two major objectives; first is to sustain robust economic growth and second to provide economic guarantee to the increasing number of senior people [11].

A continuing demographic shift comprises a key challenge for most developed countries including Malaysia. An aging and falling population caused by low birth degrees and intensified longevity will demand the organizations obtain ways to confront with a gradually aging population. In most developed countries, aging and older workers of the working population has already taken place, and is swiftly growing in countless developing countries as well [12]. While the shrinking number of younger workers, the ratio of older workers is growing. This situation gives significant challenges for many stakeholders such as government, policy makers, employers including employees as well. The major claiming is that organization will have to trust on the contribution of older workers after they are hired.

Countries with an ageing population will have fewer of working age who are productive and can contribute to the society. One of the biggest fears probably that Malaysia will end up with high numbers of elderly dependents and the possibility of the taxpayer funding their care, possibly through welfare aid. With relatively few people working, the levels of production will drop. In the long-term, population growth will bring with it the problem of an elderly population as well as the problem of overcrowding. This suggests older people should re-enter the workforce so that they become healthy, productive and successful aged citizens. Old people as they age often wish for a happy and comfortable life till the end.

2.2 Design and Development Approaches

Currently, there are three types of design and development approaches for products or services, namely User-Centered Design (UCD) [13], Participatory Design (PD) (1970), and Co-Design [14]. Each of the models has different approach to product design. However, each of the model only concern about consulting with the user, but not allowing users to make decisions, nor empowering users with the tools that the designers use. There is no work process that can support elderly employability website related to the roles provided by elderly users through co-design approach. [15] emphasises in social sciences researches on the role of the socio-economic context on shaping technology usages, and on the impact in building towards sustainable community development. The goal of the explorations in the front end is to determine what is to be designed and sometimes what should not be designed and produced. The ambiguity and chaotic nature at early front end is followed by the traditional design process where the resulting ideas for any product, service, interface, or anything else are developed first into concepts, and then into prototypes that are refined on the basis of the feedback of future users.

User-Centered Design (UCD). According to [16], user-centered design attempts to enhance the fit of product and services with how users can, wish and need to use the product/services, rather than pushing the users to alter their behavior to adapt the product and services. This approach was first described by [13] as "a philosophy based on the needs and interests of the user, with an emphasis on making products usable and understandable". However, it is now becoming possible that the UCD approach can no longer note the scale or the difficulty of the obstacles designers and researchers face today. Designers are not simply designing or inventing products for users, instead designers are inventing for the future experiences of people, communities and cultures who are now connected and notified in ways that were unconceivable even 10 years back [17]. The recent trend shows that designers are moving to designing for people's purposes rather than from the design of categories of products.

Participatory Design (PD). In Participatory Design, researchers engaged with workers and unions to explore how technology might be designed for skilled workers where it was originated in the Scandinavian Cooperative design tradition [16]. It stressed out on collaboration between the researcher and users as the approach is characterized. Its strength lies in being a movement that cuts across traditional professional boundaries. This is based on the philosophy that the environment functions better if peoples are functioning (active) and participated in its creation and management instead of being preserved as inactive users [18]. Participatory Design is said to be semi-active engagement among user.

Co-design. Co-design, a more current version of UCD and closely beyond PD, is more advanced by engaging users more actively in all stages of the design process as co-creator. Whereas participatory design demands on designers to translate users' needs, behaviors, desires and contexts to learn about their needs, co-design calls on them to enable user participation, requesting them to express their experience and knowledge directly in the design process [8]. It would therefore claim to include the user more closely in the process, and to not privilege the expertise of the designer over that of the user. Co-design aiming to intensively engage users in the design process to allow them to express their experience and knowledge. [17] stated that the terminology used until the recent obsession with what is now called as co-creation or co-design was known as participatory design. It is noted that co-design is a term used in design field while co-creation is a term used in the minds of those in the business community. Thus, it is important to note that the best known proponents of co-design originate from business or marketing field and not from design practice.

2.3 Co-design Process

According to [19] there is no single model for co-design that can be applied in all cases. The model for design of a new approach to confronting rooted problems in a particular group will be different from the re-design of existing services to better meet the needs of a well-defined group of service users [19]. However, [20] noted that co-design consists of three general work processes adopted from participatory design approach. Reference [20] suggests that the traditional participatory research design process which are plan, do, observe, and reflect be replaced by tell, make, and enact process that allows proto-typing to happen in any stage, and acknowledges that design entails movement in both directions around the process. In 'tell' process, a co-creator describes a product or concept related idea to other co-creator (designers and researcher). Whereby in 'make' process, a co-creator (elderly) make a prototype of the idea. Lastly, in 'enact' process, the created prototype spurs new ideas during the workshop conduct and serves as a basis for the next co-design cycle. There are four stages of the process in co-design [21]. Reference [21] continues that the same design sequence is always be repeated few times throughout the process until the designed product is optimal. The first phase is known as exploration [21]. In order to develop an idea about the real needs of elderly who wish to work after retirement, there is a diagnosis of elderly needs and wants. The second phase, envisioning [21] involves anticipating solutions to the matter posed to foresee or imagine what is intended to be designed, clarify the goals and capabilities of elderly people and agree on the desired outcome. The third phase, called operationalization [21] is the solution envisaged in previous phase is translated into a physical work product or prototype, which can be implemented and evaluated the usability. The last phase known as assessment and reflection phase [21] is where the iterative implementation of the prototype and systematic evaluation allows the real context for the review of the design. Co-design will be used mainly in the workshops. The study will be conducted using participant observation, interviews, and workshops. The elderly observation will be conducted as a long-term source of unspoken information as well as tacit knowledge. The interviews will be conducted to gain in-depth information from actual job seekers who are potential elderly users of the future designing.

2.4   The Roles of Users

The roles of the players in the design process from user-centered design to co-design is having an impact. The user is inactive object of study in the traditional UCD process, while the researcher commands knowledge from theories and expands more knowledge through observation and interviews. The designers then passively obtain this knowledge in the mode of a documentation and adds a grasp of technology and the creative reasoning needed to create ideas and concepts [17]. Co-design approach appoints users actively in the design process by letting them to express their personal spatial experience and needs. For example, co-design practices are used to empower users to think aloud about design ideas that are linked to their everyday life and talk with others in the user group to rationalize unusual answers that fit not their only individual users' needs and wishes, but those of other users too [16]. In co-design approach, the roles of users get mixed up where the end-user itself who will eventually be served through the design process is given the position of 'expert of his/her experience' and plays an important character in knowledge progression, idea formation and concept development. To generate insights, the researcher underpinning the 'expert of his/her experience' by stipulating suitable tools for idea generation and expression. To generate insights, the researcher supports the 'expert of his/her experience' by providing suitable tools for idea generation and expression. Plus, the designer and the researcher collaborate on the tools for ideation because design skills are very essential in the development of the tools. To date, the designer and researcher may, in fact, be the same individual. Designer or researcher still plays a critical role in giving form to the ideas [17].

2.5   Co-design Component

There are various components that need to be considered by designers and researcher while adopting the co-design approach such as active engagement by users, foster creativity, ownership, sustainability, inspired ideas, saved cost, user satisfaction and user learning (knowledge transfer) [17, 22, 23]. Table 1 summarizes the component of design approaches based on existing co-design approach.

Table 1. Literature based on component of co-design approach.

Component	UCD	PD	Co-design
Active engagement			√
Foster creativity			√
Ownership			√
Sustainability			√
Inspired ideas	√	√	√
Saved cost			√
User satisfaction		√	√
User learning (Knowledge transfer)			√

The component of active engagement is built on the doctrine that the environment works better if users are functioning and involved in its creation and management instead of being treated as inactive users [18]. In UCD approach, users are treated as passive participants. Through UCD, designers are simply designing products for users based on observation and interview. Participatory design is said to be semi-active engagement among user while in co-design approach, the line-up of user engagement is active [16].

Foster creativity aspect is comprised of various elements such as mixing and assimilating peculiar people's interpretation, improving communication and collaboration between diverse people and joint creation of new ideas [22]. [24] highlighted in order to create useful input for service innovation, the idea can be generated by the users that is where their concepts are more innovative in term of originality and better match to users' needs than the concepts generated by designers. Yet, in term of technologically feasible, designers' ideas are more accepted than the ideas of users.

In terms of ownership and sustainability, both of the components are related to the achievement of a project and its ability to become sustainable. [25] argued that a community may be prone to develop a sense of owning the artefact, which quickens the process by which it is appropriated and integrated in its practices by participating in the design of technology artefacts. [25] added to boosting a project's potential for sustainability, the co-design process itself can be instrumental. People are prone to embrace and integrate its solution in their practices by becoming involved in the initial stages of the design process.

The inspired ideas aspect may be considered with reference to the user as an expert of their experiences to cooperate creatively [20], by giving appropriate tools to express themselves in order for them to take on this role. [17] continued the generation of inspired ideas can be promoted through the trigger of probes.

In terms of user satisfaction and user learning, [22] identified people involved in co-design can engage in continuous learning and innovating. [26] mentioned the other aspects include improving idea generation through shared knowledge.

3   The Conceptual Framework

The reason of this framework is to link the concept of Co-Design as the approach to support the design strategies and development of elderly employment website. The main point of this framework is not only on the component of co-design approach but also align with the roles of elderly as a co-creator so that proper co-creation process can be used to support employment website. Figure 1 shows the proposed conceptual framework that integrates the co-design process and the context of practice which will be

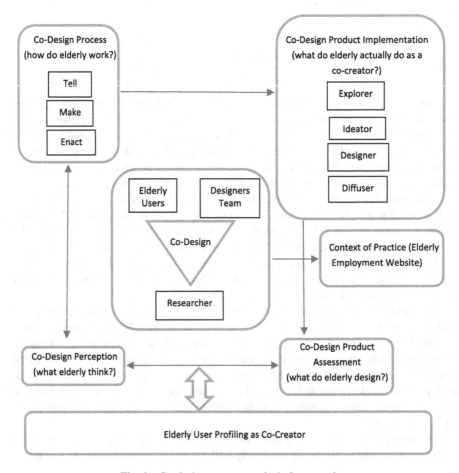

Fig. 1. Co-design process analysis framework.

employment website for elderly users. As for elderly employment website, the existing website for example Babajob (babajob.com) take advantage of mobile phone numbers as a substitute to email addresses and also involves people, who may guide the use of technology. Babajob's components include simple interface with very few and simple steps required from a job seeker, allows users to utilize directly through the site, as well as subscribe to get SMS notifications [2].

This research will be detailing out each of the elderly roles based on co-creation approach where the output of this study will discover profiling for elderly people as a co-creator in co-design approach. This research highlights the eight major components that related to co-design approach which are active engagement, foster creativity, ownership, sustainability, inspired ideas, saved cost, user satisfaction and user learning because they are commonly used in design strategies and bring benefits that can provide advantages to support elderly employment website.

Based on the innovation (or problem-solving) process [27] recognizes four distinct roles for citizens in co-creation approach namely as an explorer, ideator, designer, and diffuser. Broadly, these four roles relate to the four primary innovation phases which are identifying, discovering or defining a problem (explorer), conceptualizing a solution (ideator), designing and developing the solution (designer), and implementing the solution (diffuser) [27].

The co-design components enable several benefits. [22] reported co-design fosters joint creativity, saved costs, improved user satisfaction and user learning. Other benefits include induces ownership and sustainability [23] and promotes the generation of inspired ideas through the trigger of probes [17]. Co-design attributes matches the elderly employment website elements. Therefore, those attributes hopefully will facilitate the design and development of age-friendly employability website effectively.

As shown in Fig. 1, these dimensions are discussed from four perspectives that reinforce each other. It is a holistic model of analysis of the co-design process, which in turn allows the triangulation of data and methods, in order to preserve the study trustworthiness. For the purpose of this study, researcher is interested specifically in determine what characteristics of elderly people suitable to become co-creator. How to enable elderly people to express their experience and knowledge in order to work in co-design process as well as how far their capabilities in order to design product as job seekers. For the qualitative data analysis such as interviews, observations, field notes and post-session questionnaire, a thematic review will be used, while for the quantifiable data collection with the post-session questionnaire a content analysis will be performed. Elderly user is a major part of age friendly employability website through co-design implementation. The role of elderly as a co-creator is a major part of employability artefact implementation. The existing types of design strategies such as UCD, PD and Co-Design model have different approach to implement age-friendly employability website.

4 Conclusion

A co-design approach was proposed in order to come up with the suitable and matching design with elderly users thus develop safe and functionally appropriate employability technological website that will promote and continue independent living of elderly. Each stage of the co-design process should involve feedback to elderly participants, so they know they have been correctly heard and their input recognized as well as ongoing feedback about how the prototype is taking shape. Cooperation from elderly people is believed to help to develop a better understanding of these people's needs and wants, and to mutually develop and validate concepts for new products/services. The framework is constructed with component and benefit of employability website that is mapped from a review of the literature on the roles of elderly users, co-design approach, and elderly employability website component. The conceptual framework has potential for guiding researchers to enhance knowledge in co-design approach that can support design and development of age-friendly employability website. To end this, a conceptual framework of co-design process analysis that allows capturing the experience and knowledge of elderly people as co-creator is proposed.

5 Future Work

An elderly employability website is hoped to aid as a tool to assist elderly people who wish to re-enter the workforce. This paper discussed the need to involve elderly as a co-creator that given empowerment and able to make decisions throughout the co-design phases which suits elderly preferences. Co-design approach is proposed towards elderly participants as a co-creator in order to develop elderly employment website since there is a significant improvement of design evidence, because user's demands in different stages are considered to design process exactly. The design ideas emanated from this study as anticipated will be developed and evaluated it usefulness. One of the main challenges that designers and researcher want to consider in product design is to provide satisfaction and to understand user's needs. To understand the needs and desires of user, usually specific methods are jointed with the user. For example, elderly people with their special needs such as deteriorations including visual or mobility related disabilities and other circumstances, have specific demand from different products that they interact with. Therefore, in process of designing all of these parameters should be considered. It should be noted that the success of this process requires as complete knowledge of the user as possible, and at the beginning of the study this recognition should be considered. The future of elderly as a co-creator is promising and warrants more studies to fulfill the needs of the growing senior population.

References

1. Darvishy, A., Good, A.: Inclusive websites for the elderly: user friendly guidelines for designers and managers of websites and applications. In: Stephanidis, C. (ed.) HCI 2013. CCIS, vol. 373, pp. 226–230. Springer, Heidelberg (2013). https://doi.org/10.1007/978-3-642-39473-7_46
2. Jegede, G., Densmore, M.: Using co-design to discern and overcome barriers to employment in cape town. In: Proceedings of the 7th Annual Symposium on Computing for Development - ACM DEV 2016, pp. 1–4 (2016). https://doi.org/10.1145/3001913.3006641
3. Han, S., Moen, P.: Clocking out: temporal patterning of retirement. Am. J. Sociol. **105**, 191–236 (1999)
4. Seltzer, J.A., Yahirun, J.J.: Diversity in old age: the elderly in changing economic and family contexts (2013)
5. Nilsson, K.: Why work beyond 65? Discourse on the decision to continue working or retire early. Nord. J. Working Life Stud. **2**(3), 7–28 (2012)
6. Mann, C.L.: Information technologies and international development: conceptual clarity in the search for commonality and diversity. Inf. Technol. Int. Dev. **1**, 67–79 (2004)
7. Sahay, S.: Introduction to the special issue on IT and health care in developing countries. Electron. J. Inf. Syst. Dev. Ctries. **5**, 1–6 (2005)
8. Rizzo, F.: Co-design versus user centred design: framing the differences. In: Guerrini, L. (ed.) Notes on Doctoral Research in Design, pp. 125–132. Contributions from the Politecnico di Milano, Franco Angeli (2010)
9. Fuller, J., Jawecki, G., Muhlbacher, H.: Innovation creation by online basketball communities. J. Bus. Res. **60**(1), 60–71 (2007)
10. The Star Online: Silent 'Epidemic' of Aging, The Star Online, viewed 11th June 2017. http://www.thestar.com.my/news/nation/2015/08/09/silent-epidemic-of-ageing-malaysia-like-many-of-its-neighbours-in-asia-is-in-danger-of-getting-old-b/. Accessed 11 Jun 2017
11. Lee, R., Andrew, M.: Population Aging and the Generational Economy: A Global Perspective. Edward Elgar Publishing Limited, Cheltenham (2011). http://web.idrc.ca/openebooks/514-4/
12. Alley, D., Crimmins, E.: The demography of aging and work. In: Shultz, K.S., Adams, G.A. (eds.) Aging and work in the 21st Century, pp. 7–24. Lawrence Erlbaum Associates, London (2007)
13. Norman, D.: The Design of Everyday Things. Basic books, Olsson, New York (1988)
14. Prahalad, C.K., Ramaswamy, V.: Co-creation experiences: the next practice in value creation. J. Interact. Mark. **18**(3), 5–14 (2004). https://doi.org/10.1002/dir.20015
15. Avgerou, C.: The significance of context in information systems and organizational change. Inf. Syst. J. **11**(1), 43–63 (2010)
16. Chun, M.H., Harty, C., Schweber, L.: Comparative study of user-centred design approaches, pp. 1125–1134, September 2015
17. Sanders, E.B.-N., Stappers, P.J.: Co-creation and the new landscapes of design. Co-Design **4**(1), 5–18 (2008). https://doi.org/10.1080/15710880701875068
18. Sanoff, H.: Multiple views of participatory design. METU J. Fac. Archit. **1965**, 131–143 (2006)
19. WA Council of Social Service (wacoss). http://www.wacoss.org.au/wp-content/uploads/2017/07/Tool-5-Co-Design-process.pdf
20. Sleeswijk Visser, F., Stappers, P.J., Van der Lugt, R., Sanders, E.B.-N.: Contextmapping: experiences from practice. CoDesign **1**(2), 119–149 (2005)

21. Garcia, I., Barberà, E., Gros, B., Escofet, A.: Analysing and supporting the process of co-designing inquiry-based and technology-enhanced learning scenarios in higher education. In: Networked Learning Conference, pp. 493–501 (2014). http://www.networkedlearningconference.org.uk/abstracts/pdf/garcia.pdf

22. Steen, M., Manschot, M., Koning, N.D.: Steen, Manschot_Benefits of co-design in service design projects, **5**(2), 53–61 (2011)

23. David, S., Sabiescu, A.G., Cantoni, L.: Co-design with communities. A reflection on the literature. In: Proceedings of the 7th International Development Informatics Association Conference, 152–166 (2013). https://doi.org/10.13140/RG.2.1.2309.9365

24. Kristensson, P., Magnusson, P.: Tuning users' innovativeness during ideation. Creativity Innov. Manag. **19**(2), 147–159 (2010)

25. Ramirez, R.: A meditation on meaningful participation. J. Commun. Inform. **4**(3) (2008)

26. Roser, T., Samson, A.: Co-Creation: New Paths to Value. Promise/LSE Enterprise, London (2009)

27. Nambisan, S., Nambisan, P.: Engaging Citizens in Co-Creation in Public Services - Lessons Learned and Best Practices, pp. 1–52. IBM Center for the Business of Government, Washington, D.C. (2013)

Evaluation of Video Modeling Application to Teach Social Interaction Skills to Autistic Children

Iman Nur Nabila Binti Ahmad Azahari[✉], Wan Fatimah Wan Ahmad, and Ahmad Sobri Hashim

Computer Information Science, Universiti Teknologi Petronas, Seri Iskander, Perak, Malaysia
nabilaazahari@gmail.com, fatimhd@utp.edu.my,
sobri.hashim@utp.edu.com

Abstract. Autism Social Aid (ASD) is a mental disorder that affects a person at an early age. People with ASD show deficiencies in daily living abilities that lead to impairment in their independence skill, restrict their social involvement which leads to poor living style. This rooted from their key personal behaviours, which are impairment in social and communication skills. However, with the availability of mobile technology that engages education through video modelling, it has become more practical for educators to train daily living skills for individuals with ASD. Consequently a Video Modelling Application called 'Autism Social-Aid' was created to provide a supplementary learning material envisioned to help stimulate children with ASD in the learning process. The purpose of this study is to evaluate the effects of video modelling in teaching five children diagnosed with medium-functioning ASD to understand social interaction skills. The children went through three trials of the evaluation phases. Results revealed that video modelling was effective as all of the children were able to display positive improvements from the first trial to the third trial. As a result, all of them have reduced an average 77% of the total prompt needed to remain focus on the video lesson and an average of 70% number of errors was reduced during the quiz evaluation.

Keywords: Autism spectrum disorder children · Social interaction skill
Mobile application · Video modelling

1 Introduction

The implementation of technology especially in mobile form has proven to be dependable for society in their day-to-day activities. There has been a prompt evolution in interest concerning the use of touchscreen mobile technology as an involvement and practicality in the education field whether the goal is meant for normal children or even children with ASD. Conversely, compared to normal children, developing and designing a touchscreen application for children with autism is a delicate and crucial task as designing applications for individuals with different impairments is always puzzling because they experience different life conditions than normal people [1].

Nonetheless, technology particularly in mobile form has transformed the way children with autism learn and communicate [2]. Mobile applications have provided parents,

© Springer Nature Singapore Pte Ltd. 2018
N. Abdullah et al. (Eds.): i-USEr 2018, CCIS 886, pp. 125–135, 2018.
https://doi.org/10.1007/978-981-13-1628-9_12

teachers, and therapists various methods to teach children who develop differently from their peers. One of it is through the usage of video modelling in mobile form. This practical method can be applied in the classroom or any other daily surroundings. Video modelling technique is considered as an effective approach for educating social, communication and language, self-support as well as daily life skills to children with ASD [3].

But currently, not many existing video modelling applications are designed and proven applicable in teaching social interaction skills for children with autism. Not to mention, as stated by a local teacher from SK Sultan Yussuf's special needs education class, the current teaching materials in schools have lack of therapeutic effect on the children. The children are having a hard time to understand the lessons in schools thus giving them a setback in enhancing the soft skills. Teachers on the other hand, had to keep on changing their methods to cater the needs of the children, thus causing a time-consumption effort on developing a lesson plan. However with the assistance of mobile technology, the lessons can be more practical and become enjoyable experience for children with ASD [4].

In sequence to address the existing problems, this research have developed a Video Modelling mobile application named 'Autism Social-Aid' that would help children with ASD in learning basic social interaction skill. This will also improve the daily class's limitations via traditional education method. Moreover, this application has also included a game feature in which the children with autism will have pleasurable lessons at the same time with indulging attractive graphical user interface. Objectively, this paper is to evaluate the effects of autistic children's learning experience while using a video modelling mobile application.

2   Related Works

Autism Spectrum Disorder (ASD) is a developmental disorder that affects one in every five hundred children [5]. These children display deficiencies in social interaction skills, verbal and nonverbal communication, and demonstrate repetitive behaviours' [6]. Autism disorder has three cores of areas of difficulty, nonetheless, each autistic child is unique in their own way. The three main areas of difficulty which every person with ASD experience are known as the "Triad of Impairments" and they are; difficulty with social communication, social interaction and social imagination [7, 8]. From here, it is concluded that people with autism are mainly having trouble in social skills.

It is a battle to develop the skills of children with autism, as they are special in their individual characteristics. However, the constant practices and aids by parents, teachers and therapists are important in order to develop child's everyday skills [9].

With the help of latest technology, people with disabilities, particularly individuals with impairments in social and emotional characteristics, devote and improve their implications through usage of mobile applications that are specifically built to cater for their impairments. With the existing applications nowadays, it could assist or educate children with Autism specifically for developing their social skills and emotional aspects.

According to [10], children with Autism can now navigate well on mobile phones and tablets. They could learn while playing the mobile applications. Many people with autism are visual thinkers thus most of their thoughts are able to cooperate well with visual materials such as pictures and videos. Images are their principal language, while words are their secondary language, as stated by [11]. Supportively, one of the most promising methods in educating children with autism is visual approach, which applies videos, images or other visual items to correspond with one person to another [12]. With this, the children could definitely achieve their ultimate capability using their visual strength. Based on [13], in developing the everyday skills for individuals with autism, visual approach has been an applicable method. The recognition of the visual education practice of children with autism is becoming popular and well-practiced in the educational sector [14]. The sequences of image processes are perfect and simple to use and attract the children's attention. The evolutions and advanced growth is well defined and easy for parents, teachers and therapists to apply and keep record of the child's day-to-day progress.

Therefore, with the aid of visual approach, autistic children are more involved and are able to mature gradually as their significant strong advantages are being exercised every day. Real or actual visual items are the most applicable and easy to understand in accompanying these children. Specialists establishes that by applying actual images, children are able to improve their understanding as it is alike and associated with their environment [15].

Similar method was achieved when visual approach is implemented in technology through video modelling. Video modelling offers the children with precise and reliable examples of the target behaviour that is being presented [3]. The simplicity of employment of video modelling involves the developers to generate short video demonstrations, preferably various exemplars, with a person representing the target behaviour and offer the children with a channel on which to view the video [16], in this case on a mobile device. Furthermore, the convenience of mobile devices such as smartphones, tablets, and other handheld devices have risen the availability of video modelling, thus making it possible for the exemplar to be viewed across any settings [17]. As a result, children with autism can view the video modelling anytime and anywhere, whether it is with guidance from parents and teachers, or even self-learning.

3   Methodology

This section introduces four main subsections, which are the participants, the procedure, the application and the materials. It also discusses on the methods applied during the evaluation process.

3.1   Participants

The target participants were 5 children; 4 boys and 1 girl. All of them attended special education class in a primary school named Sekolah Kebangsaan Sultan Yussuf, Batu Gajah Perak. Each of them suffers mild-functioning ASD. They are aged from 8 to 12 years old. The evaluation could only be tested to a limited number of children, as it is difficult to gather a bigger number of medium-functioning ASD. The other children in school are characterised as low-functioning or high-functioning ASD, which are not considered as the research target focus.

3.2 Procedure

During the evaluation, children were given duration of time to play and learn Autism Social-Aid mobile application and were rated based on their reactions and responds towards the application. The evaluation was conducted to measure all aspects of the children's reactions when playing the mobile application. A teacher guided them during the process. Prior to the evaluation, the teacher had been given a full brief on how to use the application before the evaluation started.

They were seated and given a tablet with Autism Social-Aid application to study with as in Fig. 1. At the same, a videographer recorded them during the whole process. The moderator and observer were seated in front of the child to get a clear view of the child's responds.

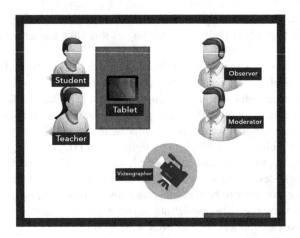

Fig. 1. The arrangement of the observation room during the evaluation. During this time, the child was aided by a teacher to ensure they feel safe and comfortable while the evaluation was conducted.

Moderator helped the child and teacher to navigate the application during the process and helped to complete a set of tasks using the application.

3.3 Application

Autism Social-Aid is a video modelling mobile application designed for the children with ASD, to teach on social interaction skills. The application was developed using iMovie, and Android Studio. The main goal of Autism Social-Aid is to assist the children to acquire and practice basic social interaction skills in their everyday activities. The development of Autism Social-Aid aims to offer a medium where children could understand and experience virtual learning anytime and anywhere. The virtual learning environment through mobile application has a wide distinguished feature compared to the old-fashioned classroom surrounding, thus building more enjoyable and interactive learning experience.

The content of the application was created based on the requirements of the children with autism. The contents were adapted from the modules and lesson plan given by Ministry of Education for children with special education. Autism Social-Aid offers an option to select between two languages, English Language or Bahasa Malaysia. These two are the standard of instruction set by the Ministry of Education in Malaysia.

Under the 'Lesson' feature the application provides a set of video modelling that teaches basic social interaction skill, which includes; Introducing Yourself, Emotions and Gestures as in Fig. 2. Each video presents a person or a group of people who demonstrate a target behaviour that must be achieved by the children. Each video lesson contains a play and repeat button where the children could choose to repeat the video. It also has a 'Record' button, where they are able to record their own voices, so they can practice basic communication and listen to their own pronunciation. This aims to promote self-learning skill for the child, as they listen and evaluate their own conversation. The application as well as the videos uses bright and lively colour to attract the children, as this will help them learn and have fun during the learning process. The features of this video modeling application also have eye-catching graphics, simple navigations, and background music that match with the current educational lessons.

Fig. 2. A sample of the 'Lesson' feature in the application. The application consists of two different features that are 'Lesson' and 'Activity'.

The 'Activity' feature consists of two simple activities, which include "Quiz Me!" and "Listen". "Quiz Me!" is an activity where the children have to match different type of emotions to the correct picture. This is to evaluate whether they understand the lessons from the video modelling and the different emotion expression. There are 10 different expressions where they have to select which one is similar to 'Happy', 'Sad' or 'Angry'. The aim of this activity is to ensure they could recognize emotions from different type of facial expressions, as most of them could not understand emotions [18].

First, the user whether the child or guardian, will direct to a Home Page as in Fig. 3 which they can choose between viewing the 'Video Lessons' or 'Play the Activities'. If they select the 'Lessons' feature, they will be directed to a page displaying three different video modelling options, which are 'Introducing Yourself', 'Emotion' or 'Gestures'. If users click any of the video option, they will be directed to a page with a video display of the specific lesson. The user will have an option to go back to the previous page or they can continue and watch the next videos. However, if the users select the 'Activity' feature, they will be directed to page with two options, which are 'Quiz Me' or 'Listen'. If users select 'Quiz Me', they will be channelled to a Quiz session on emotions. They may exit to the previous page and if they select the 'Listen' activity, the application will direct the user to an activity page where it displays a certain emotion, whether it is 'Happy', 'Sad' or 'Angry'. Here, user can learn how to pronounce the words by clicking on the button and they can also record their voice to listen whether the pronunciation is correct or false.

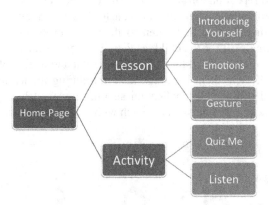

Fig. 3. The system flow of both application feature, which are 'Lessons' and 'Activity'. On the diagram above, it shows the sequences of the application.

3.4 Materials

The evaluation was guided by observing the children while they were using the application. The observations were then evaluated based on the criteria listed in the evaluation form. The evaluation form were adopted from [16, 17], where the purpose of the evaluation is to record the number of prompts for the child to attend to the video, number of verbal prompts and number of incorrect answers. The evaluation form also records the time taken for the child to provide full attention on the video, using the technique adopted by [5]. The longest duration to watch the video is 80 s as that is the full duration length of the video clips. Tables 1 and 2 displays sample of data collected from the first and the third trial evaluation with the children respectively.

Table 1. Trial one; responses from the participants during the video modelling intervention.

Student	Video number	No. of prompts to attend to the video	No. of verbal prompts	Span of attention (seconds)	No. of incorrect quiz answers
Student 1	Video 1	5	3	20	3
	Video 2	5	4	28	
	Video 3	4	1	21	
Student 2	Video 1	5	3	23	3
	Video 2	4	3	30	
	Video 3	4	4	18	
Student 3	Video 1	8	5	20	8
	Video 2	9	6	18	
	Video 3	11	5	17	
Student 4	Video 1	2	2	30	2
	Video 2	4	1	32	
	Video 3	1	1	27	
Student 5	Video 1	5	3	30	4
	Video 2	4	3	23	
	Video 3	4	4	28	

Table 2. Trial three; responses from the participants during the video modelling intervention.

Student	Video number	No. of prompts to attend to the video	No. of verbal prompts	Span of attention (seconds)	No. of incorrect quiz answers
Student 1	Video 1	1	1	58	0
	Video 2	2	2	55	
	Video 3	1	0	60	
Student 2	Video 1	0	0	72	0
	Video 2	0	0	69	
	Video 3	1	0	71	
Student 3	Video 1	3	2	59	4
	Video 2	2	3	43	
	Video 3	3	2	38	
Student 4	Video 1	1	0	59	0
	Video 2	0	1	50	
	Video 3	0	0	43	
Student 5	Video 1	2	1	50	2
	Video 2	1	2	44	
	Video 3	1	2	48	

The evaluation was conducted with each children three times in a week as they watch the three video lessons for each session respectively. In each session, the moderator and observer recorded the time taken for the children to pay attention to video and the quiz's results. After the moderator posed a question, the scene was paused and the teacher prompted the child to respond if he or she did not answer the question within 5 s or they answered incorrectly. If the child responded correctly, the video was continued to play. If the child did not respond correctly, the moderator prompted the correct response and repeated the question until the child offered the correct response. Once the child said the correct response, the moderator provided words of praises to the child and continued the video. The child were also given a quiz questions with simple responses to know whether he or she understand the previous video lessons. The number of errors when answering the quiz was also recorded.

4   Results

This section discusses the results of the evaluation. Table 1 displays the results from the evaluation of the video modelling from three different videos displayed on the first trial with the children. Whereas Table 2 shows the results from the third trial of the evaluation with the children, 6 days after the first trial was conducted.

Four criteria were evaluated, which are the number of prompts to attend to the video whereby the child were given verbal or non-verbal prompts to ensure the child view the video once they have lost their focus. Non-verbal prompts include; a show of hand towards the video, gentle pat on the child's shoulder by the teacher to regain attention or simple point towards the video. Second, number of verbal prompts; where during or at the end of video, the child were given a question by the moderator to evaluate whether he or she understand the video lesson, and the number of time they ignored and responded incorrectly to the question. Third, span of attention in seconds; the time recorded when the child was watching the video until they lost their focus and stopped watching the video. These include; the child walking away from watching the video, look at other places besides the video and start playing by themselves. Lastly, number of incorrect quiz answers; the frequent number of times where the child answer the quiz questions incorrectly was recorded.

5   Discussions

Each child displayed different response towards the video modelling lessons. Certain were fascinated to watch them, and one participant was very inactive while dodging eye contact. However, each of them showed promising results where they showed signs of eagerness and responded well at the end of each lessons. Differ situation occurred in Trial 1, where the children were in contact with the application for the first time. They were still learning to use the application and exploring the available features the video modelling application had to offer. Student 4 showed the most promising result where he scored the lowest number of prompts needed to attend to the video, number of verbal prompts and number of incorrect answers. However, Student 3 had the worst result with total of 28 prompts encountered to watch all three videos and with an attention span of 17 s as he viewed the third video. On the other hand, Student 1, 2, and 5 had much similar average results for each video. They scored 13–14 total number of prompts encountered to watch the three videos and 3–4 number of errors during the quiz session.

On the contrary, the results improved after the second and third trial evaluation. Based on Table 2, the third trial result proves that each child has lowered their prompts number and increased their span of attention in seconds to watch the video. For instance, Student 4 had successfully watched the second and third video without any prompts, and has answered all the quiz questions correctly without any error compared to the first time where he had 2 errors. Plus, Student 3 had reduced the total number of prompts from 28 times to 8 times to attend the video. Not to mention the number of incorrect answers which had been reduced from 8 times to 4 times only. The rest of the students had also demonstrated great results where they had lowered the number of prompts and increase the seconds in attention span by an average of 57%. This has shown a significant improvement of the child's attention and understanding from the first trial to the third trial. As a total, all of them had reduced an average of 77% of the total prompt needed to remain focused on the video lesson and an average of 70% number of errors was reduced during the quiz evaluation. Thus concur, the findings of this current video modelling technique to promote social living skills of individuals with autism is one of the most appropriate and effective type of method [21].

6   Conclusion

In conclusion, the results of the existing study have assisted to guarantee that application is suitable to achieve its therapeutic aims, namely using video modelling technique to train social interaction skills in children with autism. The reduction in the number of prompts from the first time the child used the application to the third time usage, has proven a promising result in using video modelling as a supplementary tool to assist parents, teachers and therapists to educate children diagnosed with ASD. They are able to focus more on the lesson and are motivated rather than when learning with the traditional methods. The core purpose of this research is to aid the Autistic children, which will improve their understanding and competencies by developing a learning video modelling application purposely in the social interaction skills that teaches how to interact with people around them. As a result from the evaluation, it was then concluded; the development of the application has become more assuring in terms of its efficiency and usability. Next improvement of the research would be developing more core areas of social lessons to be taught to children with autism. Another feature called 'Monitor', that can be developed for parents and teacher to view, monitor and evaluate the child's performance based on how he or she responds to the video lessons and game activities. Here, the guardians could keep track of the child's daily performance.

References

1. Kamaruzaman, M.F., Rani, N.M., Nor, H.M., Azahari, M.H.H.: Developing user interface design application for children with autism. Procedia - Soc. Behav. Sci. **217**, 887–894 (2016)
2. Murdock, L.C., Ganz, J., Crittendon, J.: Use of an iPad play story to increase play dialogue of preschoolers with autism spectrum disorders. J. Autism Dev. Disord. **43**, 2174–2189 (2013)
3. Hong, E.R., Ganz, J.B., Mason, R., Morin, K., Davis, J.L., Ninci, J., Neely, L.C., Boles, M.B., Gilliland, W.D.: The effects of video modeling in teaching functional living skills to persons with ASD: a meta-analysis of single-case studies. Res. Dev. Disabil. **57**, 158–169 (2016)
4. Family Center on Technology and Disability: Autism and the iPad: Finding the Therapy in Consumer Tech. Technol. Voices, pp. 1–13 (2011)
5. Eder, M.S., Diaz, J.M.L., Madela, J.R.S., Mag-usara, M.U., Sabellano, D.D.M.: Fill me app: an interactive mobile game application for children with autism. Int. J. Interact. Mob. Technol. **10**, 59 (2016)
6. Bernardini, S., Porayska-Pomsta, K., Smith, T.J.: ECHOES: an intelligent serious game for fostering social communication in children with autism. Inf. Sci. **264**, 41–60 (2014)
7. Shamsuddin, S., Yussof, H., Ismail, L., Hanapiah, F.A., Mohamed, S., Piah, H.A., Zahari, N.I.: Initial response of autistic children in human-robot interaction therapy with humanoid robot NAO. In: 8th International Colloquium on Signal Processing and its Applications, pp. 188–193 (2012)
8. Charman, T., Jones, C.R.G., Pickles, A., Simonoff, E., Baird, G., Happé, F.: Defining the cognitive phenotype of autism. Brain Res. **1380**, 10–21 (2011)
9. Ostrow, N.: Autism costs more than $2 million over a patient's life (2014)
10. Odom, S.L., et al.: Technology-aided interventions and instruction for adolescents with autism spectrum disorder. J. Autism Dev. Disord. **45**, 3805–3819 (2015)
11. Hornois, C.: Treating patients with autism spectrum disorder. Radiat. Ther. **25**, 97–100 (2016)
12. Tentori, M., Hayes, G.R.: Designing for interaction immediacy to enhance social skills of children with autism. In: Proceedings of the 12th ACM International Conference Ubiquitous Computing, pp. 51–60 (2010)
13. Shane, H.C., Laubscher, E.H., Schlosser, R.W., Flynn, S., Sorce, J.F., Abramson, J.: Applying technology to visually support language and communication in individuals with autism spectrum disorders. J. Autism Dev. Disord. **42**, 1228–1235 (2012)
14. Hodgdon, L.A.: Visual Strategies for Improving Communication: Practical Supports for Autism Spectrum Disorders (Revised & Updated Edition). Quirk Roberts, Troy (2011)
15. Willis, C.: Young children with autism spectrum disorder strategies that work. Beyond J. Young Child. Web. **64**, 1–8 (2009)
16. Carnahan, C.R., Basham, J.D., Christman, J., Hollingshead, A.: Overcoming challenges: "going mobile with your own video models". Teach. Except. Child. **45**, 50–59 (2012)
17. Cihak, D., Fahrenkrog, C., Ayres, K.M., Smith, C.: The use of video modeling via a video ipod and a system of least prompts to improve transitional behaviors for students with autism spectrum disorders in the general education classroom. J. Posit. Behav. Interv. **12**, 103–115 (2010)
18. Stone, W., Ruble, L., Coonrod, E., Hepburn, S., Pennington, M., Burnette, C., Brigham, N.: TRIAD social skills assessment. In: Assessing Children with Autism Spectrum Disorders, pp. 2–5. Vanderbilt TRIAD (2010)
19. King, S., Miltenberger, R.: Evaluation of video modeling to teach children diagnosed with autism to avoid poison hazards. Adv. Neurodev. Disord. **1**, 168–175 (2017)

20. Godish, D., Miltenberger, R., Sanchez, S.: Evaluation of video modeling for teaching abduction prevention skills to children with autism spectrum disorder. Adv. Neurodev Disord. **1**, 168–175 (2017)
21. National Professional Development Center on Autism Spectrum Disorder: Video Modeling: Step for Implementation (2010)

Investigating the Effect of Exploring Multimodal Maps at Different Orientations on Blind User's Cognitive Maps and Sense of Directions

Nazatul Naquiah Abd Hamid[(✉)], Wan Adilah Wan Adnan,
Fariza Hanis Abdul Razak, and Zatul Amilah Shaffie

Faculty of Computer and Mathematical Sciences, Universiti Teknologi MARA (UiTM),
Shah Alam, Selangor, Malaysia
nazatul84@gmail.com, {adilah,fariza,zatul}@tmsk.uitm.edu.my

Abstract. Maps have been used in different ways to facilitate traveller in way finding. Depending on the traveller's ability to translate the direction on the map of the real world, maps are normally read in different orientations. Some travellers have the ability to rotate the map mentally without having to change its original orientation while some require the map to be aligned with the direction to their intended paths as discovered in the literature. Blind people are not excluded from using maps. A multimodal map has been introduced to enable blind people to learn maps. However, the exploration of the maps using the multimodal map is restricted to a static orientation. Therefore, this study investigates the map exploration by the blind participants under two conditions; static and rotation. The aim of this study is to examine the effect of exploring maps at different orientations on blind user's cognitive maps and sense of directions. The findings of this study show the difference in the pointing accuracy of the participants in static and rotatable conditions approach significant. Results also show that blind people have the ability to build a cognitive map of the maps learned in the rotatable condition. However, the sense of direction is not correlated with the pointing accuracy for the blind participants in this study. This paper also concludes by discussing the potential of including a rotation feature on a multimodal map in order to facilitate blind people in map exploration.

Keywords: Orientation · Blindness · Cognitive maps · Sense of direction
Multimodal maps

1 Introduction

Navigating in the real world represents a significant challenge for blind people. Vision is a very powerful sense. On the one hand, a large amount of information is available simultaneously but at the same time vision can literally focus on that information which is relevant at any given time. Since blind people are unable to use this sense, other senses (notably touch and hearing) are recruited to substitute. Touch and hearing perceives information in a more sequential form. In substituting for the vision they face the so-called "bandwidth problem" that they cannot match the capacity of vision. However, if

© Springer Nature Singapore Pte Ltd. 2018
N. Abdullah et al. (Eds.): i-USEr 2018, CCIS 886, pp. 136–147, 2018.
https://doi.org/10.1007/978-981-13-1628-9_13

both senses are utilized simultaneously, they can probably provide more information to the user, as utilizing the whole may be greater than using the sum of the parts. Previous works have introduced multimodal maps that combine haptic interaction with auditory output, e.g. [1–3], in order to achieve a better learning of geographical information. Previous works have experimented multimodal maps with blind people, e.g. [1, 2, 4, 5]. The existing multimodal maps allow the blind people to access geographical information. However it only enables blind people to explore maps in a static orientation. In reality, when reaching at a corner, a person would turn to the left or right and continue walking forward. By being able to detect the orientation of the map, it is possible that when the map-user reaches the corner they can then rotate the map and continue to trace in a forward direction [6]. It is likely for a map that can be rotated to generate a more useful representation in the user's mind [7–10]. There is evidence that this kind of approach is particularly appropriate for blind people because they tend to use an egocentric spatial frame of reference [11]. Thus, the aim of this study is to further explore the accuracy of people's cognitive maps and sense of direction when using maps at different orientations.

2   Background

Maps are important to facilitate a traveller in a way finding. In order to get a direction between places, maps are usually read in different ways. For sighted people, they can use vision to perceive information at a glance. However, when the task comes to route-following between places, some prefer to get the direction align with their facing direction. Research on the use of maps by sighted people has demonstrated a strong effect on map alignment [9, 12–16]. An aligned map is one in which the points at the top of the map represents locations that are in the forward direction from the user in the environment (Fig. 1). A misaligned map is one which has been rotated in such a way that this relationship does not hold to. A map which is rotated 180° is said to be contra-aligned [17]. Judgments on direction made by participants were much more accurate when the remembered map was aligned with the environment than when it was contra-aligned [12]. This is known as map alignment effect [17]. Based on this result, it is found that sighted participants tend to encode the direction 'up' on a map as being 'forward' in the environment [12].

The problem of map alignment effect also occurred among blind people. In the literature, blind participants were found to be more accurate in directional judgments with aligned maps than with misaligned maps [17].

Increased response times with misaligned maps suggest that the participants were attempting some mental operation most probably to attain alignment. The result shows that similar to sighted people, blind people also encode maps using the 'up equals forward' assumption. This is an important finding because it establishes the consistency of the map encoding process across different types of maps (visual or tactual) used by different groups (sighted or blind people).

The blind participants in the study also reported that they used some kind of mental operations to align map images. Some of the blind participants reported that they rotate

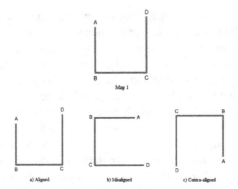

Fig. 1. The above shows (a) is aligned with Map 1, (b) is misaligned with Map 1 and (c) is contra-aligned (rotated 180°) with Map 1 [17]

themselves onto a static representation of the map while others performed the mental rotation of the map image. The participants mentioned that the mental operations would be easier if the map was aligned than misaligned. The feedback obtained from blind participants are consistent with those from sighted participants in other studies related to map alignment [9, 14, 16].

2.1 Sense of Direction

The sense of direction is defined as an individual's awareness and knowledge of the person's orientation in the environment [18–20] where this ability can be reported by the participants to a certain degree [18]. The sense of direction is primarily assessed through an interview where participants need to estimate their own abilities and complete the self-report measure. For example, Santa Barbara Sense of Direction scale (SBSOD) [21] can be used to measure user sense of direction. SBSOD scores obtained by participants mostly showed that their performance on learning the relationship between directions and landmarks [22]. Previous works had measured participants' sense of direction before they explored familiar or novel environment. Then, participants were tested on a pointing task [23]. Their scores on the sense of direction and pointing accuracy were compared to examine the relationship.

3 Objectives

The objectives of this study are threefold as the following:

1. To examine whether the cognitive map constructed on the basis of an audio-tactile map that the person is allowed to orientate as they wish is as good as those generated when the person is directed to use an aligned map.
2. To compare user pointing accuracy between static and rotatable conditions.
3. To examine the correlations between user ratings of their sense of direction and their pointing accuracy.

4   Method

4.1   Participants

There were 12 participants (4 females and 8 males) from Malaysian Association for the Blind (MAB) recruited for this study. Their ages ranged from 19 to 30 (M = 22) years. All 12 participants were totally blind (6 congenitally blind and 6 adventitiously blind). They came from different backgrounds, e.g. mobility training experience, education and work backgrounds. All of them had the experience of travelling alone in the street regularly except 1 participant. There were 9 of them who use GPS-based navigation tools (e.g. Waze) to get direction between places. All of the participants never heard and never had any experience in using tactile maps and audio-tactile maps. The participants also never used maps for planning a way finding.

5   Design

This study was a within-subject design. There were 2 independent variables (IVs) which are the map alignments and orientation conditions. There were 2 orientation conditions: (a) static map (control) and (b) rotatable map. Maps and order effects were controlled by counterbalancing the maps and the conditions. All participants were requested to try both orientation conditions. Each participant tried one condition and then the other. Half of the participants were introduced to the first condition (static map) while the others started with the second condition (rotatable map). Then the groups were effectively swapped after each condition. There were 2 dependent variables (DVs) which were participants' response to Santa Barbara Sense of Direction (SBSOD) scale [21] and pointing accuracy. The pointing accuracy was determined based on the following:

- Angular error

A measure of angular error was taken on the aligned and misalignment trials. This measure is the absolute value of the difference between the participant's response angle and the correct angle. The mean angular error measures were computed for each participant across the aligned and misalignment trials.

- Response classification

The response was classified according to the method used by previous work, see [17]. A detailed explanation on the response classification is described in Table 1 below.

Table 1. Response classification adopted from Rossano and Warren [17]

Type of response	Explanation
Correct response (CR)	For each map, the vector which represented the correct direction of travel was identified. All responses that fall within 30° of this vector were classified as correct
Misalignment error response (MI)	The error vectors representing mirror-image error was identified. Responses that fall within 30° of these vectors were classified accordingly
Alignment error response (AI)	The error vectors representing alignment error was identified and responses that fall within 30° of these vectors were classified accordingly
Undefined error response (UD)	Any response which falls outside of the labelled sectors (CR, MI and AI sectors) is called as an undefined error

6   Materials and Apparatus

6.1   Tactile Maps

A practice map and 5 test maps with different orientations (Map 1 - 0°, Map 2 - 45°, Map 3 - 90°, Map 4 - 135°, Map 5 - 180°) were used in this experiment. The test maps were constructed based on the guidelines proposed by Levine [12]. All maps were produced using a microcapsule paper in an A3 size. The practice map consists of 4 points – W, X, Y and Z. These points were presented in symbols (unfilled circles) and were identified in speech. Each point was connected through a raised line that represents a path. Similar to the practice map, the 5 test maps also consist of a path formed by 3 straight lines and 4 points with the following features – the middle line in any 5 test map (for example BC line in Map 1 in Fig. 1) is either 45°, 90° or 135° to the right or left of the longest line. The AB line is always parallel to the DC line and this is similar to other maps (Map 2–Map 5).

7   Procedure

The participants took part in the experiment individually. They were guided to the experimental room, seated at a table and were briefly introduced to the experiment. The participants' consent was obtained and they were interviewed about demographic questions. Then, the participants were required to give a rate on a Santa Barbara Sense of Direction (SBSOD) rating scale. After the interview session, the procedure of the experiment was explained. The first map was placed based on the order of the maps that have been counterbalanced. Participants in both conditions were required to familiarize with the map (Fig. 2).

Fig. 2. A participant is exploring the map in the static condition

Participants in the static condition explored the map without changing its orientation. Participants in the rotatable condition were reminded that they can orientate the turntable while exploring the map. The map exploration phase was recorded using a DSLR camera which was placed on a tripod next to the turntable and at a distance on a 45° angle to the participants. Then, the participants were given a directional task and they could start to find the direction from the start point to the target point. When they were satisfied, the participants could perform the pointing task. The participants were given a bean bag and they were told that they were required to drop the bean bag to indicate the direction of the target point (Fig. 3). The participants had to respond by turning their body, pointing directly at the target point and drop the bean bag. The angles of where the bean bags had been dropped by the participants was captured through WiFi camera which was mounted on a ceiling. There were five trials for each condition. The trials were counterbalanced between the participants. On each trial, participants only performed one directional task. The directional tasks varied from trial to trial. Participants were given a two minutes break between each trial. At the end of the study, the participants were interviewed to obtain their preference and other feedbacks on the condition that they had experienced.

Fig. 3. Bean bags dropped by a participant in the pointing task

8   Results

8.1   Error Distribution of the Pointing Task

A paired samples T-Test on the error distribution of the pointing task for static and rotatable conditions showed that the difference between the conditions approached significant ($t = 1.970$, $df = 11$, $p > 0.05$, two-tailed).

8.2   User Response on the Pointing Task

The user response on the pointing task was classified into 4 categories: correct response (CR), mirror-image error (MI), alignment error (AI) and undefined error (UD). The following Tables 2 and 3 demonstrated the results on user response for 12 participants across the 5 alignments with proportions in the parentheses.

Table 2. The frequency of responses across the 5 alignments for static condition

Static condition	Response			
	Correct	Mirror-image error	Alignment error	Undefined error
Map 1 (0°)	4 (0.33)	4 (0.33)	0	4 (0.33)
Map 2 (45°)	5 (0.42)	0	0	7 (0.58)
Map 3 (90°)	6 (0.50)	2 (0.17)	0	4 (0.33)
Map 4 (135°)	3 (0.25)	1 (0.08)	0	8 (0.67)
Map 5 (180°)	4 (0.33)	5 (0.42)	1 (0.08)	2 (0.17)
Total	22 (0.44)	12 (0.24)	1 (0.02)	25 (0.5)

Table 3. The frequency of responses across the 5 alignments for rotatable condition

Rotatable condition	Response			
	Correct	Mirror-image error	Alignment error	Undefined error
Map 1 (0°)	9 (0.75)	1 (0.08)	0	2 (0.17)
Map 2 (45°)	5 (0.42)	2 (0.17)	1 (0.08)	4 (0.33)
Map 3 (90°)	9 (0.75)	2 (0.17)	0	1 (0.08)
Map 4 (135°)	5 (0.42)	2 (0.17)	0	5 (0.42)
Map 5 (180°)	7 (0.58)	1 (0.08)	3 (0.25)	1 (0.08)
Total	35 (0.70)	8 (0.16)	4 (0.08)	13 (0.26)

Based on the result in Table 2, participants performed well for Map 3 where 6 participants got the correct response for the directional task given meanwhile Map 4 had 4 participants who got the correct response. For the mirror-image error, no error was recorded by the participants Map 2. For alignment error response, only 1 participant produced the error that is for Map 5. As for the undefined error, Map 4 recorded the highest number of participants (8) who produced the error, followed by Map 2 (7), Map 1 (4), Map 3 (4) and Map 5 (2).

The result from Table 3 shows that Map 1 and Map 3 have the highest number of correct response compared to other maps. There was 1 alignment error recorded for Map 2. Meanwhile, Map 5 has 3 participants who contributed to the alignment error. For the mirror-image error, every map of the 5 alignments recorded the error response. For the undefined error, Map 4 has the highest error response (5).

The results on the frequency of responses from the pointing task for Map 1 in static condition and total of responses for 5 alignments in the rotatable condition in this study were compared with the result for Map 1 from the study conducted by Rossano and Warren [17] (Table 4). The aim of this comparison was to examine the differences in the frequency of responses produced by participants in both studies. It needs to be highlighted that the responses from the 5 maps in rotatable condition were compared because the condition allows the user to rotate these maps to align them.

Table 4. A comparison between the frequency of user responses for aligned condition, with proportions in parentheses, from the present work and the work by Rossano and Warren [17]

Result	Response			
	Correct	Mirror-image error	Alignment error	Undefined error
Map 1 (0°) in static condition	4 (0.33)	4 (0.33)	0	4 (0.33)
Total of responses for 5 alignments (0°, 45°, 90°, 135°, 180°) in rotatable condition	35 (0.70)	8 (0.16)	4 (0.08)	13 (0.26)
Map 1 (0°) in Rossano and Warren [17]	17 (0.85)	0	0	3 (0.15)

Table 4 demonstrates the differences in the total frequency of responses for Map 1 in the static condition and the total responses for 5 alignments in the rotatable condition in the present study and from Rossano and Warren's. Map 1 in [17] has 85% correct response meanwhile the total of correct response for maps with 5 alignments in the rotatable condition is 70%. Map 1 in static condition has only 33% correct response where this percentage is lesser than the percentage obtained in Rossano's and the total responses for 5 alignments in rotatable condition in the present work. As for mirror image error response, there were no errors recorded for Map 1 from Rossano and Warren. However, there was mirror-image error response recorded for Map 1 in the static condition with 33%, and the 5 maps in rotatable condition with 16%, in the present experiment. There was also alignment error response with 8% recorded for the rotatable condition. The Map 1 in Rossano and Warren's and Map 1 in the static condition of this experiment recorded no error response for the same error. For the undefined error, both conditions (static and rotatable) in the present experiment and Map 1 from Rossano's have undefined error response. The percentage for undefined error for Map 1 in Rossano and Warren's was 15% and the 5 maps in rotatable condition in the present experiment were 26%. The error percentage obtained for Map 1 for the static condition in this experiment was 33% which is quite high compared to the percentages of Rossano's and rotatable condition. However, it can be concluded that these aligned maps from the rotatable condition of the present work and Rossano and Warren's have almost similar results despite the different proportions obtained.

8.3 Correlations Between User Sense of Direction and User Response on the Pointing Task on Static Condition and Rotatable Condition

Correlations between user scores on the sense of direction and user response on the pointing tasks on static condition and rotatable condition were calculated using Pearson test to explore the relationships between these components. From the results, there was a significant negative correlation between user scores on SBSOD and user response on static condition ($r = -.237$, $N = 12$, $p > 0.05$, two-tailed). There was also a significant negative correlation between user scores on SBSOD and user response on rotatable condition ($r = -.237$, $N = 12$, $p > 0.05$, two-tailed).

9   Discussion

The study investigated the effect of map learning using two different interaction styles (static and rotatable) on blind user cognitive maps and sense of direction.

The first objective was to examine whether the cognitive map constructed on the basis of an audio-tactile map that the person is allowed to orientate as they wish is as good as those generated when the person is directed to use an aligned map. Findings from the pointing task and map reconstruction task show that the participants were able to develop cognitive maps of the maps that they explored when using rotatable map. The result on the correct response for the maps that was rotated produced by participants was compared with the result for an aligned map (Map 1) obtained in [17]. The percentage of the correct response for the current study and in [17] was nearly similar. Based on the pointing accuracy, the blind participants who orientated the maps produced a number of correct response that was similar to participants who used an aligned map in [17]. The cognitive maps that were formed during map learning using the rotated maps contributed to participants' performance in completing the pointing task.

The second objective was to compare user pointing accuracy between static and rotatable conditions. Based on the results, a higher percentage of the correct response of the 5 alignments was produced in the pointing task for rotatable map compared to the static map. In addition, more errors, especially on the mirror-image error, were produced in the pointing task by participants in the static condition. In the work of [17], their findings also show that blind participants produced more errors in the pointing task after using unaligned map. The results obtained in this study also supported the findings of previous works where more errors are produced by blind and sighted people in a spatial task after learning an unaligned map [9, 10, 12, 15].

The third objective was to examine the correlations between user ratings on the sense of direction and user pointing accuracy. There were no correlations found between user ratings on the sense of direction and user pointing accuracy for static and rotatable conditions. Participants who rated their sense of direction with higher ratings performed well on the pointing task. In contrast, participants who rated their sense of direction with low ratings less performed on the same task. The use of the SBSOD at the beginning of the study did not affect the correlations result. As examined by Hegarty et al. [21], the correlations between SBSOD and pointing performance was not influenced by the administration order (beginning or last) of the completion of SBSOD. The result of the correlations obtained in this study was unable to be compared with previous studies since most studies used sighted participants and were conducted in a real environment. Rossano and Warren [17] investigated blind people pointing accuracy however the participants' sense of direction was not assessed. The correlation result in this study could be influenced by the factor of participants greatly overestimate their abilities which cause their self-report measures uncorrelated with the pointing performance [24]. This factor is beyond the control of the researcher in any study.

10 Conclusions and Further Work

This paper discusses the effect that influences blind user's cognitive maps and sense of direction when learning maps at a different orientation. A comparison study between learning maps in static and rotatable conditions was carried out to examine the effect of these conditions on blind user's cognitive maps and sense of direction. Results from this study has shown that the difference in the pointing accuracy of the participants in static and rotatable conditions approach significant. Moreover, results also showed that blind people have the ability to build a cognitive map of the maps learned in the rotatable condition. However, the sense of direction was not correlated with the pointing accuracy for the blind participants in this study. Relating to the findings from previous and the current works, it can be seen that map alignment plays an important role in providing the blind user with information on orientation. The current work will be extended with the use of speech and ambient sound to present landmarks on complex maps. The effect of exploring the complex maps in static and rotatable conditions on blind user's cognitive maps and their sense of direction will be evaluated. Finally, a recommendation on the design of multimodal maps for blind people can be devised.

Acknowledgment. We would like to express our gratitude to Mrs. Sumitha Thavanendran, Mr. Mohd Fazli bin Kameri, Mr. Muhammad Amjad bin Mohd Ikrom and the blind participants for their constant assistance in data gathering at Malaysian Association for the Blind (MAB), Brickfields, Kuala Lumpur. Without their help, we would not have been able to understand and write this research paper. Any opinions, findings, recommendations and conclusions expressed in this paper were those of the authors and do not necessarily reflect the opinions of MAB. We also would like to record our sincere thanks to the Universiti Teknologi MARA for the financial support of this publication under the funding of 600-IRMI/DANA 5/3/LESTARI (0137/2016).

References

1. Brock, A., Jouffrais, C.: Interactive audio-tactile maps for visually impaired people. ACM SIGACCESS Access. Comput. **113**, 3–12 (2015)
2. O'Sullivan, L., Picinali, L., Feakes, C., Cawthorne, D.: Audio tactile maps (ATM) system for the exploration of digital heritage buildings by visually-impaired individuals - first prototype and preliminary evaluation. In: Forum Acusticum (2014)
3. Paladugu, D.A., Wang, Z., Li, B.: On presenting audio-tactile maps to visually impaired users for getting directions. Audio (2010)
4. O'Sullivan, L., Picinali, L., Gerino, A., Cawthorne, D.: A prototype audio-tactile map system with an advanced auditory display. Int. J. Mob. Hum. Comput. Interact. **7**(4), 53–75 (2015)
5. Watanabe, T., Yamaguchi, T., Koda, S., Minatani, K.: Tactile map automated creation system using openstreetmap. In: Miesenberger, K., Fels, D., Archambault, D., Peňáz, P., Zagler, W. (eds.) ICCHP 2014. LNCS, vol. 8548, pp. 42–49. Springer, Cham (2014). https://doi.org/10.1007/978-3-319-08599-9_7
6. Hamid, N.N.A., Edwards, A.D.N.: Facilitating route learning using interactive audio-tactile maps for blind and visually impaired people. In: CHI, pp. 37–42 (2013)
7. Shepard, R.N., Hurwitz, S.: Upward direction, mental rotation, and discrimination of left and right turns in maps. Cognition **18**(1–3), 161–193 (1984)
8. Lobben, A.K.: Tasks, strategies, and cognitive processes associated with navigational map reading: a review perspective. Prof. Geogr. **56**(2), 270–281 (2004)
9. Seager, W., Fraser, D.S.: Comparing physical, automatic and manual map rotation for pedestrian navigation. In: Proceedings of SIGCHI Conference Human Factors Computer System – CHI 2007, p. 767 (2007)
10. Edwards, A.D.N., Hamid, N.N.A., Petrie, H.: Exploring map orientation with interactive audio-tactile maps. In: Abascal, J., et al. (eds.) INTERACT 2015. LNCS, vol. 9296, pp. 72–79. Springer, Cham (2015). https://doi.org/10.1007/978-3-319-22701-6_6
11. Millar, S., Al-Attar, Z.: External and body-centered frames of reference in spatial memory: evidence from touch. Percept. Psychophys. **66**(1), 51–59 (2004)
12. Levine, M., Jankovic, I.N., Palij, M.: Principles of spatial problem solving. J. Exp. Psychol. Gen. **111**(2), 157–175 (1982)
13. MacEachren, A.M.: Learning spatial information from maps: can orientation-specificity be overcome? Prof. Geogr. **44**(4), 431–443 (1992)
14. Hermann, F., Bieber, G., Duesterhoeft, A.: Egocentric maps on mobile devices. In: Proceedings of 4th International Workshop Mobile Computing, pp. 32–37 (2003)
15. McKenzie, G., Klippel, A.: The interaction of landmarks and map alignment in you-are-here maps. Cartogr. J. **53**(1), 43–54 (2016)
16. Rossano, M.J., Warren, D.H.: Misaligned maps lead to predictable errors. Perception **18**(2), 215–229 (1989)
17. Rossano, M.J., Warren, D.H.: The importance of alignment in blind subjects' use of tactual maps. Perception **18**(6), 805–816 (1989)
18. Kozlowski, L.T., Bryant, K.J.: Sense of direction, spatial orientation, and cognitive maps. J. Exp. Psychol. Hum. Percept. Perform. **3**(4), 590–598 (1977)
19. Harris, L.J.: Sex variations in spatial skill. In: Liben, L., Patterson, A., Newcombe, N. (eds.) Spatial Representation and Behavior Across the Lifespan, pp. 83–125. Academic Press, New York (1981)
20. Sholl, M.J., Acacio, J.C., Makar, R.O., Leon, C.: The relation of sex and sense of direction to spatial orientation in an unfamiliar environment. J. Environ. Psychol. **20**(1), 17–28 (2000)

21. Hegarty, M., Richardson, A.E., Montello, D.R., Lovelace, K., Subbiah, I.: Development of a self-report measure of environmental spatial ability. Intelligence **30**(5), 425–447 (2002)
22. Ishikawa, T., Montello, D.R.: Spatial knowledge acquisition from direct experience in the environment: individual differences in the development of metric knowledge and the integration of separately learned places. Cogn. Psychol. **52**(2), 93–129 (2006)
23. Prestopnik, J.L., Roskos-Ewoldsen, B.: The relations among wayfinding strategy use, sense of direction, sex, familiarity, and wayfinding ability. J. Environ. Psychol. **20**(2), 177–191 (2000)
24. Kruger, J., Dunning, D.: Unskilled and unaware of it: how difficulties in recognizing one's own incompetence lead to inflated self-assessments. J. Pers. Soc. Psychol. **77**(6), 1121–1134 (1999)

Adaptive Web-Based Learning Courseware for Students with Dyscalculia

Jasber Kaur$^{(\boxtimes)}$, Rogayah Abdul Majid, and Noorafini Abdul Wahab

Universiti Teknologi MARA, Shah Alam, Malaysia
{jasber, rogayah}@tmsk.uitm.edu.my, nurhaqqq@yahoo.com

Abstract. Dyscalculia is the lack of ability to acquire arithmetical or numerical skills in mathematics. Students with such learning disability fail to understand the basic concepts of mathematical problem such as addition, subtraction, multiplication, and division. This leads to lack of understanding of the problem domain in finding the correct solution to solve mathematical problems. Since the past years, the traditional teaching and learning activities have evolved to ICT-facilitated learning environment utilizing tablets and computers. Most software provided for teachers at schools are specifically for students with other forms of learning disabilities, hence lacking of specific courseware or software to cater the learning needs for dyscalculia students. Thus, this study was conducted in realization to assist dyscalculia students in their learning; i.e. development of an adaptive web-based courseware. The courseware could be used both in class and at home. The courseware conceptual model was adopted and built upon theories on cognitive learning and multisensory method of learning. User review and feedback were gathered to gauge the first-hand user experience with the courseware.

Keywords: Dyscalculia · Learning disabilities
Adaptive web-based courseware

1 Introduction

Learning disabilities are also known as having difficulties or special difficulties in learning. They occur because some humans have problems with their neurological processing. These problems can hinder basic learning skills such as language, literacy and numeracy which involve the activities of reading, writing, and also listening. It can be detected at the early stage of learning during childhood. Some examples of learning disabilities are dyslexia, dyscalculia, dysgraphia, dyspraxia, and attention deficit hyperactivity disorder (ADHD) [1].

Dyscalculia is the inability to obtain arithmetical, mathematical or numerical skills [2]. Students with dyscalculia have problems to understand the basic concept of mathematical problems such as addition, subtraction, multiplication, and division. This leads to problem in understanding and finding the correct solution in Mathematics lessons. The inability to catch up with mathematical skills and concepts could deter in utilizing mathematics and related concepts in daily living. Dyscalculia students experience difficulty in remembering major facts of numbers, formula and procedures in problem

© Springer Nature Singapore Pte Ltd. 2018
N. Abdullah et al. (Eds.): i-USEr 2018, CCIS 886, pp. 148–159, 2018.
https://doi.org/10.1007/978-981-13-1628-9_14

solving. Students are unable to interpret problems correctly and have obscurity in learning constructs of direction, sequence and time. As they cannot remember computation strategies for problem solving, therefore they cannot automatically remember basic mathematical formula and information [3, 4]. Students have the tendency to calculate with their fingers and have slow understanding of the problem domain [5].

Throughout the years, the teaching and learning activities have evolved towards the adoption of various learning techniques including utilizing ICT tools such as tablet and computer. However, most software provided for the teachers at school is specifically designed for students with general learning disabilities. There is lack of specific courseware or software for dyscalculia students at schools. Courseware is primarily defined as educational material which is being used as teaching kit for both teachers and trainers. It is a compilation of learning materials for students and usually developed to be used with computer. Hence this study attempts to develop a web-based courseware or known as *i*-Matematik to further assist teachers to teach students with dyscalculia in learning Mathematics. *i*-Matematik is not a solution but a learning tool or aid to help the students with dyscalculia especially at primary schools.

2 Literature Review

2.1 Definition

As early as 1970s, Kosc [6] suggested the first definition for developmental dyscalculia as a structural disorder of mathematical abilities originated from parts of the brain which is either in genetic or congenital disorder that can be acquired during prenatal development. These parts of the brain are called direct *anatomico-physiological substrate* which is responsible for the mathematical abilities maturity sufficient to age.

Dyscalculia has also been referred to as "number blindness". Similar to dyslexia that described as "word blindness", both represents forms of learning disabilities in children. According to Butterworth [2] a range of descriptive terms have been used, such as arithmetic learning disability, developmental dyscalculia, mathematical disability, number fact disorder, and psychological difficulties in Mathematics.

Piazza et al. [7] stated that developmental dyscalculia is one of learning disabilities which involved the knowledge acquirement of arithmetic and numbers. In another study by Mussolin et al. [8], they defined developmental dyscalculia as a persistent difficulty which involve arithmetical skill and number processing. It affects approximately 6% of school-aged children. Findings from their study showed that children with developmental dyscalculia demonstrated deficit in the cognitive system and failed to understand the concept of number magnitude compared to regular children.

2.2 Factors Affecting Numerical Difficulties

Prior studies have shown that learning difficulties in Mathematics is partly attributed to environmental factors such as the learning culture. Evans and Goodman [9] investigated children's learning difficulties aspects in Mathematics from three types of antecedents; child characteristics, teaching method or teacher, and the teaching subject.

Study findings shows that under-achieved children in Mathematics resulted from the following reasons; difference in gender, difference background culture, dyscalculia, family experience, poor in language skills, poor in mathematics, poor in self-image, prone to dyslexic-type difficulties, and learning style. In a later study by Marzocchi et al. [10], he confirmed that children whom are found to experience mathematical (arithmetical or numerical) learning difficulties are also prone to other learning difficulties such as dyslexia.

Several other studies explored factors from scientific experiments related with brain development. McLean and Hitch [11], Camos [12] and Schuchardt et al. [13] reported a close relationship between developmental dyscalculia and spatial working memory. Meanwhile, Rosselli et al. [14] claimed children with dyscalculia have deficit in visual spatial memory. Rotzer et al. [15] conducted an experiment to explore brain activity related to spatial working memory processes between two groups of 8–10 years old children who have developmental dyscalculia, and regular children as control group. The task involved spatial working memory processes which restrained the spatial number representations formation and also storing and retrieving the arithmetical facts. As a result, children with developmental dyscalculia group showed slower neural activation compared to regular children.

2.3 Information and Communication Technology Intervention for Dyscalculia

In this new era, Information and Communication Technology (ICT) and multimedia-based learning have become important learning tools in classrooms. Computer software, internet and web-based tool have big potential in making teaching and learning process more accessible, fun and interesting [16, 17]. Various ICT tools are developed to assist children with learning disabilities [19, 22, 32]. Adaptive game software is another successful method in approaching dyslexia children. Similar adaptive game software was developed using appropriate cognitive and algorithmic principles for dyscalculia. It was successfully being adapted to children's performance including their difficulty level and maintained their success rate closer at the targeted rate.

Wilson et al. [18] designed an adaptive computer game called "The Number Race" to improve the arithmetical or mathematical or numerical magnitude representations in dyscalculia children. The final outcomes proved a positive enhancement in their performance on core number tasks. This also indicated an improvement in their arithmetical or mathematical or numerical confidence in mathematical abilities. Waiganjo and Wausi [19] revealed that ICT usage in classroom could enhance the mathematical performance in dyscalculia students in Kenya. It must be supported by the teacher's attitude and experience, and also assisted by the use of technological software and hardware. Hence, they recommended the government of Kenya to furnish hardware and software facilities to primary schools and provide workshops and trainings for Mathematics teachers.

According to Amiripour et al. [20], the use of mathematical software like "Math Explorer" can improve mathematical performance of students with dyscalculia. They indicated that such software could attract students to find the problem solution; students felt that they require no help from teachers or parents, hyperactive students gave more focus on the software screens, and students did not require any use of fingers or figures in calculation. Another type of software known as therapy software was developed based on neuro-cognitive models which aimed at enhancing basic skills of under-standing number and its concepts [21].

Such diverse range of assistive technology could aid students with different types of dyscalculia to manage their learning difficulties. The use of assistive technology can be implemented in the mathematics lessons as it enables independent learning mode [22]. Different approaches in intervention have wide prospective to inculcate positive value to dyscalculia children. Computer based intervention are proven for being helpful and efficient in optimizing learning difficulties [23, 31]. Consequently, incorporating and integrating multimedia in software program brings greater advantages to children with dyscalculia. They are able to relate them with daily activities and help to improve their understanding of arithmetic or numeric concepts.

3 Research Design

3.1 Conceptual Framework for Dyscalculia

Several frameworks were developed for learning disabilities in Malaysian environment. Savitha and Nur Athirah [24] developed a prototype of assistive courseware project called Malay Sign Language (eBIM) courseware which specialized for hearing-impaired children in Malaysia. It utilizes static graphics and animations to attract the young deaf children in using the courseware. eBIM used 3D characters to display alphabet signs where students can rewind, stop, and pause the display. A search engine function is also provided for the user to perform searching in the database. An observation was conducted among a group of young deaf children (age ranging from 4 to 6 years old) and they demonstrated improved understanding and high interest to the courseware. This was due to colors and design usage, easy and simple navigation method, and also the use of 3D images with animation and video. In another study by Azirah et al. [25], they claimed that elements like colors and 3D images are connected with user's emotion and need to be considered during development of software.

MEL-SindD is a another form of multimedia courseware developed by Yussof and Paris [26] that supports Down syndrome children learning Malay language. The courseware uses scaffolding modeling to incorporate; navigation and explorative modules, reading and listening to stories, and using sub-modules to stimulate capa-bilities for thinking. The project outcome showed that scaffolding models had enhanced the confidence level of the Down syndrome children.

Mahidin [27] constructed a courseware model called "E-Z Dyslexia" to support children with dyslexia in reading. This model was developed based on previous studies on dyslexia and computer assisted learning. It integrates suitable teaching and learning methods for dyslexic children. Several cognitive areas that were deemed important and related to children with dyslexia was incorporated such as, active learning, attention and perception, encoding (Mayer dual coding theory), locus of control, memory, and motivation. The courseware was further tested with a group of children from 7 to 11 years old with dyslexia.

Hence, given the frameworks as discussed in this section, elements for design and development were adapted for this study. As previous studies have indicated that students with dyscalculia may lack both literacy and numeracy skills thus dyscalculia students have similar traits with dyslexia students. A report by Dyslexia Sydney Support Group [28] showed that 50%–60% of students with dyslexia have problems with Mathematics subject. Therefore, this study builds upon theories from cognitive learning and multisensory method as the conceptual model for *i*-Matematik, which is discussed in the following section.

3.2   *i*-Matematik Conceptual Model

Two relevant theories were adapted as the foundation in designing this courseware; cognitive learning and multisensory method theory [29, 30]. Cognitive learning theory was deemed appropriate to address cognitive areas that are suitable for dyscalculia student that includes (1) attention and perception, (2) locus of control, (3) motivation and (4) working memory. According to Marcia [29] and Eze Manzura [27], multisensory theory has been used and proven for students with learning disabilities. It stimulates learning by engaging students by the use of multiple ways of teaching methods. A multisensory teaching technique means helping a student to learn through more than one sense as compared with traditional teaching techniques that focuses either visual or auditory. Multisensory teaching method involves a simultaneous links between visual, auditory and kinesthetic ways to enhance learning and memory [29]. The student's sight is used for reading information, looking at text, pictures or reading information from board whilst hearing sense is used to listen to what a teacher says.

Thus, elements from both cognitive and multisensory theories are incorporated in *i*-Matematik courseware design. The framework serves as a guideline in designing an online courseware for dyscalculia student as illustrated in Fig. 1. As shown in Fig. 1, the interface design incorporates elements of;

- **Audio Elements.** Audio elements are implemented to support the teaching and learning activities. This is another way to engage the student in using the courseware.
- **Suitable Color Selection.** Dyscalculia is mainly related to weaknesses of various cognitive functions implemented by the extended brain network. Suitable group of colors are selected to reduce the student working memory in processing their activities.
- **Kinesthetic Elements.** Encourage two way interactions between the student and the courseware.
- **Left Marker.** To specify the left side of the interface encourages students to read from left to right.
- **Segmentation.** To cluster the data on the interface in segmentation.
- **User Control Navigation.** This feature will give full control to the student in navigating the courseware.
- **Visual Elements.** Include the texts that are supported with simple graphics. These help the dyscalculia student to understand better.
- **White Space.** Segmentation will help to provide more white space on the interface. This will help to reduce the working memory.

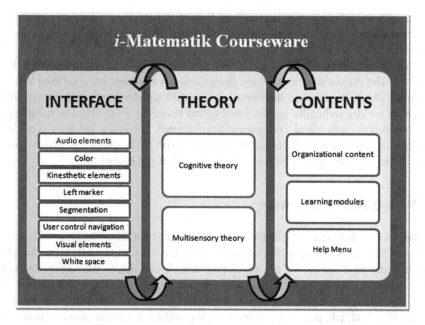

Fig. 1. *i*-Matematik courseware conceptual model

There are three parts in the content structure design of the courseware as following;

- **Organizational Content.** The courseware content design is presented in visual and auditory elements which include supported kinesthetic elements that encourage interaction between student and the courseware. Based on an initial interview with the teacher, it is important to incorporate hands on activities into learning materials to sustain dyscalculia student's attention. As related to the cognitive theory, this feature supports the principles of attention and perception, locus of control, motivation and working memory for dyscalculia students.
- **Learning Modules.** The learning modules are based on national co-curriculum of Malaysian Education for Standard 4, Standard 5 and Standard 6. However, the organization of material is designed to follow the logical order where it begins with most basic elements and progress accordingly to more difficult material.
- **Help Page.** It is vital to include Help page in designing courseware. This will assist the student, teacher and parents in using the courseware.

4   Design and Development of Courseware

The developed conceptual model (Fig. 1) was used as guideline to design the user interface for *i*-Matematik web-based courseware. This is vital to ensure the web-based courseware development meet the system requirement and the mockup interfaces are designed based on system requirements. The aim of this system design is to design *i*-Matematik web-based courseware based on the perceived guidelines. Balsamiq Mockups software was used as a tool for creating interface design mockups in this phase.

The development phase is conducted when all requirements needed has been collected. The phases such as analysis, design and development are combined into one integrated phase because the development is conducted iteratively and continuously. A website builder and editor software tool called Wix.com is identified as suitable tool for *i*-Matematik web-based courseware development. Interview sessions were conducted with dyscalculia students and their teacher to obtain feedback and respond about the web-based courseware which will be discussed at the end of Sect. 5.

5 Web-Based Courseware

i-Matematik web-based courseware is designed to adapt both desktop and mobile platform. Thus, there are two views available; desktop view and mobile view. Adaptive design is the best option for the development as it can detect the screen size upon loading and will select the most appropriate layout for the user. It is useful for the user especially when they are using mobile devices. Dyscalculia student can use various devices like iPad, tab, personal computer, laptop and even a smart phone to access the web-based courseware. There are six pages designed in this web-based courseware, Home Page, Topic Page, Notes Page, Learning Video Page, Exercise Page, and Help Page. Password is required to ensure that only dyscalculia student can use this web-based courseware. Pop-up screen is used for user to key-in password.

The *i*-Matematik web-based courseware is available at http://nurhaqqq.wix.com/i-matematik. It can be both viewed via desktop and mobile devices.

5.1 Home Page

At the home page (Fig. 2), user can access through the main menu using menu tabs as Main Page (*Laman Utama*), learning modules for Year 4, 5 and 6, and Help menu (*Menu Bantuan*). Some graphics are displayed to attract the dyscalculia student and they can also download the diagnostic test from the Main Page. The standard features are the main menu, header and footer. Password is provided to grant access to users. The pop-up screen for the user to enter password as illustrated in Fig. 3.

5.2 Topic Web Page

Password is provided The Topic Page displays the selection of topics for each Year 4, 5 and 6. Users click on their topic based on their level. Figure 4 shows the mobile view for Topic Page with similar functionalities as the desktop view. The standard features are the main menu, header and footer.

Fig. 2. Home page - desktop view (left) and mobile view (right)

Fig. 3. Pop-up screen to enter password

5.3 Learning Video Web Page

The Learning Video Page is where user can watch uploaded videos on learning materials. There are two buttons for Previous and Next to enable the user to navigate their notes based on their learning abilities. The standard features are the main menu, header and footer. Figure 5 illustrates the learning video page.

5.4 User Review and Feedback

An evaluation was conducted involving user feedback and review that were collected upon the completion of their tasks. The questions provided focused on the website features, functionalities and website interface design. In this case, the website design and functions were analyzed to check on their functionalities.

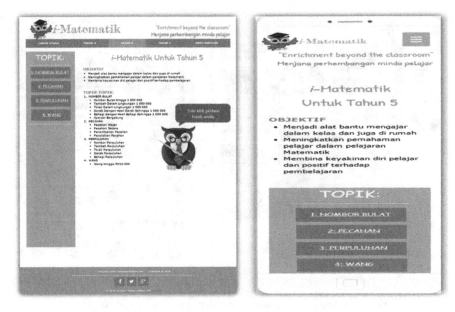

Fig. 4. Topic web page - desktop view (left) and mobile view (right)

Fig. 5. Learning video web page - desktop view (left) and mobile view (right)

Based on the user feedback, the choice of colors and interface design is suitable and consistent. They are neither too bright nor too dull for dyscalculia students hence it is able to attract them. Fewer graphics are important and the web-based courseware is found to be easier to read. It is very vital to emphasize on the white space as the dyscalculia student need to read slowly without interference on the reading space. All functionalities on the web-based courseware worked perfectly and they performed exactly how they are expected to do. All users agreed that *i*-Matematik web-based courseware is appropriate and easy to be used by the dyscalculia student. It is able to assist the teacher or parent in teaching the dyscalculia student either at school or home.

Nevertheless, there were suggestions to include more features such as animation, interactive functionalities and audio to enhance dyscalculia students' understandability. Overall the feedback gained for website interface design is good where users are satisfied with the website design as it has clean and simple interface, suitable selection of colors and the information is easy to understand.

6   Conclusion

i-Matematik web-based courseware was developed using conceptualized model built upon theoretical grounds and educational courseware guidelines for student with dyscalculia. The design and structure of the website is very vital in this project. The most important criteria for dyscalculia student are their accessibility to the web and how the information is presented to them.

The design features such as colors selection, font type, font size and space for reading are very important. Dyscalculia students have slight reading problems and they tend to lose focus when they have difficulty to read. As a result, they lose their interest in learning. It becomes a challenge for both parents and teachers to ensure dyscalculia student motivated and interested in their learning.

Repetition is another important criterion for dyscalculia student. This web-based courseware is designed with Previous and Next buttons for easier navigation. In addition, it is to ensure the dyscalculia student to be on track and able to repeat their lesson via the web-based courseware.

Graphics are amusing and fun for student but too much graphics will interfere the dyscalculia student's thinking. Their way of thinking is linear, similar with how they do their counting. It is best to have fewer graphic for easier reading and understanding. It also helps dyscalculia student to focus more on their lesson.

Future studies to address on learning disabilities could investigate in-depth on how these dyscalculia students respond to the web-based courseware. The student-system interaction could help us to further understand difficulties faced by students during their interaction experience using the web-based courseware. The study has limitation as the selected website software builder used in this project has limited functionalities on web customization. It is best to have more features added to this project such as animation and interactive games or simulation.

References

1. Wellbeing Team: Understanding Specific Learning Difficulties (SpLD). University of West London, Ealing (2014)
2. Butterworth, B.: Dyscalculia Screener Highlighting Pupils with Specific Learning Difficulties in Maths (Age 6–14 Years). Nfer-Nelson Publishing Company Limited, Great Britain (2003)

3. Hasselbring, T.S., et al.: Technology-Supported Math Instruction for Students with Disabilities: Two Decades of Research and Development. American Institutes for Research, Washington, D.C. (1988)
4. Shepard, R.N., Cooper, L.A.: Mental Images and Their Transformations. MIT Press/Bradford Books, Cambridge (1982)
5. Gersten, R., et al.: Early identification and interventions for students with mathematics difficulties. J. Learn. Disabil. 38(4), 293–304 (2005)
6. Kosc, L.: Psychology and psychopathology of mathematical abilities. Stud. Psychol. 12, 159–162 (1970)
7. Piazza, M., Facoetti, A., Trussardi, A.N., Berteletti, I., Conte, S., Lucangeli, D., Dehaene, S., Zorzi, M.: Developmental trajectory of number acuity reveals a severe impairment in developmental dyscalculia. Cognition 116(1), 33–41 (2010)
8. Mussolin, C., Mejias, S., Noël, M.P.: Symbolic and nonsymbolic number comparison in children with and without dyscalculia. Cognition 115(1), 10–25 (2010)
9. Evans, R., Goodman, K.: A review of factors associated with young children's difficulties in acquiring age-appropriate mathematical abilities. Early Child Dev. Care 114(1), 81–95 (1995)
10. Marzocchi, G.M., Lucangeli, D., De Meo, T., Fini, F., Cornoldi, C.: The disturbing effect of irrelevant information on arithmetic problem solving in inattentive children. Dev. Neuropsychol. 21, 73–92 (2002)
11. McLean, J.F., Hitch, G.J.: Working memory impairments in children with specific arithmetic learning difficulties. J. Exp. Child Psychol. 74(3), 240–260 (1999)
12. Camos, V.: Low working memory capacity impedes both efficiency and learning of number transcoding in children. J. Exp. Child Psychol. 99(1), 37–57 (2008)
13. Schuchardt, K., Maehler, C., Hasselhorn, M.: Working memory deficits in children with specific learning disorders. J. Learn. Disabil. 41(6), 514–523 (2008)
14. Rosselli, M., Matute, E., Pinto, N., Ardila, A.: Memory abilities in children with subtypes of dyscalculia. Dev. Neuropsychol. 30(3), 801–818 (2006)
15. Rotzer, S., Loenneker, T., Kucian, K., Martin, E., Klaver, P., von Aster, M.: Dysfunctional neural network of spatial working memory contributes to developmental dyscalculia. Neuropsychologia 47(13), 2859–2865 (2009)
16. Segers, E., Verhoeven, L.: Multimedia support of early literacy learning. Comput. Educ. 39, 207–221 (2002)
17. Gauss, B., Urbas, L.: Individual differences in navigation between sharable content objects and evaluation study of a learning module design. Br. J. Edu. Technol. 34(4), 499–509 (2003)
18. Wilson, A.J., Dehaene, S., Pinel, P., Revkin, S.K., Cohen, L., Cohen, D.: Principles underlying the design of "The Number Race", an adaptive computer game for remediation of dyscalculia. Behav. Brain Funct. 2, 19 (2006)
19. Waiganjo, S., Wausi, A.: Using ICT to assist dyscalculia students: situation analysis for primary schools in Kenya: a case study of Starehe District Nairobi County. Int. J. Innov. Educ. Res. 1(1), 74–83 (2013)
20. Amiripour, P., Bijan-zadeh, M.H., Rostamy-Malkhalifeh, M., Najafi, M.: The effects of assistive technology on increasing capacity of mathematical problem solving in dyscalculia students. J. Appl. Math. 8(4(31)), 47–55 (2012)
21. Kaser, T., et al.: Therapy software for enhancing numerical cognition. Interdisc. Perspect. Cogn. Educ. Brain 7, 207–216 (2011)
22. Nagavalli, T., Fidelis, P.J.: Technology for Dyscalculic Children. Sri Sarada College of Education, Salem (2012)

23. Kucian, K., Grond, U., Rotzer, S., Henzi, B., Schönmann, C., Plangger, F., et al.: Mental number line training in children with developmental dyscalculia. Neuroimage **57**, 782–795 (2011)
24. Savita, K.S., Nur Athirah, A.P.: Malay sign language courseware for hearing-impaired children in Malaysia. World Appl. Sci. J. (Spec. Issue Comput. Appl. Knowl. Manag.) **12**, 59–64 (2011)
25. Azirah, S.A., Fauziah, R., Rogayah, A.M.: Usability evaluation of academic record system at the International Islamic College (IIC). In: 2015 IEEE Conference on e-Learning, e-Management and e-Services (2015)
26. Yussof, R.L., Paris, T.N.S.T.: Reading activities using the scaffolding in MEL-SindD for down syndrome children. Proc.-Soc. Behav. Sci. **35**, 121–128 (2012)
27. Mahidin, E.M.M.: Preliminary courseware conceptual model for dyslexic children. Int. J. Innov. Educ. Res. **2**(8), 54–60 (2014)
28. Dyslexia Sydney Support Group: Mathematics Dyslexia and Dyscalculia (2015)
29. Marcia, K.H.: Structured, sequential, multisensory teaching: the Orton legacy. Ann. Dyslexia **48**(1), 1–26 (1998)
30. Schunk, D.H.: Learning Theories: An Educational Perspectives, 6th edn. Pearson New International Edition (2012)
31. Hazlina, A., Fauziah, R.: Evaluating students' emotional response in video-based learning using Kansei engineering. In: 4th International Conference on User Science and Engineering, i-USEr (2016)
32. Saud, S.F., Nasruddin, Z.A.: Design of e-learning courseware for hearing impaired (HI) students. In: 4th International Conference on User Science and Engineering, i-USEr (2016)

Technology and Adoption

Gamification and Augmented Reality Utilization for Islamic Content Learning: The Design and Development of Tajweed Learning

Nurtihah Mohamed Noor[1(✉)], Rahmah Lob Yussof[2],
Fakhrul Hazman Yusoff[1], and Marina Ismail[1]

[1] Universiti Teknologi MARA, Shah Alam, Selangor, Malaysia
nurtihah_83@yahoo.com
[2] Universiti Teknologi MARA, Kuantan, Pahang, Malaysia

Abstract. Gamification and augmented reality are among the technologies that promise a lot of advantages to the learners. Previous studies have shown that both can motivate learners and make a learning process enjoyable. Nevertheless, Islamic content learning such as tajweed is claimed to be a very dry and plain content. The statement is affirmed by the outcome of our preliminary investigation that reveals tajweed learning is not attractive and it needs to be revolutionized as to make it more attractive and interesting to the present digitally native generation. Producing a high-quality tajweed learning tool is possible through good design and development process. Therefore, this study utilized a gamification and augmented reality in the design and development of tajweed learning in order to make the learning more captivating and meaningful. The ADDIE model was employed to conduct the design and development processes. Hopefully, the combination of the two technologies can attract the learners, particularly the children, and engage them in the tajweed learning process.

Keywords: Gamification · Augmented reality · Tajweed · Learning

1 Introduction

For decades, the utilization of technological approach has been proven to benefit many fields, including the learning field. There are many applications, systems, and approaches developed to facilitate the learners in learning no matter what learning contents the applications conveyed [1]. Among the technologies and approaches that are currently well-known are gamification and augmented reality [2]. Gamification is an infant concept that emerged in the early of 2010s and gained its popularity in several fields [3], such as business, learning, and education. It emphasizes the use of the game elements for non-gaming environment, in other words, the usage is more on the serious or non-gaming environment [4]. Game elements such as the rules, gameplay, and mechanics (point, badges, leaderboard, unlocking items, and many more) can be utilized in the non-gaming context [5]. The utilization ensures a learner to enjoy and then engage in a learning process in which later will bring positive outcomes in the learning. Moreover, the utilization of augmented reality in a learning process has also been proven to deliver positive outcomes to the

© Springer Nature Singapore Pte Ltd. 2018
N. Abdullah et al. (Eds.): i-USEr 2018, CCIS 886, pp. 163–174, 2018.
https://doi.org/10.1007/978-981-13-1628-9_15

learners [6]. Augmented reality enables the virtual contents to be overlaid in the real environment and exhibits high experiential learning processes to the learners [7]. In relation to gamification, previous studies have shown the attempts of utilizing augmented reality in gamification [2, 8]. Augmented reality and gamification adaptation in learning can be utilized in different ways as proposed by the previous studies [2, 8]. However there is a need for empirical studies to investigate the effectiveness of both techniques in the learning process [2]. The utilization of gamification and augmented reality in learning process is able to bring enjoyment to the users through experience and motivation [4, 6]. Augmented reality and gamification can help the processes to be attractive, engaging, and facilitating the learners with limited visual imagination and understanding.

Learning something which is related to religious contents, particularly Islam, is always dry and plain [9]. In spite of the fact that there is much knowledge to be learnt and comprehended by a learner, Islamic content learning is always left far behind than other learning subjects such as science, language learning, medical, or any other critical subjects, especially in Malaysia. One of the anticipated Islamic contents that can be highlighted for technological employment is tajweed learning for Al-Quran recitation [10]. In Islam, a precise Al-Quran recitation is highly demanded as mentioned in the following verse:

"...and recite Al-Quran clearly with tartil (in a distinct and measured tone)." [Al-Muzammil: verse 4]

Our preliminary studies revealed that the performance of Al-Quran recitation with accurate tajweed is low among 33 children and some of them are found to be uninterested in the learning process. Nevertheless, previous studies have shown that the employment of the technological approaches, such as gamification and augmented reality in learning, can motivate the learners to learn [4, 10, 11]. Therefore, this paper discusses a proposed approach to gamification and augmented reality adoption for tajweed learning to motivate learners, particularly children, to learn accurate tajweed articulation for Al-Quran recitation. Section one presents the introduction. Several backgrounds on the topics are discussed in the sections two until four. Section five elaborates the design and development of the proposed approach by using instructional system design methodology, ADDIE; and finally, section six concludes the discussed topics in the paper.

2   Tajweed Learning

Linguistically, the term "tajweed" in Arabic is defined as the proficiency or skilfully exhibiting expertise in doing something; while in relation to Al-Quran recitation, tajweed means to articulate the Al-Quran verses with correct pronunciations within the determined rules. There are many rules that need to be understood by a reciter. The rules have their own names such as the rules of Idgham Bilaghunnah, Idgham Maalghunnah, Ikhfak Hakiki, and many more. Meanwhile, there are also methods that concentrate on the accurate pronunciations or sounds of the letters, rather than to highly concentrate on the rule name memorization in the earlier years of Al-Quran introduction to the learners [12]. Table 1 shows the tajweed in Al-Quran recitation.

Table 1. The types of tajweed in Al-Quran [12].

Types
▪ The pronunciation of letters (makhraj), especially the letters that are not included in the Malay language (ث ج ح د ذ ش ص ض ط ظ ق ل)
▪ Thick (Istiklal) and thin (Istifal) pronunciation
▪ Long or short recitation: 2, 4, 5 and 6
▪ With nasalization or without nasalization (Idgham, Ikhfak, and Izhar)

In fact, there are many studies that reveal the poor performance of accurate Al-Quran recitation in any age levels, either in primary or secondary schools, and in higher education institutions [10, 13–15]. In Malaysia, there are many approaches that have been compiled, especially for primary and secondary schools. However, since the current generation is a digitally native generation, there are a lot of possibilities for employing a more sophisticated approach to tajweed learning.

3 Gamification

Gamification is the utilization of the game elements in the non-game environment context. The non-game environment context can be myriad such as for military, business, marketing, social relationship, and of course, the learning field [16]. Game elements discussion is very broad as many researchers tend to propose various features and characteristics for the elements such as challenge, control, rules and goals, mystery, sensory stimuli, and fantasy [17]; rules, system, fun, mechanics, dynamic, aesthetics [18]; and many more. However, [5] clearly explained that there are five important elements of gamification; namely goal and rules, gameplay, feedback, game space design, and storyline.

Additionally, gamification emphasizes the employment of the game mechanics [2, 4], which are in the feedback elements [5]. Points, badges, leaderboard, unlocking items, level, and title are examples of the game mechanics [4]. Gamification's effectiveness has been long discussed for engaging the learners in the learning environment [6], and to be engaged, it provides enjoyment to its learners as myriad game elements and mechanics have been utilized in the approach. Previous studies have designed many styles of gamification approaches in the learning process, but the most important is the process can make the learners learn, make assessment, have activities, social relationships, show progression, and exhibits enjoyable and interesting processes [19]. Gamification can be deployed for learning the content [20] or for accelerating the learning process requirements for a curriculum [1]. In fact, transferring the game elements in the learning environment is innumerable. For instance, the learners perform activities, download learning materials, and then evaluate by giving the mechanics, which can also be deployed by exposing the learners to an exact digital game application in the gamified learning process for content learning [19, 20]. Previous studies have also shown that gamification can be deployed with myriad technologies and approaches to make the learning more interesting and attractive [2].

4   Augmented Reality

Augmented reality is a technology that overlays the virtual contents in the real world and often used in the learning field [6]. It enables the learners to portray the unseen materials and objects on the spot while the learners interact with the augmented reality application [2]. By using the myriad types of learning process designs, previous studies indicate the employment of the augmented reality technology for explaining the learning content [6] or as a game [21]. However, the utilization of augmented reality as a real game seems very complicated for certain age level.

This technology also exhibits many impressive characteristics that can bring enjoyment and engagement to the learners. Augmented reality makes the learners immersed in the learning process and gets the feeling of presence in the developed application. Of course, the information provided by the virtual contents evoke the learners' imagination and interpretation, which is essential for a learning process [2].

5   Design and Development

For designing and developing the proposed approach, gamification and augmented reality employment for tajweed learning, an instructional design model was applied to guide the processes systematically. Known as Analysis, Design, Development, Implementation, and Evaluation (ADDIE), this type of instructional design methodology is very reliable, guides the instructional design effectively [22], and has been well accepted in designing the instructional technology for learning [23]. Hence, next subsections elaborate the steps involved in this study.

5.1   Analysis

Basically, this phase is related to figure out the needs and problems, and then make a rough planning to cater to the problem within its context, environment, and focus of the study [22]. For that matter, this phase determines the current situations in tajweed learning among children. A preliminary investigation was conducted and it showed that there is a need to propose the current technological approach for attracting the learners to learn the Islamic content, which permits enjoyment and engagement in the process. As the current generation is very deeply involved in the technology, it is very relevant to any religious or Islamic content learning to be kept updated with the current transformation [9]. Besides the preliminary investigation analysis, this phase also issued a user role model [23] to give a rough overview of the relationship between the user and the proposed gamification and augmented reality approach for tajweed learning. Table 2 shows the overview.

Table 2. The user role model.

Tajweed learning and the children's role	
Context	The learning can be formal or informal; conventional learning is always dry and plain; basically related to self-motivation and awareness to master; very important knowledge; end with accurate pronunciation of letters and verses
Characteristic	Requires recognition, understanding, and practices; sounds of each letter and verse are critical; performance will improve with comprehension and practices
Criteria	Understand the cognitive level; attractive and interesting way of learning; accurate knowledge of the learning, particularly the sounds (pronunciation)

5.2 Design

This phase will look into the designs of the proposed approach or processes, including the objectives and goals, learning types, learning activities, and the required media and features for supporting the proposed approach processes [22]. Tajweed learning can be categorized as the intellectual skill type of learning. Each letter or verse in Al-Quran recitation has certain rules, concepts, and conditions that need to be understood before taking any action (recite) [12], which suits the intellectual skill type of learning division [24]. Table 3 elaborates the classification of intellectual skill for tajweed learning. Furthermore, some related theories are referred to in ensuring the proposed approach is guided and effectively designed.

Table 3. The intellectual skill types of learning.

Step	Intellectual Skill Division	Description	Employment in Tajweed Learning (Qolqolah as an example)
1.	Discriminations	Telling that the stimulus is different.	Telling the discrimination of Qolqolah recitation letters and verses.
2.	Concrete concept	Grouping for similar characteristics.	Emphasize the three types of Qolqolah recitation styles.
3.	Defined concepts	Classify the rules for the defined characteristics.	The recitation styles of the three types; clear, lightly, and plodding.
4.	Rule learning	Apply the rules.	Apply the recitation for each type of the Qolqolah recitation verses.
5.	Problem solving	Encounter other problem-solving.	Apply the recitation for myriad verses and mixed recitation styles.

As enjoyment is important in any learning process, particularly for children's learning, the motivational and experiential theories have been utilized. Experience and motivation are the key factors in bringing enjoyment to a process or activity [3]. Experience can be evoked from interactive interactions while the adoption of technology and the gamification approach can bring the feeling of experience to the users [25]. This is where the elements of both gamification and augmented reality are determined so that the elements' availability can be used to maximize the usage in giving meaningful experience to the learners. Goals and rules, gameplay, feedback, storyline, and game space determination are important elements required for gamification in learning [5], while the virtual content and real-time interaction are the most interesting elements provided by augmented reality in facilitating a learning process [26]. In gamification, [5] discussed that the goal explains the objectives and targets that need to be accomplished in the process. Rules require certain structures to make the learning interesting whereby the learners must follow the rules to successfully complete the proposed approach. Gameplay is the planning on how the learners complete all the required activities and tasks, and basically consists of the above-mentioned goal and rules, as well as the challenges and interaction. Feedback consists of the feedback in the game structure, instructional feedback, assessment feedback, and challenges feedback. The game mechanic elements in gamification are included in the feedback element. Lastly, the

Table 4. The adoption of Malone's motivational theory in the proposed approach.

Element	Description	Adoption in the proposed approach
Challenge	(i) Goals - ensure to have clear goals, challenge by levels appropriate to users (ii) Uncertain outcomes - difficulty is variety, hidden information but selective revealed, randomness (iii) Performance feedback - Clear, frequent, constructive, and encouraging performance feedback (iv) Self-esteem - positive feedback to promote competence and social relevance to users	- The goals are to master the tajweed by recognizing and understanding the types and sounds (pronunciation) - Scaffold the contents for several levels, from easy to difficult - Provide feedback to the learners - Emphasize the utilization of game mechanics in the process - Positive feedback for the success and provide social relationship between the learners within the activity
Curiosity	(i) Sensory curiosity- audio and visual utilization (ii) Cognitive sensory - incompleteness of competence	- Utilize all the multimedia elements for learning - Learners cannot proceed to other levels and module if they do not achieve the determined target
Fantasy	(i) Emotional aspect - employ storylines, characters (ii) Cognitive aspect - provide appropriate metaphors or analogies for the learning content	- There are storylines in the proposed process, to help a character complete a mission - The learning contents have been chunked and organized in appropriate metaphors
Control	(i) Contingency - responsive environment (ii) Choice - emphasize the user's choice (iii) Power - produce powerful effect	- Learners can control the process by themselves but must start with the augmented reality environment in order to collect points, badges, and other activities

game space elements require the determination of the environment used to implement the gamification approach.

Additionally, a motivational theory proposed by [27] was used to guide the design and development of the proposed approach. Table 4 explains the adoption of the theory in the proposed approach and the next figure shows the learning activities that will be implemented in general (see Fig. 1).

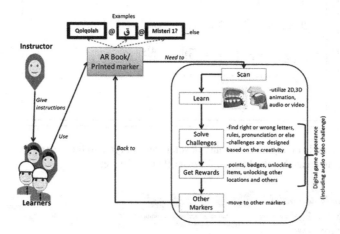

Fig. 1. The tajweed learning activity design in the gamification and augmented reality proposed approach.

5.3 Development

There are three stages involved in the development phase, namely pre-production, production, and post-production. Pre-production is related to the creation of storyboard, scripting, and multimedia elements, which are used for determination and casting (if any). Meanwhile, production ensures all the needed sources are developed and produced including utilization of many software and hardware, and lastly, post-production stage needs all the produced resources from the production stage to be merged in a platform [28]. The next subsections show the activities in the stages.

Pre-production. In the pre-production stage, storyboard for developing the application was developed. In view of this study utilizing several platforms, different storyboards were developed by using Microsoft PowerPoint to facilitate the development process (see Figs. 2 and 3). This study employed augmented reality, digital game, and audio and video recording application to complete the gamification approach. Besides that, an expert in Al-Quran and tajweed pronunciation was also involved in order to record all the audio related files in the application. The same person was used to record the narrations in the application. In relation to that, scripts for the narration and tajweed-related pronunciation were deployed. In addition, the resources for digital games were also determined in this stage including its rules, storyline, and feedback, which highlight the use of game mechanics and theories as mentioned in the previous sections.

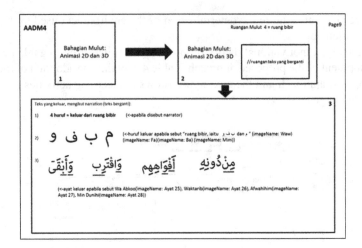

Fig. 2. An example of augmented reality development storyboard for the proposed approach in tajweed learning created in the Microsoft Power Point software.

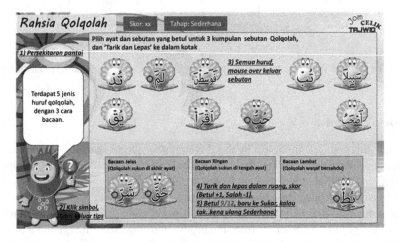

Fig. 3. An example of a digital game development storyboard for the proposed approach in tajweed learning created in the Microsoft Power Point software.

Production. This stage produced all the planned resources in the pre-production stage [28]. In this stage, the graphics, animations, and videos were developed; and the narrations as well as tajweed pronunciations were recorded for both of the digital game and augmented reality platform (see Fig. 4). A digital game was developed for the end-product application. Basically, various types of software were used in this phase such as Autodesk 3DMax, Adobe Premier CS 6, Adobe Photoshop CS 6, Adobe Flash CS 6, Audacity, and BuildAR software.

Fig. 4. The examples of activities involved in the production processes including audio recording in Audacity, graphics creation in Adobe Photoshop CS6, and a digital game development in Adobe Flash CS 6.

Post-production. The post-production stage is the final stage in a development process [28]. In this stage, all the developed resources were combined in the main platform, which is Adobe Flash CS6. The function of augmented reality, digital game, and assessment (audio/video recording) were put together in the main platform (see Fig. 5).

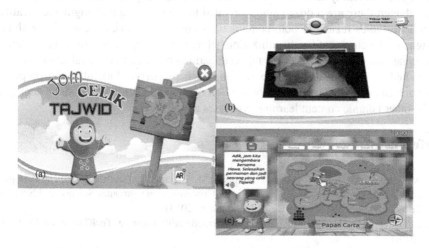

Fig. 5. The main page of the application for the proposed approach (a). The examples of interfaces including the augmented reality and digital game interface (b) and (c).

5.4 Implementation

After completing the development phase, the proposed approach will then be implemented in the real setting in which it is focused on. This approach will be implemented in the real environment soon, particularly for summative evaluation and the activities will be as stated in the previous figure (see Fig. 1).

5.5 Evaluation

Evaluation is divided into two types, which are the formative and summative evaluation [22]. Formative evaluation is deployed while in the production stage in order to investigate any dysfunctional or error in the application. Meanwhile, summative evaluation is employed after the implementation in the real environment. This study had gone through several debugs in the production stage. However, the summative evaluation will be deployed later on.

6 Conclusion

Tajweed learning is demanded in Islam as the Muslims have Al-Quran to be recited and comprehended. In view of the Al-Quran in the Arabic language, there are certain recitation rules to be followed so that the pronunciations are accurate and bring the exact meaning in the verses. However, a dry learning process for a plain learning content as tajweed sometimes make the learning process unattractive and uninteresting, particularly for children. Our preliminary studies proved it as the children stated that the current learning process is very bland and need to be revolutionized. Therefore, this study suggests a gamification and augmented reality use in the learning process. Gamification and augmented reality have been proven to motivate and engage learners in the process. Even though there are a dozen studies related to gamification and augmented reality, empirical studies related to both combinations are fewer. Thus, we came out with the design and development for the utilization before conducting an experimental design to investigate the effectiveness of the tajweed learning process. Later, evaluations will be conducted to investigate the proposed approach properly. Hopefully, the proposed approach can change the learners' perception of tajweed learning and can be deployed in the other Islamic content learning processes as well.

References

1. Amriani, A., Aji, A.F., Utomo, A.Y., Junus, K.M.: An empirical study of gamification impact on e-learning environment. In: International Conference on Computer Science and Network Technology, pp. 265–269. IEEE Xplore, Dalian (2013)
2. Dunleavy, B.M.: Design principles for augmented reality learning. TechTrends **58**(1), 28–35 (2014)
3. Deterding, S.: The lens of intrinsic skill atoms: a method of gameful design. Hum.-Comput. Interact. **30**(3–4), 294–335 (2015). Special Issues HCI Digital Games
4. Noor, N.M., Yusoff, F.H., Ismail, M., Yussof, R.L.: Adaptation of enjoyment in learning through gamification. Am. Sci. Lett. **24**, 1455–1459 (2018)
5. Hoe, T.W.: Gamifikasi Dalam Pendidikan, 1st edn. Penerbit UPSI, Tanjung Malim (2015)
6. Abas, H., Badioze Zaman, H.: Visual learning through augmented reality storybook for remedial student. In: Zaman, H.B., Robinson, P., Petrou, M., Olivier, P., Shih, Timothy K., Velastin, S., Nyström, I. (eds.) IVIC 2011. LNCS, vol. 7067, pp. 157–167. Springer, Heidelberg (2011). https://doi.org/10.1007/978-3-642-25200-6_16

7. Huang, T.C., Chen, C.C., Chou, Y.W.: Animating eco-education: to see, feel and discover in an augmented reality-based experiential learning environment. Comput. Educ. **96**, 72–82 (2016)

8. Villagrasa, S., Fonseca, D., Duran, J.: Teaching case: applying gamification techniques and virtual reality for learning building engineering 3D arts. In: 2nd International Conference on Technological Ecosystems for Enhancing Multiculturality, pp. 171–177 (2014)

9. Jusoh, W.N.H., Jusoff, K.: Using multimedia in teaching Islamic studies. J. Media Commun. Stud. **1**(5), 86–94 (2009)

10. Ismail, M., Diah, N.M., Ahmad, S., Rahman, A.A.: Engaging learners to learn tajweed through active participation in a multimedia application (TaLA). In: 3rd International Conference on Advances in Computing, Control and Telecommunication Technologies, pp. 88–91. Institute of Doctors Engineers and Scientists (IDES), Jakarta (2011)

11. Chen, C., Shih, J., Ma, Y.: Using instructional pervasive game for school children's cultural learning. Educ. Technol. Soc. **17**(2), 169–182 (2014)

12. Hassan, S.S.: Talaqqi – Asas Sebutan Huruf Al-Quran, 3rd edn. REHAL, Petaling Jaya (2014)

13. Awang, A., Mat, A.C., Yaakub, A.N.: Tahap Pembacaan Al-Quran Dalam Kalangan Pelajar di UiTM Terengganu. Asean J. Teach. Learn. High. Educ. **3**, 83–100 (2011)

14. Hassan, S.S., Zailani, M.A.: Khatam Al-Quran in Islamic education curriculum in Malaysia. Procedia – Soc. Behav. Sci. **103**, 558–566 (2013)

15. Hassan, S.S., Zailani, M.A.: Analysis of tajweed errors in Quranic recitation. Procedia – Soc. Behav. Sci. **103**, 136–145 (2013)

16. Noor, N.M., Yusoff, F.H., Yussof, R.L., Ismail, M.: The potential use of augmented reality in gamification. In: 5th International Conference on Computing and Informatics Proceedings, Istanbul, Turkey, pp. 159–167 (2015)

17. Garris, R., Ahlers, R., Driskell, J.E.: Games, motivation and learning: a research and practice model. Simul. Gaming **33**(4), 441–467 (2002)

18. Hunicke, R., LeBlanc, M., Zubek, R.: MDA: A Formal Approach to Game Design and Game Research (2004). http://www.aaai.org/Papers/Workshops/2004/WS-04-04/WS04-04-001.pdf?utm_source=cowlevel. Accessed 28 Jan 2015

19. Miure, M.: Gamification: A Guideline for Integrating and Aligning Digital Game Elements into a Curriculum. Bowling Green State University, Bowling Green (2012)

20. Brown, K., Anand, C.: Gamification and serious game approaches for introductory computer science tablet software. In: 1st International Conference on Gameful Design, Research and Applications – Gamification Proceedings, pp. 50–57. ACM Press, Toronto (2013)

21. Blum, L., Wetzel, R., Mccall, R., Oppermann, L., Broll, W., Coudenhove-kalergi, R.R., Augustin, S.: The final TimeWarp: using form and content to support player experience and presence when designing location-aware mobile augmented reality games. In: Designing Interactive System Conference Proceedings, pp. 711–720. ACM, Newcastle (2012)

22. Gustafon, K.L., Branch, R.M.: What is instructional design? In: Trends and Issues in Instructional Design and Technology, pp. 17–25 (2002)

23. Noor, N. M.: Al-Adab: Islamic sex education courseware using cognitive theories. Unpublished thesis. Univeriti Utara Malaysia, Sintok, Kedah (2012)

24. Gagne, R.M.: Learning outcomes and their effects: useful categories of human performance. Am. Psychol. **39**(4), 377–385 (1984)

25. Selinger, M., Kaye, L.: ICT tools and applications. In: Leask, M., Pachler, N. (eds.) Learning to Teach Using ICT in the Secondary School - A Companion to School Experience, 3rd edn., pp. 82–99. Routledge, Taylor & Francis Group, New York (2014)

26. Chao, K., Lan, C., Chang, K., Sung, Y.: Knowledge management & e-learning augmented reality in a fundamental design course. Knowl. Manag. e-Learn. **6**(2), 123–139 (2014)

27. Malone, T.W., Lepper, M.R.: Making learning fun: a taxonomy of intrinsic motivations for learning. In: Snow, R.E., Farr, M.J. (eds) Aptitude, Learning and Instruction Volume 3: Conative and Affective Process Analyses, Hillsdale, New Jersey, London, pp. 223–253. (1987)
28. Escobar, G., Kirsh, L.H.: Authoring Tools for Multimedia Application and Network Delivery, 5, 659, 793 (1997)

Adoption of Customer Centered Service in Public University: A Case Study in Malaysia

NorHapiza Mohd Ariffin[1](✉) and Norfarizan Mohd Daud[2]

[1] Faculty of Computer and Mathematical Sciences, Universiti Teknologi MARA,
Shah Alam, Selangor, Malaysia
hapiza@tmsk.uitm.edu.my
[2] Universiti Malaysia Pahang, Kuantan, Pahang, Malaysia
farizan@ump.edu.my

Abstract. The Information and Communication Technology (ICT) represents a basis for the development of academic institution in public sector. Thus, there is a huge emerging from the traditional academic institution into technological environment based. ICT implementations indirectly will represent the major changes of the business processes. In term of providing the best ICT facilities and infrastructure, there are often issues about service delivering, customer expectation, utilization of infrastructure, knowledge sharing and matters regarding ICT services. Therefore, this study was conducted to analyze the adoption of customer centered service for ICT services in Malaysian public university. There are two main objectives of this study which first, to identify the current status of customer centered service for ICT services and second, to identify the impact of adoption of customer centered service for ICT services. About 10 public universities in Malaysia involved in this study. Interview and questionnaires were used for collecting data. The findings showed that 80% of public universities in Malaysia have adopted customer centered services to facilitate the ICT services and facilities in their universities and this study revealed about the positive impact of customer centered service to the ICT services. Suggestions as to what future research should indicate are also discussed.

Keywords: Customer service · Public university · ICT service delivery

1 Introduction

In public administration literature, there is a long study about adoption of Information Technology and Communication [1]. For example, the higher education in the United Kingdom has witnessed a considerable change resulting from a number of successive initiatives such as the education reform act in the mid-1980s and the information systems and technology value for money study in the late 1990s [2]. The ICT represents a basis for the development of academic institution in public sector [3]. In addition, emerging from the traditional academic institution into technological environment based, the public university in public sector became heavily reliant

© Springer Nature Singapore Pte Ltd. 2018
N. Abdullah et al. (Eds.): i-USEr 2018, CCIS 886, pp. 175–182, 2018.
https://doi.org/10.1007/978-981-13-1628-9_16

on information and communication technologies (ICTs) in order to consider major changes in "patterns of demand and competition" for higher education [3].

Regarding to the emergence and innovation of the ICT, the education institution in public sector is growing from the customer perspective. Furthermore, the customer service orientation in the ICT service can influence on the expectations towards university services. In term of providing the best ICT facilities and infrastructure, there are often issues about service delivering, customer expectation, utilization of infrastructure, knowledge sharing, information inquiring and matters regarding ICT services. Therefore, there is a need to investigate the impact of the issues to the university.

Currently, due to the tremendous growth in customer oriented services, educational institutions are not excluded in restructuring and re-engineering their operating processes to cut costs and become more efficient while responding and interacting with their customer.

In Malaysia, Higher Learning Institutions are more related to representing an involvement with diversify stakeholders and services. This shows that Higher Learning Institutions are more critical in managing interactions with their customers. Thus, this study focused in public universities and can be represented as a small world of education community.

In order to operate efficiently, the organizations need to be supported by ICT facilities and services in 24/7 environment. The administration, teaching learning process and research development activities must be run seamlessly. The investment in ICT development should be a foundation to optimize the operation cost and increase productivity and profit of the university. This responsibility usually handled by ICT department. The facilities and services can be categorized as Application System, IT equipment maintenance and support, networking and security and telecommunication.

University environment is divided into divisional boundaries such as by departments, faculties, and units. At the same time there are multiple level of customers such as student, academic staff, non-academic staff, alumni, and government agencies. This environment becomes a challenge to the IT department in order to maintain good services and customer satisfaction as a non-profitable basis. This environment not only contributes to different challenge in term of functional, but must be also considered the geographical issue, manpower, skills and interest.

Recently, in Malaysia, there are about 20 public universities all around the states. As the growth of the technology, most of the university is using IT/ICT department to manage and facilitate the ICT services for the whole university. Due to more and less issues regarding ICT services, there suppose a bridge between the ICT departments as service provider to the customer who are using all the ICT facilities and services. This study intends to examine about the adoption of Customer Centered Services to facilitate the ICT services. The focus of this study is ICT services in public University in Malaysia and University Malaysia Pahang (UMP) as a case study.

2   Literature Review

Delivering the best ICT facilities and infrastructure required a new invention of service delivery. Transforming ICT into a service oriented organization required a good model to be approached. [4] has proposed Service Accession Model. This model is designed specifically for IT service delivery whereby it considered the maturity stages in terms of both operational delivery and customer orientation. The model called as Accession model because it assists IT department to attain a particular succession of competency stages, each of which builds on what has gone before. The model can be used to define what is needed and to chart progress towards its achievement.

There are four stages to define the service accession. All of the stages are demonstrating the life cycle maturity of an organization. Each maturity level covers the one beneath it and so can be regarded as a cumulative or progressive status rather than something that is radically different from its predecessor. This model represents the continuous progression in delivering ICT services from bottom left to top right, based on how much of the maturity of the next stage is displayed. However, regarding to [4], the operation is possible to be operated at intermediate points.

Besides that, there are a lot of best-practice frameworks and methodologies to guide ICT operations and services such as Application Services Library (ASL), Capability Maturity Model (CMM), ICT Infrastructure Library (ITIL), and Microsoft Operations Framework [5]. ICT departments are increasingly viewed as service providers to business users and improving service quality and user satisfaction has been a concern of ICT researchers and practitioners [6]. As stated earlier, one example of ICT service framework is ITIL. ITIL has originally developed in the 1980s in UK. According to [4], ITL was an international standard framework that is applicable to commercialize the organization as well as government bodies and much of the contents are written by the expert from ICT industry all over the world. Nevertheless, it has become most widely accepted approach to service management and quite relevant to ICT department to imply the ICT infrastructure of the business processing around the firm interactions with its customer services.

By optimizing the ICT service delivery, the performance management of the infrastructure is important to ensure the stable ICT services for the existing and any new ICT practices [7]. The stable ICT services involve two management area which are the "Service delivery front offices that have a customer focus for the service delivery" and "Supported product back offices which is focusing on operational efficiency". According to them, "Service delivery front office is more into "end-to-end" ICT service group. Customer service can be defined as the way in which an organization handles the interaction between itself and its customers [8]. [9] asserts the customer service is an organization's ability to consistently meet the needs and expectations of its customers.

In the corporate world, the emphasis on customer service has been described as a marketing concept of business management. When an organization has adopted the marketing concept, it "moves from a product orientation to a customer orientation". The foundation of the marketing concept is a business philosophy that leaves no doubt in the mind of every employee that customer satisfaction is of primary importance. All energies are directed toward satisfying the customer [10]. As general understanding, ICT

Customer Service Unit/Department will be referred to the people or person who performs the services to the customers.

According to [11], there are six functions of centered customer to make the center being excellent in their services such as monitor service performance; provide self-help facilities; receive problem report and establish ownership; allocate problem to the correct team; establish root cause of problem and resolve it; and inform customer that problem has been resolved.

In the private sector, profit and growth are the outcomes, not goals. Profit and growth are generated by customer loyalty. Loyalty is generated by customer satisfaction. Customer satisfaction is the goal that companies should seek and focus on, because high customer satisfaction, as a matter of course, produces customer loyalty and subsequently profit and growth.

In educational or higher learning environment, there are some issues related to quality service delivery regarding ICT service hierarchy and service delivery architecture. One of the prime quality measures in ICT infrastructure service delivery is service availability. To the customers or the end users, the important thing is to be able to access the end destination, which provides the ICT services such as e-learning materials, online databases, wireless and others. Hence, the service provider is to provide the means of accessibility in whatever way possible taking into consideration the latest technology in end devices.

Availability can be defined in two ways, first the extension of coverage and second, the up time of the services offered. The service accessibility has to be provided at any time (or all the time), anywhere and by whatever means possible (anyhow) [12].

Extending the coverage of ICT service and facilities is a policy of the university. Since the university has targeted that all of the population of the university, including off-campus students and staff can access on line information provided by the university, the ICT plans should incorporate this requirement. The first challenge in providing this coverage is the considerable finance needed to deploy the services. This is followed by determining the right technology and approach to implement. If the planning and design are not done properly, then ultimately the service provider will meet with the situation where services are unavailable (down) for the provided (covered) services most of the time. The rapid change in technology has caused a gap between end users' competency in handling their devices and the technology they adopt. For the service provider, the rapidly changing technology has also impacted the management of the ICT services wherein the limited resources of ICT personnel have to be constantly retrained to ensure their competencies is in pace with technology.

This nature has been characterized by existence of multiple help desks and customer service center, which makes resolution to incidences time consuming, untraceable and impedes improvement. This phenomenon is further compounded by ICT units or department acting in silos especially in resolving incidences and problems. Therefore, to eliminate or decrease these problems, it is important to investigate about the adoption and impact of customer centered service for ICT services in universities. The result of this study can be used to develop future growth of customer service in education perspective and ICT services.

3 Research Aim

The aim of this research is to investigate the ICT services provided for public university community. In term of improving the services, customer centered service is shown as one of the solution that suit to be analyzed. The result of the research can be used to develop future growth of customer service in Public University ICT services. The objectives of the study are first, to identify the status of the adoption of customer centered service for ICT services in public university and second; to identify the impact of the adoption of customer centered service (CSS) for ICT services in public university.

4 Methodology

This study uses interviews and questionnaires for collecting data. The location of this study is at public universities in Malaysia. A set of phone interviews was conducted among 10 public universities in Malaysia. The purpose of the phone interview is to answer the first objective of this study. The structured interview was used to gain information about the adoption of customer centered service in ICT departments of the public university. The questions in the structured interview were validated by pilot test based on its content validity. The respondents are randomly selected from ICT departments of the selected universities. The interview took about 15 to 20 min per call by answering seven questions regarding their centralized customer service. Ten of ICT staff from each university involved in this phone interview session.

Questionnaire has been used to gather information for the second objective which is adapted from [13]. For this stage, Universiti Malaysia Pahang (UMP) has been selected as a case study to investigate the impact of customer centered service for ICT services in public university. The questionnaire has been measured using Cronbach Alpha reliability test during the pilot study and showed the indication of the high level of consistency across scale of 0.85.

The questionnaire has been divided into three (3) parts and using five point Likert Scale (1-Strongly Disagree, 2-Disagree, 3-Neither, 4-Agree, 5-Strongly Agree). The first part is about the service and environment of ICT services of the university. The second part is a about the service and quality towards delivering ICT services and relationship with the centered customer services. The third part is about the impact of the adoption of customer centered service towards the delivering of ICT services in the university.

The questionnaires have been distributed among 70 respondents from University Malaysia Pahang. Forty of them are the customers who are the user of ICT department in UMP and thirty of them are the ICT staffs of ICT department in UMP.

5 Findings

For the purpose of collecting data, the total of ten universities and eighty respondents were directly involved in this study through interview and questionnaires methods. Based on the data collection, about eight (8) of ten (10) public university in Malaysia have been implementing the customer centered service in their organization. Only two (2) universities did not use the customer centered service for ICT services. Besides that, most of the ICT departments in public university classified non-academic, academic staff and student as their customer. From eight (8) university that implement customer centered service, seven (7) are operating their service center within office hours in the weekdays. But only one university operates their service center until 10.00 pm and during weekend.

This summary of phone interview session shows that almost 80% of public university in Malaysia have adopted customer centered service to facilitate the ICT services and facilities in their universities. Furthermore, they also agreed that the customer centered service can reflect their services to the customer and the universities.

The results from descriptive analysis investigated via questionnaires are represented in several tables below. Table 1 below represents the results of service and quality of the ICT services in UMP ICT department whereas Tables 2 and 3 represent the results of two different groups of respondents' perception towards the impact of Customer Centered Services of the ICT services in UMP ICT department. These results are ranked using Friedman test which is used to analyze and ranks the question based on the mean rank level.

Table 1. Descriptive statistics results of service and quality of the ICT services in UMP ICT department.

Rank	Question	Mean
1	The customer service representative is very polite	3.95
2	On-site technical support is knowledgeable and professional	3.87
3	The customer service representative appears knowledgeable and competent	3.85
4	Sufficient information was available to solve my problem	3.85
5	The customer service representative is able to assist and very helpful	3.77
6	The customer service representative can handle issues with courtesy and professionalism	3.77
7	The service always in a best quality	3.72
8	The customer service representative handled my call quickly	3.70
9	The process of getting problem resolved was very quick	3.65
10	My phone call was quickly transferred to the person who could best assist me	3.42

Table 2. Descriptive statistics of users' response towards the adoption of customer centered service (CCS) in UMP ICT department.

Rank	Question	Mean
1	CCS is a medium to improve IT service performance	4.22
2	CCS is important in providing IT services	4.20
3	CCS is medium to understand the IT service needs of the organization	4.15
4	CCS is the main factor to increase the quality of IT services	4.15
5	CCS is a medium to create the relationship between the IT department and the user	4.12
6	CCS can help to increase knowledge in IT	3.97
7	CCS can provide sufficient information about IT facilities in the campus	3.97
8	CCS helps to understand the cause and the solution to the problem	3.92

Table 3. Descriptive statistics of ICT staffs' response towards the adoption of customer centered service (CCS) in UMP ICT department.

Rank	Question	Mean
1	CCS is important in providing IT services	4.63
2	CCS is the main factor to increase the quality of IT services	4.43
3	CCS is a medium to create the relationship between the IT department and the user	4.36
4	CCS can provide sufficient information about IT facilities in the campus	4.30
5	CCS helps to understand the cause and the solution to the problem	4.30
6	CCS is medium to understand the IT service needs of the organization	4.30
7	CCS is a medium to improve IT service performance	4.23
8	CCS can help to increase knowledge in IT	4.16

The overall mean for Table 1 which represents the results of service and quality of the ICT services in UMP ICT department is 3.76. This result which is below than the level of agreement shows that the respondents are perceived unsatisfactory towards the service and quality of the ICT services in UMP ICT department. Furthermore, this study intends to make a comparison between the users' responses and ICT staff responses towards the utilization of centralized customer services at UMP ICT department. Thus, using Friedman test, it shows that, ICT staff perceived (mean 4.34) that they are more influenced by the utilization of customer centered service compared to the users (mean 4.09). Both agreed that customer centered service contribute to the positive impact for managing and facilitating all the problems and matters regarding the ICT services. The customer service representatives are the primary contact point between the ICT department and customers in providing information, problems solving and sharing the knowledge.

6   Conclusions

This study shows that majority of public university in Malaysia has adopted customer centered service for ICT services in the university. Based on the analysis, most of the operation hours for the customer service are similar to the office operation hour which is between 8.00 am to 5.00 pm on weekdays.

Based on the analysis, the lowest rank of the service and quality is about the effectiveness in answering phone call. Thus, to improve call management of the center, they can provide more than one general line. They can also find the best alternative to implement the telephony system for the university. The second lowest of the rank is the resolution time of the problem. This issue can be solved by giving more training to the customer service staff and increase their awareness about the important of timely resolution time. Apparently, all of these findings give a hint that the service and quality of the customer centered service in public universities need to be improved. The ICT department should take into consideration about this matter. It might be related to the poor ability of technical skills or lack of staff.

Beside to these two main issues, the customer service should consider other matters such as the representative appearance, communication skills, knowledge, competency and others. This study suggests that the quality of service can be a measurement to evaluate the performance of ICT department regarding the satisfaction of the customer especially the student. This suggestion also supported by [14].

There are several impacts of the adoption of customer centered service for ICT services that can be highlighted from this study. This study elicit that the customer centered service is an important component in providing the ICT services to the university. The impacts of the adoption of customer centered service are such as increase the quality of IT services to the university and increase knowledge in IT among their customers. Hence, customer centered service will act as a medium to improve IT service performance and understand the IT services needs of the organization by providing sufficient information about IT services and facilities and technical support to the campus citizen.

References

1. Christopher, M.: Logistics and Supply Chain Management, 5th edn. Prentice Hall, New York (2016)
2. Clarke, T.: The knowledge economy. Educ. Train. **43**(1), 189–196 (2001)
3. Begusic, D., Rozic, N., Dujmic, H.: Development of the communication/information infrastructure at the academic institution. Comput. Commun. **26**(5), 472–476 (2003)
4. Wheatcroft, P.: World Class IT Service Delivery. The British Computer Society, Swindon (2007)
5. Mark, L.: Enterprise Architecture at Work: Modelling, Communication and Analysis. Springer, Berlin (2017)
6. Kettinger, W., Lee, C.: Perceived service quality and user satisfaction with the information services function. Decis. Sci. **25**(6), 737–766 (1994)
7. Wiggers, P., Kok, H., De Boer-de Wit, M.: IT Performance Management. Computer Weekly (2004)
8. Jenny, H., Frances, D.: Managing Customer Service. Gower Publishing Ltd., Brookfield (1998)
9. Miao, H., Wang Bassham, W.: Embracing customer service in libraries. Libr. Manag. **28**(1), 53–61 (2006)
10. Kaliski, B.: Ethics in Management. Encyclopedia of Business and Finance, 2nd edn. New Macmillan, New York (2006)
11. Trigger, J., Harrison, M.: Six steps to excellent customer service. BT Technol. J. **24**(1), 117–126 (2006)
12. Chucks, D., Sussan, U., Darlina, C.: Availability and accessibility of ICT in the provision of information resources to undergraduate students in Babcock University Library. Res. Humanit. Soc. Sci. **4**(14), 29–34 (2014)
13. John, W.M., Michael, J.T., Michael, J.K.: Development and validation of the customer-centered behavior measure. Serv. Ind. J. **34**(13), 1075–1091 (2014)
14. Rezaei, A., Çelik, T., Baalousha, Y.: Performance measurement in a quality management system. Scientia Iranica **18**(3), 745–752 (2011)

The Implementation of Gamification in Massive Open Online Courses (MOOC) Platform

Nur Fatihah Abu Bakar[✉], Ahmad Fadhil Yusof, Noorminshah A. Iahad,
and Norasnita Ahmad

Faculty of Computing, Universiti Teknologi Malaysia, Johor Bahru, Johor, Malaysia
nfatihah.ab@gmail.com

Abstract. The development of Massive Open Online Course (MOOC) platform
has opened more opportunities for students around the world to learn and many
education institutions have taken up this initiative in their effort to widen target
students scope. However, MOOC faces a huge challenge whereby its students'
engagement rate is decreasing. Implementing gamification component in MOOC
is said to be beneficial in engaging students, hence providing a solution to MOOC
main challenge. Therefore, the purpose of this study is to present the implementation of gamification specifically in MOOC platform. This ongoing research
features review of MOOC and gamification, mapping of gamification elements
in MOOC, as well as design of the prototype.

Keywords: Gamification · MOOC · Implementation · Rewards · Design
Prototype

1 Introduction

The development of Massive Open Online Course (MOOC) platform has been seen as
a huge potential for the education field, given its advantage to reach wider audience from
various fields. MOOC is different from the e-learning and it is known for its openness
and massiveness [1, 2]. MOOC was originally created in 2008 and is still expanding as
of today. Examples of popular MOOC platforms include Coursera, UdaCity and edX
[1]. Despite displaying effective results over its establishment, many MOOC platforms
have failed to keep their students motivated and endure the course they enrolled for until
the end [2–5].

Gamification uses elements in games to reach goals or in other words, as motivators.
The purpose of gamification, irrespective of where it is applied to is still the same, that
is to increase motivation, learning or to solve problems [5–7]. Progress tracking serves
as guidance for students to see their progress in that particular course towards the
learning goal. There are usually several goals to be met, during the course duration and
at the end of the course. By implementing gamification in MOOC, study modules are
released in stages, either by deadline or unlock able activities and this would motivate
students to keep checking their course progress [6, 7]. On the other hand, the reward
system introduced allows students to collect points and digital badges. These points are

N. Abdullah et al. (Eds.): i-USEr 2018, CCIS 886, pp. 183–193, 2018.
https://doi.org/10.1007/978-981-13-1628-9_17

displayed in a leaderboard and would provide a sense of competitiveness between students and their online course mates [6–8].

2   Methodologies

After initial problem background review, the researcher proceeds to do a thorough literature review using 40 journals retrieved from reliable databases including Scopus, IEEE, ScienceDirect and SpringerLink. Most journals referred to and being reviewed was published between 2008 and 2016. Keywords used to search for related papers include "Gamification", "MOOC" and "Gamification in MOOC". The review began by finding the problems regarding MOOC, followed by solution to the related problems, which then led to gamification implementation in MOOC. To further understand the usage of MOOC and how it can be improved, the researcher reviewed several MOOC platforms, including Coursera, edX, Udacity and OpenLearning. Then, the researcher acquires experts' validation for suitable gamification elements to be implemented in MOOC. Experts' validation is also acquired for the prototype development.

3   Massive Open Online Courses (MOOC)

MOOC is a free or a low-cost online class that is available to anyone from different backgrounds, given that they have an Internet access. In MOOC, lectures consist of short videos with online tests and forums where students and lecturers are able to communicate with each other [8, 9]. Basically, any form of communication to and from lecturers to students that were usually done in a conventional classroom way, is now being delivered via the internet in MOOC. Contents in MOOC include 10–15 min video lecture, computerized tests that may or may not be segmented according to level of difficulty and online interaction between lecturers and students. Although most MOOC platforms have the standard online tests with multiple-choice answers, which are usually graded automatically, there is other form of MOOC platforms where students have to do group assignment in order to be graded [9–11]. Despite displaying effective results over its establishment, many MOOC platforms have failed to keep their students motivated and endure the course they enrolled for until the end. The major disadvantage of MOOC is the environment of MOOC that treats all students equally, regardless of their knowledge level. Hence, it might be difficult for students with low knowledge level to learn and catch up with the rest [2, 3]. Even though MOOC is packed with multimedia aid such as video lectures, computerized evaluation and energetic participation from other students, the registration-to-completion ratio is still comparatively low. Most students decide to leave the course as soon as they register for it [12–14]. From statistic perspective, MOOCs have a mean of completion rate of less than 10%. Among plausible causes include the decrease of students' interest, which will lead to their disappointment in the course. This may be due to how the course content is created and executed within the MOOC platform. It is also reported that only 5-10% of the students managed to pass and complete the course despite only needing a passing rate of 60%. These numbers may be due to the fact that some students only join the MOOC for information and are not interested to take the tests given. It can also be contributed to the decline of students' motivation caused by lengthy and boring course content. Although the former cause is not within MOOC's control as it is up to students, the latter can be addressed by making the course more interesting and elevating the students' motivation level [15–17].

4   Gamification in MOOC

The implementation of gamification in MOOC is deemed as the most suitable approach to achieve the objective of retaining students' enrollment in MOOC and eventually increasing courses' completion rate [18, 19]. Gamification can be defined as "the application of gaming metaphors to real life tasks to influence behavior, improve motivation and enhance engagement" [6]. It is equal to integrating game-based techniques and mechanics, which is done to make the contents and activities more interesting thereby engage students to keep coming back to complete the course [14]. In spite of the fact that there is no particular meaning of gamification in terms of learning or particularly MOOC, MOOC with gamification segment can be comprehended as the reconciliation of amusement components, for example, computerized identifications and point in educational setting of MOOC. Games have remunerated frameworks where users get rewards for accomplishing an objective or overcoming a deterrent. Examples include points and badges [10]. SAPS (Status, Access, Power and Stuff) are the term used to differentiate various types of rewards available [20, 21]. Students are given reward after they successfully complete a task, which is also regarded as the course's objective milestone for the students in term of course's knowledge level. The instructors or lecturers usually set a few staged learning goals at the beginning of the course, during the course and at the end of the course, where they serve as time pressure for students. Students may see their progress through the progress-tracking bar [21, 22]. Besides points, students may acquire digital badges or tokens throughout the course. Accomplishments that qualify for digital badges include tasks completion, active participation and skill mastery [22, 23]. These digital badges are displayed as icons or logos in MOOC and can be collected throughout the course.

Identifying students' preference based on audience analysis is one of the steps needed in order to implement gamification in MOOC. Audience analysis is a crucial part of gamification because it can identify all motivational aspects needed and the students' knowledge base. Occasionally, gamification in MOOC involves group or team assignment; hence the students' tendencies towards competition and cooperation should be identified. Before creating the course content for MOOC, lecturers are advised to find as much information as he can to ensure smooth learning process for all students [23, 34]. Scope, rewards, game objectives and structure can be identified via distribution of questionnaires to intended audience. Depending on whether it is used for education or business, there are several gamification approaches, including voluntary participation for business models [24–26]. The purpose of gamification in education is for grading purpose where students are compulsory to involve in gamified activities. Game leveling is created to signify students' completion within the course [27–29].

Upon recognizing how gamification can improve students' motivation level while engaging with the courses, well-known MOOC platforms such as Udacity, edX and Coursera started to implement reward system as the gamification component within their platform. However, only a few courses are implemented with the gamification component [30–33]. The feeling of fun and flow experience while using MOOC will result in higher time spent in MOOC, thus this gamification design should be made a priority when it is implemented in MOOC platforms. Gamification is reported to have big potential in elevating students' learning experience while using MOOC [34–37]. To foster human nature that feels the need to be in a community, the implementation of social component as part of the gamification element in MOOC is also necessary. This will encourage them to help each other and gain more understanding in the process [38]. To implement gamification in MOOC platforms, instructors or lecturers have to take into account several things including suitable activities and types of reward. As per the gamification design factors for MOOC platforms, there are three types of interactivity, including [39, 40]:

(a) Learner–content interaction
(b) Learner–learner interaction
(c) Learner–instructor interaction.

5   Prototype Design

This section discusses design of the prototype that includes suitable gamification elements based on literature review. Initial prototype will be developed using Gametize.com. Eventually the prototype will be embedded into the real MOOC when it is rolled out. The design consists of two perspectives, which are users or students and administrators or lecturers. Basically, the administrator is able to control all features in the MOOC, including rewarding students based on their accomplishment during the course (see Fig. 1). Administrators are able to create content and time the release of the topics to students. They can also put deadlines to challenges to give a sense of time pressure. On the other hand, students are required to complete course materials and challenges to earn points and badges. Students are able to discuss with fellow students throughout the course and votes other students' challenges completion (See Fig. 2).

5.1   Prototype Modules

The researcher develops a few modules for the purpose of the MOOC prototype with embedded gamification elements. Figures 1 and 2 show the flow of the system for both administrators or lecturers and students. Modules developed for both actors are listed as the following.

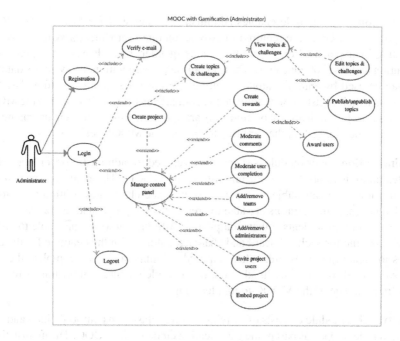

Fig. 1. Administrator control.

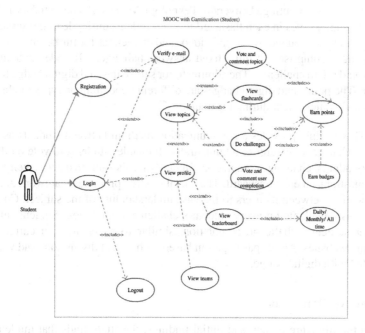

Fig. 2. Students' activity diagram.

Registration. This module enables administrators and students as first time MOOC users to register. Users are required to provide unique username, password as well as providing their personal details such as name, gender, birth date, address, education institution and level of education. These details are stored within the system's database and can be used by administrators for future reference. Users are able to update their details once their registration is activated via e-mail verification. To login to the MOOC system, users (administrators or students) are required to key in their username and password. Once logged in, they are free to explore the MOOC features.

Administration. This module is specially developed for administrators or lecturers. It enables administrators to control all features in MOOC. The control panel enables administrators to create subjects, topics, activities and challenges. Within these topics and challenges, administrators are able to create specific points and digital badges that will be awarded to students if they complete it. Administrators are also able to control the release time for each flashcard and challenge, along with the deadline for the challenges to create time pressure. When required, administrators can complete the challenges on behalf of students. In addition, this module enables administrators to invite users from outside of the MOOC to join learning.

Activity. This module consists of activities such as flashcards, tutorial video and challenges. It is developed as part of the gamification elements in MOOC. The main activity, which is flashcard, is based on syllabus from System Analysis and Development subject from Faculty of Computing, Universiti Teknologi Malaysia. The syllabus is broken down into simpler notes in each flashcard to ease students during learning session. The flashcards are accompanied by tutorial videos and challenges for further understanding. The challenges comprised of quiz, fixed answer challenge, QR code challenge, poll challenge and photo challenge. The administrator sets points and digital badge for every challenge. The points and digital badges are different depending on types of challenges and students' achievement during the course.

Social. This module provides a communication medium between students as well as between students and lecturer or administrator. It enables students to vote on the topic and other students' challenge completion. Students are also able to discuss their opinions and ask questions on each flashcard. The social module promotes teamwork and active communication between its users to increase understanding of the subject. Comments section is also available on every student's challenge completion. Students may also vote other students' challenge completion, similar to an element in current social networking websites. Active participation based on frequent discussions and votes may be awarded with digital badge.

5.2 Prototype Development

Based on the literature review and initial findings, the study finds that implementing gamification elements in MOOC leads to better learning performance. The study determines the gamification elements that are suitable to be implemented in MOOC, which are, activities, levels, badges, points, leaderboard and peer discussion. However, for the developed prototype, the researcher decided to change peer discussion method from forum to comments and votes section. This is due to constraint by the development tool, as well as providing more convenience to communicate between students. Levels could not be implemented as well due to development tool constraint. The prototype was developed using a free gamification development software named Gametize (See Fig. 3). Using Gametize, the researcher managed to develop a prototype that includes all suitable elements for MOOC.

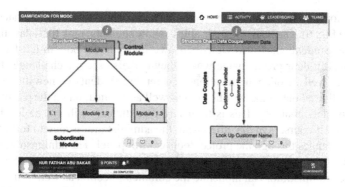

Fig. 3. Flashcards (activity)

There are five digital badges to be earned throughout the topic in this prototype. Digital badges cause students to be more motivated to study. These badges are listed under unlock able achievements. Achievements are virtual items that users can unlock when they reach certain milestones in the topic. These badges may be acquired by completing challenges (See Fig. 4). They include Beginner badge, Pioneer badge, Superstar Badge, Think Machine badge and Photogenic badge (See Fig. 5).

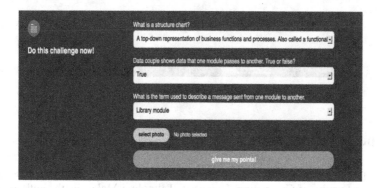

Fig. 4. Challenge

Fig. 5. Digital badges

This prototype also includes a leaderboard based on the points accumulated by each student (See Fig. 6). The leaderboard is able to show students' rank for today, this month and all-time. Students may also view their own points at the bottom left-hand side of the page, nearby their profile name where they can also see the challenges they have completed as well as other notifications. To remind students of new flashcards, the prototype will send out e-mail notification as well as notification on the prototype itself informing of new contents. This is to ensure that students will not be left behind in completing their course. On the other hand, the administrator is able to form teams for the topic challenges through the project tools control panel. The administrator can also award bonus points to students. For example, if they have done well for all challenges. Besides, the administrator can moderate the comments section as well as user completions where inappropriate completions can be removed while excellent completions may be rewarded with extra points.

Fig. 6. Leaderboard.

6   Experts Validation

Since the prototype will be developed based on System Analysis and Design subject, a course from Faculty of Computing, Universiti Teknologi Malaysia, the authors gained validation on the design from two experts. The experts are lecturers who have been teaching the course since 2009 for both undergraduate and postgraduate students. Interview with the experts consists of questions regarding suitable gamification elements to be implemented in MOOC and the overall flow of the design for the prototype. The authors listed activities such as flashcards, rewards such as points and badges and social elements as the gamification elements. Both experts agreed that these elements are suitable for the intended MOOC, provided that the content must be aligned with the course syllabus, taking note of suitable challenges for the course. The experts also agreed that the implementation of rewards would make learning more interesting, as well as incorporating social elements where students can communicate with fellow students and the lecturers. The feature that enables lecturers to control type of rewards and time of rewards is also a key element, whereby it would enable lecturers to award points or badges to students with excellent participation or task completion.

7   Conclusions

The decreasing rate of students' engagement while using MOOC has been seen as an opportunity to explore gamification field. Gamification should be implemented in MOOC according to the target audience or content for it to be effective. It should also have easy navigation for both students and lecturers to explore. Developing the prototype based on the design and finally deploying it into the real MOOC will be further developed in this ongoing research.

References

1. Al-Qahtani, A.A.Y., Higgins, S.E.: Effects of traditional, blended and e-learning on students' achievement in higher education. J. Comput. Assist. Learn. **29**(3), 220–234 (2013). https://doi.org/10.1111/j.1365-2729.2012.00490.x
2. Armier, D.D., Shepherd, C.E., Skrabut, S.: Using game elements to increase student engagement in course assignments. Coll. Teach. **64**(2), 64–72 (2016). https://doi.org/10.1080/87567555.2015.1094439
3. Barak, M., Watted, A., Haick, H.: Motivation to learn in massive open online courses: examining aspects of language and social engagement. Comput. Educ. **94**, 49–60 (2016). https://doi.org/10.1016/j.compedu.2015.11.010
4. Bíró, G.I.: Didactics 2.0: a pedagogical analysis of gamification theory from a comparative perspective with a special view to the components of learning. Proc. – Soc. Behav. Sci. **141**, 148–151 (2014). https://doi.org/10.1016/j.sbspro.2014.05.027
5. Blohm, I., Jan, P., Leimeister, M.: Massive open online courses. Bus. Inf. Syst. Eng. **6**, 111–114 (2014). https://doi.org/10.1007/s12599-014-0313-9
6. Brophy, J.: Motivating Students to Learn, 2nd edn. Erlbaum, Mahwah (2004)
7. Brigham, T.J.: An introduction to gamification: adding game elements for engagement. Med. Ref. Serv. Q. **34**(4), 471–480 (2015). https://doi.org/10.1080/02763869.2015.1082385
8. Buckley, P., Doyle, E.: Gamification and student motivation. Interact. Learn. Environ. **24**, 1–14 (2014). https://doi.org/10.1080/10494820.2014.964263
9. Chang, J., Wei, H.: Exploring engaging gamification mechanics in massive online open courses. J. Educ. Technol. Soc. **19**, 177–203 (2016)
10. Chauhan, J.: Enhancing MOOC with augmented reality, adaptive learning and gamification, pp. 348–353 (2015)
11. Clarà, M., Barberà, E.: Learning online: massive open online courses (MOOCs), connectivism, and cultural psychology, **7919** (2016). http://doi.org/10.1080/01587919.2013.770428

12. Collazos, C.A., Cauca, U., González, C.S., García, R.: Computer supported collaborative MOOCS: CSCM (2014)
13. Coryell, J.E., Chlup, D.T.: Implementing e-learning components with adult English language learners: vital factors and lessons learned. Comput. Assist. Lang. Learn. 20(3), 263–278 (2007). https://doi.org/10.1080/09588220701489333
14. Cox, M.J.: Formal to informal learning with IT: research challenges and issues for e-learning. J. Comput. Assist. Learn. 29(1), 85–105 (2013). https://doi.org/10.1111/j.1365-2729.2012.00483.x
15. Danforth, L.: Gamification and libraries. Libr. J. 136(3), 84 (2011)
16. De Smet, C., Schellens, T., De Wever, B., Brandt-Pomares, P., Valcke, M.: The design and implementation of learning paths in a learning management system. Interact. Learn. Environ. 4820, 1–21 (2014). https://doi.org/10.1080/10494820.2014.951059. (June 2015)
17. De-Marcos, L., Garcia-Lopez, E., Garcia-Cabot, A.: On the effectiveness of game-like and social approaches in learning: comparing educational gaming, gamification & social networking. Comput. Educ. 95, 99–113 (2015). https://doi.org/10.1016/j.compedu.2015.12.008
18. Endut, A., Isa, P.M., Rahayu, S., Aziz, A., Nor, M., Jono, H.H., Aziz, A.A.: E-learning for Universiti Teknologi MARA Malaysia (UiTM): campus wide implementation and accomplishments. Proc. – Soc. Behav. Sci. 67(3), 26–35 (2012). https://doi.org/10.1016/j.sbspro.2012.11.304
19. Faghihi, U., Brautigam, A., Jorgenson, K., Martin, D., Brown, A., Measures, E., Maldonado-Bouchard, S.: How gamification applies for educational purpose specially with college algebra. Proc. Comput. Sci. 41, 182–187 (2014). https://doi.org/10.1016/j.procs.2014.11.102
20. Hew, K.F., Cheung, W.S.: Students' and instructors' use of massive open online courses (MOOCs): motivations and challenges. Educ. Res. Rev. 12, 45–58 (2014). https://doi.org/10.1016/j.edurev.2014.05.001
21. Gamage, D., Perera, I., Fernando, S.: A framework to analyze effectiveness of e-learning in MOOC: learners perspective, pp. 236–241 (2015)
22. Gené, O.B., Nuñez, M.M.: Gamification in MOOC: challenges, opportunities and proposals for advancing MOOC model (n.d.)
23. Grünewald, F., Meinel, C., Totschnig, M., Willems, C.: Designing MOOCs for the support of multiple learning styles. In: Hernández-Leo, D., Ley, T., Klamma, R., Harrer, A. (eds.) EC-TEL 2013. LNCS, vol. 8095, pp. 371–382. Springer, Heidelberg (2013). https://doi.org/10.1007/978-3-642-40814-4_29
24. Hamari, J., Shernoff, D.J., Rowe, E., Coller, B., Asbell-Clarke, J., Edwards, T.: Challenging games help students learn: an empirical study on engagement, flow and immersion in game-based learning. Comput. Hum. Behav. 54, 170–179 (2016). https://doi.org/10.1016/j.chb.2015.07.045
25. Lebron, D., Shahriar, H.: Comparing MOOC-based platforms: reflection on pedagogical support, framework and learning analytics. In: 2015 International Conference on Collaboration Technologies and Systems (CTS). https://doi.org/10.1109/cts.2015.7210417
26. Hew, K.F., Huang, B., Chu, K.W.S., Chiu, D.K.W.: Engaging Asian students through game mechanics: findings from two experiment studies. Comput. Educ. 92–93, 221–236 (2016). https://doi.org/10.1016/j.compedu.2015.10.010
27. Lai, H.F.: Determining the sustainability of virtual learning communities in e-learning platform. In: 5th International Conference on Computer Science and Education, Final Program and Book of Abstracts, ICCSE 2010, pp. 1581–1586 (2010). http://doi.org/10.1109/ICCSE.2010.5593772
28. Hoy, M.B.: MOOCs 101: an introduction to massive open online courses. Med. Ref. Serv. Q. 33, 85–91 (2016). https://doi.org/10.1080/02763869.2014.866490

29. Hurst, E.J.: Digital badges: beyond learning incentives. J. Electron. Resour. Med. Libr. **12**(3), 182–189 (2015). https://doi.org/10.1080/15424065.2015.1065661
30. Imazeki, J., Imazeki, J.: Bring-your-own-device: turning cell phones into forces for good. J. Econ. Educ. **45**, 240–250 (2016)
31. Jäntschi, L., Bolboacă, S.D., Marta, M.M., Laszlo, A.: E-learning and e-evaluation: a case study. In: 2008 Conference on Human System Interaction, HSI 2008, pp. 840–845 (2008). http://doi.org/10.1109/HSI.2008.4581552
32. Jayasinghe, U., Dharmaratne, A.: Game based learning vs. gamification from the higher education students' perspective. In: International Conference on Teaching, Assessment and Learning for Engineering, pp. 683–688, August 2013. http://doi.org/10.1109/TALE.2013.6654524
33. Kelleher, J.: Current State of Massive Open Online Courses in Malaysia, 23 October 2015. http://www.opengovasia.com/articles/6606-current-state-of-massive-open-online-courses-in-malaysia. Accessed 13 Apr 2017
34. Khalid, S.U., Basharat, A., Shahid, A.A., Hassan, S.: An adaptive e-learning framework to supporting new ways of teaching and learning. In: International Conference on Information and Communication Technologies, ICICT 2009, pp. 300–306 (2009). http://doi.org/10.1109/ICICT.2009.5267175
35. King, C., Doherty, K., Kelder, J., Mcinerney, F., Walls, J., Robinson, A., Vickers, J.: "Fit for Purpose": a cohort-centric approach to MOOC design. Int. J. Educ. Technol. High. Educ. **11**(3), 108–121 (2014). Open Educational Resources Initiatives in Oceania
36. De Langen, F., Van Den Bosch, H.: Massive Open Online Courses: disruptive innovations or disturbing inventions? **513** (2016). http://doi.org/10.1080/02680513.2013.870882
37. Landers, R.N.: Developing a theory of gamified learning: linking serious games and gamification of learning. Simul. Gaming **45**(6), 752–768 (2014). https://doi.org/10.1177/1046878114563660
38. Landers, R.N., Armstrong, M.B.: Enhancing instructional outcomes with gamification: an empirical test of the technology-enhanced training effectiveness model. Comput. Hum. Behav. 1–9 (2014). http://doi.org/10.1016/j.chb.2015.07.031
39. Laubersheimer, J., Ryan, D., Champaign, J.: InfoSkills2Go: using badges and gamification to teach information literacy skills and concepts to college-bound high school students. J. Libr. Adm. **56**, 1–15 (2016). https://doi.org/10.1080/01930826.2015.1123588
40. Leaning, M.: A study of the use of games and gamification to enhance student engagement, experience and achievement on a theory-based course of an undergraduate media degree. J. Med. Pract. **16**(2), 155–170 (2015). https://doi.org/10.1080/14682753.2015.1041807

Data Analysis on the Performance of Technology Sector in Malaysia with Entropy-TOPSIS Model

Lam Weng Siew[1,2,3(✉)], Lam Weng Hoe[1,2,3], and Liew Kah Fai[1,3]

[1] Department of Physical and Mathematical Science, Faculty of Science,
Universiti Tunku Abdul Rahman, Kampar Campus, Jalan Universiti,
Bandar Barat, 31900 Kampar, Perak, Malaysia
lamws@utar.edu.my
[2] Centre for Business and Management, Universiti Tunku Abdul Rahman,
Kampar Campus, Jalan Universiti, Bandar Barat,
31900 Kampar, Perak, Malaysia
[3] Centre for Mathematical Sciences, Universiti Tunku Abdul Rahman,
Kampar Campus, Jalan Universiti, Bandar Barat,
31900 Kampar, Perak, Malaysia

Abstract. Technology sector plays an important role in a country since the development of the technology can affect the reputation of the country. The financial performance of the technology companies is important because they represent the overall performance of technology sector in Malaysia. The objective of this study is to propose a conceptual framework to evaluate, rank and compare the financial performance of the companies from the technology sector based in Malaysia using Entropy-Technique for Order of Preference by Similarity to Ideal Solution model. The data analysis on the performance of the companies is assessed by current ratio, debt to assets ratio, debt to equity ratio, earnings per share, return on asset and return on equity. The results of this study show that MPI, GTRONIC, KESM and ECS are ranked as the top four technology companies in Malaysia. This study is significant because it helps to determine the financial performance of the companies from the technology sector in Malaysia with the proposed conceptual framework based on entropy-TOPSIS model.

Keywords: Financial performance · Multi-criteria decision making
Conceptual framework · Ranking

1 Introduction

Technology sector plays an extremely important role in the development of the country. Nowadays, it is obvious that more modern organizations are largely depending on the technology for their daily business operations. Development of the technology is an ongoing process and also a challenging task for every country that may give some competitive advantages. However, development of advanced technology is a recurring decision that faced by every modern organization in this fast-paced world.

© Springer Nature Singapore Pte Ltd. 2018
N. Abdullah et al. (Eds.): i-USEr 2018, CCIS 886, pp. 194–203, 2018.
https://doi.org/10.1007/978-981-13-1628-9_18

The past studies focus on the operational performance of technology and manufacturing companies. The analysis on the financial performance of the companies is usually ignored. However, the analysis on the financial performance is crucial to the companies as it can clearly reflect the overall performance of the companies. Moreover, the study on the companies' financial performance is important to ensure the sustainability and development of the company in long-term. Therefore, the analysis on the companies' financial performance should be investigated. Therefore, this paper aims to propose a conceptual framework to measure the listed technology companies' financial performance in Malaysia with Entropy-TOPSIS model. TOPSIS is decision making model which helps to solve multi-criteria decision making problem (MCDM) [1–3]. Entropy weight method is proposed by Shannon [4] in assigning the weight for each decision criterion based on the data analysis and amount of information obtained.

TOPSIS model has been widely applied in the field of automobile [5], bank [6, 7], coal mines [8], financial company [9, 10], information system selection [11], oil and gas [12], power companies [13], power grid enterprise [14], suppliers [15, 16], site selection [17] and mobile network operator selection [18]. The objective of this paper is to propose a conceptual framework to measure, rank and compare the technology companies' financial performance in Malaysia with Entropy-TOPSIS model. The rest of the paper is organized as follows. Section 2 discusses about the data and methodology of the study. Then, the next section presents the empirical results of this study. Finally, conclusion is drawn in the last Sect. 4.

2   Data and Methodology

2.1   Conceptual Framework

Table 1 presents the proposed conceptual framework to evaluate the technology sector companies' financial performance in Malaysia with Entropy-TOPSIS model.

Table 1 shows the conceptual framework in this study which consists of the main objective, decision criteria and decision alternatives for the evaluation on the technology companies' financial performance in Malaysia. As shown in Table 1, the decision criteria such as CR, DAR, DER, EPS, ROA and ROE are considered in this

Table 1. Proposed conceptual framework.

Level	
Objective	Evaluation on the technology companies' financial performance
Decision criteria	Current ratio (CR)
	Debt to assets ratio (DAR)
	Debt to equity ratio (DER)
	Earnings per share (EPS)
	Return on asset (ROA)
	Return on equity (ROE)

(*continued*)

Table 1. (*continued*)

Level	
Decision alternatives	AMTEL
	CENSOF
	CUSCAPI
	DIGISTA
	ECS
	EFORCE
	ELSOFT
	GRANFLO
	GTRONIC
	INARI
	JCY
	KESM
	MPI
	NOTION
	PANPAGE
	UNISEM
	VITROX
	WILLOW

study [19–21]. The listed technology sector companies in Malaysia stock market is investigated in this study and their data is obtained from the technology companies' annual report from year 2012 until 2016 [22].

Based on the past study, the six decision criteria such as CR, DAR, DER, EPS, ROA and ROE are considered in this study [23–27]. In this study, the decision criteria such as CR, EPS, ROA and ROE are needed to be maximized in order to identify the best ideal alternatives. On the other hand, the decision criteria such as DAR and DER are needed to be minimized.

2.2   Entropy-TOPSIS

Multi-criteria decision making (MCDM) problem involves decision analysis on different alternatives based on multiple criteria [28–30]. TOPSIS model is a decision tool which helps to solve MCDM problem [1, 2]. The major advantage of the TOPSIS model is to rank the alternatives comprehensively based on the separation distance between each alternative and the positive ideal solution (PIS) as well as the negative ideal solution (NIS). The NIS comprises all worst values attainable from the criteria. On the other hand, the PIS consist of all best values attainable from the criteria. The best alternative selection would be the one that is farthest from the NIS and nearest to the PIS.

In this study, Entropy-TOPSIS model involves the following 10 steps based on the past data-driven data analysis [1].

Step 1: Determination of weight of the decision criteria via entropy weight method. Compute the proportion "p_{ij}" of index value of alternative m under criteria n.

$$p_{ij} = \frac{x_{ij}}{\sum\limits_{i=1}^{m} x_{ij}}, \ i = 1, 2, \ldots, m, \ j = 1, 2, \ldots, n \tag{1}$$

Step 2: Computation of the entropy "e_j" of alternative m.

$$e_j = -k \sum\limits_{i=1}^{m} p_{ij} \cdot \ln(p_{ij}), \ j = 1, 2, \ldots, n \tag{2}$$

Where

$$k = \frac{1}{\ln(m)}$$

Step 3: Computation of the entropy weight "w_j" of alternative m.

$$w_j = \frac{1 - e_j}{\sum\limits_{j=1}^{n} (1 - e_j)}; \ j = 1, 2, \ldots, n \tag{3}$$

Step 4: Establish the decision matrix $((x_{ij})_{m \times n})$:
A $m \times n$ decision matrix is formed. m refers to the alternatives and n refers to the criteria.

Step 5: Calculate a normalized decision matrix:
Normalization method is used to form a normalized decision matrix $R = (r_{ij})_{m \times n}$.

$$r_{ij} = \frac{x_{ij}}{\sqrt{\sum\limits_{i=1}^{m} x_{ij}^2}}, \ i = 1, 2, \ldots, m, \ j = 1, 2, \ldots, n \tag{4}$$

Step 6: Determine the weighted decision matrix (T):
The weighted normalized decision matrix is formed.

$$T = (t_{ij})_{m \times n} = (w_j r_{ij})_{m \times n}, \ i = 1, 2, \ldots, m \tag{5}$$

Step 7: Identify the positive ideal solution (PIS) and negative ideal solution (NIS):

$$\begin{aligned} \text{PIS} = \{ &<\min(t_{ij}|i = 1, 2, \ldots, m)|j \in J_- >, \\ &<\max(t_{ij}|i = 1, 2, \ldots, m)|j \in J_+ > \} \equiv \{t_{bj}|j = 1, 2, \ldots, n\}, \end{aligned} \tag{6}$$

$$\begin{aligned} \text{NIS} = \{ &<\max(t_{ij}|i = 1, 2, \ldots, m)|j \in J_- >, \\ &<\min(t_{ij}|i = 1, 2, \ldots, m)|j \in J_+ > \} \equiv \{t_{wj}|j = 1, 2, \ldots, n\}, \end{aligned} \tag{7}$$

where J_+ is associated with the positive impact criteria and J_- is associated with the negative impact criteria.

Step 8: Calculate the separation distance of each alternative from the PIS and NIS:

$$d_{ib} = \sqrt{\sum_{j=1}^{n} (t_{ij} - t_{bj})^2}, \; i = 1, 2, \ldots, m \tag{8}$$

$$d_{iw} = \sqrt{\sum_{j=1}^{n} (t_{ij} - t_{wj})^2}, \; i = 1, 2, \ldots, m \tag{9}$$

Step 9: Measure the relative closeness to the ideal solution (s_{iw}):
Calculate the relative closeness to the ideal solution (s_{iw}).

$$s_{iw} = \frac{d_{iw}}{d_{ib} + d_{iw}}, \; 0 \leq s_{iw} \leq 1, \; i = 1, 2, \ldots, m \tag{10}$$

Step 10: Rank all the decision alternatives in descending order according to the s_{iw} and select the best decision alternative with the largest s_{iw}. The decision alternative that has the closest distance to the PIS and farthest from the NIS is the best alternative.

3 Empirical Results

Figure 1 shows the weights of all decision criteria on the technology companies' financial performance evaluation in Malaysia.

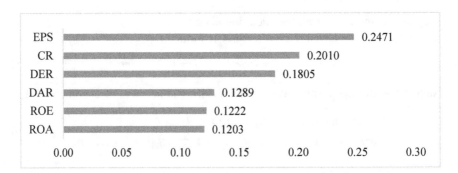

Fig. 1. Weights of financial ratios on the technology companies' financial performance evaluation in Malaysia.

As presented in Fig. 1, the weights of financial ratios on the technology companies' financial performance evaluation in Malaysia are EPS (0.2471) followed by CR (0.2010), DER (0.1805), DAR (0.1289), ROE (0.1222) and lastly ROA (0.1203). This implies that EPS, CR and DER are the most important financial ratios on the technology companies' financial performance evaluation in Malaysia.

The PIS and NIS for each decision criterion are determined by using the Eqs. (6) and (7) respectively. Figure 2 shows the PIS and NIS for each decision criterion.

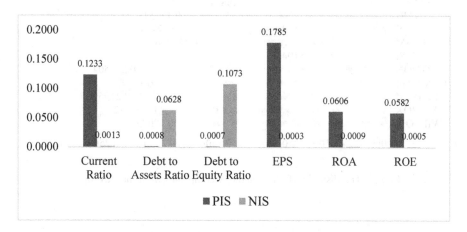

Fig. 2. The PIS and NIS for each decision criterion.

As shown in Fig. 2, the PIS that determined by the Entropy-TOPSIS model for CR, DAR, DER, EPS, ROA and ROE is 0.1233, 0.0008, 0.0007, 0.1785, 0.0606 and 0.0582 respectively. On the other hand, the NIS for CR, DAR, DER, EPS, ROA and ROE is 0.0013, 0.0628, 0.1073, 0.0003, 0.0009 and 0.0005 respectively.

The distance of all decision alternatives from the PIS (d_{ib}) and the distance of all decision alternatives from the NIS (d_{iw}) are calculated by using the Eqs. (8) and (**9**) respectively. Figure 3 presents the distance of all decision alternatives from the PIS (d_{ib}).

Based on Fig. 3, the distance of the technology companies from the PIS (d_{ib}) is determined by comparing the decision criteria of the company with the PIS. MPI has the least distance from the PIS among the other technology companies. This indicates that MPI is closed to the PIS. On the other hand, CENSOF shows the longest distance from the PIS with a value of 0.254091.

Figure 4 presents the distance of all decision alternatives from the NIS (d_{iw}).

As presented in Fig. 4, the distance of technology companies from the NIS (d_{ib}) is determined by comparing the decision criteria of the company with the NIS. CENSOF shows the shortest distance from the NIS with a value of 0.016599. This indicates that the distance of CENSOF from the NIS is the closest among the technology companies in this study. In contrast, MPI has the farthest distance from the NIS compared to other technology companies.

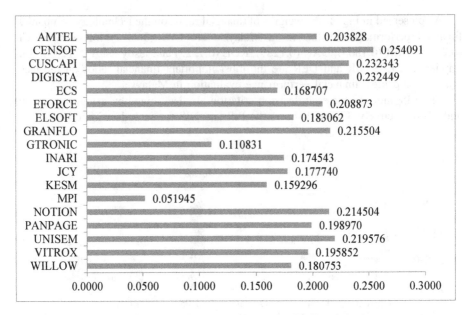

Fig. 3. The distance of all technology companies from the PIS (d_{ib}).

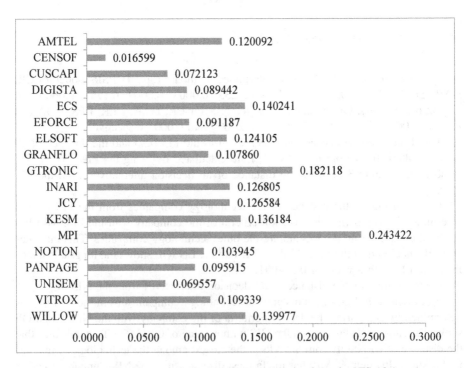

Fig. 4. The distance of all technology companies from the NIS (d_{iw}).

The technology companies' overall performance is determined by using the Eq. (10). Table 2 presents the technology companies' overall performance in Malaysia.

Table 2. Technology companies' overall performance in Malaysia

Companies	s_{iw}	Rank, T
MPI	0.824133	1
GTRONIC	0.621672	2
KESM	0.460890	3
ECS	0.453931	4
WILLOW	0.436433	5
INARI	0.420793	6
JCY	0.415951	7
ELSOFT	0.404030	8
AMTEL	0.370746	9
VITROX	0.358264	10
GRANFLO	0.333555	11
NOTION	0.326410	12
PANPAGE	0.325263	13
EFORCE	0.303897	14
DIGISTA	0.277864	15
UNISEM	0.240570	16
CUSCAPI	0.236883	17
CENSOF	0.061322	18

As shown in Table 2, the s_{iw} for each technology company and the overall ranking of companies are determined by using Entropy-TOPSIS model. MPI achieves the first ranking among the technology companies with s_{iw} of 0.824133 which is the highest among the companies. The s_{iw} for GTRONIC, KESM and ECS are 0.621672, 0.460890 and 0.453931 respectively. Therefore, GTRONIC, KESM and ECS obtained the second, third and fourth ranking respectively. On the other hand, the s_{iw} for UNISEM, CUSCAPI and CENSOF are 0.240570, 0.236883 and 0.061322 respectively. Thus, these companies get the lowest ranking in this study.

4 Conclusion

In conclusion, the proposed conceptual framework is able to measure, compare and rank the technology companies' financial performance in Malaysia effectively. In this study, MPI achieves the best performance followed by GTRONIC, KESM and ECS. In addition, the results of this study show that EPS is the most important decision criterion followed by CR, DER, DAR, ROE and lastly ROA. The significance of this study is to measure the technology companies' financial performance in Malaysia with the proposed conceptual framework based on entropy-TOPSIS model.

Acknowledgment. This study is supported by Universiti Tunku Abdul Rahman Research Fund.

References

1. Hwang, C.L., Yoon, K.: Multiple Attribute Decision Making. Springer, Berlin (1981). https://doi.org/10.1007/978-3-642-48318-9
2. Celen, A.: Comparative analysis of normalization procedures in TOPSIS method: with an application to Turkish deposit banking market. Inform. (Neth.) **25**(2), 185–208 (2014)
3. Mandic, K., Delibasic, B., Knezevic, S., Benkovic, S.: Analysis of the financial parameters of Serbian banks through the application of the fuzzy AHP and TOPSIS methods. Econ. Model. **43**, 30–37 (2014)
4. Shannon, C.E., Weaver, W.: The Mathematical Theory of Communication. The University of Illinois Press, Urbana (1947)
5. Tewari, P.C., Prakash, U., Khanduja, D., Sandeep: Ranking of sintered material for high loaded automobile application by applying Entropy-TOPSIS method. In: 4th International Conference on Materials Processing and Characterization, vol. 2, no. 4–5, pp. 2375–2379 (2015)
6. Lam, W.S., Liew, K.F., Lam, W.H.: Evaluation on the financial performance of the Malaysian banks with TOPSIS model. Am. J. Serv. Sci. Manag. **4**(2), 11–16 (2017)
7. Elsayed, E.A., Dawood, A.K.S., Karthikeyan, R.: Evaluating alternatives through the application of TOPSIS method with entropy weight. Int. J. Eng. Trends Technol. **46**(2), 60–66 (2017)
8. Li, X.X., Wang, K.S., Liu, L.W., Xin, J., Yang, H.R., Gao, C.Y.: Application of the entropy weight and TOPSIS method in safety evaluation of coal mines. Proc. Eng. **26**, 2085–2091 (2011)
9. Liew, K.F., Lam, W.S., Lam, W.H.: Financial analysis on the company performance in Malaysia with multi-criteria decision making model. Syst. Sci. Appl. Math. **1**(1), 1–7 (2016)
10. Kharusi, S.A., Basci, E.S.: Financial institutions performance evaluation in a unique developing market using TOPSIS approach. Banks Bank Syst. **12**(1), 54–59 (2017)
11. Huang, J.W.: Combining entropy weight and TOPSIS method for information system selection. In: Proceedings of the IEEE International Conference on Automation and Logistics, Qingdao, pp. 1965–1968 (2008)
12. Yadav, S.K., Kapoor, R., Dhaigude, A.S.: Financial performance ranking of oil and gas companies in India using TOPSIS method. Int. J. Appl. Bus. Econ. Res. **14**(6), 4463–4473 (2016)
13. Li, X.G., Gao, Z.J.: Application of improved entropy TOPSIS to competitive performance evaluation of power companies. In: International Conference on Computational Science and Engineering, pp. 183–188 (2015)
14. Zhang, Y.F.: TOPSIS method based on entropy weight for supplier evaluation of power grid enterprise. In: 2nd International Conference on Education Reform and Modern Management, pp. 334–337 (2015)
15. Lam, W.H., Lam, W.S., Chen, J.W.: A study on the performance of the retailers in Malaysia with TOPSIS model. Int. J. Econ. Theory Appl. **5**(1), 7–12 (2017)
16. Lam, W.H., Din, M.A., Lam, W.S., Chen, J.W.: Evaluation on the performance of suppliers in Malaysia with TOPSIS model. J. Fundam. Appl. Sci. **10**(6S), 406–415 (2018)
17. Asadzadeh, A., Sikder, S.K., Mahmoudi, F., Kotter, T.: Assessing site selection of new towns using TOPSIS method under entropy logic: a case study: New towns of Tehran Metropolitan Region (TMR). Environ. Manag. Sustain. Dev. **3**(1), 123–137 (2014)
18. Lam, W.S., Bakar, M.A., Lam, W.H., Liew, K.F.: Multi-criteria decision making in the selection of mobile network operators with AHP-TOPSIS model. J. Eng. Appl. Sci. **12**(23), 6382–6386 (2017)

19. Price, J.E., Haddock, M.D., Brock, H.R.: College Accounting, 10th edn. Macmillan/McGraw-Hill, New York (1993)
20. Akguc, O.: Financial Statement Analysis, 13th edn. Arayis Publication, Istanbul (2010)
21. Khrawish, H.A.: Determinants of commercial banks performance: evidence from Jordan. Int. Res. J. Financ. Econ. **81**, 148–159 (2011)
22. Bursa Malaysia: Company Announcements—Bursa Malaysia Market (n.d.). Accessed http://www.bursamalaysia.com/market/listed-companies/company-announcements/#/?category=all
23. Lam, W.S., Liew, K.F., Lam, W.H.: An optimal control on the efficiency of technology companies in Malaysia with data envelopment analysis model. J. Telecommun. Electron. Comput. Eng. **10**(1), 107–111 (2018)
24. Hoe, L.W., Siew, L.W., Fai, L.K.: Improvement on the efficiency of technology companies in Malaysia with data envelopment analysis model. In: Badioze Zaman, H., et al. (eds.) IVIC 2017. LNCS, vol. 10645, pp. 19–30. Springer, Cham (2017). https://doi.org/10.1007/978-3-319-70010-6_2
25. Liew, K.F., Lam, W.S., Lam, W.H.: An empirical evaluation on the efficiency of the companies in Malaysia with data envelopment analysis model. Adv. Sci. Lett. **23**(9), 8264–8267 (2017)
26. Lam, W.S., Liew, K.F., Lam, W.H.: An empirical comparison on the efficiency of healthcare companies in Malaysia with data envelopment analysis model. Int. J. Serv. Sci. Manag. Eng. **4**(1), 1–5 (2017)
27. Lam, W.S., Liew, K.F., Lam, W.H.: Investigation on the efficiency of financial companies in Malaysia with data envelopment analysis model. In: Journal of Physics: Conference Series, vol. 995, no. 012021, pp. 1–10 (2018)
28. Siew, L.W., Wai, C.J., Hoe, L.W.: Data driven decision analysis in bank financial management with goal programming model. In: Badioze Zaman, H., et al. (eds.) IVIC 2017. LNCS, vol. 10645, pp. 681–689. Springer, Cham (2017). https://doi.org/10.1007/978-3-319-70010-6_63
29. Lam, W.S., Bishan, R.S., Lam, W.H.: An empirical study on the mold machine-tool selection in semiconductor industry with analytic hierarchy process model. Adv. Sci. Lett. **23**(9), 8286–8289 (2017)
30. Chen, J.W., Lam, W.S., Lam, W.H.: Optimization on the financial management of the bank in Malaysia with goal programming model. J. Fundam. Appl. Sci. **9**(6S), 442–451 (2017)

Human Centered Computing

Usability Evaluation and Recommendation According to Factors Affecting Purchase Intention: Qlapa.Com–An Indonesian Local Handmade Marketplace

Rahma Khairunisa Nursalamah, Harry Budi Santoso[✉],
and R. Yugo Kartono Isal

Faculty of Computer Science, Universitas Indonesia, Depok, Indonesia
rahma.khairunisa@ui.ac.id, {harrybs,yugo}@cs.ui.ac.id

Abstract. This study aims to evaluate Qlapa.com, a marketplace for Indonesian local crafts, according to factors affecting purchase intention. Factors affecting purchase intention used in this study are usability factors and handmade purchase factors. The evaluation was conducted with usability testing and contextual interview. Data were analyzed using the thematic analysis method. The result shows that the current Qlapa.com has issues in all usability factors. It is recommended for Qlapa.com to consider the handmade purchase factors in some areas and be more selective in delivering its content, since it has a specific line of products. Frequent, deliberate user research and usability evaluation is also needed for Qlapa.com to make sure its platform can respond to users' purchase intention.

Keywords: Handmade · Marketplace · Purchase intention · Usability

1 Introduction

The e-Commerce environment in Indonesia is played by not only established ones, but also newcomers [1–3]. The competition is tight [1, 2] as they may have the same target of customers. One of these e-Commerce players is Qlapa.com, a C2C e-Commerce which only sells Indonesian handmade products. Qlapa.com, which was established in 2015, sets growing Indonesian creative industry as its goal [4, 5]. In Indonesia, creative industry is considered as the pillar of Indonesian economics with the handmade industry as one of three biggest subsections of creative industry, bearing export value of 93 trillion Rupiahs [6–9]. The opportunity in this industry is obviously big. Based on a personal study, from emerging players such as Tokopedia and Bukalapak to big players such as Lazada have handmade products or local crafts in their line of products. Not only against handmade-focused e-Commerce, Qlapa.com also has to face other e-Commerce sellers with a broader variety of products.

In order to win the competition, e-Commerce players should at least have a good usability [10, 11]. Paying attention on how users interact with the system, especially in reaching their goals, is necessary for Qlapa.com as an e-Commerce business organization. Evaluation is needed to understand what does not work or what can potentially be improved. Although evaluation can be done with non-users [12], real users are still

© Springer Nature Singapore Pte Ltd. 2018
N. Abdullah et al. (Eds.): i-USEr 2018, CCIS 886, pp. 207–218, 2018.
https://doi.org/10.1007/978-981-13-1628-9_19

the ones who determine how good the usability of the system is. However, no endeavor by real users has been conducted to evaluate Qlapa.com.

Previous studies have shown that usability can significantly affect users' purchase intention in e-Commerce [13–17]. Unless stated otherwise, users can only interact with products through the system, either to search for the right products, communicate with the sellers or pay for the products. Having limited product information or slow loading time, for example, can hinder users to buy products. It could get worse if such situation happens during the first time a user visits the e-Commerce. Low-usability website may reflect a poor image of the company, which eventually result in a lower users' intention to return to the platform.

A purchase occurs when a user has the intention to purchase. Purchase intention can be planned [18], which means either user has the intention when visiting a system or it can be obtained after users are exposed by certain information [19]. Even so, users might lose their intention to purchase if they have problems in using the system. In a condition when users' goals are to make a purchase, an e-Commerce is considered as having a good usability if it can create and/or keep its users' purchase intention.

This research aims to evaluate usability of Qlapa.com according to factors affecting purchase intention. Factors affecting purchase intention used in this research are usability factors and handmade purchase factors. The handmade purchase factors are used because the specific type of products which Qlapa.com sells can affect its users' expectation and perception [15]. Also, knowing that users are the one who determine the rate of usability of the system, User-Centered Design (UCD) was adopted in this study. This study is hoped to give Qlapa.com, or other handcraft-focused e-Commerce sellers, the insights to have a more efficient and effective design and development effort by knowing which area to improve and which area is important to users' purchase intention, especially for handmade products. This study also contributes to human-computer interaction related studies in Indonesia, since currently such studies are still limited in number. This paper is organized in five parts; (1) the introduction explains about the background and objective of this study, (2) the literature review discusses the literature review results which are related to the study, (3) method consists of relevant techniques which have been used, (4) the discussion and results which show the result of this study, and (5) the conclusion which explains the main points of this study and also ideas for further research.

2   Literature Review

2.1   Usability and Purchase Intention

In an e-Commerce, users can only interact with the product through the system. Previous studies [15, 18] showed that users' past experience with the system can affect their intention to return, especially to make a purchase. Given these situations, factors affecting purchase intention are used in order to see how the issue may affect the purchase intention. This study used ten usability factors affecting purchase intention which have been identified by Lee and Kozar [16] to later map the issues found in the evaluation of Qlapa.com's platform.

2.2 Purchase Intention for Handmade Products

Adjusting the system environment to the real environment (according to its context) is important as users might have the expectation that the system is act like the real shop [20]. Knowing this, the type of products sold by an e-Commerce seller may as well affect the interaction design of the system, as they automatically become the content in the system [15]. Thus, factors affecting someone to buy a handmade product (later will be referred to as handmade-purchase factors) are also used in this study to give more clarity of what to improve in regards of purchase intention for handmade product. This study used the nine handmade-purchase factors which have been identified by Yi and Anh [21]. Factors and their descriptions can be found in Table 1.

Table 1. Handmade-purchase factors by Yi and Anh [21]

Factor	Description	Factor	Description
Symbol status	Consumption of product with the intent of displaying wealth in public	Love conveyance	Craftman's love and passion for his work
Uniqueness	Product's difference compared to other products	Personal level sales service	Service provided during or after the product has been sold to ensure trouble-free product
Creativity	Exceptional value of the product	Environment friendliness	Impact of the product to the environment
Quality	The quality of the product	Artisan & local community support	Opportunity to support artisan or local community by purchasing the product
Customization	The ability to carry out specific requirement from customer		

2.3 Usability Evaluation

To reach certain understanding of usability of a product, evaluation should be done [22]. Usually, companies implement analytics to track the usage of their products. While analytics can show the numbers and trends, evaluation of product's usability can answer how or why those events have occurred.

Methods have been developed to evaluate product's usability [23]. This study used usability testing [24] and contextual interview [25] to evaluate Qlapa.com's usability. Specifically, the usability testing used the thinking-aloud protocol [26]. Contextual interviews were undertaken when and after each usability testing session was carried out to generate richer insights.

In evaluating a product's usability and making sure the insights are valid, it has to involve the right participants. In this context, participants are the ones who use Qlapa.com. Therefore, before usability of a product can be conducted, understanding the users is an important process. This attempt of understanding users is referred to as user research [27].

3 Methodology

3.1 Participants

Participants in each iteration were chosen with convenience sampling from online questionnaire respondents. Convenience sampling was done based on personas, which will be briefly described in Sect. 4.1. Convenience sampling was used because this study adopted UCD and since the personas represented the users, participants who conveniently match the personas are required [28, 29]. From the sampling, five people were chosen for each persona, making the total participants for each iteration to be ten. The number of five was based on a previous study [30] which has shown that the number of participant is enough to discover the majority of usability problems.

3.2 Data Collection Procedures

This study adopted two-phase approach which combines quantitative and qualitative research [32–34]. Participant selection model was used in user research and later taxonomy development model was used in generating insights from usability evaluation findings. In user research, online questionnaire insights (quantitative) were gathered to identify and select participants for usability evaluations (qualitative). Meanwhile in generating insights from usability evaluation, findings (qualitative) were classified into themes and predefined factors (quantitative).

The evaluation of Qlapa.com was first started with understanding who the users are through user research. Since there was no previous endeavor in identifying users by Qlapa.com and since Qlapa.com is an online platform, people who have visited Qlapa.com at least once were assumed to be the users. Online questionnaire was conducted to collect data and develop insights about users, including their goals in using Qlapa.com, their pain points and their workarounds to overcome them. User research was also carried out with usability evaluation on existing Qlapa.com platform. The usability evaluation was conducted to 8 respondents of the online questionnaire. The number 8 was chosen to add more variation to the insight.

In order to gain more clarity on who the users are, persona is created. It is then followed by task analysis. The result of task analysis is the tasks and scenarios [35] which indicate users' intention to purchase in Qlapa.com.

There are two iterations explained in this paper. After users and tasks were identified, the evaluation of Qlapa.com was followed by the first iteration. This iteration mainly focused on identifying issues on existing Qlapa.com. The second iteration focused on generating alternative design of Qlapa.com and identifying its issues. The alternative design was delivered in high-fidelity prototype [36]. High-fidelity prototype was chosen to enable users to have more realistic interaction with the design. The alternative design was created as recommendation to address the issues found in previous iteration.

Identifying issues in both iterations was done with usability evaluation, using usability testing and contextual interview. Usability testing was done by asking participants to do the predefined tasks. Questions asked in contextual interview are as follows; do you have any feedbacks regarding purchasing products?, do you have any feedbacks regarding adding favorite products?, do you have any feedbacks regarding finding help?, do you have any feedbacks regarding tracking orders?, can you tell me the obstacles or unmet expectation you have when using this platform?, can you tell me the satisfaction you feel when using this platform?, and finally do you have any feedbacks regarding overall of this platform?. Translation from issues identified by the answers into recommendation will further be explained in Sect. 3.3.

3.3   Data Analysis

The collected data, referred to hereafter as findings, from usability evaluation were qualitative data which covers participants' comments, errors in doing tasks and observation regarding participants' behavior in doing tasks. These findings were analyzed using thematic analysis method, utilizing affinity map in the process. Firstly, findings were clustered by the task in which they occurred and by their theme. After that, these flows were prioritized by mapping them under which usability factors they affected. This will generate an insight of which task affecting which factor. The flow not mapped under the usability factors will be considered as low priority to address. Otherwise, the ones mapped under usability factors will be put as high priority. Each finding, based on prioritized tasks, was then assigned with relevant handmade purchase factors, along with various design theories such as 10 Usability Heuristics for User Interface Design [37] and Basics of User Experience [38]. The result of the mapping contributed in the creation of alternative design.

4   Results and Discussion

4.1   User Research

User research started from collecting data and then developed into insights of users. There was a total of 587 participants for online questionnaire. Majority of online questionnaire respondents were at the age between 25 and 34 (212 people), followed by the group of 35–44 (166 people), then the group of 18–24 (103 people) and lastly, the group of people in their late 40 s (91 people). Most of them (235 people) answered that they usually visit Qlapa.com during office hours, after office hours (146 people), and the rest answered only when they have the time to or the need to (191 people). By intention, 306 people mentioned that they visited Qlapa.com out of lifestyle needs, 283 people mentioned because they have to fulfil daily needs and 196 responded that they just want to look for information. 328 people mentioned that what usually stops them from purchasing a product is because they cannot find the product they want at the website they visited, 233 people mentioned that the reason is because the product they want exceeds their budget, 177 people mentioned that the product they want has limited information, 71 people mentioned that their previous dissatisfying experience affects them, 45 people mentioned that their reason is because the navigation is confusing, 33 people mentioned that the reason is because of the shipping policy, 16 people mentioned that they have difficulties in adding the product into the cart, and 15 people mentioned that they have difficulties in doing the checkout.

From the user research, two personas and four tasks were generated, which can be found in Tables 2 and 3 accordingly. The two personas were differentiated by their purchase intentions in Qlapa.com. Occasional buyers were identified as people who purchase products only when there is an occasion, such as gifts or daily needs, while handmade collectors are people who purchase products to fulfil their lifestyle needs or people who purchase products rather impulsively.

Table 2. Personas

	Occasional buyer	Handmade collector
Demographics	18–34 years old Employee	>35 years old Entrepreneur
Goals/motivation	Buy gifts Fulfil daily needs	Collect goods Fulfill lifestyle needs
Pain points	No time to visit offline store Unclear product information Hard to find budget products with good quality	No time to visit offline store Unclear product information Limited product variation in offline store
Workarounds	Shop online Use sort and filter features Shop somewhere else	Shop online Contact customer support Wait until new products arrive

Table 3. Task analysis results

Task	Subtasks	Scenario	Justification
Purchase products	• Search products to purchase • Add to cart • Checkout	"Now you're looking at the Qlapa.com homepage. You may look around and then buy any product you like with a budget of IDR500,000.-"	The main task of an e-Commerce
Add favorite product	• Search products to mark as favorite • Mark products as favorite	"You've found the product you like, but unfortunately you cannot purchase it for the time being. What will you do?"	Adding favorite products indicates a planned purchase intention [18]

(continued)

Table 3. (*continued*)

Task	Subtasks	Scenario	Justification
Find help	Find customer support contact	"You're thinking of purchasing it, but the description is unclear and you want to ask for further detail about the product. What will you do?"	Related to how users address their problems in the system
Track order	• See all transactions • See the detail of the tracked order	"You suddenly remember about the purchase you've made some time ago and you want to see how it has progressed so far. What will you do?"	Related to users' expectation after they pay for their products

4.2 Iteration I

With the new understanding of users, the evaluation process was then started. The alternative design had not been made in this iteration yet. The object evaluated was still the existing Qlapa.com. Since there were two personas, usability evaluation was conducted to ten participants (5 participants representing one persona) in which each participant was asked to do the aforementioned tasks while sharing their thoughts out loud regarding what they think or feel while doing each task.

From this iteration, it was found that for every usability factor, the existing Qlapa.com has at least one issue. This is considered detrimental, since these factors affect users' purchase intention. In other words, having issues in those factors can also prevent users to develop and/or keep their intention to purchase. The summary of findings from this iteration can be found in Table 4.

The mapped issues were then addressed with recommendations along with relevant handmade-purchase factors. In certain flow, page or section of page, these factors are important. For example, in purchasing a product, if "clearer and more understandable terms" were to be implemented, "love conveyance", "uniqueness" and "quality" are suggested to be considered. Product detail, where the recommendation can be implemented, should show the users how unique the product is compared to other products or the extent of effort the craftsman had done to bring the best quality out of his/her product. This information is needed, because they are part of the reason why users would want to buy handmade products [21]. The recommendations can be found in Table 5.

Other than findings regarding the usability issues, more understanding of both personas was also obtained. Occasional buyers were identified as users who start searching and purchase products only when they need them. They also have a rather strict budget (price-sensitive) and expectation of shipping time as they are in the need of the purchased products. On the other hand, handmade collectors are users who start searching or purchase products even when they do not actually need them at that moment. They are more flexible in budget and shipping time, since they understand there is a manual process in creating handmade products. While the occasional buyers are more functional-driven users, handmade collectors are value-driven users.

Table 4. Summary of iteration I findings

Task	Total issue	Task	Total issue
Consistency		Navigability	
Purchase products	1	Purchase products	1
Content relevance		Track order	1
Purchase products	4	Telepresence	
Readability		Purchase products	1
Purchase products	12	Credibility	
Add favorite products	1	Purchase products	4
Find help	2	Interactivity	
Track order	2	Purchase products	2
Simplicity		Supportability	
Purchase products	2	Purchase products	1
Track order	1	Find help	1
Learnability		Interactivity	
Purchase products	3	Purchase products	2

Table 5. Recommendations addressed with handmade-purchase factors

Recommendation	Usability factors	Handmade-purchase factors
Purchase products		
Clearer and understandable terms	Consistency, simplicity, learnability	–
	Content relevance, readability, navigability	Status symbol, uniqueness, creativity, quality, customization, love conveyance, personal level sales service, environment friendliness, artisan & local community support
Add discussion feature	Telepresence, credibility, interactivity, supportability	Customization, personal level sales service
Add favorite product		
Clearer and understandable terms	Readability	-
Find help		
Fix content layout	Readability, supportability	-
Track order		
Clearer and understandable terms	Readability, simplicity, navigability	Personal level sales service
Fix information architecture	Readability, navigability	Personal level sales service
Fix content layout	Readability, simplicity	Personal level sales service

4.3   Iteration II

In the second iteration, user research was not conducted since the needs had been identified in the first iteration. According to the same personas, usability evaluation in this iteration was also conducted to ten participants with usability testing and contextual interview. However, usability testing in this iteration was focused more on task purchasing products, while the rest of the tasks were evaluated through contextual interview.

Findings in the evaluation were also mapped in the same fashion as the previous iteration. Issues decreased after recommendations were implemented, in which only content relevance, readability, learnability, and credibility on the purchase products task were the ones producing issues by one per factor. Users who understand that the product being sold is handmade know what to expect from the product. For example, they can relate why certain products may only available in pre order, since usually users only want in-stock products when shopping online. It indicates that considering handmade-purchase factors in the design may improve users' perception of the products. It is also expected that when users have a better understanding of a product, they can make a better judgement of the product [13–15], and therefore developing and/or keeping their intention to purchase. Table 6 shows recommendations for future improvement of Qlapa.com platform.

Table 6. Recommendations addressed with handmade-purchase factors

Recommendation	Usability factors	Handmade-purchase factors
Purchase products		
Content standardization	Content relevance, readability	Status symbol, uniqueness, creativity, quality, customization, love conveyance, personal level sales service, environment friendliness, artisan & local community support
Clearer and understandable terms	Readability	
Curated discussion	Credibility	Quality, personal level sales service
Find help		
Fix content layout	Readability, simplicity	Personal level sales service

5   Conclusion

This study aims to evaluate Qlapa.com's usability platform in accordance to factors affecting purchase intention. Factors used in this study are usability factors and handmade-purchase factors. This study shows that the existing Qlapa.com's platform has issues on every usability factor, with the task of purchasing a product having the most issues. These issues, especially in purchasing a product, may hinder users in reaching their goal through the platform. It can even reduce users' purchase intention to nothing, and thus may hinder Qlapa.com from keeping its position within Indonesia's e-Commerce landscape.

On the other hand, e-Commerce sellers that focused on handmade products need to be more selective in choosing the content of their platform since they sell handmade products. Some words might be too confusing for users or more details are needed for a product. Thus, understanding why users would want to purchase handmade products and identifying the utilizing factors affecting them are important in the favor of having optimal usability.

However, this study still needs further research in some other aspects, such as the extent of usability factors and handmade-purchase factors affecting users' purchase intention in handmade-focused e-Commerce platforms. Also, this study only considers usability factors and handmade-purchase factors to help evaluate the usability. In the future, other factors or calculation might be needed to optimize the result and can be used as a framework to evaluate a handmade-focused e-Commerce.

References

1. Kinasih, R.: Indonesia's e-commerce landscape: 6 takeaways from Indonesia's online battle field (2016). https://ecommerceiq.asia/indonesia-ecommerce-landscape-ecommerceiq/. Accessed 13 May 2017
2. Prasatya, A.: A snapshot of Indonesia's ecommerce scene as companies brace for Amazon's arrival (2017). https://www.techinasia.com/talk/ecommerce-indonesia-brace-amazon. Accessed 18 Aug 2017
3. Firdaus, F.: E-Commerce booming in Indonesia, survey finds (2014). http://jakartaglobe.id/business/e-commerce-booming-in-indonesia-survey-finds/. Accessed 13 May 2017
4. Wijaya, K.K.: Dengan dukungan engineer Silicon Valley, apakah Qlapa bisa menjadi solusi bagi perajin Lokal? (2015). https://id.techinasia.com/qlapa-marketplace-produk-kerajinan-tangan. Accessed 13 May 2017
5. Freischlad, N.: Qlapa, Indonesia's marketplace for handicrafts, wants to avoid Etsy's mistakes (2015). https://www.techinasia.com/qlapa-indonesia-handicraft-marketplace-like-etsy. Accessed 13 May 2017
6. Gareta, S.P., Ratomo, U.T.: Ini kontribusi industri kreatif di perekonomian Indonesia (2015). https://www.antaranews.com/berita/511673/ini-kontribusi-industri-kreatif-di-perekonomian-indonesia. Accessed 17 May 2017
7. Kementrian Perindustrian RI: Menperin: Industri kreatif tumbuh 7% per tahun (2015). http://www.kemenperin.go.id/artikel/12797/Menperin:-Industri-Kreatif-Tumbuh-7-Per-Tahun. Accessed 17 May 2017
8. Sindo Weekly: Nilai ekspor industri kreatif siap salip migas (2017). https://ekbis.sindonews.com/read/1206676/34/nilai-ekspor-industri-kreatif-siap-salip-migas-1495266760. Accessed 1 Jun 2017
9. Endarwati, O.: Industri kreatif sumbang Rp642 triliun PDB Indonesia (2017). https://ekbis.sindonews.com/read/1188405/34/industri-kreatif-sumbang-rp642-triliun-pdb-indonesia-1489505337. Accessed 16 May 2017
10. Lee, S., Koubek, R.J.: The effects of usability and web design attributes on user preference for e-commerce web sites. Comput. Ind. 329–341 (2010). https://doi.org/10.1016/j.compind.2009.12.004

11. Kuan, H.H.: Comparing the effects of usability on customer conversion and retention at e-commerce websites. In: The Proceedings of the 38th Hawaii International Conference on System Sciences, Hawaii (2005)

12. Simon, D.P.: The art of guerrilla usability testing (2017). http://www.uxbooth.com/articles/the-art-of-guerrilla-usability-testing/. Accessed 27 Oct 2017

13. Perdana, R.A., Suzianti, A.: Analysis of usability factors affecting purchase intention in online e-commerce sites. In: The International Conference on Information Technology and Digital Applications (2017)

14. Hausman, A.V., Siekpe, J.S.: The effect of web interface features on consumer online purchase intentions. J. Bus. Res. **62**, 5–13 (2009). https://doi.org/10.1016/j.jbusres.2008.01.018

15. Wang, Y.-M., et al.: The relationships among presentation mode, product type, consumers' product knowledge, and consumers' purchase intention in the e-commerce environment. In: 37th Annual Computer Software and Applications Conference (2013)

16. Lee, Y., Kozar, K.A.: Understanding of website usability: specifying and measuring constructs and their relationships. Decis. Support Syst. **52**, 450–463 (2011). https://doi.org/10.1016/j.dss.2011.10.004

17. Vila, N., Kuster, I.: The role of usability on stimulating SME's on line buying intention: an experiment based on a fictitious web site design. Dig. J. Qual. Quant. **46**, 117–136 (2012). https://doi.org/10.1007/s11135-010-9332-x

18. Al-Lozi, E., Papazafeiropoulou, A.: Intention-based models: the theory of planned behavior within the context of IS. In: Dwivedi, Y.K., et al. (eds.) Information Systems Theory: Explaining and Predicting 219 Our Digital Society, vol. 2, pp. 219–239. Springer, London (2012). https://doi.org/10.1007/978-1-4419-9707-4_12

19. Lim, Y.J., et al.: Factors influencing online shopping behavior: the mediating role of purchase intention. Proced. Econ. Finance **35**, 401–410 (2015). https://doi.org/10.1016/S2212-5671(16)00050-2

20. Preece, J., et al.: What is interaction design?. In: Interaction Design. Wiley (2015)

21. Yi, H., Anh, N.N.: The handmade effect: what is special about buying handmade? Int. Rev. Manage. Bus. Res. **5**, 594–609 (2016). ISSN: 2306-9007

22. Cockton, G.: Usability evaluation (nd). https://www.interaction-design.org/literature/book/the-encyclopedia-of-human-computer-interaction-2nd-ed/usability-evaluation. Accessed 1 June 2017

23. Usability.gov: Usability evaluation methods (nda). https://www.usability.gov/how-to-and-tools/methods/usability-evaluation/index.html. Accessed 12 May 2017

24. Usability.gov: Usability testing (ndb). https://www.usability.gov/how-to-and-tools/methods/usability-testing.html. Accessed 28 May 2017

25. Interaction Design Foundation: Contextual interviews and how to handle them (2016). https://www.interaction-design.org/literature/article/contextual-interviews-and-how-to-handle-them. Accessed 28 May 2017

26. Nielsen, J.: Thinking aloud: The #1 usability tool (2012). https://www.nngroup.com/articles/thinking-aloud-the-1-usability-tool/. Accessed 28 May 2017

27. Usability.gov: User research basics (ndc). https://www.usability.gov/what-and-why/user-research.html. Accessed 28 May 2017

28. Sauro, J.: Do you need a random sample for your usability test? (2010). https://measuringu.com/random-sample/. Accessed 22 April 2018

29. Matthews, T., et al.: How do designers and user experience professionals actually perceive and use personas? (2012). Accessed 22 Apr 2018

30. Nielsen, J.: How many test users in a usability study? (2012). https://www.nngroup.com/articles/how-many-test-users/. Accessed 28 May 2017

31. Allwood, C.M.: The distinction between qualitative and quantitative research methods is problematic. Qual. Quant. **46**, 1417–1429 (2011). https://doi.org/10.1007/s11135-011-9455-8
32. Gelo, O., et al.: Quantitative and qualitative research: beyond the debate. Integr. Psychol. Behav. **42**, 266–290 (2008). https://doi.org/10.1007/s12124-008-9078-3
33. Gelo, O., et al.: Quantitative and qualitative research: beyond the debate. Integr. Psychol. Behav. **43**, 406–407 (2009). https://doi.org/10.1007/s12124-009-9107-x
34. Usability.gov: Personas (ndd). https://www.usability.gov/how-to-and-tools/methods/personas.html. Accessed 28 May 2017
35. Usability.gov: Scenarios (nde). https://www.usability.gov/how-to-and-tools/methods/scenarios.html. Accessed 28 May 2017
36. Pernice, K.: UX Prototypes: Low fidelity vs. high fidelity (2016). https://www.nngroup.com/articles/ux-prototype-hi-lo-fidelity/. Accessed 28 May 2017
37. Nielsen, J.: 10 Usability heuristics for user interface design (1995). https://www.nngroup.com/articles/ten-usability-heuristics/. Accessed 26 May 2017
38. Kurtuldu, M.: Basics of user experience (2017). https://developers.google.com/web/fundamentals/design-and-ux/ux-basics/. Accessed 26 May 2017

Preliminary Study of JunoBlock: Marker-Based Augmented Reality for Geometry Educational Tool

Julio Cristian Young and Harry Budi Santoso[✉]

Faculty of Computer Science, Universitas Indonesia, Depok 16424, Indonesia
harrybs@cs.ui.ac.id

Abstract. Augmented reality (AR) is one from many multimedia technologies which allows computer-generated content to be seamlessly overlaid and mixed into humans' perceptions of the real world. In educational field, many researchers believe AR technology can improve user interface technology and has a huge potential implication as well as numerous benefits from the virtual augmentation of learning environments or even a teaching process. However, in the earlier researches about AR geometry educational tool, researchers did not use any pedagogical approach in its application design process. In fact, a pedagogical approach is needed for creating an effective educational application to make sure students' learning time is spent productively. In this research, we try to create AR geometry educational tool by using design-based learning and game-based learning approach to create a better geometry educational tool. Furthermore, the application also used iterative software development lifecycle that requires a series of prototype to find the best AR game mechanics in geometry learning process.

Keywords: Augmented reality · Design-based learning · Game-based learning
Technology-supported learning

1 Introduction

Augmented reality (AR) is one from many multimedia technologies which allows computer-generated content to be seamlessly overlaid and mixed into humans' perceptions of the real world [1]. AR as technology is often associated with expensive hardware that requires significant processing capability, head-mounted displays (HMDs), or even wearable computers. In recent years, with the rapid advances of mobile technologies, a wide variety of AR technology can be implemented by much simpler solutions, such as a laptop with web camera or even a mobile phone [2]. For example, researchers have created location-based AR application which used location-based service on two different mobile operating systems, iOS and Android [3].

In educational field, many researchers believe AR technology can improve user interface technology and has a huge potential implication as well as numerous benefits from the virtual augmentation of learning environments or even a teaching process [1, 4–6]. The number of possible educational benefits regarding the use of AR is related to; being safer and cheaper to reproduce and virtual objects that can easily be animated

© Springer Nature Singapore Pte Ltd. 2018
N. Abdullah et al. (Eds.): i-USEr 2018, CCIS 886, pp. 219–230, 2018.
https://doi.org/10.1007/978-981-13-1628-9_20

(engage students into learning process), be modified and transformed by users' actions (create interactive learning process), be combined seamlessly with other media (can be integrated with another multimedia technologies) and not constrained by the law of physics like a real object (enable students to have private sandbox for learning). As a technology in educational field, AR is often used to increase the students' interest in certain subjects through the implementation of AR books, games, discovery-based learning apps, object modelling apps, and skill training apps [1].

For example, in discovery-based learning, researchers have created the EXPLOAR project that involves visitors of science museums and science centers in extended episodes of playful learning [4]. By using personalized wearable system that enhances conventional teaching with natural types of learning with virtual content, EXPLOAR is proven to be able to increase intrinsic motivation of the learners. In addition, after using an additional device, to increase users' intrinsic motivation, EXPLOAR also took peda-gogical design to use AR system as content delivery system for informal learning for quite diverse target groups. The pedagogical design is implemented in EXPLOAR by allowing the users to easily adjust the information's complexity level of the presented content to meet their learning background.

In another research, through the implementation of object modelling approach, researcher has created Construct3D, a collaborative application that uses see-through head-mounted displays for implementing AR-based geometry education tool [7]. Construct3D also promotes and supports discovery-based learning through dynamic geometry construction using a stylus as an input tool to AR system. Just like EXPLOAR [4], Construct3D is also proven to enhance students' understanding by enabling visu-alisation and observation of virtual objects to the real world.

In this research, JunoBlock tries to create an AR system by putting object modelling approaches and discovery-based learning approach into a game. The focus of this appli-cation is to help the students' learning process about geometry objects. JunoBlock tries to improve the learning process by allowing its users to construct virtual 3D objects to the real world using a 3D object's general properties (nodes and edges). Unlike Construct3D [7] and EXPLOAR [4], JunoBlock is designed to work on mobile devices. JunoBlock takes this approach since three-quarters of all children aged 8 and below have access to some type of "smart" mobile devices at home [8]. By using mobile devices, we are also improving the accessibility level of JunoBlock. Although the system is designed for mobile devices, we keep the performance high so it still provides a better and reliable user experience.

2   Previous Works

Before the design and software implementation of JunoBlock is conducted, our research team conducted a review from the earlier researches related to AR technology in geom-etry learning. Based on the results of the review, we found some related research that could be used as references in creating a better geometry learning tool. The general information related to these researches can be seen in the Table 1.

Table 1. AR technology implementations in geometry learning.

Title	Context	Limitations	Findings
Collaborative Augmented Reality in Education	First use of AR technology in geometry education	Performance, size and weight of hardware technology in early 2000	See-through HMD is preferable by users. AR applications that uses see-through HMD can cause several usability problems
Development of an Interactive Book with Augmented Reality for Teaching and Learning Geometric Shapes	Interactive AR book to support learning of main geometric shapes	Only focusing on spatial visualization	AR book capable of contributing effectively to the development of educational supportive system. AR book also has a highly promising resource compared to other educational system with AR
Geometry Learning Tool for Elementary School using Augmented Reality	AR application for creating virtual protractor to measure angle	Only focus on line and angle visualization Application user interface is not well defined	The use of AR technology increases students' motivation in geometry learning. AR could make learning process become faster compared to using conventional method
Cyberchase Shape Quest: Pushing Geometry Education Boundaries with Augmented Reality	AR game for elementary school children	The game requires a set of printed physical paper block	AR can cause a major problem related to game mechanics that involves AR. Designing AR games requires an iterative design process. AR developers need to conduct testing early and often as well as to involve different domain experts in the development process
An Augmented Reality Application with Hand Gestures for Learning 3D Geometry	Framework for learning geometry using AR and hand gestures recognition technologies	Framework needs additional devices to recognize users' hand gestures as an input	AR technology can be well integrated with other technologies. Combination of AR technology and hand gesture recognition devices can increase students' level of understanding in geometry learning application

As we can see from the Table 1, first use of AR technology as geometry learning supportive tools was done in 2003 [7]. In this research, researchers created mobile collaborative AR system called Construct3D. Construct3D focuses on improvement in the learners' spatial abilities at high school and university level. Construct3D takes a basic assumption that the learning process will take place naturally through the simple exploration and discovery of the virtual environment. Based on this basic assumption, Construct3D takes the constructivist theory to create such system that enables the learning activities through process of building 3D objects. To achieve natural communication among its users and combine virtual objects into real world, Construct3D uses see-through HMDs that is connected via cable to single distributed system that has a capability to overlay computer-generated images into the real world [7, 9].

By the Construct3D evaluation process, there are several problems related to the technical aspect and affective parameter in the uses of AR technology. The problems are related to unpredictable software's response time, the requirement of the software which is little time to learn, and motion sickness that is caused by several factors such as accommodation problems; low frame rate and lag or bad fitting helmets. Despite of the negative effects, majority of students think Construct3D is "easy to use", "encourages learners to try new functions" and "can be used consistently". Although the researchers have not yet focused on evaluating the use of AR, the researchers have a thesis that mentioned by working directly in a 3D space provided by AR technology, complex spatial problems can be better understood and faster compared to traditional methods [9].

In 2012, researchers have developed an interactive AR book for learning geometric shapes called GeoAR [10]. GeoAR enriches the contents presented in a traditional book by the uses of AR markers to augment virtual 3D objects into the real world. GeoAR uses images, animations, 3D objects, narrated explanations and sound effects to explain basic concepts of Geometry related to the main geometric shapes and its calculations. GeoAR utilization requires GeoAR printed book and a computer with a webcam and a video monitor. Through the evaluation process of GeoAR, researchers consider that the use of AR book has a great capability to contribute effectively in supporting the teaching and learning process.

The next two years after GeoAR research, other researchers, have created a geometry learning tool to visualise (augmenting digital lines to the real world) and measure 180-degree angle by the uses of AR marker as a vertex [11]. As the researchers have concluded, because students and teachers do not need to redraw the lines every time the vertex changed, the learning process becomes faster. This research uses a projector, a wooden box with mirror as a projection's reflector from a projector, computer that runs the application and a webcam. The research found that AR can be used to increase the students' interest in mathematics and to make the learning process become faster compared to conventional methods.

In 2015, researchers have created a collection of mini games that contain AR games as one of its collection, known as Cyberchase Shape Quest [12]. Cyberchase Shape Quest is a free game that is available for camera-enabled Android, iOS and Kindle tablets. The AR game in Cyberchase Shape Quest has a focus in solving 3D geometry and spatial cognition problem. The core idea of the game is to encourage children to engage in spatial problem thinking in a fun puzzle game environment. The game is built based on game design theory, the flow channel. At the beginning of the game, the puzzle inside the game is relatively easy, later it become more challenging as players gain mastery.

The evaluation process confirmed that AR game can deliver learning material through multiple levels in the game in a fun way and reinforce students' learning motivation to beat multiple puzzles that are provided in game.

Besides the findings about AR application on geometry learning process, researchers who created the Cyberchase Shape Quest also mentioned a Software Development Lifecycle method that can be used for creating AR application. This SDLC method involved a team of producers, game designers, technological experts and educational specialists in the earliest stage of the software design process. The group of experts discussing about which math topic was best suited for AR technology and its potential as well as the game mechanics which utilize AR technology. After the discussion session, this team of experts also created a series of prototype. Each of the prototypes is evaluated to the target users to find the best mechanics, usability and level design provided in the final game.

Recent researches related to AR technology in learning have been done by researchers in 2017 [13]. The focus of this research was to develop an AR and hand gesture based application for learning 3D geometry in an easy and convenient way. With combination of both technologies, the students can understand the basic concepts of 3D objects interactively and intuitively through AR ability to provide a dynamic visualization of 3D structures in a real world and direct 3D objects manipulation using their hand gesture. The application offers several functions related to 3D geometry learning process including constructive solid 3D geometry using union, subtraction and intersection operation as well as 3D construction process from a set of 2D shapes. Based on the evaluation process, AR application with hand gestures recognition is proven to provide an easy and convenient way of learning 3D geometry compared to traditional method by the uses of pen, paper and imagination. Researchers also suspect that through the addition of collaborative method (remote cooperation between students) in AR application will improve the learning quality in it.

The use of HMD devices in AR application can surely raise several problems as mentioned by other researchers [9]. However, referring to the capabilities of HMD devices to naturally combine virtual objects into the real world, preferably, an AR application is designed to support the usage of HMD devices. To solve several technical problems in the use of HMD devices, unpredictable software response time and all technical factor that cause motion sickness in AR application must be identified. AR application should be developed by the uses of fundamental and optimal process of AR application [14, 15]. In addition to the uses of see-through HMD devices, to increase interactivity between player and AR application, AR application can be integrated with hand tracking recognition devices [13]. The combination of AR technology with these devices is certainly able to increase students' motivation in geometric learning through the immersive experience.

To keep students' motivation high along with the increasing level of difficulty of the material presented in the AR application, an application can be designed as a game [12]. By putting students into game's flow channel, a game will reinforce students to stay focus in solving the learning material as its difficulty level increased. However, many researchers [16, 17] state that designing a flow channel that fits every player's skill and its development is a very challenging process. Fortunately, using software development lifecycle (SDLC) method that has been used by the earlier research [12], AR game's flow channel could be developed to fit target users' needs.

By creating AR application that supports see-through HMD as well as hand tracking recognition devices and the use of SDLC method for creating game's flow channel that fits target users' needs, an AR application is expected to be able to reinforce students' motivation and all the good benefits mentioned in the earlier researches [7, 10–12].

3   Proposed Augmented Reality Design Methodology in Geometry Learning

Design process of JunoBlock follows some requirements needed in designing process of an educational application. Previous researcher stated that design process of an educational application requires pedagogy approach to make sure that the application used by students is spent productively during students' learning time [18]. In application design process, all criteria based on the chosen pedagogy approach are defined. In addition to the definition from pedagogical approach, the design phase also describes how AR technology is implemented to integrate with other technologies, as well as benefits of such integrations.

3.1   Pedagogy Approach

Although previous researchers did not really mention any pedagogy approach used in the earlier researches, it was found that the previous studies primarily used design-based learning pedagogy to interact and deliver the subject to the students. Design-based learning (DBL) is rooted in the educational principles of problem-based learning (PBL) and found as constructionist pedagogical paradigm [19, 20]. In the context of higher education, PBL takes learner-centered active method as its educational principles. The benefit from learner-centered active method is to encourage learners to gather information and apply knowledge by conducting explorations, generating data and evaluating the learning process [21]. On the other hand, constructionist pedagogical paradigm has been shown to improve student learning outcomes in the domain of practice [19].

DBL is an educational approach that engages students in solving real-life design problems while reflecting the learning process using design activities as means of acquiring engineering knowledge [22]. DBL approach consists of the design element through interactive or iterative methodology; open-ended, hands-on, authentic and multidisciplinary design tasks, teachers who facilitate both the process of gaining domain-specific knowledge and the process to propose innovative solutions, assessment by both formative and summative assessment, and the social context of DBL projects [23]. As a pedagogy approach, design-based learning (DBL) can increase student's performance, conceptual understanding and desire to learn about a specific subject.

According to previous research, there are several mechanisms found on DBL that have positive effects. Through several mechanisms such as discussing, problem-solving, theorizing, and drawing conclusions, these mechanisms can promote intellectual quality of the students. Another mechanism such as conceptual analytic is also proven to improve students' depth of understanding [24]. Like the previous research that has been done, JunoBlock is also designed using DBL approach.

As many researchers' state that optimal solution for AR system may not reside on one pedagogy approach but rather a blending of pedagogy approaches [6, 19, 25], Juno-Block adapts game-based learning (GBL) as a complementary pedagogy. In previous researches, GBL is proven to create high and active engaging system as well as pace tailored system for each individual student [26]. Other researches also mention that GBL can increase development level of critical thinking, creative thinking and problem solving of the students [2]. GBL through its environments can provide all benefits mentioned above because it improves a person's motivation and engagement level, draws individual or thousands of students into a kind of focused, highly engaged state of mind, a pleasant and self-motivating condition called "flow" as well as improves expertise and expert performance of a learner by facilitating the development of learner's mental models and schemata [27–30].

The design process of GBL is very different compared to pure entertainment games. The formation of GBL requires the designer to combine game formal and dramatic elements with elements of learning aspects [28]. There are seven core elements of well-designed games in terms of learning. Those elements are presented below [31]:

1. Interactive problem solving: requires an architecture that enables interaction between the player and the game by series of problems and creates those series of problems to dance around the outer limit of player's abilities [32].
2. Specific goals/rules: have rules to follow and consist of series of goal that guide the player to focus on what to do and when, on their discovery and application through virtually embodied transactions in the game itself. Goals can be implicit or explicit.
3. Adaptive challenges: balance difficulty level to match player's ability and keep the player just at the edge of their capabilities [33].
4. Control: encourages player's influence over gameplay, game environment and learning experiences. The element of control indicates that players should have a sense of control over the characters and movements in the game world and game interface.
5. Ongoing feedback: provides timely information to players about their performance.
6. Uncertainty: evokes suspense and player engagement. If a game "telegraphs" its outcome, or be predictable, it will lose its appeal.
7. Sensory Stimuli: combine all kind of multimedia content, such as graphics, sounds, and/or storyline to excite the players' senses.

3.2   Application Design

To interact with users, JunoBlock uses marker-based augmented reality. Marker-based augmented reality is used since application is designed to be able to run on mobile devices. On mobile devices, real-time computer vision for area learning and depth perception are computationally expensive, even for an algorithm dedicated to solve a very specific problem [34]. By using a specific marker that has been designed to be easily recognized by computer, application can take advantage of the remaining resources left for virtual objects transformation and animation process.

Not only designed to work on mobile devices, JunoBlock also supports the uses of see-through HMD device and hand-gestures recognition device on mobile devices by the integration with GoogleVR SDK and LeapMotion SDK. With GoogleVR SDK, users can choose to play a game using Google Cardboard (virtual reality platform used with a head-mount for smartphone) or just a fully functioning AR game without it. If a user chooses to play using Google Cardboard, they can also choose to extend their playing experience using hand-gestures recognition device.

To implement DBL approach as well as to fulfill the criteria of design elements through interactive and iterative methodology, JunoBlock uses GBL approach as a second pedagogy approach since GBL approach can create highly and actively engaged system [26]. To fulfill the rest of DBL criteria, application will provide free exploration mode where students can create any 3D object that they want using unlimited resources (nodes and edges). Through free exploration mode, teacher can create both formative and summative assessment to help both the process of gaining domain specific knowledge and the process to propose innovative solutions. The social context of DBL can also be achieved by enabling users to collaborate with one another to build a specific object in a free exploration mode.

To implement GBL approach in the application, the application needs to be developed as a game. For an application to be considered as a game, the application needs to have an essential structural function of a game or known as game's formal elements [35]. In JunoBlock, each of the formal element and its implementation are presented as below:

1. Players: players can play a game as a single player or multiplayer. Based on Bartle taxonomy of player types, JunoBlock will target players who love to interact with other players or game's environments (socializers and explorers) [36].
2. Objectives: in normal game mode, players have an objective to build a specific 3D object with some limited resources given. In free exploration mode, players have no objective and can create any 3d objects that they want.
3. Procedures:
   a. players start the game by clicking the game's icon,
   b. players can adjust background music volume and sound effects volume through settings menu,
   c. players choose the game mode that they want (normal or free exploration mode),
   d. players choose to play alone (single player mode) or together with their friends (multiplayer mode),
   e. in play mode, players must direct their device's camera to a predefined marker to play a game over the marker,
   f. players can build a node by touching a generated platform when marker is detected,
   g. players can select a node by touching a node,
   h. connect each node, lifting and lowering the node's position, remove node and connections and create another node above the currently selected node via the UI button provided on the screen,

     i. in normal mode, players will be given 3 opportunities to evaluate the 3d objects they have created and given unlimited opportunities in free exploration mode.

4. Rules:

    a. in normal mode, every time players make a wrong evaluation, players will lose some of their score and one opportunity,

    b. if players' opportunities have run out, they will lose the game,

    c. if players evaluate correctly, their score will increase and they will move to the next stage,

    d. if players have completed all the stages, their score will be recorded into the leaderboard.

5. Resources: player's opportunities to evaluate the 3d objects they have created.

6. Conflict: players must complete several levels provided by them before their chances run out.

To apply seven core elements of well-designed games in terms of learning, implementation details that applied to each element are presented below [31]:

1. Interactive problem solving and adaptive challenges: game presents several levels in which the levels of difficulty will increase in each level.

2. Specific goals/rules: game presents a formal element related to the objectives, procedures, and rules in the game completely in a section above.

3. Control and ongoing feedback: game provides the actions needed to complete all levels within the game via input directly onto the platform that have been provided or through buttons that have been provided. Every time players perform an action (pressing a button, making a mistake or moving to the next level) then the game will emit a specific sound as a feedback to them.

4. Uncertainty: the game will automatically select a problem from several alternative problems on each level related to a geometrical concept that is introduced within it. By doing this step, every level in the game will become unpredictable by the player and keep the player interested to finish it.

5. Sensory Stimuli: game uses 3d low poly assets that attract children's attention, sound effects as feedback to users and background music with soothing rhythm to increase players' concentration.

6. Conflict: players must complete several levels provided to them before their chances run out.

Based on the DBL and GBL approach as well as the application design definition above, all images from the first prototype that has been developed can be seen in the Fig. 1 below.

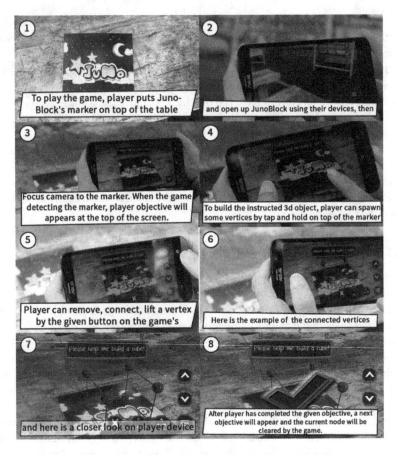

Fig. 1. First prototype of JunoBlock

4   Conclusion

By the proposed design methodology, the first prototype of JunoBlock has been success-fully created and ready to be evaluated. The focus of this first prototype evaluation is to find some issues related to appropriateness of AR technology as an educational tool. By using DBL and GBL in the application design process, JunoBlock is expected to increase students' learning motivation. Furthermore, with AR technology, JunoBlock is also expected to support students in understanding learning materials through the visualiza-tion of interactive virtual objects in the real world.

5   Future Works

After the evaluation of the first JunoBlock prototype, JunoBlock will be improved based on user suggestions related to aspects of usability, design or mechanics in the application.

Moreover, Junoblock will also be integrated with VR technology through the help of Google Cardboard SDK. By the integration with VR technology in the application, the comparison between AR and VR technology as educational tool and the discovery of the advantages and disadvantages for each technology can be done.

References

1. Yuen, S.C., Yaoyuneyong, G., Johnson, E.: Augmented reality: an overview and five directions for AR in education. J. Educ. Technol. Dev. Exch. **4**(1), 119–140 (2011)
2. Owen, M., Owen, S., Barajas, M., Trifonova, A.: Pedagogic issues and questions from the science centre to go, augmented reality, project implementation. In: Augmented Reality in Education, Proceedings of the "Science Center To Go' Workshops, pp. 3–15. Ellinogermaniki Agogi, Greece (2011)
3. Geiger, P., Schickler, M., Pryss, R., Schobel, J., Reichert, M.: Location-based mobile augmented reality applications: challenges, examples, lessons learned. In: 10th International Conference on Web Information Systems and Technologies, pp. 383–394, Spain (2014)
4. Gargalakos, M., Rogalas, D. EXPLOAR: visualizing the invisible, augmented reality in education. In: Proceedings of the "Science Center To Go' Workshops, pp. 51–61, Greece (2011)
5. Shelton, B.E., Hedley, N.R.: Using augmented reality for teaching earth-sun relationship to undergraduate geography students. In: The First IEEE International Augmented Reality Toolkit Workshop pp. 1–8, Germany (2002)
6. Klopfer, E., Squire, K.: Environmental detectives—the development of an augmented reality platform for environmental simulations. Educ. Technol. Res. Dev. **56**(2), 203–228 (2006)
7. Kaufmann, H.: Collaborative augmented reality in education. In: Proceedings of Imagina 2003 Conference, pp. 1–4, Monaco (2003)
8. Holloway, D., Green, L., Livingstone, S.: Zero to eight: young children and their internet use, LSE. EU Kids Online, London (2013)
9. Kaufmann, H., Schmalstieg, D.: Designing immersive virtual reality for geometry education. In: IEEE Virtual Reality Conference, pp. 51–58, Alexandria (2006)
10. Kirner, T.G., Reis, F.M.V., Kirner, C.: Development of an interactive book with augmented reality for teaching and learning geometric shapes. In: 7th Iberian Conference on Information Systems and Technologies, pp. 1–6, Madrid (2012)
11. Purnama, J., Andrew, D., Galinium, M.: Geometry learning tool for elementary school using augmented reality. In: International Conference on Industrial Automation and Information & Communications Technology, pp. 145–148, Indonesia (2014)
12. Radu, I., Doherty, E., DiQuolo, K., Tiu, M.: Cyberchase shape quest: pushing geometry education boundaries with augmented reality. In: The 14th International Conference on Interaction Design and Children, pp. 430–433 (2015).
13. Le, H.Q., Kim, J.I.: An augmented reality application with hand gestures for learning 3D geometry. In: IEEE International Conference on Big Data and Smart Computing, Shanghai, China (2017)
14. Jain, P., Manweiler, J., Choudhury, R.R.: OverLay: practical mobile augmented reality. In: 13th Annual International Conference on Mobile Systems, Applications, and Services, pp. 331–344, New York (2015)
15. Barfield, W.: Fundamentals of Wearable Computers and Augmented Reality, 2nd edn. CRC Press, Florida (2015)
16. Schell, J.: The Art of Game Design: Book of Lenses, 1st edn. CRC Press, Florida (2008)

17. Shabalina, O., Mozelius, P., Malliarakis, C., Tomos, F., Balan, O.C., Blackey, H., Gerkushenko, G.: Combining game-flow and learning objectives in educational games. In: 8th European Conference on Games-based Learning (2014)
18. Aldrich, C.: Learning by Doing: A Comprehensive Guide to Simulations, Computer Games, and Pedagogy in e-Learning and Other Educational Experiences, 1st edn. Pfeiffer, San Francisco (2005)
19. Bower, M., Howe C., McCredie N., Robinson, A., Grover, D.: Augmented reality in education – cases, places and potentials. In: International Council for Educational Media, pp. 1–15, Singapore (2013)
20. De Graaff, E., Kolmos, A.: Characteristics of problem-based learning. Int. J. Eng. Educ. **19**(5), 657–662 (2013)
21. Gomez Puente, S.M.: Design-based learning: exploring an educational approach for engineering education, pp. 171–195 (2014). Chap. 8
22. Gómez Puente, S.M., van Eijck, M., Jochems, W.: A sampled literature review of design based learning approaches: a search for key characteristics. Int. J. Technol. Des. Educ. **23**(3), 717–732 (2013)
23. Gómez Puente, S.M., van Eijck, M., Jochems, W.: Empirical validation of characteristics of design-based learning in higher education. Int. J. Eng. Educ. **29**(2), 491–503 (2013)
24. Van Haren, R.: Engaging learner diversity through learning by design. E-learn. Dig. Media **7**(3), 258–271 (2010)
25. Tarng, W., Ou, K.-L.: A Study of campus butterfly ecology learning system based on augmented reality and mobile learning. In: IEEE 7th International Conference on Wireless, Mobile and Ubiquitous Technology in Education, pp. 62–66, Takamatsu (2012)
26. Trybus, J.: Game-based learning: what it is, why it works, and where it's going. New Media Institute, Pittsburgh, Pennsylvania (2014)
27. Ifenthaler, D., Eseryel, D., Ge, X.: Assessment for game-based learning. In: Ifenthaler, D., Eseryel, D., Ge, X. (eds.) Assessment in Game-Based Learning, pp. 1–8. Springer, New York (2012). https://doi.org/10.1007/978-1-4614-3546-4_1
28. Loh, C.S.: Information trails: in-process assessment of game-based learning. In: Ifenthaler, D., Eseryel, D., Ge, X. (eds.) Assessment in Game-Based Learning, pp. 123–144. Springer, New York (2012). https://doi.org/10.1007/978-1-4614-3546-4_8
29. Csikszentmihalyi, M.: Beyond Boredom and Anxiety, 1st edn. Jossey-Bass, San Fransisco (1975)
30. Pausch, R., Gold, R., Skelly, T., Thiel, D.: What HCI designers can learn from video game designers. In: Conference on Human Factors in Computer Systems, pp. 177–178, Boston (1994)
31. Shute, V.J., Ke, F.: Games, learning, assessment. In: Ifenthaler, D., Eseryel, D., Ge, X. (eds.) Assessment in Game-Based Learning, pp. 43–58. Springer, New York (2012). https://doi.org/10.1007/978-1-4614-3546-4_4
32. Zimmerman, B.J., Schunk, D.H.: Models of self-regulated learning. In: Zimmerman, B.J., Schunk, D.H. (eds.) Self-regulated Learning and Academic Achievement, pp. 1–25. Springer, Heidelberg (1989). https://doi.org/10.1007/978-1-4612-3618-4_1
33. Gee, J.P.: What Video Games have to Teach us About Learning and Literacy, 2nd edn. St. Martin's Griffin, New York (2007)
34. Pulli, K., Baksheev, A., Kornyakov, K., Eruhimov, V.: Real-time computer vision with OpenCV. Commun. ACM **55**, 61–69 (2012)
35. Fullerton, T., Swain, C., Hoffman, S.: Game Design Workshop: a Playcentric Approach to Creating Innovative Games, 2nd edn. Morgan Kaufmann, San Francisco (2006)
36. Bartle, R.: Hearts, clubs, diamonds, spades: players who suit MUDs. J. MUD Res. **1**(1), 19–42 (1996)

Importance of User Experience Aspects for Different Software Product Categories

Harry Budi Santoso[1(✉)] and Martin Schrepp[2]

[1] Faculty of Computer Science, Universitas Indonesia, Depok, Indonesia
harrybs@cs.ui.ac.id
[2] SAP SE, Cloud Platform User Experience, Walldorf, Germany
martin.schrepp@sap.com

Abstract. A good user experience is a must for modern software products. However, in software product design we have to often deal with conflicting requirements. A new software product feature may increase efficiency, but on the other hand decrease learnability of the product. Such types of conflicts often cause lengthy discussions, since it is often not clear which user experience aspect has the higher importance or priority for the software product. Thus, to make valid design decisions in such situations requires an understanding of the importance of different user experience aspects for different types of software products. We present a study that investigates the importance of 16 commonly used user experience aspects for a range of 15 common software product categories. The results show that the importance of the user experience aspects vary heavily between different product categories. Results can be directly used by product designers to derive some conclusions about the relative importance of different design requirements for their projects and thus help them to make good design decisions.

Keywords: User experience · UX aspects · UX measurement

1 Introduction

In today's competitive markets a good level of user experience (short UX) is a prerequisite for the commercial success of software products. UX is a very subjective impression, so in principle it is difficult to measure [1]. In addition, UX is clearly a multi-dimensional concept [2], i.e. it is based on a huge number of different aspects of a software product, for example the beauty of the interface design, the efficiency of the interaction, how easy it is to learn how to use the product, and many other aspects [3].

Within this paper, we conceptualize user experience as a set of semantically independent UX aspects or UX quality criteria. The overall UX impression of a person towards a software product will result as a consequence of the detailed perception of these UX quality aspects [4].

However, not all UX aspects will be of equal importance for different types of products [5]. For example, for a web shop, intuitive use is of central importance. A user must be able to place an order without reading instructions or help. Efficiency, for such a shop is most likely not a central user experience requirement, i.e. as long as the

© Springer Nature Singapore Pte Ltd. 2018
N. Abdullah et al. (Eds.): i-USEr 2018, CCIS 886, pp. 231–241, 2018.
https://doi.org/10.1007/978-981-13-1628-9_21

interaction is intuitive users most likely do not complain about a few unnecessary clicks. For a programming tool or business software that is used the whole day by user, efficiency is clearly the most important UX aspect, while users typically accept to learn how to use the software product, thus intuitive use is, in general, not expected for such products. Another example which shows this dependency of the importance of UX aspects on the product type or product category, are games. Here, fun of use is a central UX aspect, which is of course not relevant at all for an online banking app, a spread sheet or word processing application.

The concrete dependencies between UX aspects and product types are not much known in the moment. We present a study that tries to clarify the importance of common UX aspects for typical product categories.

A detailed knowledge of the importance of UX aspects can help in designing products [6]. Often different UX requirements contradict each other. For example, a new product feature can add complexity and make it harder to learn how to use the product, but on the other hand this feature may increase efficiency. If we design a business software and know that efficiency is much more important than learnability for this type of products we can easily solve this design conflict and save time by reducing unnecessary discussions.

It must also be considered that the importance of an UX aspect for a certain type of product may vary in different cultures [7]. Thus, it is important to collect data concerning the importance of UX aspects in different countries.

2   User Experience Aspects

So how can we determine a list of suitable UX aspects? As a basis for such a list of aspects described in the international norm DIN EN ISO 9241-210 [8], the dimensions used in typical user experience questionnaires or an own list of relevant aspects for a special product category can be used. The DIN EN ISO 9241-210 lists a number of different UX dimensions in an attempt to define the term user experience more precisely. These include user specific factors, e.g. skills, behaviors or personal goals, but also product related properties that support a good user experience.

Questionnaires for the measurement of user experience define UX dimensions in the form of scales, i.e. sub-groups of items that are assumed to measure a common aspect, which is usually described by the scale name. For example, the user experience questionnaire (UEQ) contains the scales *Attractiveness, Perspicuity, Efficiency, Controllability, Stimulation* and *Originality* [4] (an Indonesian translation of this questionnaire is described by [9]). The SUMI [10] contains scales *Efficiency, Affect, Helpfulness, Control*, and *Learnability*. Here *Efficiency* in the UEQ and SUMI describe the same UX aspect, and this is also true for *Controllability* (UEQ) and *Control* (SUMI), respectively *Perspicuity* (UEQ) and *Learnability* (SUMI). The other UEQ dimensions have no counterpart in the SUMI and vice versa. In addition, there are several highly-specialized questionnaires, which measure only a single UX dimension, for example the VISAWI [11] that measures visual aesthetics.

The advantage of standardized questionnaires, like the UEQ or the SUMI, is that they can be used directly and efficiently to get a UX measurement for a product.

However, each questionnaire defines by the selection of the scales an own variant of the concept of user experience, i.e. some UX aspects are not measured at all, since a corresponding scale is not available. Thus, for practical purposes it is often required to use more than one UX questionnaire to measure all UX aspects that are of interest in the context of a product evaluation. An analysis of all the currently available questionnaires can provide quite a good overview about the UX aspects that are considered as relevant in the field.

For the study described in the next section, we refer on a list of UX aspects created by [5, 12]. In [5] a list of 22 UX factors were extracted from the analysis of existing UX questionnaires, a broad literature review and by interviewing some UX experts. This list was then used in a first empirical study to investigate the importance of these UX aspects for different products. Based on the results this list was reduced to a list of 16 aspects, which was again [12] validated in an empirical study. The original list of UX aspects is in German, we show in the following list a careful English translation of the aspect names and descriptions:

- **Content Quality:** The information provided by the product are always actual and of good quality.
- **Customization:** I can adapt the product to my personal preferences or personal work style.
- **Perspicuity:** It is easy to understand and learn how to use the product.
- **Efficiency:** I can achieve my goals with minimal time and physical effort. The product responds quickly to my input.
- **Immersion:** When I deal with the product, I forget the time. I completely sink into the interaction with the product.
- **Intuitive Usage:** I can use the product directly without any learning or the help of other people.
- **Usefullness:** Using the product brings me advantages. It saves me time and effort and makes me more productive.
- **Novelty:** The design of the product is interesting and unusual. The original design catches my attention.
- **Beauty:** The product is beautiful and attractive.
- **Identity:** The product helps me to make contacts and to present myself positively.
- **Controlability:** The product always reacts predictably and consistently to my input. I always have full control over the interaction.
- **Stimulation:** I find the product stimulating and exciting. It's fun to deal with the product.
- **Clarity:** I find the user interface of the product looks tidy and clear.
- **Loyality:** Even if there are other equivalent products for the same tasks, I would not change the product.
- **Trust:** My given data is in safe hands. The data will not be misused to harm me.
- **Value:** I find the product makes a high-quality and professional impression.

The results of the study [12] showed that participants could understand the UX aspects and their corresponding descriptions without problems. In addition, they were able to judge the importance of these UX categories for several product categories. Thus, the list is a good candidate to be applied as a basis for our study in Indonesia.

3 Study to Determine the Importance of UX Aspects

3.1 Participants

One hundred and fourteen students of Faculty of Computer Science, Universitas Indonesia (64 male, 50 female) participated in the study. The mean age was 21.34 years.

The students enrolled in Human-Computer Interaction course. The course is mandatory and it is available for the third-year (junior level) students. The lecturer explained the importance of UX aspects in the middle of the semester after they learned about Data Gathering topic. It was intended to provide a better understanding about data collection process.

The students were given around one week to complete the judgment process because it takes times to make a good judgment based on their reflection upon particular software products. The students who completed the task by judging the importance of UX aspects received an additional score for their participation.

3.2 Material

The participants should judge the importance of the UX aspects described in the previous section for 15 product categories. The product categories were chosen to represent a broad range of available products. The categories were described by a category name and several examples of concrete products from that category:

- **Word Processing:** Ms Word, MS Power Point, LaTex, Writer (Open Office)
- **Spreadsheet:** MS Excel, Calc (Open Office)
- **Messenger:** WhatsApp, Facebook Messenger, Snapchat
- **Social Network:** Facebook, Xing, LinkedIn
- **Video Conferencing:** Skype, Google hangout
- **Web Shops:** Tokopedia, Bukalapak, Shopee
- **News Portals:** detik.com, liputan6.com
- **Booking Systems:** Traveloka, Trivago
- **Info web pages:** http://www.ui.ac.id, http://smartcity.jakarta.go.id/
- **Learning platforms:** Udemy, Udacity
- **Programming tools:** Eclipse, Visual Studio
- **Image processing:** Photoshop, CorelDraw, gimp
- **Online banking:** m-BCA, mandiri mobile, jenius
- **Video portals:** Youtube, Netflix
- **Games:** DoTA2, Mobile Legend

Examples represent common or popular products of the corresponding category in Indonesia. The examples are quite important to make sure that the participants get a clear understanding of the meaning of the product category.

3.3   Procedure

An MS Excel list containing the 16 UX aspects as rows and the product categories as column headers was available on a learning management system (LMS) used at the faculty. The enrolled students were asked to download, fill out, and upload the Excel file through the LMS. All texts were translated to Indonesian, so participants could fill the information in their natural language. As descriptions for the UX aspects the translated version of the texts shown in the previous section were used.

Each cell could be filled with the answer categories: *Meaningless* (this should be used if the UX aspect did not make sense at all for the product category), *Extremely unimportant* (1), *Somewhat unimportant* (2), *Slightly unimportant* (3), *Neutral* (4), *Slightly important* (5), *Somewhat important* (6), *Extremely important* (7). With 16 UX aspects and 15 product categories the participants had thus to fill 240 cells, i.e. had to make 240 decisions. As demographic data, sex and age were asked in two separate input fields inside the Excel list.

The concrete instruction for filling out the MS Excel was: *In the following, several quality criteria for interactive products are given. Your task is to decide how important these quality criteria are for the overall assessment of different product categories. Of course, all quality criteria describe positive aspects of a product. But please do NOT classify them therefore all as important. Use the category "Meaningless" only if the formulation of the quality criterion makes absolutely no sense from your impression. In all other cases please provide an importance rating! Consider exactly per product category and quality criterion how you would personally rate the importance. There are no objectively correct or wrong answers. Your personal assessment counts!*

3.4   Results

First, we look at the mean values of the importance ratings per UX aspect and product category. These values are shown in Fig. 1 as bar charts. The exact numeric values and standard deviations are shown in Table 1.

The different product categories vary massively concerning the importance of the UX aspects. But we also can see that product categories that are similar concerning use cases and usage scenarios show similar profiles. This is true, for example, for word processing and spreadsheet or programming tools and image processing. Some product categories, for example games, show quite distinct profiles.

Concerning interindividual differences it was observed that the standard deviations for the means range between 0.64 and 1.86 (average over all standard deviations was 1.31). Thus, different persons vary heavily concerning their subjective impression of the importance of the UX aspects. In addition, this also depends on the product category and dimension. Thus, for some combinations of product category and UX aspect the level of agreement between subjects is much higher than for others (see Table 1).

Some UX aspects show consistently a high rating over different product categories. These are mainly pragmatic quality aspects, e.g. *Content Quality, Perspicuity, Efficiency, Usefulness, Controllability, Clarity* and to some extent *Value*. For others, for example *Identity*, the rating varies massively between product categories.

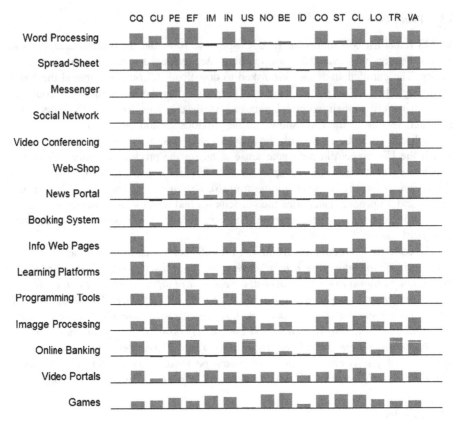

Fig. 1. Means for the importance ratings for the UX aspects Content Quality (CQ), Customization (CU), Perspicuity (PE), Efficiency (EF), Immersion (IM), Intuitive Use (IN), Usefulness (US), Novelty (NO), Beauty (BE), Identity (ID), Controllability (CO), Stimulation (ST), Clarity (CL), Loyalty (LO), Trust (TR), Value (VA).

The data set was also split into male and female participants to check if there are differences between these groups concerning the importance ratings. However, except for one combination of product category and UX aspect, no significant differences were found between male and female participants for the other 239 combinations of UX aspect and product category on the 5% level (t-test, two-sided). Thus, the sex of the participants seems to have no influence of the importance ratings.

Now we look at the similarity of UX aspects. Similarity in this context means that two UX aspects show similar importance ratings over all investigated 15 software product categories.

We use multi-dimensional scaling (short MDS) [13] to visualize similarity between UX aspects. A MDS is based on a set of objects (in our case the UX aspects) and a matrix that shows for each pair of objects their similarity. In our case the similarity index is calculated on the basis of the correlations of the importance ratings over all product categories, i.e. the higher this correlation is the more similar are the UX aspects.

Table 1. Means (top) and standard deviations (bottom) of the importance ratings.

	CQ	CU	PE	EF	IM	IN	US	NO	BE	ID	CO	ST	CL	LO	TR	VA
Word processing	5.64	5.24	6.62	6.48	3.75	5.91	6.55	4.22	4.35	4.02	6.03	4.42	6.27	5.30	5.75	5.98
	1.27	1.65	0.68	0.64	1.47	1.13	0.69	1.59	1.40	1.64	1.08	1.50	0.96	1.46	1.40	1.11
Spreadsheet	5.67	5.12	6.51	6.54	3.87	5.75	6.58	4.21	4.28	3.95	6.02	4.39	6.27	5.15	5.80	5.96
	1.29	1.69	0.79	0.67	1.52	1.27	0.77	1.53	1.48	1.59	1.07	1.48	1.00	1.58	1.37	1.16
Programming tools	5.70	5.82	6.34	6.23	4.65	5.66	6.25	4.79	4.58	4.15	6.14	5.13	6.02	5.04	5.44	5.99
	1.37	1.69	1.08	0.95	1.59	1.04	1.33	1.07	1.11	1.38	1.10	1.28	0.84	1.33	0.88	1.40
Image processing	5.45	5.72	5.96	5.98	4.79	5.46	6.03	5.06	5.19	4.09	5.93	5.14	6.06	5.19	5.12	5.79
	1.21	1.36	0.92	1.22	1.59	1.03	1.37	1.03	1.03	1.25	1.21	1.21	0.92	1.38	1.10	1.39
Booking system	6.53	4.67	6.35	6.51	4.28	6.13	6.12	5.61	5.84	4.33	6.06	5.06	6.33	5.75	6.40	6.04
	1.36	1.50	1.08	1.06	1.51	1.24	1.10	1.40	1.47	1.57	1.23	1.41	0.96	1.42	1.04	1.35
Online banking	6.24	3.93	6.36	6.38	3.87	6.03	6.38	4.50	4.61	4.26	5.98	4.36	6.03	4.88	6.65	6.22
	1.01	1.75	0.96	0.92	1.58	1.06	1.35	1.11	1.02	1.71	1.19	1.34	0.70	1.58	0.91	1.27
Web-shop	6.36	4.47	6.24	6.29	4.86	5.92	5.86	5.72	5.94	4.50	5.82	5.33	6.44	5.56	6.46	6.00
	0.85	1.67	1.46	1.48	1.59	1.29	1.49	1.30	1.23	1.71	1.55	1.51	1.14	1.65	1.55	1.34
Messenger	5.67	4.77	6.22	6.25	5.26	6.19	5.88	5.71	5.71	5.38	5.98	5.46	6.37	5.61	6.58	5.51
	0.77	1.77	0.86	0.78	1.75	0.92	1.23	1.19	1.06	1.72	1.14	1.50	0.94	1.36	1.11	1.21
Social network	5.84	5.38	6.14	5.83	5.57	5.95	5.39	5.91	5.98	5.78	5.89	5.77	6.28	5.48	6.39	5.61
	0.81	1.67	1.33	1.48	1.60	1.39	1.40	1.19	1.17	1.73	1.68	1.57	1.18	1.65	1.68	1.38
Video conferencing	5.44	4.65	5.83	6.12	4.88	5.74	5.91	5.03	5.10	4.92	5.68	5.19	6.06	5.11	6.19	5.50
	0.84	1.53	0.96	1.02	1.51	1.15	0.69	1.27	1.19	1.52	1.07	1.54	1.05	1.60	1.35	1.24
Learning platforms	6.56	5.12	6.35	6.12	4.86	5.89	6.44	5.13	5.25	4.99	5.91	5.39	6.26	4.90	5.91	6.04
	1.28	1.22	1.09	1.01	1.67	1.30	1.14	1.50	1.43	1.73	1.06	1.53	1.10	1.49	1.64	1.11
Video portals	5.75	4.63	5.57	5.46	5.74	5.47	5.22	5.50	5.54	4.99	5.54	5.92	6.11	5.33	5.68	5.38
	1.36	1.42	1.37	1.09	1.65	1.41	1.26	1.31	1.23	1.67	1.21	1.40	1.00	1.43	1.75	1.16
News portal	6.53	3.78	5.26	5.26	4.74	5.51	5.14	5.29	5.39	3.99	5.09	4.85	5.90	4.76	5.38	5.68
	1.23	1.83	0.97	0.83	1.72	1.10	0.92	1.59	1.48	1.73	1.35	1.66	1.15	1.72	0.80	1.12
Info web pages	6.45	3.92	5.57	5.26	4.08	5.45	5.50	5.23	5.31	4.12	5.15	4.61	5.96	4.31	5.61	5.71
	1.21	1.64	1.28	1.34	1.45	1.45	1.51	1.18	1.18	1.52	1.33	1.20	0.93	1.47	1.34	1.36
Games	5.15	5.17	5.64	5.14	5.92	5.67	4.22	6.03	6.22	4.70	5.96	6.03	5.95	5.30	5.08	5.15
	1.68	1.69	1.35	1.67	1.60	1.41	1.86	1.30	1.15	1.80	1.27	1.38	1.23	1.82	1.86	1.63
Average	5.93	4.83	6.06	5.99	4.74	5.78	5.83	5.20	5.29	4.55	5.81	5.14	6.15	5.18	5.90	5.77

An MDS shows the objects as points in a two-dimensional space, so that the Euclidean distance between the points reflects the similarity of the objects as close as possible. Thus, it is mainly a visualization technique to show groups or clusters of similar objects in the data set.

The results of the MDS for our data set are shown in Fig. 2. Please note that the exact position of an UX aspect in the diagram is meaningless, only the distances between the points can be interpreted in the sense that a smaller distance represents a higher similarity.

We can clearly see a group of hedonic non-task related aspects [14] on the right (*Beauty, Novelty, Identity, Stimulation, Immersion*) and a group of pragmatic task related aspects [14] at the lower left corner (*Usefulness, Efficiency, Perspicuity, Controllability, Customization*).

What is a little bit surprising is the position of *Intuitive Usage* and *Clarity*. First, they are seen by the participants as very similar concerning their importance for the

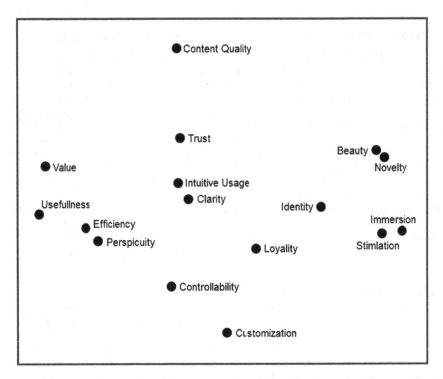

Fig. 2. Multi-dimensional scaling of the UX aspects. The smaller the distance between two UX aspects is, the more similar are their importance ratings over all 15 product categories.

investigated 15 product categories. From the semantic meaning of *Intuitive Usage,* one would expect a much closer connection to *Perspicuity*, since if a product is intuitive to use it is not necessary to learn it as it is easy to understand. However, this connection is not true in the other direction, i.e. a product that shows a high level of *Perspicuity* must not at all be intuitive.

Content Quality is quite different from the other aspects, which is also natural given its definition. The two aspects *Trust* and *Loyalty* are somewhere between pragmatic and hedonic qualities. *Value* is heavily related to the pragmatic qualities, i.e. a high-quality impression is strongly related to the task-oriented product quality.

Using the same technique, we can also visualize the similarity of the product groups. Thus, we consisted two product categories as similar if they show similar importance ratings over all 16 investigated UX aspects. This corresponds to similar profiles in Fig. 1, i.e. participants expect the same pattern of UX aspects for both products.

We can see that Games, Video Portals and Social Networks have not much similarity to any other group. Image Processing and Programming Tools have similar expectations concerning their important UX aspects and built a group. The rest of the products shows similar profiles, but we can see inside this cluster some sub-groups, for example Word Processing and Spreadsheet (Fig. 3).

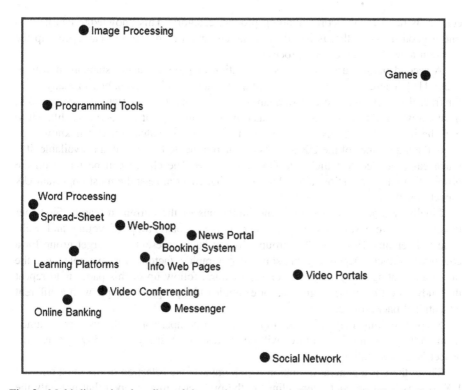

Fig. 3. Multi-dimensional scaling of the product categories. The smaller the distance between two product categories is, the higher is their similarity concerning the importance rating for all 16 UX aspects.

4 Discussion

We investigated how important the different common UX aspects are considered for common types of products. Thus, participants in a study rated the importance of 16 UX aspects taken from another study [12] to a list of 15 common product categories.

Results showed that different product categories varied heavily concerning the importance rating of the UX aspects, thus which UX aspect is important or unimportant varies massively with the type of product.

So how can UX designers or UX researchers make use of this results?

As already mentioned, quite often a certain product feature or design element has a positive impact on one UX aspect and a negative impact on another UX aspect. Therefore, a design conflict occurs. The designer must decide if the product feature should be implemented or not. Such a decision requires knowledge about the relative importance of the two affected aspects. In an ideal situation, users can be contacted and interviewed, and the decision can be based on this feedback. But in the real project, it is often not so easy to organize. Sometimes this is due to time restrictions or sometimes because it is not easy to find users who can give feedback. In such situations, it can be quite helpful to know how the importance of the UX aspects affected by the design conflict is rated for the corresponding product category. This knowledge can help to find a good decision that is based on some empirical evidence and can speed up the decision as well as the design process.

A second natural use case is the evaluation of products using standard questionnaires [15]. There are a huge number of such questionnaires available, in many cases for free. But each of these questionnaires offers different scales (which correspond in most cases to the UX aspects investigated in this paper), so it is practically difficult to find the best matching UX questionnaire for a product evaluation. But if knowledge about the importance of the UX aspects for the product to be evaluated is available, it is much easier to decide which questionnaire to use. The choice can be based on the observation which questionnaire offers scales that cover at least the most important UX aspects for the product.

Finally, we have to mention some limitations of the current research. First, our target group were students, i.e. a rather homogeneous group of young and well-educated persons. However, this group may not be a representative target group for a concrete product. Depending on some demographic factors, for example age, the importance ratings may vary. Therefore, a natural follow up of this paper is to repeat the study for different target groups, for example older people or people with a different educational background.

Second, culture may have an impact, thus a comparison with answers obtained from participants in other cultures will be interesting. A study which investigates this aspect is in preparation.

Third, there is a general limitation which impacts the selection of the most relevant UX aspects for a product. Depending on the product it may happen that not only the UX aspects relevant for the end users are important for the design, but that other UX criteria required for marketing the product must be considered. For example, assume we have a tool for programming. We see in our data that hedonic aspects like beauty or originality are not seen as relevant by users. However, if this product is new and should prominently be shown on marketing events or conferences targeted at developers, these aspects may be very important for the commercial success of the company that builds the product. Thus, such specific requirements may change the view on the importance of UX aspects. But in fact, they are easily to get in the sense that product management will articulate them directly when a product design process starts. Thus, the list of UX aspects relevant for users can easily be expanded to also consider such marketing specific needs.

References

1. Law, A.L., Schaik, P.V., Roto, V.: Attitudes towards user experience (UX) measurement. Hum.-Comput. Stud. **72**, 526–541 (2014)
2. Lallemand, C., Gronier, G., Koenig, V.: User experience: a concept without consensus? Exploring practitioners' perspectives through an international survey. Comput. Hum. Behav. **43**, 35–48 (2015)
3. Preece, J., Sharp, H., Rogers, Y.: Interaction Design – Beyond Human-Computer Interaction. Wiley, Chichester (2015)

4. Laugwitz, B., Held, T., Schrepp, M.: Construction and evaluation of a user experience questionnaire. In: Holzinger, A. (ed.) USAB 2008. LNCS, vol. 5298, pp. 63–76. Springer, Heidelberg (2008). https://doi.org/10.1007/978-3-540-89350-9_6

5. Winter, D., Schrepp, M., Thomaschewski, J.: Faktoren der User Experience: Systematische Übersicht über produktrelevante UX-Qualitätsaspekte. In: Endmann, A., Fischer, H., Krökel, M. (eds.) Mensch und Computer 2015 - Usability Professionals, pp. 33–41. De Gruyter Oldenbourg, Berlin (2015)

6. Winter, D., Bittenbinder, S.: UX-Controlling in der Produktentwicklung: Gezielt zum Produkt mit positiver User Experience (2014). http://www.germanupa.de/events/mensch-und-computer-2014/agile-ux/ux-controlling-in-der-produktentwicklung.html

7. Santoso, H., Schrepp, M., Hinderks, A., Thomaschewski, J.: Cultural differences in the perception of user experience. In: Burghardt, M., Wimmer, R., Wolff, C., Womser-Hacker, C. (Hrsg.) Mensch und Computer 2017 – Tagungsband, pp. 267–272. Gesellschaft für Informatik e.V., Regensburg (2017)

8. DIN EN ISO 9241-210: Ergonomie der Mensch-System-Interaktion - Teil 210: Prozess zur Gestaltung gebrauchstauglicher interaktiver Systeme (2011)

9. Santoso, H.B., Schrepp, M., Isal, R.Y.K., Utomo, A.Y., Priyogi, B.: User experience questionnaire: development of an Indonesian version and its usage for product evaluation. J. Educ. Online-JEO 13(1), 58–79 (2016). ISSN 1547-500X

10. Kirakowski, J., Corbett, M.: SUMI: the software usability measurement inventory. Br. J. Edu. Technol. 24(3), 210–212 (1993)

11. Moshagen, M., Thielsch, M.T.: Facets of visual aesthetics. Int. J. Hum Comput Stud. 68(10), 689–709 (2010)

12. Winter, D., Hinderks, A., Schrepp, M., Thomaschewski, J.: Welche UX Faktoren sind für mein Produkt wichtig? In: Hess, S., Fischer, H. (Hrsg.) Mensch und Computer 2017 - Usability Professionals. Gesellschaft für Informatik e.V., Regensburg (2017)

13. Torgerson, W.S.: Theory and Methods of Scaling. Wiley, New York (1958)

14. Hassenzahl, M.: The effect of perceived hedonic quality on product appealingness. Int. J. Hum.-Comput. Interact. 13(4), 481–499 (2001)

15. Santoso, H.B., Schrepp, M., Basaruddin, C., Isal, Y.C., Sadita, L.: User experience evaluation of student centered e-learning environment for computer science program. In: Proceedings i-USEr Conference (2014)

Designing a Mobile-Based Solution
for Self-management of Chronic Pain

Fatma Meawad[1(✉)], Su-Yin Yang[2], Fong Ling Loy[2],
Ee Joe Chang[1], and Muhammad Halim Isryad[1]

[1] School of Computing, University of Glasgow, Singapore, Singapore
fatma.meawad@glasgow.ac.uk
[2] Pain Management Clinic, Tan Tock Seng Hospital, Singapore, Singapore
{su_yin_yang,fong_ling_loy}@ttsh.com.sg

Abstract. Chronic pain or simply defined as non-malignant pain which last more than 3 months, remains one of the most difficult medical conditions to treat in current times. There is no known cure for chronic pain whereby self-management approaches are often encouraged as part of treatment delivery. A multi-modal bio-psychosocial approach is the key in managing this complex condition. However, such treatments are usually delivered in specialist clinics with long waiting list and high costs. There is also usually a time lag between the patient's pain experience and the consultation from the clinic. The increasing accessibility of mobile technology platforms in recent years makes them appealing tools for promoting personal health and fitness. Numerous applications (apps) have been designed to track activity levels, set exercise routines, and encourage healthy eating as well as other lifestyle changes. Within the context of chronic pain management, a mobile application incorporating a multidisciplinary treatment model may be able to help people with chronic pain to self-monitor their pain and engage in real-time pain management strategies. This is in addition to addressing the access barriers and costs. It may also support the maintenance of long-term treatment that has been inconsistently achieved with conventional face-to-face sessions. This paper describes the design, development, and evaluation of a first prototype app that includes features to bridge the current gaps in mobile solutions for pain management. Specifically, features that integrate health professional input, elements that address the multidimensional nature of pain and tailored behavior change strategies.

Keywords: Personal health technologies · Chronic pain management
Smart mobile applications · Human computer interaction

1 Introduction

The estimated global prevalence of chronic pain stands at 28% of the world's adult population [5]. This prevalence, although much lower in individual countries in East and Southeast Asia (7% to 15%) [4, 11], it still remains high by any healthcare standard and should contribute to a global healthcare priority.

© Springer Nature Singapore Pte Ltd. 2018
N. Abdullah et al. (Eds.): i-USEr 2018, CCIS 886, pp. 242–251, 2018.
https://doi.org/10.1007/978-981-13-1628-9_22

Chronic pain is expensive to treat, compared to typical healthcare; the cost is almost 3 times higher for people with chronic pain than those without [10]. An estimate of US $16.4 billion [15] and £584 million alone is spent annually in the United States and in the United Kingdom [2, 9] respectively on pharmacological treatments for pain. In Singapore, an estimate of S$8.4 billion annually was reported to be spent on managing head and body pain [13].

As at current, there is no known cure for chronic pain. An interdisciplinary, self-management treatment model, focused on reducing pain interference is recommended as a standard model of care [6]. Such programs however require intensive health professional involvement, incur high costs, time commitment and often result in high attrition rates. Measured treatment outcomes are also reliant on patients' self-reports. Such reports may be subjected to many biases and may not present an objective reference of patient's actual pain and pain-related experiences.

1.1 Mobile Health Applications

Smartphone applications, which have been popularly utilized in many settings including healthcare, can contribute to an enhanced delivery of the current standard model of care for chronic pain. There already is a variety of chronic pain-related mobile applications in the market [8]. These applications allow the user to monitor and acquire information about a specific pain condition. Users are however required to give input on a series of information before an output response is generated. As for the pain applications available in the market at current, 54% provide general information, 24% include some form of tracking program, and only 17% include specific information related to pain management. Specific information includes types of exercises to do and the types of activities to avoid keeping the pain under control. Majority of the pain applications (58.5%) include only a single self-management function and lack healthcare professional participation in the application.

The mobile penetration rate in Singapore in 2016 was reported at 149.8%, with 12.86 petabytes of mobile data utilized across the country[1]. Such high recorded rates of mobile data penetration and utilization provide an excellent opportunity for collecting useful contextual data to design appropriate mobile applications for patients with pain in Singapore. Smartphone applications designed for the self-management of chronic pain for this context should be easy to use, perceived to be useful by the user, appropriate for tracking symptoms, allow real-time pain measurement and management, offer a platform for patients to communicate with their health professional team and provide sufficient information and interaction that can increase the confidence of patients to self-manage pain [16].

1.2 A New Focus

In this paper, we introduce a new chronic pain management system designed to allow patients to monitor their pain progress, not only through (1) self-recording of daily

---

[1] https://www.imda.gov.sg/industry-development/facts-and-figures/telecommunications#9x.

pain events, but also through (2) an interactive communication portal with the professional either via an instant messaging or through a community forum and (3) a notification feature to remind patients to engage in specific tailored activities as recommended by their health professionals. These recommendations include management of pain medications and outpatient appointments, exercise, and psychology-based management strategies.

Our main objective of designing this system was to establish the feasibility and usefulness of the system by assessing its (1) adequacy to provide self-management strategies that may allow the patient to reduce their dependence on the health professional; (2) the usability of the system, focusing especially on whether it is easy to use as compared to other existing application; (3) the usefulness in helping the patient to cope with their daily activities and (4) the system - if used on a regular basis by chronic pain patient - will be useful to them in the long run.

2   The Pain Management System

The system discussed in this paper, was designed following an iterative design process in participation with healthcare professionals in pain management. The system targets patients between the age of 21 and 65. Multiple requirement analysis and prototype refinement meetings were conducted by the designers with participation from the healthcare professionals. In order to further understand the context, the designers observed pain assessment and consultation sessions done by the healthcare personnel. The continuous feedback from the professionals steered the design of the system to focus on decreasing the level of interference of pain in patients' lives, improving patients' adherence and enabling some sort of social support among patients and ex-patients with light moderation from healthcare professionals. The resulting features were grouped into three main themes; (a) tracking of pain-related events and their parameters, (b) automated reminders and follow-ups to assist further in the management process and (c) establishing a platform for regularized communication and discussions to introduce some sort of social support. The final theme features revolve around developing a trusted community for chronic pain patients, which fills a clear gap in existing chronic pain management systems.

A thin mobile client application was built for Android based mobile devices. The application is thin since all the logic and data are maintained on an online server to keep the mobile application lightweight. The mobile client uses REST to invoke PHP server-side web services running on Apache web server using a PostgreSQL database.

One important design requirement is to keep the self-reported data entry to a minimum value to maintain a high rate of commitment. In the meantime, the entered data should be sufficient for use later by the professionals, and for generating useful follow-ups or reports. Based on the input from pain professionals and patient observations, the pain event was divided to include a set of mandatory and optional questions. Moreover, several design decisions were made to assist in simplifying the process. In the following subsections, we unpack the discussed themes and discuss their features in terms of value and design decisions.

2.1 Tracking Events

A thorough review of existing applications and the discussions with professionals led to defining three events that are of most value to the pain management process; pain episode, medicine intake and doctor appointment. Figure 1 shows the main screens related to these events. For each event, we keep the mandatory data entry to a minimum. Moreover, we allow patients to complete or modify information at any time and use the features offline. The main entry to all events is a calendar view (Fig. 1a), where all patients' events are visualized and color coded. The calendar view acts as a homepage summary of the patients' activity as it additionally shows the number of steps done by the user every day. The device's accelerometer is used to capture this value.

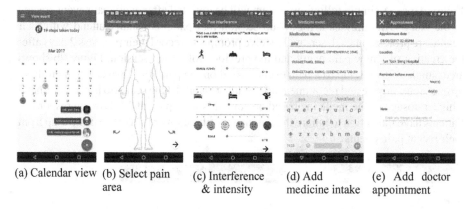

| (a) Calendar view | (b) Select pain area | (c) Interference & intensity | (d) Add medicine intake | (e) Add doctor appointment |

Fig. 1. The main screens related to tracking events in the pain management systems

To create a pain diary, the only mandatory options are specifying the pain area, intensity and the time. All other parameters are optional, for example, ranking pain areas per intensity, interferences level, pain duration or notes taking. Patients are given a chance to enter multiple notes either as text or even audio, which can be an alternative to typing which many patients are not comfortable with. A field trial of a similar personal health application showed that the text entry on the phone was never used by the patients [1]. In this application, all optional data entry can be skipped and replaced by these free-form multimodal notes. Relying only on audio will affect the automatic summary insights but could contribute to a better commitment to maintain the diary due to its simplicity.

For the medicine intake event, more mandatory fields are required, for example, medicine name, medicine type, date, frequency, and dosage. Based on the input from professionals, this element of pain management is challenging since patients tend to take random doses of medicine and forget to report their precise intakes during the consultation. However, to improve the experience, these fields are developed as either auto-complete or with common defaults to improve the entry process.

2.2   Feedback and Follow-Ups

Existing work in personal health technologies revealed that simple mechanisms for reminders and follow-ups with the patients can ensure adherence on the part of the user for personal health technologies [1]. We discuss three added features to support this dimension in our application.

Automatic Reminders. Skipping medication is an issue for current chronic pain patients. For the medicine intake event, multiple automatic notifications are scheduled to remind the patients of the intakes. For doctor appointments, patients can schedule special reminders by creating an appointment.

Follow-Ups. A simple follow-up system will be initiated after every pain event created in the diary. This mimics a follow-up session that patients usually attend with their healthcare professionals. Users will receive prompts to record their progress 2 days after the creation of a new pain event and the previous follow-up session. Figure 2b shows an example of follow-up to a pain event. Based on the patient's answers to the follow-up questions, advice and recommendations are presented. One scenario is to recommend a higher dosage of the medicine based on comparison of patients' follow-up responses. Patients have the option to ignore the reminder notification or turn off the follow up from their recent pain events.

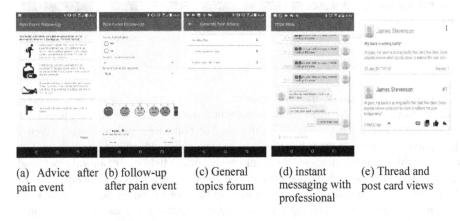

(a) Advice after pain event   (b) follow-up after pain event   (c) General topics forum   (d) instant messaging with professional   (e) Thread and post card views

Fig. 2. The main screens related to follow-ups (a–b) and communication (c–e) in the pain management systems.

Tailored Advice. A short pain-related advice generated after each successful creation of a pain event is meant to provide useful self-management tips and strategies. This includes information about (1) taking medicine as prescribed, (2) performing daily exercises as instructed by their health professionals, (3) reinforcing activities pacing, (4) monitoring of pain and progress update (see Fig. 2a).

2.3 Regularized Communication and Interaction

Social support is known to have a positive impact on recovery and adaptation of pain among patients [14]. Integrating mobile applications with current social media platforms does not preserve patients' privacy or give them confidence for sharing sensitive information and questions. Therefore, we integrate such connection to social support in our system by enabling peer support with the involvement of professionals. Our solution for communication consists of two main modules: instant chat and forums. The forums are organized as a repository for useful information organized into several categories and subcategories, to ensure that the correct resources and content are easily recorded and accessible. Creating main topics can only be done by the healthcare professionals. Textual and media content of any type can be shared on the forums to help the patients, for example; an exercise animated image can be added to guide patients to do their exercises properly. The discussions with the professionals steered the design of the forums to give administration access to professionals, but at the same time invite participations from all patients and ex-patients. The aim here is to create a trusted community for the patients where they can share their experiences and expect sensible replies knowing that the forum is managed by the professionals. In the meantime, patients can create new discussion topics, which are presented as forum threads, or post a response to another thread as a reply to other patients.

The instant messaging function enables communication between the patients and doctors. This allows for a quick response to simple questions about the patient's condition. The instant messaging function is similar to other mobile application such as WhatsApp or Telegram. However, in this case, the instant messaging is restricted to patients and professionals. The professionals are identified by their role (psychologists, physiotherapist, etc.), not their real names.

3 Evaluation

An initial evaluation of the pain management application was conducted to investigate HCI and feasibility related issues. Ten subjects that meet the inclusion criteria were recruited to participate in the evaluation of the Pain Management System. The inclusion criteria were; (1) within the age 21 and 65 years, (2) familiar with an Android smartphone and (3) were one of the stakeholders of the mobile application. The subjects evaluated the system as potential users suffering from some form of pain condition. The system was pre-installed on a standard Google Nexus 6P smartphone.

The main objectives of the evaluation were to determine the usability of the system, and the usefulness of the system in helping users better manage their pain. The following aspects were considered:

1. The usability of this new system
2. The possibility of using this new system on a regular or daily basis
3. The adequacy and usefulness of the self-management advice in allowing users to be more independent in managing their pain.

3.1 Methods

User feedback was collected using two questionnaires and a semi-structured interview. Usability was assessed with the System Usability Scale (SUS) [10], and utilized the questions from the USE questionnaire [11]. The 7-point Likert scale used in the USE questionnaire was modified to a 5-point scale for simplification. Standard questions were used in the semi-structured interview, and a qualitative analysis was conducted on the responses. The evaluation was conducted in one session format where a standard introduction was completed for each subject. Each subject was given time to familiarize themselves with the mobile application and explore the features. Subsequently, each subject was given six tasks to complete using the mobile application: (1) Creating a pain diary, (2) Creating a medicine reminder, (3) Creating a medical appointment reminder, (4) Creating a new discussion on the forum, (5) Creating a message on the Instant Messaging, and (6) Completing a pain follow-up. Upon completion of the tasks, the subjects completed the questionnaires and the semi-structured interview.

3.2 Results

The usability scores for the 6 tasks are presented in Table 1. The average rating for "Ease of Use" ranged from 3.7 to 4.2, while those for "Usefulness" ranged from 3.7 to 4.3. From these scores, we can conclude that the participants found that the overall ease of use and usefulness of the system are very good. This matches the overall indication by most of the subjects (80%) of their satisfaction with the system as "Satisfied" or "Very Satisfied". However, the interviews exposed several concerns about the system's usability as will be discussed in the following subsection. Finally, the participants indicated high likeliness to use our system frequently with an average rating of 3.8 on a scale of 1 (Unlikely) to 5 (Likely).

Table 1. The rating results for ease-of-use on a scale from 1 (Difficult) to 5 (Easy) and usefulness on a scale from 1 (Not useful) to 5 (Useful).

Tasks	Ease of use	Usefulness
Creating a pain diary	3.9	4.3
Creating a medicine reminder	3.9	4.1
Creating a medical appointment reminder	4.2	4.3
Creating a discussion on the forum	3.7	3.7
Creating a message on instant messaging	3.8	3.8
Completing a pain follow-up	3.9	4.2

3.3 Qualitative Feedback

The feedback collected from the participants could be categorized into two main themes: (1) Display and functionality and (2) Privacy and medical-legal concerns. We will discuss positives, negatives, and recommendations for each theme.

Display and Functionality. Despite the overall high satisfaction with the system, nine of the subjects had concerns about the display and overall user-friendliness of the system. Specifically, they suggested that (1) the overall design could be more intuitive for easy completion (2) instructions to complete the requirements on the app could be made more readily available and (3) fewer steps should be needed to enter medicine events or recurring pain events. Six of the subjects commented about the visual displays; more distinctive colors could be used to differentiate different events more clearly, and animation could be added to improve the effectiveness of exercise instructions. During the interviews, P6 (a physiotherapist), believed that the system would eventually help the patients if used on a daily basis, stating:

> *"I believed that this system will help patient if used frequently, however there is still room for improvement. One of which is the populating of graph which will help us to pinpoint pain trigger for them. It would be good to recommend different type of exercise if patient pain still persists for a long duration."*

A few subjects suggested including to include functions that would present the data more visually and showing the trend through time. This could be more informative for prospective users with pain, and that might help in sustaining their interest in the system. Furthermore, such feature will help doctors pinpoint the actual triggers of pain which could allow them to propose better treatments for the patients. One subject suggested the inclusion of a data export function that could allow the collated information to be sent to the user's health care provider. Other recommendations included the addition of a customizable display, unique reminders to take a stretch break and incorporating other existing functions in the phone like a pedometer would be useful. P4 commented that more work should be done in reminding patients to move around to help mitigate their pain. P4 continues:

> *"It would be good if there is a way to remind the patient to stand up and do some stretching after a long period of sitting".*

As mentioned earlier, the device's accelerometer works as one of the sensors used in the system as a pedometer. By tracking the number of steps taken by the patient, we can derive the number of steps taken which provides useful insights about the activity level in relation to the pain events. The information are also used for the follow-up scenario.

Privacy and Medical-Legal Concerns. The participants found it useful to have features such as a forum to share media content. However, half of the subjects surveyed had some concerns about the privacy and the regulation of the discussion forums and Instant Messaging. They were concerned that the freely accessible messaging and forums might be construed as means of accessing urgent pain advice. They suggested including prominently placed disclaimers, the expected response time by a health professional, and an explicit note that the system would not replace the usual access to urgent medical care. As explained by one of the participants:

> *"There should be a disclaimer to inform the patient to prevent any misconception of the feature provided within the application. This is to prevent any legal issue whenever we post advice into the forum. The patient should only use the messaging application for non-urgent enquiry."*

A few subjects suggested including features that would require the users to be enrolled, and health professionals to be only identified with their clinical identities. The current system provides special gesture-based login and one-time registration using an identification given by the healthcare provider. However, this feature was not tested in this initial evaluation. Additionally, the participants suggested that the health professionals should be allowed to exercise administrative rights to manage offensive content. Integrating terms and conditions within the application feature might assist in mitigating such issues. Clearly, there is a need emphasized by the participants to examine potential medico-legal implications related to health advice that could be posted by the health professionals.

4   Discussion and Conclusion

Mobile technologies hold much promise for designing personal healthcare services, especially for the scenarios that require long-term adherence and motivation from patients, such as chronic pain management. For such systems to be successful, the user experience, ease of use and usefulness as perceived by the patients and the professionals should be carefully designed early in the development process. This paper has reported on a new mobile application for chronic pain management and a one day evaluation trial by 10 participants (nurse clinicians, psychologists and physiotherapists). The discussed system was designed with strong input from healthcare professionals with sole focus on helping patients to better manage their pain with the least interference to their daily activities. In this trial, we studied the situation from different aspects including the ease of use, usability and usefulness of the system. This work has allowed an initial exploration of the needs and benefits of mobile-based pain management with more attention given to the professional's view of the problem. Healthcare professionals' evaluation of our proposed system has shown that the system is feasible to be used in helping patients manage their pain journey. This was evidenced from the rating scores on ease of use and system usability as well as supported by results from participant interviews.

The app developed is currently an initial prototype with much room for improvement. The conducted trial has given a rich list of recommendations for future enhancements. Providing clinical evidence of improvement to patients' pain management capabilities and consequently, their quality of life requires a carefully planned longitudinal field study. A long-term field study of the application to assess the real impact of our system in patient management is necessary. Integrating ambient tracking capabilities where data entry is supported by sensor tracking in the background for example, mood tracking from facial expressions and patients' activity level from speed or type of motion are equally important to assess the usability of our app in effective pain management.

References

1. Bardram, J.E., Frost, M., Szántó, K., Faurholt-Jepsen, M., Vinberg, M., Kessing, L.V.: Designing mobile health technology for bipolar disorder: a field trial of the monarca system. In: Proceedings of the SIGCHI Conference on Human Factors in Computing Systems, pp. 2627–2636. ACM (2013)
2. Belsey, J.: Primary care workload in the management of chronic pain: a retrospective cohort study using a GP database to identify resource implications for UK primary care. J. Med. Econ. **5**, 39–52 (2000)
3. Brooke, J.: SUS-A quick and dirty usability scale. Usability Eval. Ind. **189**(194), 4–7 (1996)
4. Cardosa, M.S., Gurpreet, R., Tee, H.G.T.: Chronic Pain: The Third National Health and Morbidity Survey 2006, vol. 1, p. 262. Institute of Public Health, Ministry of Health Malaysia, Kuala Lumpur (2008)
5. Elzahaf, R.A., Tashani, O.A., Unsworth, B.A., Johnson, M.I.: The prevalence of chronic pain with an analysis of countries with a Human Development Index less than 0.9: a systematic review without meta-analysis. Curr. Med. Res. Opin. **28**(7), 1221–1229 (2012)
6. Gatchel, R.J., McGeary, D.D., McGreart, C.A., Lippe, B.: Interdisciplinary chronic pain management: past, present and future. Am. Psychol. **69**(2), 119–130 (2014)
7. Guillory, J., Chang, P., Henderson Jr., C.R., Shengelia, R., Lama, S., Warmington, M., Gay, G.: Piloting a text message-based social support intervention for patients with chronic pain: establishing feasibility and preliminary efficacy. Clin. J. Pain **31**(6), 548 (2015)
8. Martínez-Pérez, B., De La Torre-Díez, I., López-Coronado, M.: Mobile health applications for the most prevalent conditions by the World Health Organization: review and analysis. J. Med. Internet Res. **15**(6) (2013)
9. Maniadakis, N., Gray, A.: The economic burden of back pain in the UK. Pain **84**, 95–103 (2000)
10. Moore, R.A., Derry, S., Taylor, R.S., Straube, S., Phillips, C.J.: The costs and consequences of adequately managed chronic non-cancer pain and chronic neuropathic pain. Pain Pract. **14**(1), 79–94 (2013)
11. Nakumara, M., Nishiwaki, Y., Ushida, T., Toyama, Y.: Prevalence and characteristics of chronic musculoskeletal pain in Japan: a second survey of people with or without chronic pain. J. Orthop. Sci. **19**, 339–350 (2014)
12. Lund, A.M.: Measuring usability with the use questionnaire12. Usability Interface **8**(2), 3–6 (2001)
13. Straits Times. www.straitstimes.com/singapore/health/suffering-from-pain-costs-singapore-more-than-8-billion-each-year-study. Accessed 20 June 2017
14. Subramaniam, V., Stewart, M.W., Smith, J.F.: The development and impact of a chronic pain support group: a qualitative and quantitative study. J. Pain Symptom Manag. **17**(5), 376–383 (1999)
15. Turk, D.C., Theodore, B.R.: Epidemiology and economics of chronic and recurrent pain. In: Lynch, M.E., Craig, K.D., Peng, P.W.H. (eds.) Clinical Pain Management: A Practical Guide, pp. 6–13. Wiley-Blackwell, West Sussex (2010)
16. Vardeh, D., Edwards, R.R., Jamison, R.N., Eccleston, C.: There's an app for that: mobile technology is a new advantage in managing chronic pain. Pain: Clin. Updates **21**(6) (2013)

HCI and IT Infrastructure

A Pattern to Predict the Occurrence
of Moment of Information Overload During
Online Information Searching

Natrah Abdullah[✉] and Nur Amirah Mustapar[✉]

Faculty of Computer and Mathematical Sciences, Universiti Teknologi MARA,
Shah Alam, Malaysia
natrah@tmsk.uitm.edu.my, mira.mustapar@gmail.com

Abstract. Scholars have identified that individuals are confronted with information overload while searching for the information in the virtual library. They
sometimes do not realize that they are overloaded until the symptoms appear.
Moreover, previous literature claimed that information overload will also lead to
the changes in physiological signal of an individual which later results in
decreased efficiency of information processing. Several scholars have analyzed
this phenomenon and investigated its causes, symptoms, effects and countermeasures of information overload but there are lacking of empirical data to
detect moment of information overload as moment can be represented as a point
that happens along the chronological continuum at which certain effects occur.
Therefore, the primary purpose of this research is to detect the existence and the
occurrence of moment of information overload among individuals during
searching in virtual library, focusing on the pattern reflected in the physiological
data that can potentially be used as indicator of moment of information overload.
This study adopts user testing methods and methods from psychophysiology.
Collected empirical data were analyzed using quantitative analysis and were
presented using graphs and tables. Study findings revealed that heart rate
measurement is the best measure compared to other physiological measurement
and the underlying pattern of moment of information overload is presented in a
form of matrix. From the study findings, the recommendation of the future work
was made which outlined that the detected pattern can be used to design an
application which monitors the information load among the individuals.

Keywords: Information overload · Moment · Psychophysiology

1 Introduction

In most studies, the concept of information overload suggests that individuals have
limited capacity for information processing [1–6]. When the information received
exceeds the limited information processing capacity, people are subjected to cognitive
constraints that lead to information overload.

Figure 1 as discussed in previous study [7] shows the inverted U-curve of information overload from Schroder [8]. It shows that when the information received
exceeds the limited human information processing capacity, it leads to information

© Springer Nature Singapore Pte Ltd. 2018
N. Abdullah et al. (Eds.): i-USEr 2018, CCIS 886, pp. 255–265, 2018.
https://doi.org/10.1007/978-981-13-1628-9_23

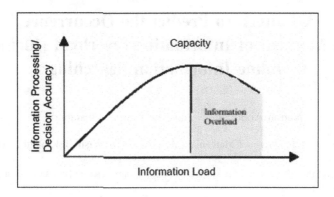

Fig. 1. The inverted U-curve of information overload

overload. The point where information processing has reached its peak, and starts to decline, is the individual's capacity for information processing. Any information received beyond that point will not be processed [3, 9, 10].

2 Problem Statement

Several scholars have analyzed the phenomenon of information overload and investigated its causes, symptoms, effects and countermeasures of information overload but lack of empirical data on moment of information overload. Xu [11] noted that in his formulae, moment is an element of an outcome. An event is the outcome of what happened before, which is the event's antecedent or also known as a cause. Event's antecedents has the outcome that happened which makes it appropriate to classify the event as occurring at a moment in time. Moment is fixed as the point in time at which the event's antecedent had the outcome [12]. Thus, the "moment" of an event then can be represented as a point that happens along the chronological continuum at which certain outcome occurs. This assertion is supported by Littmann [13] who found that there is a strong intuition that when something in the world changes, there is a moment at which the change occurs. The importance of moment of information overload is that it can be an indication for the information overload to occur. By knowing when and how the moment of information overload may affect the individuals, the causes of information overload can be diverted. By the same token, when the moment of information overload has been identified, it can prevent the overload problem from getting worse. Early identification of this overload problem will form a preventive strategy. Therefore, the primary purpose of this research is to detect the moment of information overload. Additionally, although a handful of studies on information overload have revealed the causes, symptoms, effects and countermeasures of information overload, a moment of information overload is still absent. Researcher intends to fill this gap with a study focusing on detecting moment of information overload.

3 Research Background

3.1 Information Searching

Information search process is the constructive process of a human in finding the meaning from information in order to extend human knowledge on a particular problem which consists of different stages. It incorporates three areas which are the affective (feelings), the cognitive (thoughts), and the physical (actions) common to each stage. There are six stages included in the information search process which are initiation, followed by selection, then continue with exploration, followed by formulation, proceed with collection and lastly presentation [14, 15]. In defining search task difficulty, there is no single meaning of task difficulty. With the various definitions of search task difficulty available by the previous studies, the current research agrees with Kim [16] in which she argued that task difficulty relies on individual perception, understanding and judgment of the objective task complexity. She examined the searcher's characteristics such as search experience, and topic of knowledge, intrinsic task characteristics such as specificity of target information and information sources, and intrinsic search process characteristics which is assessing or navigating a website and locating information on a webpage as the contributing factors to the perceived task difficulty. Issues experienced during the search process were recognized by the study subjects as the main reason for a posteriori perception of tasks as difficult [17]. Therefore, the difficulty of the search task could vary among people as people have different psychological abilities and searching skills. This research tries to examine the difficulty of the search task by comparing the difficult and easy task in a few types of databases (single database vs. multiple databases) used in finding the desired information.

3.2 Psychophysiology

Psychophysiological measures are often used to study emotion and attention responses to the given task, during exertion, and increasingly, to better understand cognitive processes [18]. There are several possible methods to represent the psychological state of the user. This study uses a combination of cardiovascular measurement which are heart rate (HR), blood pressure (BP), and body temperature (BT) measurement in order to measure the physiological states of an individual. These combinations of measurements are also known as vital sign which is the measurements of the body's basic functions. The advantages of using psychophysiological indices are that their measures are covert and implicit, and their changes are continuous [19]. It only deals with the available information when the user interacts with the computer system without any explicit communication or input device. This psychophysiological measure is a precise one-to-one representation of a significant or relevant psychological dimension such as task engagement, mental effort, and frustration.

4 Research Methodology

To address a research question which is "What is the pattern of moment of information overload during information searching in virtual library?", researcher's approaches to tackle research issue related to information overload are to merge knowledge and method from psychophysiology and adopt user testing method. The user testing methods seek to record performance of a user when dealing with the system, and preference or satisfaction of a user with the system being used [20].

4.1 Research Framework

This research proposes extended cognitive-fit framework (Fig. 2). The framework visualizes three important aspects required to conduct this research which are personal factor, searching environment (task-difficulty) and the physiological states of an individual. The task difficulty is related to its level of complexity. The level of complexity is different in terms of the scope of search (the breadth and depth), the amount of input/information provided, and the extent of the output required. Difficulty of the search task could vary among people as people have different psychological abilities and searching skills. This research examines the difficulty of the task by comparing the easy and difficult task in how much information is supplied during finding the desired information. When the information received by the individuals do not fit with their brain capacity which means the individuals received more information than they can digest, it will lead to information overload and will cause the changes in the physiological states of an individual that finally will reveal the moment of information overload.

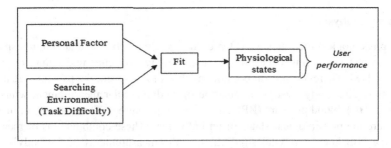

Fig. 2. Research framework

4.2 Data Collection

To get the empirical data on moment of information overload, researcher used the combinations of cardiovascular measurement which are heart rate (HR), blood pressure (BP), and body temperature (BT) measurement. Researcher used ProComp Infiniti encoder to measure the changes of physiological signals of the participants. To assess individual differences in facing information overload, researcher measured physiological signals of the participants on a task in a controlled situation. Researcher had constructed a task situation in which information overload could be reached and the output would be measurable and quantifiable. After analysing a few task environments to choose, a journal-searching task environment was chosen. The participants were required to search latest journals (ranging from the year 2012 to 2015) of certain topics need within a restricted time of 60 min (30 min for each level) in a certain repository (e.g. EZAccess UiTM). Time acts as a constraint in this research. It consisted of two levels, which are easy and difficult. For the easy level, participants were only allowed to do the searching task in a single browser while for the difficult level, participants were required to do the searching task in multiple browsers at the same time. There is no single meaning of task difficulty. Previous studies claimed that task difficulty is subjective as people have different psychological abilities and searching skills. This research determines the difficulty of the task by comparing the easy and difficult task in how much information is supplied during the process of finding the desired information. The amount of the data accessed by using single browser is less than data accessed by using multiple browsers. This condition is expected to give different impact to the participants. Figure 3 below shows the summary of data collection.

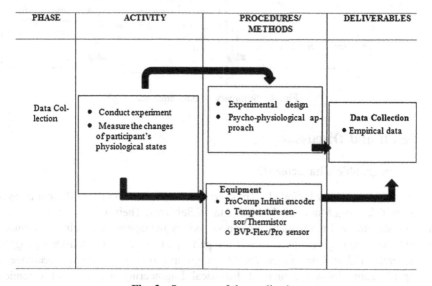

Fig. 3. Summary of data collection

4.3   Data Analysis

In the process of analyzing the signals retrieved using quantitative analysis, each recorded signal of blood pressure (BP), body temperature (BT) and heart rate (HR) underwent a pre-processing phase in which all the signals from the "Physiological Suite" software were converted into data set and transferred into Microsoft Excel. All the data set from 12 participants were combined into one sheet in order to see the differences among them. The data set were then converted into specified data set by finding their mean and then transformed them into a graph. Later the data underwent an extraction phase where the graphs were divided into 10 min interval to show the changing pattern that lies in the graphs for fifteen participants. The pattern lies in the graphs had been compared between easy and difficult task. This is to get the changes occurred in the patterns during easy and difficult searching task as according to Gerin and Zawadzki [21], people who are stressed will have an increased reading of blood pressure (BP) and heart rate (HR) as well as the body temperature (BT) [22, 23] and these are some of the effects of the information overload. Thus, with the changes of the reading in the three empirical data, the moment of information overload can be revealed. In this extraction phase, the different patterns of the empirical data had been classified. Figure 4 below shows the summary of data analysis.

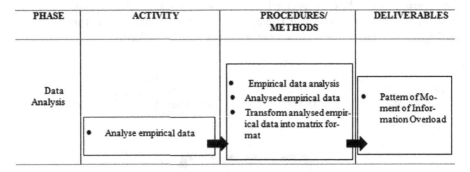

Fig. 4. Summary of data analysis

5   Result and Discussion

5.1   Demographic Characteristic

Participants in this study included 15 post graduate students from four different areas in Universiti Teknologi Mara (UiTM Shah Alam), Selangor. Their backgrounds are in the area of computer and mathematical sciences, policy management, electrical engineering, and chemical engineering. Most of the participants were in the master's program (80%), female (73.3%) and in the 25–34 age group (86.7%). An equal percentage of participants came from the area of Electrical Engineering and area of Chemical Engineering (6.7%), while approximately 90% of all participants were either in the area of Computer and Mathematical Sciences (66.6%) or the area of Administrative Science and Policy Studies (20%).

5.2   Result on Physiological Measure

Blood Pressure (BP). In this research, the autonomic nervous system was assessed through blood pressure (BP). Mean blood pressure (BVP) readings showed no major differences within 30 min of task completion for both levels. Most of the participants had a slight decrement in their BP readings at the first 10 min compared to their initial readings but did not have any changes during the last 20 min of the searching task. When comparing number of participants' changes in BP during easy level and the difficult level, most of the participants showed a constant slight increment and decrement in their BP readings. Based on the analysis of the result, moment of information overload could not be demonstrated by using this study measure. Even though the readings showed some variations in the values, but the values still fall in the range of their initial BP reading. This is supported by American Heart Association (2014), which claimed that there are no clear links between stress which is the symptoms of information overload and blood pressure even though stress definitely affects our bodies. There was a statistically non-significant difference from Easy Level (M = 35.35, SD = 0.48) to Difficult Level (M = 35.62, SD = 0.480, t(14) = −1.776, p > 0.0005). The eta squared statistic (.475) indicated a moderate effect size.

Body Temperature (BT). Body temperature has been monitored in this study in order to demonstrate the moment of information overload. When comparing number of participants' changes in body temperature (BT) during the easy level and the difficult level of the searching task, most of the participants showed a constant decrement in their BT readings. Even though the readings showed some variations in the values, moment of information overload could not be demonstrated by using this study measure. Prior to exposure to stress, the body temperature of the participant is expected to rise but the experiment showed a different result as experiment was held in the cold room. Body temperature readings of the participants were affected by the external factor which is the temperature of the room. Hence the readings of the participants' body temperature are below the normal human body temperature as the body loses more heat than it can generate. Even though body temperature may increase temporarily when people are stressed, participants' body temperatures were already affected by the external environment. Hence this study needs more physiological measures in order to demonstrate the moment of information overload. The next physiological measure is by using heart rate.

Heart Rate (HR). Heart rate shows a major difference within 60 min of task completion for both levels. When comparing the participants' heart rate readings during the easy and difficult of the searching task, most of the participants had a rapid change in their heart rate readings during the task completion in difficult level. The heart rate of the participants increased gradually over the minutes compared to the heart rate readings in the easy level of the searching task. Table 1 shows the pattern of moment of information overload through heart rate (HR) measure.

Most of the participants had a rapid occurrence of heart rate (HR) readings ranging from 100 ≤ 150 beats per minute (bpm) for both levels of easy and difficult in the first 10 min of the task. However, the total number of participants who reached a maximum range of heart rate (HR) readings which is 150 ≤ 200 (bpm) increased from 8 participants to 12 participants in the difficult level. In this first 10 min, total number of occurrences of abnormal readings from easy and difficult levels increased from 21 occurrences to 27 occurrences. Then after 20 min in easy level of the task, most of the participants started to reach maximum range of heart rate (HR) readings which is

Table 1. Pattern of moment of information overload through heart rate (HR) measure.

No.	Easy Level				Difficult Level			
Range	100≤150 (bps)		150≤200 (bps)		100≤150 (bps)		150≤200 (bps)	
Pattern								
First 10 minutes								
R1		/		/		/		/
R2			/			/	/	
R3		/	/			/	/	
R4		/			/			
R5		/			/		/	
R6		/				/	/	
R7						/		/
R8	/					/		
R9	/		/			/		/
R10		/		/		/		/
R11		/		/		/		/
R12		/		/		/		/
R13		/	/			/	/	
R14	/					/		
R15		/				/	/	
TOTAL (Participant)	3	10	4	4	2	13	6	6
TOTAL ALL (Occurrence)	21				27			
Next 20 minutes								
R1	/			/		/		/
R2	/		/			/		/
R3		/	/			/	/	
R4		/	/		/		/	
R5		/	/			/	/	
R6		/			/		/	
R7						/		/
R8	/					/	/	
R9		/	/	/		/		/
R10		/		/		/		/
R11		/		/		/		/
R12	/			/		/		/
R13		/	/			/	/	
R14	/					/	/	
R15		/			/		/	
TOTAL (Participant)	5	9	6	5	3	12	8	7
TOTAL ALL (Occurrence)	25				30			
Last 30 minutes								
R1		/		/		/	/	
R2	/		/		/		/	
R3		/	/			/	/	
R4						/		/
R5	/					/	/	
R6	/		/			/	/	
R7		/		/		/		/
R8				/		/	/	
R9		/		/		/		/
R10		/		/		/		/
R11		/		/		/	/	
R12		/	/			/	/	
R13	/		/			/	/	
R14			/			/	/	
R15		/	/			/		/
TOTAL (Participant)	4	8	7	6	1	14	10	5
TOTAL ALL (Occurrence)	25				30			

150 ≤ 200 (bpm). Meanwhile in difficult level of the task, most of the participants had a rapid occurrence of heart rate (HR) readings ranging from 100 ≤ 150 (bpm). However, at this period, the total number of participants who reached a maximum range of heart rate (HR) readings increased from 11 participants to 15 participants in

the difficult level. Hence, the total number of occurrences of abnormal readings from easy and difficult levels increased from 25 occurrences to 30 occurrences. In the last 30 min, compared to easy level, most of the participants had a rapid occurrences for both abnormal readings of heart rate (HR), $100 \leq 150$ and $150 \leq 200$ (bpm) in the difficult level and the total number of the participants who reached a maximum range of heart rate (HR) readings increased from 13 participants to 15 participants in the difficult level. Hence, it can be concluded that, in between easy and difficult level, most of the participants had the most occurrence of abnormal readings during the difficult level of the task. Based on the results above, a paired sample t-test was conducted to evaluate the differences of occurrence of abnormal readings between easy and the difficult level of the searching task. There was a statistically significant increase from Easy Level (M = 4.73, SD = 1.53) to Difficult Level (M = 5.80, SD = 0.41, t(14) = −3.096 p < 0.0005). The eta squared statistic (.475) indicated a moderate effect size.

Table 2. Pattern of moment of information overload

Information Searching Environment	Easy Task	Difficult Task
Pattern of occurrence of abnormal reading ($100 \leq 200$ bpm)		

Table 2 above shows the matrix of patterns during moment of information overload. There are two patterns of moment of information overload which are easy and difficult level of the searching task. During easy level of the task, the occurrence of abnormal heart rate reading is less than the occurrence of abnormal heart rate reading during difficult level of the task. During difficult level, most participants had a rapid occurrence of abnormal heart rate reading. It is due to the amount of information supplied is higher than they can digest. With the limited searching time duration and too many information are supplied, the participants were overwhelmed by the amount of information and this lead them to experience information overload. Based on the analysis of the empirical data retrieved and the post-experiment questionnaire, most of the participants had stress in the difficult level of the task and the result of the empirical data shows that heart rate is the best measure compared to blood pressure and body temperature of the participants. This is parallel with the claims from Gerin and Zawadzki [21] which mentioned that people who are stressed will have an increased reading of heart rate. This is supported by Newell [23] who advocated the view that stress can cause a rapid and large increase in heart rate.

6 Conclusion

The association between difficulty of the task and the participants' overall performance may be explained from the perspective of individual's behaviour, mental states or cognitive abilities. Difficult task produces higher degrees of mental workloads resulting in higher arousal of stress than easy task [24]. The empirical contribution from the finding of this research is that the detection of pattern of moment of information overload through physiological measure is best measured by heart rate. Other than that, this research also provides empirical support to the developed conceptual framework of information overload in order to establish the relationship between the components of the framework. Hence, it provides the empirical justification of the usefulness of the developed framework verified by one-to-one experimental testing with the user. This research finding is effectively relevant to the practitioner in the related area as it offers the applicability of the framework.

7 Future Work

The findings reported in this research have implications for future research. The result of the experiment can be used to design an application which controls the information load among the individuals. Other than that, this research can look further into symptoms of information overload. By having empirical data of moment of information overload, it can provide a great basis to the justification of the symptoms of information overload. A deep and better understanding of the information overload problem will give many benefits to the society as it can lead to better performance of an individual.

Acknowledgement. The authors would like to thank Universiti Teknologi MARA (UiTM), Malaysia for partly funding the study by given the BESTARI PERDANA grant (600-IRMI/DANA 5/3/BESTARI (P) (091/2018)). The authors would also like to thank USE Lab, Faculty of Computer and Mathematical Sciences, Universiti Teknologi Mara, Shah Alam and all the respondents who had contributed to this study.

References

1. Ji, Q., Sypher, U.: The role of news media use and demographic characteristics in the prediction of information overload. Int. J. Commun. **8**, 699–714 (2014)
2. Pentina, I., Tarafdar, M.: From "information" to "knowing": exploring the role of social media in contemporary news consumption. Comput. Hum. Behav. **35**, 211–223 (2014)
3. Whelan, E., Teigland, R.: Transactive memory systems as a collective filter for mitigating information overload in digitally enabled organizational groups. Inf. Organ. **23**(3), 177–197 (2013)
4. Chen, C.-Y., Pedersen, S., Murphy, K.L.: The influence of perceived information overload on student participation and knowledge construction in computer-mediated communication. Instr. Sci. **40**(2), 325–349 (2012)
5. Memmi, D.: Information overload and virtual institutions. AI Soc. **29**, 1–9 (2012)

6. Ayyagari, R.: Impact of information overload and task-technology fit on Technostress. In: Proceedings of the Southern Association for Information Systems Conference, pp. 18–22 (2012)

7. Mustapar, N.A., Abdullah, N., Md. Noor, N.: A review towards developing a moment of information overload model. In: The 4th International Conference on User Science and Engineering (i-USEr), Melaka, pp. 222–226 (2016)

8. Schroder, H.M., Suedfeld, P.: Personality Theory and Information Processing. Ronald Press, New York (1971)

9. Sasaki, Y., Kawai, D., Kitamura, S.: The anatomy of tweet overload: how number of tweets received, number of friends, and egocentric network density affect perceived information overload. Telemat. Inform. **32**(4), 853–861 (2015)

10. Eppler, M.J., Mengis, J.: A framework for information overload research in organizations. Report, Università Della Svizzera Italiana, pp. 1–42 (2003)

11. Xu, M.: Actions as events. J. Philos. Log. **41**, 765–809 (2012)

12. Rodopi, B.V.: Wholeness: The Character Logic. Amsterdam (2004)

13. Littmann, G.: Moment of change. Acta Analytica **27**(1), 29–44 (2012)

14. Kuhlthau, C.C.: Inside the search process: information seeking from the user's. Perspective **42**(5), 361–371 (1991)

15. Wiley, C., Williams, J.: Librarian as advisor: information search process of undecided students and novice researchers. **35**(1), 13–21 (2015). http://doi.org/10.12930/NACADA-14-008

16. Kim, J.: Task difficulty in information searching behavior: expected difficulty and experienced difficulty (2002)

17. Gwizdka, J., Spence, I.: What can searching behavior tell us about the difficulty of information tasks? Study Web Navig. **43**, 1–13 (2016)

18. Shad, K.F.: What is psychophysiology? Where to go next?, vol. 1, pp. 1–2 (2014)

19. Knaepen, K., Marusic, U., Crea, S., Rodríguez, C.D., Vitiello, N., Pattyn, N., Meeusen, R.: Human movement science psychophysiological response to cognitive workload during symmetrical, asymmetrical and dual-task walking. Hum. Mov. Sci. **40**, 248–263 (2015)

20. Hasan, L.: The usefulness of user testing methods in identifying problems on university websites. JISTEM J. Inf. Syst. Technol. Manag. **11**(2) (2014). http://dx.doi.org/10.4301/S1807-17752014000200002

21. Gerin, W., Zawadzki, M.J.: Stress and blood pressure dysregulation. 531–535 (2012). http://dx.doi.org/10.1016/B978-0-12-375000-6.00344-X

22. Mientka, M.: Chronic Stress Can Cause Fever And Fatigue; New Neural Understanding May Offer Help, pp. 1–4 (2015)

23. Newell, L.: A High Heart Rate and Stress. Livestrong.com (2015). http://www.livestrong.com/article/172324-a-high-heart-rate-and-stress/

24. Adler, R.F., Benbunan-Fich, R.: The effects of task difficulty and multitasking on performance. British Computer Society. Advanced Access Publication (2014). https://doi.org/10.1093/iwc/iwu005

A Comparison of Gestural and Touch-Based Interface for Designing a Virtual Percussion Instrument

Hoo Yong Leng, Noris Mohd Norowi[✉], and Azrul Hazri Jantan

University Putra Malaysia, 43400 UPM
Serdang, Selangor Darul Ehsan, Malaysia
gs44389@student.upm.edu.my,
{noris,azrulhazri}@upm.edu.my

Abstract. The paper presents an exploratory study to design a new virtual musical instrument for *Kompang*, using the natural hand for interaction purpose. The study first explores the potential technologies that are low-cost, easy to access and most importantly, these technologies use hand-based interaction. Two input devices that fulfil these requirements are selected, and then developed as low-fidelity interfaces. A study was conducted to identify which interface was preferable by the user for future development. A set of design criteria was also identified at the end of study for development of a virtual *Kompang* instrument.

Keywords: Virtual musical instrument · Natural User Interfaces
Human-Computer Interaction · Evaluation · Design criteria

1 Introduction

Advances in the size, power, and cost of computer hardware allow human to go beyond using mouse and keyboard and start to use more natural form of interactions to communicate with computer interfaces. Such form of interaction is also known as the Natural User Interface (NUI). It aims to make the computer interface behaves in a way that users can operate through intuitive actions related to daily life human behaviours.

In broader term, the Touch User Interface (TUI) is considered as a type of NUI which allows users to interact with objects by simple tapping and dragging input. It is also the main approach of interaction with computer devices, such as tablets or smartphones. Direct feedbacks provided by TUI makes it seems more natural than traditional input devices such as keyboard and mouse, to interact with object on the screen. Nevertheless, research interests on TUI are then shifted to other field in which the interaction form is more natural and intuitive. The most notable example is the gestural interface which uses the implementation of motion sensor to capture human body movement, typically hand movements as the primary source of data input [1]. The motion sensors track and transmit image data to computer to capture human motions. Command is executed based on the gestural input done by the user. Examples of such devices are the Microsoft's Kinect, Leap Motion sensor, and Wii Remote.

© Springer Nature Singapore Pte Ltd. 2018
N. Abdullah et al. (Eds.): i-USEr 2018, CCIS 886, pp. 266–276, 2018.
https://doi.org/10.1007/978-981-13-1628-9_24

In the musical context, the emergence of NUI-equipped technologies has opened a wide range of possibilities in the creation of Digital Musical Instruments (DMI). Thus, a plethora of research works was found in describing technical features and novelty of the designed musical interfaces or instruments. The following examples show various types of musical instruments designed by past researchers. They are the Radio Baton [2], Reactable [3], Smule's Ocarina [4], and Song Walker [5]. Nevertheless, very few works were found on evaluation of the effectiveness of these technologies in helping to emulate the similar experience of playing the real instrument.

This paper presents an exploratory study on development of a virtual percussion instrument that offers natural playing experience using bare hands. The study wants to identify which existing input devices can support better drumming experience with natural hand input. To explore this idea, a prototype named Virtual Kompang is created. *Kompang* is a traditional Malay instrument in Malaysia. The main reason it is selected for the study is because it uses bare hands to play. A touch and gestural interface are designed and evaluated to identify which of these are preferred by the *Kompang* musicians. Concurrently, a post-interview is conducted. The outcomes of this paper include the comparison data of the two interfaces based on user preferences and a set of initial design criteria which guided the development of the virtual *Kompang* are identified.

2   Literature Review

2.1   Evaluation and Human-Computer Interaction

Evaluation appears to be the main problem in developing a DMI. Throughout review on previous studies, it was found that limited numbers of research works were done concerning the evaluation method on the digital instrument. This is because the contributions in this domain are mainly related to the artistic novelty of the new musical instrument. Stowell et al. [6] for example, stated that the evaluation method done by past researchers on user experience were self-created without following any related methodologies. As proven by Schmid [7] who also indicated that many papers focused on the novelty of their product and might skip or informally described the evaluation part.

Concurrently, several studies indicated the potential of borrowing Human-Computer Interaction (HCI) approach to investigate the experiences of musicians who use the musical interface. An early example was done by Wandarley and Orio [8]. They adapted usability testing from HCI to evaluate input devices for musical expression. Kiefer et al. [9] followed the similar approach to evaluate their musical controller. However, they noticed that this method was lacked in providing real-time quantitative data concerning the participants' experience on the instrument. This is because there was lack of technology and methodology at the time to measure user experience quantitatively and qualitatively.

More recently, few published papers began to take mixed evaluation method approaches in collecting relevant qualitative and quantitative data to evaluate user experience on DMI. An early example of such work was done by Stowell et al. [10], as they evaluated user experience on the system using Discourse Analysis (DA) and Turing Test to obtain qualitative and quantitative data. Xambo et al. used video analysis to evaluate musical tabletops based on users' feedbacks and questionnaire to measure the frequency of behaviour patterns [11]. More recently, Deacon et al. [12] took a combination of interview, video analysis, and questionnaire to assess user experience towards the interactive music virtual environment. From these studies, it indicated that the implementation of quantitative approach, complementary with qualitative findings help to evaluate the musical system from different perspectives.

2.2 Design Criteria for Virtual Musical Instrument

The software designers have certain goals in mind to decide the necessary characteristics to develop the musical instrument so that it will behave the way it is supposed to be. However, it is also important to consider why they develop the system in such a way. Identifying the design criteria are the explicit goals that designers should find out to ensure the system they designed is a successful one. The effort has benefited the designers in two ways. It helps to explicit designers' intention or goals and facilitates evaluation of the system according to the criteria set.

A huge amount of literatures consider design criteria for DMI. One of the criteria that are often highlighted in papers is the ease of use. An early example of such paper was conducted by Wessel and Wright [13] as they examined on the virtuosity of the musical instrument. They stated that the system should provide ease of use to motivate musicians to develop high-level skills with the system. Nevertheless, in more recent years, McDermott et al. [14] argued that the designers should clearly identified the concept of ease to use for the system as there were various dimension of difficulties to evaluate. Blindly applied interaction techniques to the system might cause the interface to turn out to be uninteresting to the musicians.

Reviews on the past works also indicated that intimacy was another key criterion for designing a musical instrument. Intimacy is referred to the degree in which the musicians feel in control of the instrument in the similar way like they play with the real one. Fels [15] argued that there are four characteristics that determine the intimacy of instrument; response, control, reflection, and belonging. Later, Johnston [16] implemented similar approach to measure intimacy level of the instrument using structured questionnaire. McDermott et al. also highlighted the importance of intimacy in evaluating expressive interfaces [17].

In fact, there are more design criteria such as consistency, expressivity, and diversity that can be used to guide development of a musical instrument. It is important to know that the developed instrument is not expected to meet all criteria generally. Until today, the key ideas to develop a virtual percussion instrument, specifically for *Kompang* remains unknown. Efforts to identify criteria in this study will help to develop the system that meets users' expectation in the following user studies.

3   Interface Design

Siswanto et al. indicated that there were two common sounds produced by a *Kompang* [18]. The *Kompang* (see Fig. 1) produces *bum* and *pak* when hit on different positions of the *Kompang* membrane. For example, hitting the edge of membrane with closed fingers will produce *bum* while hitting on the center of membrane with open fingers will produce *pak*. An illustration on the techniques to hit *Kompang* is shown in Fig. 2 (a) and (b).

Fig. 1. The *Kompang*

Two low-fidelity prototypes including gestural and touch-based interface are developed for the study. The gestural interface is implemented with Leap Motion controller while the touch-based interface is designed on mobile device. These devices are selected because they are relatively inexpensive and easy to set up compare to other hand tracking devices.

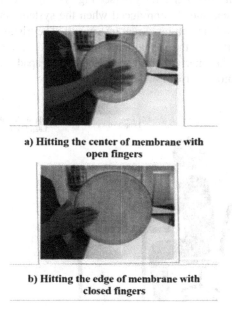

a) Hitting the center of membrane with open fingers

b) Hitting the edge of membrane with closed fingers

Fig. 2. Hand position when player hit (a) 'Pak' and (b) 'Bum'.

3.1 Gestural Interface

The gestural interface is a desktop application using gestural interaction based on the Leap Motion to simulate a *Kompang* in a virtual room setting (see Fig. 3). The Leap

Motion controller is a sensor-based optical tracking device that can capture the fine movement of hands and fingers. It works with infrared cameras and LED as depth sensor in a limited field of view. As the device detects hands within the field of view, it provides updates in frames of data. Each frame has a list of detailed data which covers hand characteristics such as fingers, palms and arms, and velocity profiles.

Fig. 3. Gestural interface of the virtual *Kompang*.

To play the gestural interface, user must plug the Leap Motion device into the desktop and place it in front of the monitor (see Fig. 4). The interface shows user where the fingers are in space. Sound is produced when the system detects the virtual hand colliding with the membrane of the virtual instrument. The triggered sound is different, depending on what position the virtual hand has collided on the membrane of *Kompang*. In this study, the interface runs on a Lenovo Ideapad z50 laptop with AMD A10-7300 1.9 GHz processor and 8 GB RAM.

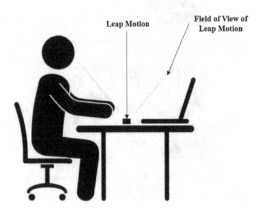

Fig. 4. Desktop setup for gestural interface using Leap Motion controller.

3.2 Touch-Based Interface

The touch-based version of the music system is a mobile application. The default interface is a *Kompang* at top view. Similar to the gestural interface, sound is triggered when the hand hits on the *Kompang* membrane. '*Bum*' is triggered when user touched on the edge of membrane while '*pak*' is triggered when touched on the center of membrane. An illustration of the touch-based interface design is shown in Fig. 5.

Fig. 5. The touch-based interface of the virtual *Kompang*.

The mobile application developed for this paper is implemented on a consumer mobile device, the ASUS Zenpad 8.0 tablet with Octa-core Snapdragon 410 processor and 2 GB of RAM. Its' mobile operating system is the Android 5.0 Lollipop.

4 User Study

The user study intends to evaluate user experience on the selected interface. From this study, several topics of interest are also highlighted as follow:

- How are the musicians' experience on gestural interface and touch-based interface?
- What are the design criteria for designing a virtual musical instrument for *Kompang*?

To answer the question on the key design criteria for the virtual *Kompang*, the study follows the similar approach as done by Johnston [16] by analyzing the notes made by the observer during the study. A mixed-method approach is utilized by collecting qualitative video recordings and quantitative questionnaire data for answering the questions above.

The analysis of video which captured subjects' experience and informal insights throughout the session were done. It is also a method from HCI field because it aims at understanding human interaction with technology through verbal and non-verbal communication [11]. Among challenges faced in this study is to extract useful data from videos in order to identify consistent themes and patterns and to make sense of the information. By analyzing the video data, it helps to identify a set of design criteria for development of virtual instrument for *Kompang*. Techniques from the grounded-theory method [19] were therefore used in order to achieve this goal. The reason for using this method is because it helps in forming theories closely related to the evidence from rich qualitative data.

A questionnaire was administered to ask about subjects' experience in playing with the two interfaces, in terms of control, ease of use, enjoyment, and complexity of music production. The study also collected five-point Likert scale questionnaire data that investigates the playing experience on the instruments, ranging from 'Strongly Agree' to 'Strongly Disagree'. Questions were repeated to capture participants' opinions towards the gestural and touch-based interface. The data provide a complementary layer of information to explain which interface is preferable to the *Kompang* musicians.

Ten *Kompang* musicians (five men and five women) were recruited for the study. All of them have a minimum of 3 years of experience in playing the *Kompang*. When describing their *Kompang* skills, 2 subjects selected 'advanced', 6 participants chose 'intermediate' and 2 chose 'beginner'. Due to the higher degree of expertise, the number of participants is considered sufficient to provide detailed feedback about the experience of interacting with the interfaces.

At the beginning, participants were shown the functionalities of the touch-based and gestural interface. The focus of this study was what the participants are able to do with the interfaces, what are the impacts of using them for making music, which interface do they prefer to make music and if there is any suggestion for improvement. Thus, there were no specific musical tasks to perform by participants. They were told in simple terms how the interfaces worked and then asked to explore and make music with them. Participants were allowed to answer the questions at any time during the session. A post interview was conducted before the session ended to capture feedbacks on the experience of interacting with the two interfaces.

5   Results

5.1   Participants' Interface Preference

The preference on touch-based interface was clearly observed, since nine out of ten participants preferred this interface. Some participants responded that they felt the sense of touching on *Kompang* when they tapped the screen to trigger the sounds. In addition, participants had the feeling of being in control of the instrument as they were able to locate the position to make *bum* and *pak* sound.

On the other hand, it was observed that the majority faced problems when they were playing gestural interface via the Leap Motion controller. Some participants noticed that the Leap Motion controller could not track hand movement when they performed the fast swing hit. The device might miss a swing hit when tracking of hand movement was lost and subsequently regained after the hand left the membrane of virtual *Kompang*. Occlusion is another error that was noticed from the study. Similar to finding observed by Silva et al. [20], some participants had to adjust the hand position to ensure they could hit on the various positions on the membrane of the virtual *Kompang*. These bugs caused frustrations in participants as they felt it was inconvenient to play a sequence of rhythm with the gestural interface.

Reflecting on the questionnaire data, the preference data was statistically significant (see Table 1). The Wilcoxon Signed-Ranks Test was used to compare mean value of each statement for touch-based (A0) and gesture-based (A1) interface. At a significant level of 0.05, the means for all statements on the two interfaces are statistically significant.

Table 1. Summary of participants' comments in average and Chi-test p-value obtained from questionnaire.

Keywords	Statements	A0	A1	P-value	U-value	Z-score
Control	I feel in control of the application	4.5	2.6	0.003	10	2.986
Complexity	The application allowed me to create complex musical	3.9	2.3	0.014	17	2.457
Enjoyment	It is fun to play the application	4.1	2.4	0.003	10	2.986
Ease of use	The application is easy to use in overall	3.9	2	0.002	9	3.062

5.2   Design Criteria for Development of a Virtual *Kompang*

The study found that all participants did not approach the instruments in the same way. By using grounded theory for analyzing the qualitative data, the study was able to find consistent patterns of expectations towards the instrument. The study was made of YouTube's captioning service by adding caption on each word that was mentioned by musician. The caption files were then downloaded and saved as Word file. An extra effort is made to translate each statement into English as each session was conducted in Malay, which subjects felt comfortable with. Interview data are organized into a series of codes that capture the meaning of the statement. The codes are combined and contrasted to develop categories that group similar codes together thereby generating a series of theory that described the design criteria for virtual *Kompang*. An example of generation of codes from raw interview data is shown in Table 2.

The study indicates that some criteria are interrelated to each other. In the following section, each of these criteria will be introduced:

Criterion 1: The Way to Interact with the Virtual Percussion Instrument Should be Natural

What is meant by 'natural' is that the interaction using this instrument should be directly and naturally use hand input. The interaction design for the instrument should implement hand-based interaction. The intention is to make the user to feel intuitive connection between playing the virtual *Kompang* and the actual one.

Criterion 2: The Virtual Percussion Instrument Should be Able to Respond Consistently

The concept of consistent means the designed instrument responds like the real instrument. The physical *Kompang* would use hand to make sound, so should the

Table 2. Example of generation of themes from raw interview data

Statement	Codes	Theme
"Usually we hold a Kompang with one hand, hit the Kompang with another hand. By doing that, we had the feeling of playing a Kompang"	Realism	The way to interact the instrument should be able natural
"I had similar feeling like playing a real Kompang as I swing my hand to make hit"		
"I have the feeling of hitting an actual Kompang when playing with the mobile version of Kompang"		
"If played the virtual Kompang with two hands, we can imagine the Kompang on our hand. That make us feel like hitting a kompang"	Natural	
"I had similar feeling like playing an actual Kompang as I swing my hand to make hit. It is better we can grab on something when we play the gestural interface"		
"The touch-based interface is better. We can be hold it to play"	Physical play	
"The experience of playing gestural interface is different as playing with the actual Kompang. We can hold the drum when we played"		
"The way to play is different between this application and the actual Kompang. We use palms or fingers to play the actual Kompang"		

virtual instrument. In terms of triggered sound, the instrument should also have the same effect as the real *Kompang*. It is necessary for the player to have confidence to play with the instrument.

Criterion 3: The Virtual Percussion Instrument Should be Simple Yet Allows Player to Create New Rhythm

A good interface should be as simple as possible yet attractive, so should the virtual *Kompang*. One core issue elicited by the participant in the study was that the touch-based interface (see Fig. 3) was not interesting though it was simple. This is because the instrument could only trigger sound according to the button touched by the user. Thus, adding extra functionality to the instrument without affecting the live performance reliability will facilitate user to create complex *Kompang* rhythm.

Criterion 4: The Virtual Percussion Instrument Should be Interesting and Engaging the Musician to Play on It

This criterion is related to Criterion 2. The designer should ensure the instrument to engage and motivate the user. It makes user to continue trying on the instrument.

Criterion 5: The *Kompang* Player Should Feel in Control of the Instrument

Majority of the participants had similar experience elicited that they suffered from latency issue when they played the gestural interface. A sensitive and responsive virtual instrument can cope with sudden time signature change, enabling user to feel in control to play various rhythm.

Criterion 6: The Virtual Percussion Instrument Should Encourage a Playful, Exploratory Experience for Musicians

This criterion is related to Criterion 3. Participants were hoping that the virtual *Kompang* could offer playful experience to stimulate the sense of exploring the instrument. Nevertheless, the additional ideas should not decrease the reliability so that they could enjoy playful and interesting experience without affecting the live performance.

Criterion 7: The Playing Experience Between the Actual Instrument and the Virtual Percussion Instrument Should be Apparently Similar to the Musician

Findings from the study showed that participants tend to compare playing experience on the physical instrument with the application. This is because they were looking after for the commonalities between both instrument. Designing a virtual instrument that nearly replicate the characteristics of a physical instrument brings several advantages to the user. Firstly, it helps to understand the acoustics of the physical instrument through simulation. Secondly, it also provides an optional tool to users who do not have the instrument in real life.

6 Conclusion

In this paper, a study was conducted with the aim to identify which interfaces either by using gestural or touch-based interaction is preferred by the users. Through this study, it was found that majority of the participants are more likely to prefer the touch-based interface. By analyzing opinions elicited by the participants, a set of design criteria could be decided, especially for designing *Kompang* instrument. This set of criteria will work as a guideline for the design of any percussion instrument that use hand input for interaction. This study is also hoped to help propose key criteria in evaluating the performance of a DMI.

References

1. Macaranas, A., Antle, A.N., Riecke, B.E.: What is intuitive interaction? Balancing users' performance and satisfaction with natural user interfaces. Interact. Comput. **27**(3), 357–370 (2015)
2. Mathews, M.V.: The radio baton and conductor program, or: pitch, the most important and least expressive part of music. Comput. Music J. **15**(4), 37–46 (1991)
3. Jordà, S., Geiger, G., Alonso, M., Kaltenbrunner, M.: The reacTable: exploring the synergy between live music performance and tabletop tangible interfaces. In: Proceedings of the 1st International Conference on Tangible and Embedded Interaction, pp. 139–146 (2007)
4. Wang, G.: Designing Smule's Ocarina: the iPhone's magic flute. In: NIME, pp. 303–307 (2009)
5. Bouwer, A., Holland, S., Dalgleish, M.: Song walker harmony space: embodied interaction design for complex musical skills. In: Holland, S., Wilkie, K., Mulholland, P., Seago, A. (eds.) Music and Human-Computer Interaction. SSCC, pp. 207–221. Springer, London (2013). https://doi.org/10.1007/978-1-4471-2990-5_12

6. Stowell, D., Plumbley, M.D., Bryan-Kinns, N.: Discourse analysis evaluation method for expressive musical interfaces. In: NIME, pp. 81–86 (2008)
7. Schmid, G.M.: Measuring musician's playing experience: development of a questionnaire for the evaluation of musical interaction. In: Practice-based Research Workshop at the 2014 Conference on New Interfaces for Musical Expression (2014)
8. Wanderley, M.M., Orio, N.: Evaluation of input devices for musical expression: borrowing tools from HCI. Comput. Music J. **26**(3), 62–76 (2002)
9. Kiefer, C., Collins, N., Fitzpatrick, G.: HCI methodology for evaluating musical controllers: a case study. In: NIME, pp. 87–90 (2008)
10. Stowell, D., Robertson, A., Brayn-Kinns, N., Plumbley, A.: Evaluation of live human-computer music-making: quantitative and qualitative approaches. Int. J. Hum. Comput. Stud. **67**(11), 960–975 (2009)
11. Xambó, A., Laney, R., Dobbyn, C., Jordà, S.: Video analysis for evaluating music interaction: musical tabletops. In: Holland, S., Wilkie, K., Mulholland, P., Seago, A. (eds.) Music and Human-Computer Interaction. SSCC, pp. 241–258. Springer, London (2013). https://doi.org/10.1007/978-1-4471-2990-5_14
12. Deacon, T., Barthet, M., Stockman, T.: Subjective experience in an interactive music virtual environment: an exploratory study. In: 12th International Symposium on Computer Music Multidisciplinary Research, São Paulo (2016)
13. Wessel, D., Wright, M.: Problems and prospects for intimate musical control of computers. Comput. Music J. **26**(3), 11–22 (2002)
14. McDermott, J., Gifford, T., Bouwer, A., Wagy, M.: Should music interaction be easy? In: Holland, S., Wilkie, K., Mulholland, P., Seago, A. (eds.) Music and Human-Computer Interaction. SSCC, pp. 29–47. Springer, London (2013). https://doi.org/10.1007/978-1-4471-2990-5_2
15. Fels, S.: Designing for intimacy: creating new interfaces for musical expression. Proc. IEEE **92**(4), 672–685 (2004)
16. Johnston, A.: Beyond evaluation: linking practice and theory in new musical interface design. In: Proceedings of the International Conference on New Interfaces for Musical Expression, pp. 280–283, June 2011
17. McDermott, J., Sherry, D., O'Reilly, U.M.: Evolutionary and generative music informs music HCI—and *Vice Versa*. In: Holland, S., Wilkie, K., Mulholland, P., Seago, A. (eds.) Music and Human-Computer Interaction. SSCC, pp. 223–240. Springer, London (2013). https://doi.org/10.1007/978-1-4471-2990-5_13
18. Siswanto, W.A., Wahab, C., Akil, W.M., Yahya, M.N., Ismail, A.E., Nawi, I.: A platform for digital reproduction sound of traditional musical instrument Kompang. In: Applied Mechanics and Materials (2014)
19. Fencott, R., Bryan-Kinns, N.: Computer musicking: HCI, CSCW and collaborative digital musical interaction. In: Holland, S., Wilkie, K., Mulholland, P., Seago, A. (eds.) Music and Human-Computer Interaction. SSCC, pp. 189–205. Springer, London (2013). https://doi.org/10.1007/978-1-4471-2990-5_11
20. Wallis, I., Ingalls, T., Campana, E., Vuong, C.: Amateur musicians, long-term engagement, and HCI. In: Holland, S., Wilkie, K., Mulholland, P., Seago, A. (eds.) Music and Human-Computer Interaction. SSCC, pp. 49–66. Springer, London (2013). https://doi.org/10.1007/978-1-4471-2990-5_3

The Issues of Halal Inspection Process from the Perspective of Demand and Supply Side in Malaysia Halal Certification System

Mohd Zabiedy Mohd Sulaiman[✉], Nurulhuda Noordin, Nor Laila Md. Noor,
Ahmad Iqbal Hakim Suhaimi, and Wan Abdul Rahim Wan Mohd Isa

Faculty of Computer and Mathematical Sciences, Universiti Teknologi MARA (UiTM),
40450 Shah Alam, Selangor, Malaysia
zabiedy.s@outlook.com,
{hudanoordin,norlaila,aiqbal,wrahim2}@tmsk.uitm.edu.my

Abstract. *Halal* inspection (HI) allows the auditor to perform a physical evaluation on the inspection site to ensure it follows the related standards and Islamic guidelines. HI is carried out as part of several important processes in *Halal* certification (HC) system where the end product is issued in the form of *halal* certificate and logo. But, HI is not an easy procedure and the complexity of it has become part of the major factor that contributes to several issues in HC field. Many scholars have studied the issues in HC but there are still lacking extensive research that focuses on HI process. This article attempts to describe the issue in HI which elaborated from the perspective of demand and supply side of HC in Malaysia. The key motivation of this study focuses on the changes to be implemented on HI process via the use of information technology such as virtual technology. The study is carried out based on the Work System Framework and Computer-Supported Cooperative Work as the research basis where the data is collected via interviews and observations focusing on the HI process. The results will provide exposure on HI problems which should be considered for the better use of today's technological advancement in HC field. As technology advances, HC will have to adapt to fit current technology. This is a new innovation in HI process; *halal* virtual inspection is a worthwhile topic to study so that the quality of services in HC sector can be improved for the future.

Keywords: *Halal* · *Halal* inspection issue · *Halal* virtual inspection
Halal certification system · Work System Framework · CSCW

1 Introduction

Halal industry has a huge market and its diversity is beneficial to many areas. It is important to perform verification and certification measures in every process and activities in production. This is because, it helps to guarantee that the end-product is *halal* and produced according to the Islamic law [1]. However, *halal* industry became more challenging since people are not always have the same knowledge regarding the *halal* compliance. Geographical settings, local needs and cultural differences contribute to

© Springer Nature Singapore Pte Ltd. 2018
N. Abdullah et al. (Eds.): i-USEr 2018, CCIS 886, pp. 277–288, 2018.
https://doi.org/10.1007/978-981-13-1628-9_25

variations of views of *halal* concepts adopted by Muslims around the world [2]. In Islam, Muslims are familiar with the *halal* concepts which means something that permissible, pure and abides with Islamic teachings. In this context, everything must be *thoyyib* (meaning something wholesome and free from any hazards) [3]. *Halal* concept is emphasized through the Islamic dietary laws and aims to prevent mankind (Muslims) from consuming unnatural foods product which may affect their health [4]. This concept is applied to almost everything from food to cosmetics, healthcare and pharmaceutical products as well as human actions and deed [5].

The *halal* industry creates a new environment and grabbing the world's attentions as the demand of *halal* products and services is now increase due to the remarkable growth of the world's Muslim population [6]. As a result, many countries take advantages on this profitable industry such as Australia (beef), New Zealand (lamb), Brazil (poultry), Thailand (processed food), and Malaysia (processed *halal* food, ingredients and non-food products) [7]. The trend in the *halal* industry makes it essential to preserve *halal* for the benefit of Muslim and non-Muslim consumers. One of the factor is due to "the growing awareness of consumers concerning the importance of Halal Certification (HC)" [1]. HC consists of several systematic evaluation processes. In order to maintain '*halal*', it is vital to handle HC system properly and efficiently. Unfortunately, there are a lot of issues, problems and challenges often encountered by the relevant authority along the process which become the incompetence factor of HC system. Among all processes in the HC system, *Halal* Inspection (HI) process is the most vital part and strict procedure of the system [8]. This is because, HI allows the authority to physically evaluate and ensure that every component in production are handled according to the related standards and requirements. In this respect, everything must be free from non-*halal* elements, contaminations and hazards [9]. Without HI process, it is difficult for the auditor to obtain the necessary information (evidence) before the issuance of the HC [8]. As many researchers concerned about the *halal*-related issues such as the difficulties in implementation and enforcement of *halal* laws [5], the misuse of *halal* certificate (fake) and logo, inappropriate placement and mixing of *halal* and non-*halal* products [10] as well as lack of unified *halal* guideline for the global uses [11], there are still lacking of extensive research conducted to highlight the issue in HI process.

This paper aims to determine the issues in HI process; from the perspective of the demand and supply side of HC system. This study is conducted via interviews and observations on the HI focusing on the evaluation process of small and medium size food outlets in Malaysia. This article will identify the problems which should be considered in utilizing information technology such as *virtual technology* in HC field. The objective is to perform the inspection process through a better way to achieve the inspection goals; effectively and efficiently. HI virtualization is unique compare to other inspection process as it is needed to be viewed from many aspects of Islamic perspective. As long as this innovative approach abides with all *halal* requirement; *halal* virtual inspection is not something impossible to be implemented although there will be some boundaries that will be encountered along the journey. This article is arranged into sections begins with introduction, literature review, methodology, data analysis, results and conclusion.

2 Literature Review

2.1 Halal Certification System

Halal certification (HC) represents valuable products, nutritious and protection of consumers' rights which is to assure the product's conformity to the Islamic dietary laws and *halal* standards as well as provides guarantee of permitted elements for Muslims consumption. HC gives a 'hint' to show the consumers that products are produced based on *halal* methods and with HC, any unwanted (*haram*) products can also be determined [12]. HC is beneficial to many sectors and can be seen as a new source of the economic growth [7]. There are many aspects that will be evaluated mainly on the hygienic, quality and safety of certain food products or goods. The evaluation criteria includes the preparation, handling and processing activities in the production, the ingredients and raw materials, packaging, storing and so forth [11]. HC is considered as an Islamic - version of safety assurance system which is now become the major part of Muslim consumers' needs. It is not enough for Muslims to just rely on other existing assurance system such as the Good Manufacturing Practices (GMP), Good Hygiene Practices (GHP) and the Hazard Analysis Critical Control Points (HACCP) to evaluate the products and services, especially in the food sector. This is because, Muslims have some restriction in product consumption due to their needs to seek for a good source of physical and spiritual development [13]. However, HC adapts those assurance systems in its evaluation process together with some special criteria in regard to religious matters.

HC system has developed as a significant force in Muslims and non-Muslims countries which created a regional market environment all over the world. It is issued by *Halal* Certification Body (HCB) which comprises of government-controlled departments, non-profit organizations, private for-profit businesses and mosques [14]. In the recent year, many countries have implemented the necessary actions to strengthen its *halal* market. One of the promising market is in Southeast Asia where countries like Indonesia, Brunei, Singapore and Malaysia play major roles in *halal* development. Different country may have different way of conducting HC since there is no unified *halal* verification standard that can be implemented globally. In fact, such integrated framework is still in a working progress by the Organisation of Islamic Cooperation (OIC) [14]. Indonesia, the world's largest Muslim population is using its *halal* laws such as *Halal* Product Guarantee Law (Act no. 33) to enforce its *halal* sector. Recently, Indonesian government has passed the authority of certifying *halal* products from the Indonesian Ulema Council (MUI) to the newly formed body; the *Halal* Product Certification Agency (BPJPH) [15]. Meanwhile in Brunei, HC is enforced by the Religious Council Brunei Darussalam (MUIB) based on several laws and guidelines such as *Halal* Meat Act, *Halal* Meat Rules 2008, *Halal* Certificate and *Halal* Label Order 2005, the Guidelines for *Halal* Certification. The Islamic Religious Council of Singapore (MUIS) in Singapore is the responsible body for Singapore's HC based on Section 88(A) of Administration of Muslim Act (AMLA) [12]. These countries have some similarities and differences in HC implementation but still comply with the Islamic guidelines and *halal* requirement. Muslim-majority country like Malaysia; has strongly promoted and recognized the need for HC to verify the foods, products and services. Malaysia's *halal* regulations (i.e. Malaysian *Halal* Standards, and Manual Procedure for Malaysia *Halal* Certification (MPPHM) (3rd Revision) 2014) have become the contributor that position the country as the lead nation in *halal* development. HC in this country is conducted by several government departments and agencies at the federal and state level. HC is managed and issued by the Department of Islamic Development Malaysia (JAKIM); which is the sole authorized Islamic body to produce Malaysia's HC. JAKIM is working together with the State Islamic Religious Department (JAIN), State Islamic Religious Council (MAIN), other government departments (i.e. Ministry of Health, Department of Chemistry Malaysia, etc.), non-government organizations (NGO), *halal* centres, public and private universities [16]. Basically, HCB issues *Halal Certificate* and/or *Halal Logo* which will be given to the HC applicant. In most countries, HC is not a mandatory requirement for business establishment [5]. But, HC gives a perception of healthy choices for consumers which influenced business practitioners to obtain *halal* certificate as it helps to boost-up profit and improve economic growth.

Malaysia Halal Certification System. *Halal* certification in Malaysia is conducted based on the Manual Procedure for Malaysia *Halal* Certification (MPPHM) (3rd Revision) 2014; the latest standard operating procedure (SOP) used by the JAKIM and other Malaysian *halal* authorities. In general, HC is carried out under four main stages; (i) application of *halal* certificate, (ii) *Halal* Inspection (HI) (consists of documents approval and premise inspection), (iii) application approval by *halal* certification panel and (iv) enforcement and monitoring [4]. It all started after the HCB receiving an HC application, HI process will be carried out by the HCB where all supporting documents will be verified. This process also known as application and documents approval or Off-site Inspection process. Then, premise inspection process (also known as On-site Inspection) will be conducted. This is the main process in HI where *Halal* Auditor will search for evidence of non-compliance in accordance to the certification requirements. At least two *Halal* Auditors are required for each HI; one Shariah *Halal* Auditor (expert in Islamic studies) and one Technical *Halal* Auditor (food technologist) [9]. This is the minimum requirement for each HI process. Then, the inspection findings will be recorded to be presented to the *Halal* Certification Panels at the monthly panels meeting. If approved, the applicant will be awarded with the certification or will be informed regarding the rejection of the application. Finally, the certificate holder will be monitored and enforcement process will be conducted. This is a continuous process that will be carried out from time to time. Among all of the processes, HI process is the most critical part of HC system which should be handled carefully. This is because, HI process is the procedure that will be the determinant factor of approval or rejection of certain application [8] since any non-compliance evidence found during HI will affect the status of the application. To date, it is common that the HCB conduct the inspection process manually; through the physical visual inspection process on the applicant's premises. Besides, other factors such as hygiene and safety level at the premise, HCB (*Halal* Auditor) usually will observe, check and identify if there is any non-*halal* element can be found in the premise. If any, the findings will be recorded, evidence and sample will be taken if necessary for further analysis at the laboratory, and proper recommendation will be given by the auditors. Figure 1 simplifies the certification process.

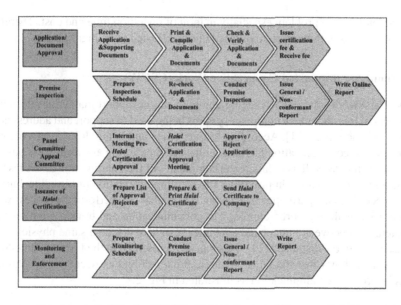

Fig. 1. *Halal* certification process [4].

2.2   Halal Certification Issues and Information Technology Application

For many years, scholars have discussed numerous *Halal* Certification (HC) issues and the reason to implement the necessary actions of improvement. Shafie and Othman [17] stated that the HC issues include the variation of '*halal*' definition, misuse of *halal* logo and Islamic brand names which lead to consumers' confusion. These issues believed to be the trigger that sparks the problems and incompetence of HC system. In this case, information technology (IT) can be the best option to overcome the problem. IT is evolving from time to time and has been used in many areas [18]. However, the study on IT application in HC is still quite rare. Kadir et al. [19] proposed a method for product consumer to verify HC held by the business practitioner by simply 'close-scanning' the chip-embedded *halal* certificate using Near Field Communication (NFC) technology; a common feature in today's smartphones. Yuniarti et al. [18] proposed a system that can assist the consumer to identify the *halal* products based on the Optical Character Recognition (OCR) technology using mobile device's camera. Both systems [18, 19] aim to make *halal* detection more end-user friendly that can be 'linked' with *halal* databases. Furthermore, as the consumers' awareness on *halal* matters is increasing, many scholars are encouraged to look for the best method to reduce HC issue. QuikHalal; the world's first mobile apps that specially designed to help *halal* authority in conducting *Halal* Inspection (HI) process [20]. It enhances the auditor's productivity by eliminating the need to prepare the HI checklist and inspection report for the auditor. The technology such as NFC, OCR and QuikHalal prove how IT application in the HC field can be helpful to eliminate HC issues. As the key element in HC system, HI process require some special attention of improvement. Some claims that HC is complex, time-consuming and high cost [9, 20]. In this research, conducting HI process virtually is believed may cut the problem especially in term of operation time and cost. Therefore, as a primary action, the issues often faced during HI need to be highlighted.

2.3 Computer Supported Cooperative Work (CSCW)

CSCW framework offers wide-ranging communication support making it relevant for this research. It is about how computer systems being used to support and addresses any collaborative activities [21]. According to Carstensen and Schmidt [21], offering good interaction and communication facilities, enhanced monitoring and awareness possibilities to the actors as well as reducing the complexity of the coordination activities to be conducted is an alternative in providing CSCW. Implementation of virtual technology involves people as the participants in a work system that will perform the process where the computer as the support technology of communication and transmission medium. The interaction between human and computer "can take place on same physical space and also place in the distance" [22]. This can be represented in the form of Time-Space Matrix which shows that the human-computer interaction can occur via synchronous and asynchronous communication as illustrated in Fig. 2.

	Same Time	Different Time
Same Place	Face-to-face interaction	Asynchronous interaction
Different Place	Synchronous distributed interaction	Asynchronous distributed interaction

Fig. 2. Johansan's time-space matrix [22].

CSCW technology applied to optimizing space, reduce cost, improve performance, efficiency and satisfaction [22]. Researchers believe the interaction between time human and technology that must be considered in term of time and place making this theory is suitable for this study. In this respect, conducting *Halal* Inspection process through the use of virtual technology and digital mediator can be performed at the real time which is same time and place; same time and different place; or different time and place.

3   Methodology

3.1   Interview

Five *Halal* Auditors have been selected to be the respondent of this study and have been interviewed in three separate meetings; Interview 1 (*Halal* Auditor 1 and 2), Interview 2 (*Halal* Auditor 3 and 4) and Interview 3 (*Halal* Auditor 5). The selection of the respondent is based on their experience in *Halal* Certification (HC) field. After making appointment, one-hour semi-structured interview has been conducted at the respondents' office. This is to provide comfortable environment during the interview sessions. The interview is conducted according to the questions which have been designed early that focusing on the research topics. The interview questions are focusing on the processes and activities in *Halal* Inspection (HI) process, the participants (actors) involved, the technology used and the information related to the HC and HI process. Notes have been taken for further analysis and the sessions were voice-recorded with the respondents' permission which then transcribed and analysed. The respondent details are described in Table 1.

Table 1. Respondent details.

Respondent	Background and experience in *halal* certification field
Halal Auditor 1	• Assistant Director, JAKIM/*Halal* auditor/Islamic affairs officer • Academic: Bachelor of Islamic Studies (Shariah), UKM • Experience: 4 years of service in JAKIM
Halal Auditor 2	• Assistant Director, JAKIM/*Halal* auditor/Islamic affairs officer • Academic: Bachelor of *Usuluddin*, Al-Azhar University • Experience: Audit Unit, JAKIM
Halal Auditor 3	• Assistant Director, JAKIM/*Halal* auditor • Academic: Bachelor of Food Science and Technology, UPM • Experience: involved in *halal* certification since 2009
Halal Auditor 4	• Assistant Director, JAKIM/*Halal* auditor • Academic: Bachelor of Science (Chemical Sciences and Food Technology), UKM, Diploma in Laboratory Technology, USM • Experience: involved in *halal* certification since 2011
Halal Auditor 5	• Assistant Director, JHEAINS/*Halal* auditor/Islamic affairs officer • Academic: Bachelor of Shariah, UM • Experience: appointed as *halal* auditor since 2012 and as assistant director since 2014 in MGI unit of JHEAINS

3.2   Observation

The observations were conducted to obtain more information to strengthen researcher's understanding on *Halal* Inspection (HI) process. Besides, it is also to acquire some experience on how the auditor performs the inspection process and determine the aspect that will be inspected (observed). For that purpose, 10 food premises (4 chain restaurants, 1 hotel kitchen or restaurant, 4 food kiosks and 1 franchise restaurant) located in Selangor and Kuala Lumpur, Malaysia have been selected for the observation.

The observations were carried out in four working days; 1st day (Premise 1), 2nd day (Premise 2 and 3), 3rd day (Premise 4, 5, and 6) and 4th day (Premise 7, 8, 9, and 10) together with 14 *Halal* Auditors from Malaysian *Halal* Certification Body (6 are the expert in Islamic studies (*Shariah*) and 8 are the experts in technical aspect (food technologist)). A special 'checklist' has been designed and used during the observations to help the researcher in identifying the inspection details. On the other hand, it is also to determine any issues encountered by the *halal* auditor during the process. Notes have been taken and the duration of each inspection has been recorded for further analysis. Table 2 shows the summary of the observations.

Table 2. Summary of observation.

Premise	Type	Duration	Area of inspection (observation)
Premise 1	Chain restaurant	• 1 h, 5 min	Kitchen, preparation area, storage
Premise 2	Hotel (kitchen or restaurant)	• 1 h, 40 min	Main kitchen; Chinese kitchen; pastry kitchen, butcher kitchen, food preparation area, storage facilities, racks, waste disposal, workers hygiene
Premise 3	Chain restaurant	• 30 min	Dining & serving area, food handling and preparation area, food racks, stock storage
Premise 4	Food kiosk	• 45 min	Handling area, kitchen, dining area
Premise 5	Food kiosk	• 18 min	Food handling area, mini kitchen, dining area, storage, racks, cabinets
Premise 6	Franchise restaurant	• 1 h, 20 min	Kitchen, storage room, dining area, dishes washing area, food processing, handling & preparation area
Premise 7	Chain restaurant	• 1 h, 10 min	Pastry products and cakes section, dining area (open area & air-conditioned area)
Premise 8	Food kiosk	• 10 min	Storage (containers & cabinets), food serving area
Premise 9	Chain restaurant	• 55 min	Kitchen, dining area, food handling and preparation area, workers lockers, storage
Premise 10	Food kiosk	• 15 min	Storage (containers & cabinets), food serving area

4   Analysis and Results

4.1   Interview Analysis

The collected data is transcribed and analysed using thematic interview analysis. From the interviews, the *Halal* Certification (HC) process has been identified. The certification starts by the application process from the applicant which then will be inspected by the *Halal* Certification Body (HCB). Firstly, on the documentations (desk-checking) followed by the issuance of service charges letter to the applicant. After the payment has been made, the inspection schedule will be prepared and the premise inspection will be carried out. At this point, *Halal* Auditor will start the inspection with opening meeting session at the applicant's premise for a quick briefing. They will conduct documents re-checking and verification. Then, the evaluation of the premise begins where all documentation, the product used in food processing and production, and so forth will be evaluated. This process ends with a closing meeting between the *Halal* Auditor and the applicant where the findings as well as the recommendation will be given. The findings from *Halal* Inspection (HI) process will be presented at the panel meeting for approval or rejection of the application. If complete, *halal* certificate will be issued to the applicant which will be monitored from time to time. For each HI, the number of *Halal* Auditor that perform the process is depending on several factors such as the category and size of the premise, the location, the availability of the auditors and type of certification scheme. During this process, usually *Halal* Auditor will use common equipment such as digital camera, stopwatch (for inspection at the slaughter houses), sampling apparatus, torchlight, and mobile computing devices (i.e. computers, tablets, smartphones, etc.). The related guidelines also used as reference during HI such as the Manual Procedure for Malaysia *Halal* Certification (MPPHM) (3rd Revision) 2014, Malaysian *Halal* Standards, Food Act and Food Regulation, and many more.

4.2 Observation Analysis

The data collected from the observations has been analysed using comparison table by focusing on the *Halal* Inspection (HI) process. This will help the researcher in identifying the related issues in HI. From the observations, more detailed HI processes have been determined. Firstly, during HI, the auditor will introduce themselves to the representative at the premise before requesting the supporting documents of HC application. Then, they will make some preparation for inspection. After that, they will begin the process with opening meeting (quick briefing to the applicant). At this point, they will also conduct the document re-checking to ensure the informations provided at the premise are similar with the one in the online application system. Then, the auditor conducts physical inspection on the premise. Notes will be taken during the process and all evidence will be recorded. Next process is the final evaluation where the auditor will complete the inspection forms and auditors will discuss the findings with the applicant. Finally, the HI process ends with the closing meeting (the findings will be presented to the applicant and auditor gives recommendations of improvement/comments). From the observations, it can be summarized that the HI process usually performed at the rate of two to five food premises per day. In this case, the inspection has been performed at premise located in the same area or near to each other. For example, there are three food premises that have been inspected and observed within the same day including 2 chain restaurants (kiosks) and 1 franchise restaurant (see Table 2). These premises are located in the same building which make it easier for the auditor to move from one premise to another. In term of duration, there are situation which takes about 10 min up to 2 h for each inspection to be completed. This is depending on the current situation which can be influenced by many factors such as weather condition, traffic, type of premise, and collaboration between auditors and the applicant or representative at the food premise.

4.3 Halal Inspection Issues

As a result, the issue in *Halal* Inspection (HI) process has been uncovered. The result is categorized into two perspectives; demand side and supply side of *Halal* Certification (HC). From the perspective of demand side of HC, HI issues are (i) the availability of the HC applicant. Sometimes, the applicant is not available during inspection (i.e. taking sick leave, etc.). On top of that, there are situation where (ii) the applicant is not ready for the HI process due to certain factor such as busy (peak hour), limited staff available and lack of HC knowledge. Besides, incomplete information in the online application system provided by the applicant also affecting the smoothness of HI process. There are some materials identified in the premise but not mentioned in the online system. Improper documentation also delays the HI process as the applicant will take some time for preparation. Furthermore, (iii) there is also difficulty in communication between the present parties. Sometimes, non-local applicant is not able to properly communicate with auditors due to language differences which leads to misunderstanding during HI. (iv) There is situation where the applicant used unclear labelling and halal status of critical raw materials (i.e. source, cheese, meat product, etc.). In this case, the auditor need to take some samples for further analysis. Finally, (v) in term of the premise management; insufficient Muslims workers, company information is outdated (i.e. changes of the company's administration), improper outlet layout and product storage also are the major factors that will affect the HI results.

From the supply side perspective, it is also identified that (i) HI can be a time-consuming process. Sometimes, it is difficult for the auditor to identify the location of the applicant's premise which slows down the inspection process. In addition, the environmental factors such as (ii) the distance of the inspected premises and traffic jam (urban area) (i.e. shopping mall; busy during peak hour) also delays the inspection process. On top of that, (iii) unsystematic documentation and incomplete premise details (i.e. address provided is simple, etc.) make it harder for the auditor to identify the premise's location. Furthermore, in term of (iv) the unexpected last-minute issues while conducting the HI process. There is situation where the premise is not operational at the time of inspection (information provided not up-to-date). Sometimes, the auditor will also receive a last-minute assignment (i.e. urgent meeting, etc.) which forced them not to proceed with the current inspection planning and reschedule the HI. Finally, in term of (v) the evidence of non-compliance during HI. *Halal* Auditor identified non-*halal* products at the premise (even for temporary storage purposes). For the inspection process for the *Halal* Certificate holder, the auditors also detected some repeated mistakes (non-compliance) at the outlet although the applicant was reminded during the previous inspection process. It is important to emphasize these issues which can be seen as part of the vital elements which should be considered in virtualizing the inspection process. This will help to determine the best approach that can be implemented to enhance the existing HC system. Table 3 simplifies the issues in HI process.

Table 3. Halal inspection issues.

No.	Demand side (applicant)	Supply side (*halal* auditor)
1	Availability of applicant	Time-consuming process
2	Readiness for inspection	Environmental factors
3	Miscommunication issues (language factor)	Incomplete information provided
4	Unclear *halal* status	Unexpected issues
5	Poor premise management	Evidence of non-compliance

5 Conclusion

In short, *halal* is a concept associated with religious belief. The increase of Muslims population clearly leads to the rising demand of *Halal* Certification (HC). As an important process in HC system, *Halal* Inspection (HI) acts as a tool for evaluating and verifying the effectiveness of control measures in the certain organization. However, current inspection method relies on the auditor's consistency, observational judgement, skills and experience in order to be effective. The complexity of HC and HI process requires better approach in line with the advancement of information and communication technology. This article has revealed several issues in HI process via an exploratory research which clarified from the perspective of demand and supply side of HC. This includes the issues of the applicant's availability and readiness for HI, miscommunication between the involved parties, unclear *halal* status, poor premise management, time-consuming HI process, environmental factors, incomplete HC information, unexpected issues and finally, the presence of the non-compliance evidence at the applicant's premise. Reducing such issues can be the 'boost-up factor' that may remove inefficiency element in the HI process. In order to the HI virtualization to be successful, these issues should be considered and given special attention as it may affect the expected outcomes of the virtualization process. Implementing virtual technology in HC field is not an easy process and several limitations will be encountered along the journey. This is because, the relevant *halal* requirements must not be compromised at any circumstances. Still, this approach cannot be denied due to its benefit in making our life better and efficient. Hopefully, HI virtualization will help us to improve the existing HC system.

Acknowledgment. Our thanks to the Ministry of Higher Education Malaysia for funding this research under the grant RAGS/1/2015/ICT04/UITM/02/1, Universiti Teknologi MARA (UiTM), Malaysia, Department of Islamic Development Malaysia (JAKIM) and other authorities for supporting this study.

References

1. Dube, F.N., HaiJuan, Y., Lijun, H.: Halal certification system as a key determinant of firm internationalisation in the Philippines and Malaysia. Asian Acad. Manag. J. **21**, 73–88 (2016)
2. Edbiz Consulting: Global halal industry: an overview. In: Global Islamic Finance Report 2013, pp. 140–159 (2013)
3. Zakaria, Z., Ismail, S.Z.: The trade description act 2011: regulating "halal" in Malaysia. In: International Conference on Law, Management and Humanities (ICLMH 2014), Bangkok, Thailand, pp. 2011–2013 (2014)
4. Noordin, N.: Efficiency factors and ecosystem framework in Malaysian halal food certification system (2013)
5. Buang, A.H., Mahmod, Z.: The issues and challenges of halal certification bodies in Malaysia. Shariah J. **20**, 271–288 (2012)
6. Reuters, T., Standard, D.: State of the global islamic economy: 2014–2015 report (2015)
7. Halal Industry Development Corporation [HDC]: The Halal Industry - The New Potential Market (2016)
8. Mohamad, P.M.D.M.N., Othman, N.: Audit pengesahan halal - kajian di Jabatan Kemajuan Islam Malaysia (2004)
9. Ab. Rahman, L.: Shariah & Malaysian halal certification system. J. Penyelid. Islam. **18**, 15–36 (2005)
10. Abdul Wahab, N., Mohd Shahwahid, F., Ab. Hamid, N.A.: Issues, challenges and strengths of the halal industry in Singapore: MUIS's experience. In: Proceeding of the 2nd International Conference on Economics & Banking 2016, 2nd ICEB, Selangor, pp. 82–91 (2016)

11. Batu, A., Regenstein, J.M.: Halal food certification challenges and their implications for Muslim societies worldwide. In: International Periodical for the Languages, Literature and History of Turkish or Turkic, Turkish Studies, Ankara, Turkey, pp. 111–130 (2014)
12. Asa, R.S.: Malaysian halal certification: It's religious significance and economic value. Shariah J. **25**, 137–156 (2017)
13. Syed Marzuki, S.Z., Hall, C.M., Ballantine, P.W.: Restaurant managers' perspectives on halal certification. J. Islam. Mark. **3**, 47–58 (2012)
14. Evans, A., Syed, S.: Halal Goes Global, Geneva, Switzerland (2015)
15. The Jakarta Post: Government ends MUI's authority to issue halal certificates. http://www.thejakartapost.com/news/2017/10/13/government-ends-muis-authority-to-issue-halal-certificates.html. Accessed 24 Apr 2018
16. Abdul Majid, M.A., Zainal Abidin, I.H., Mohd Abd Majid, H.A., Tamby Chik, C.: Issues of halal food implementation in Malaysia. J. Appl. Environ. Biol. Sci. **5**, 50–56 (2015)
17. Shafie, S., Othman, P.D.M.N.: Halal certification: an international marketing issues and challenges. In: Proceeding Int. IFSAM VIIIth World Congress, pp. 1–11 (2006)
18. Yuniarti, A., Kuswardayan, I., Hariadi, R.R., Arifiani, S., Mursidah, E.: Design of integrated latext: Halal detection text using OCR (Optical Character Recognition) and web service, pp. 1–5 (2017)
19. Kadir, E.A., Shamsuddin, S.M., Rahim, S.K.A., Rosa, S.L.: Application of NFC technology for premise Halal certification. In: 2015 3rd International Conference Information Communication Technology ICoICT 2015, pp. 618–621 (2015)
20. Illyas Tan, M.I.: A QuikHalal – A solution to Halal Certification Process for Industry. http://www.utm.my/research/2017/10/05/quikhalal-a-solution-to-halal-certification-process-for-industry/. Accessed 31 Jan 2018
21. Carstensen, P.H., Schmidt, K.: Computer supported cooperative work: new challenges to systems design. In: Itoh, K. (ed.) Handbook of Human Factors, pp. 619–636 (1999)
22. Penichet, V.M.R., Marin, I., Gallud, J.A., Lozano, M.D., Tesoriero, R.: A classification method for CSCW systems. Electron. Notes Theor. Comput. Sci. **168**, 237–247 (2007)

Towards Achieving the Efficiency in Zakat Management System: Interaction Design for Optimization in Indonesia

Muharman Lubis$^{(\boxtimes)}$ and Anik Hanifatul Azizah

Telkom University, Telekomunikasi 1, 40257 Bandung, Indonesia
{muharmanlubis, anikhanifazizah}@telkomuniversity.ac.id

Abstract. There is great potential in the Zakat Management System (ZMS) to increase social welfare that requires government attention. Using the appropriate technological advances to administer zakat process might improve the efficiency to optimize the potential. Therefore, several related factors must be considered such as human, environment, culture, language, literacy and regulation to improve the effectiveness of interaction and communication among stakeholders. This study discusses several journals and articles that focused on various problems faced by zakat institution in 5 (five) stages namely; planning, collecting, organizing, distributing and disbursing the zakat. The design for interaction can provide clear views of the system's weaknesses to improve decision making by generating the proper strategy to produce an efficient process.

Keywords: Zakat · Interaction design · Optimization · Efficiency

1 Introduction

Historically, Indonesian had to pay zakat directly to the recipient, through masjid (Muslim's place of worship) or with religious figures separately until KH. Ahmad Dahlan suggested the establishment of Zakat institution as an intermediary for the ZMS structurally before independence. Zakat is obligatory payment made annually under Islamic law on certain kinds of property which will be used for charitable and religious purposes. At practical level, many Indonesians paid zakat to their families or poor people close to their homes. Alternatively, ZMS through the organization has been recognized by the Ministry of Religious Affairs to have many benefits, such as ensuring the discipline of zakat payers, reducing social and technical problems related to zakat receiver, assessing the priority target and increasing the potential of the zakat fund where the specific objective have not been achieved. Based on the BPS (Indonesian Central Bureau of Statistics) report in April 2011, the total number of Indonesian population was 237.6 million with 119.6 million males and 118 million females with a growth level of 1.36% between 2010 and 2016. Meanwhile, BPS has projected in 2017, the total population will reach 261.89 million with 56% in Java Island. In addition, the percentage of poor citizens reached 10.64% (27.77 million) in March 2017, in which unemployment rate increased 5.5% since February-to-August 2017 at around 6.79% (17.78 millions) in cities and 4.01% (10.5 millions) in villages. Interestingly, the

N. Abdullah et al. (Eds.): i-USEr 2018, CCIS 886, pp. 289–301, 2018.
https://doi.org/10.1007/978-981-13-1628-9_26

economic growth in East Java was 5.62% above the national average (5.18%) in the second quarter of 2016.

In general, there are two types of zakat, which are required by Muslim in certain period of time to provide some portion of their primary food and wealth; zakat Fitr (before Shalat Idul Fitr) and Zakat Mal (after 1 year of unused belonging and reach the limit/nishob). Zakat is different with other voluntary charities such as shodaqoh (giving alms freely), infaq (building masjid) and waqf (freeing properties for the sake of community/ummah) in which qualified people should perform 2.5% (zakat mal) and 1 sha' or around 2.5 kg (zakat fitr) obligatorily. The government of Indonesian issued Act No. 38/1999 to accommodate the need for effective and efficient ZMS, which establishes BAZ (Zakat Organizer Body) in section 6 and LAZ (Zakat Organizer Institution) in section 7 as the institutions that have the authority to administer zakat and strengthen the position of Amil (zakat organizer) to be more professional. It is expected that its establishment increase the zakat payers' awareness which help deliver the efficient distribution. In addition, it also maintains the updated data related to 8 (eight) mustahiq (eligible person) such as those who has huge debts (gharimin), in huge needs (faqir) or do long trip (musafir) [1, 2].

Another interesting aspect is the reduction for taxable income, namely in Article 13 subsection 3 where the act stipulates that the portion of zakat payment to BAZ or LAZ can be exempted from taxation. Although, in Indonesia there is controversy regarding this policy as tax collection is considered prohibited based on shari'ah law but zakat as a deduction for taxable income is confirmed legal with establishment of Act No. 17/2000 on Income Taxes. It is stated in chapter VIII about the obligation to all zakat institutions to keep the record accurately else they have to pay the sanction up to Rp. 30 million if the institution does not perform its duties properly. In actual fact, the mechanism of ZMS is rather flexible and dynamic which is based on the case of Caliph Umar who once considered the specific policy to not share the zakat to muallaf (revert to Islam) while during the reign of Caliph Usman, he delegated to the trusted representative as response to the spread of Islam. Currently, BAZ DKI Jakarta has decided that Amil and Riqab will not receive zakat [3] because it is extremely difficult to identify the complete zakat recipients in accordance to strict criteria. There are also communication gaps between zakat institution and recipient such as embarrassment, being cheated, bureaucracy in administration and they also believe that the process adds more problems than solutions [2]. Therefore, this study investigates requirement analysis of ZMS in Indonesia that focus on the interaction of the relevant stakeholders, the related application, the required infrastructure and the task role.

2   Literature Review

2.1   Zakat Awareness

The efficiency of the zakat system cannot be seen only in regard to the level of trust between zakat payers and zakat institutions, but its main purpose in reducing the poverty of society [4]. As fundamental pillar of sharia, the obligation to pay zakat must be believed as a way to obtain reward from Allah Ta'ala. As the home to the largest

Muslim population in the world, Indonesia's zakat potential is expected to be at around Rp. 7.3 trillion per year according to PIRAC (Public Interest Research and Advocacy Public) and Rp. 17.5 trillion according to FOZ (Forum of Zakat), however the realization is only 3.3 trillion per year [5], although it should be greater at estimation of more than Rp. 286 trillion [14]. Those numbers can grow further beyond prediction if the Muslims are aware of the benefits such as equity in economic circulation and stimulation of the wheels of the transaction, not only by practising zakat, but also infaq, waqf and shodaqah [6]. Interestingly, since the issuance of new regulation of Act no. 23/2011 (ZMS), there have been around 180 of LAZ being registered as member of FOZ and hundreds of BAZ under government instruction along with other thousands of unregistered charity bodies were identified, causing high concern from managerial perspective. However, it is of no use without synergy between relevant institutions to provide suitable coordination as well as collaboration in terms of providing accurate and consistent information about zakat recipients or cooperating with financial support to expand the coverage of zakat distribution with logistic, warehouse and accommodation [5, 6].

According to poverty level defined by World Bank standard of income at the average of US$ 1.25/day/person, there are around 1.6 billion (29%) of the world population living as poor people. BAZ and LAZ play critical role to raise awareness among stakeholders by giving full control for them to determine the modes in delivering zakat to recipient, in which the institutions support in terms of operational, financial and growth control in data monitoring [7]. In addition, as mentioned by the Director General of the Islamic Community Guidance and Hajj Affairs, no. D/291 of 2000 on technical guidelines for ZMS still has problems such as there is no sanction for dereliction of duty [8]. Meanwhile, the aspect of trust is also important to attract zakat payers to utilize BAZ/LAZ as common channel in allocating payment to recipient. Majority of Indonesians want improvement in responsibility, transparency and accountability in ZMS [9]. Zakat empowerment are absolutely necessary to be implemented in efforts to conduct ventures to build infrastructure in remote area, providing vehicle to help the poor people to work, develop educational center, and provide vocational skill to the unemployed person [10, 11]. There is also lack of understanding on zakat mechanism, whereby some assume that zakat is equal to donation or voluntary act, not to be forced but based on sincerity [12]. The problem mentioned above has indirect result for low level of awareness in zakat payers to pay through zakat institution or even give directly to recipients.

2.2 Zakat Collection

In detail, there are many non-governmental approaches used to collect zakat namely Dhuafa Wallet (Dompet Dhuafa), Zakat Home (Rumah Zakat), Islamic boarding school (Pesantren), masjid and individual zakat payers besides BAZ which collects zakat on national, province and district level under supervision of Ministry of Religious Affairs. Unfortunately, even with huge number of zakat collectors which is supposed to translate into huge zakat collection, the realization only reached 6% (Rp. 1.3 trillion) [12]. As comparison, the target for tax revenue based on the APBN-P 2016 (State Budget-changes) was at Rp. 1,355 trillion with 81.6% realization but the expenses were at Rp. 2,095 trillion. The tax revenue takes up about 70% from the overall composition of APBN, which consist two types namely central tax (PPh, PPN, PPnBM, PBB, Bea Meterai, etc.) and local tax (parking, billboard, cigarettes, water surface, gasoline, etc.). There are total of around 500 office units and 39,000 employees in Directorate General of Taxation under Ministry of Finance to handle the process of tax collection [13], which consume a lot of total revenue. Thus, government should perceive the benefits of zakat compare to taxation in providing financial budget for national development. Many Indonesian have initiative to do or give voluntarily for charitable work such as infrastructure funding due to support from ustadz or respected religious leaders, thus making the marketing cost to be less compared to high amount of budget to educate the nation on taxation for example; tax seminar, socialization or counselling. In addition, the tax system applied in Indonesia can be considered as an overburden for majority of the people as they should pay zakat in the regular basis, though the tax reduction has been implemented [12]. There is also no certain punishment for those who refuse to pay zakat even though the shariah law demand hard punishment to those who choose not to pay as it is an act of disobedience to Allah Ta'ala. The first Islam caliph, Caliph Abu Bakar during his reign declared war and imposed death penalty to the community who rejected the obligation to pay zakat.

In Indonesian's social life, everything is uncertain thus making it difficult to esti-mate the situation, but through measurement of exponential smoothing in predicting trend based on pessimistic level, the zakat collection can reach up to Rp. 3.75 trillion, in moderate level up to Rp. 4.16 trillion and optimistic one about 4.24 trillion. By using multiplicative decomposition approach, the zakat collection is predicted to reach up to Rp. 5 trillion in 2020 and Rp. 8.33 trillion in 2029 [14]. It is really unfortunate that the optimization of zakat collection can only reached out less than 3% of its potential, in the range of 1.5% until 2.9% in the next decade. Thus, serious concern is needed from Ministry of Religious Affairs to coordinate and supervise BAZ and LAZ to improve public trust to lead to greater result of zakat collection [15] with several supportive programs. It can involve various communities to develop local potential, fellowship program for outstanding students, subsidy for da'wah training in isolated area such as in the mountains and villages, health care monitoring for disabled or critical patient and economic recovery compensation after calamities or natural disasters. Most zakat organizers have inaccurate data about zakat recipient and there is no proper document to record the process of collection conducted by respective body [2, 4, 16]. However, the organization that handle public interest should provide transparency in their finances (incomes and outcomes) as mandated by regulation [17]. It is aligned with the research that found out religious indicator as critical attribute to raise awareness of individual to protect the unity of society [18]. Therefore, there is significant relation-ship between level of understanding, literacy, attitude and intention of zakat payers [19]. In addition, there is no official officer in certain cities and villages due to lack of transportation and resources. There is also the high cost of manual process involving the operational and coordination cost due to the great distance from ZMS center or big city, resulting to certain location has been neglected without proper delegation mechanism [20].

2.3   Zakat Organization

The role of zakat organization is to maintain social affordability and ensure the economic sustainability. Therefore, process of organizing zakat faces various challenges due to environmental changes in modern societies whereby some people are reluctant to adopt technology innovation and application of new technique [4]. The good corporate governance in zakat organization requires the development of internal control structure, which relates to the provision of accuracy and consistency of data where management need to consider the basic principles namely fairness, transparency, accountability, responsibility and independence [9]. Unclear jurisdiction conflict in terms of vague definition between functions of regulation, supervision and implementation of the zakat organization bring incoordination and indetermination [12]. Importantly, the spirit of defending Islam as religion for all human beings should be inspired in the business activity and objective of the organization to become the basic principles based on the roles of responsibilities and accountability [21]. However, certain operation of organization process in Indonesia involves family business' way of thinking instead of professional code, which somehow endangers their future and success [22]. It is really difficult to punish or be harsh against family if they make mistake or perform badly.

In practice, there are several problems associated with verification and validation of zakat collection and distribution, which has a gap of nearly 40%. Meanwhile, there is no data integration among zakat agency that leads to complexity in finding relevant recipient to improve their quality of life [23]. Some application has been developed to solve various issues in organizing zakat such as decision support system using Analytical Hierarchy Process (AHP), Weight Product Method (WPM), Taxation System, Geographical Information System, Social Society Approach, etc. [2, 20, 23, 24]. Therefore, those applications will be useless if the zakat institution still do not want to improve their business plan and process. On the other hand, there are many complaints made by public that zakat did not reach the targeted group due to lack of publicity by the authority or lack of knowledge on the other part of the community [25].

2.4   Zakat Distribution

The satisfaction in the process of distributing zakat is positively correlated with the adherence to the zakat payment, emphasizing various capacities and performances. An independent or proactive approach of zakat distribution can be the most effective way to assure the better quality of life for zakat recipients [21]. Interestingly, big data maturity model is proposed to support zakat institution evaluate their implementation level in sending enormous amount of money to the zakat beneficiaries [26]. Meanwhile, strengthening cooperation with educational institution and developing the application or solution can increase the capacities to cover large areas in distributing zakat to remote areas. In addition, financial statements should be published periodically to maintain loyalty and enhance stakeholder's satisfaction [27]. Too much bureaucracy is another problem that slows down all operations and makes it time consuming [28]. Among example of this problem is requesting evidence letter of poverty from district office. The high population of urbanized villagers in big city such as Jakarta also poses other problems in the zakat distribution especially with regard to maintaining the accuracy of recipients' identity or personal data [29]. Hence, the zakat funds are now used as income-generating initiatives, a modern development approach to release the poor community permanently from poverty. The redefinition of recipients' category and the introduction of new ways of disbursement, along with the economic perspective of poverty eradication is one step closer towards translating what the scholars have been imagined [4].

Another problem that has been acknowledged is the shortage of personnel and experts in zakat institutions with respect to numerous tasks they bear under their responsibility. This limitation may lead to inefficiency and ineffectiveness of ZMS performed by the zakat institutions such as lack of commitment, concern or motivation [2]. On the other hand, it is common for the recipients to not possess bank account or temporary address, which cause difficulty to locate their position or updating their status to distribute zakat directly. To some extent, zakat recipients receive an announcement from the neighborhood representative or masjid about the time and location, and then they go straight to the place according to the schedule. Unfortunately, there are cases where several of them ask for debt to pay for their transportation cost. Meanwhile, Hairrunizam and Radiah [30] suggested the concept of localization to optimize the distribution process that is the responsibility of the local committee. This provides several benefits such as the effective, efficient and fair allocation of zakat distribution based on the onsite identification or recognition of their unregistered neighbors. To reduce the complexity at the operational level such as registration and documentation the local committee can easily visit the zakat recipient directly unlike the previous system which has constraint regarding coverage, cost and accuracy.

2.5 Zakat Disbursement

A further possible reason preventing the zakat institution to disburse effectively is the problem in identifying the entire eight types of zakat recipient. There were several cases reported that the zakat payers were not satisfied with zakat distribution because the institution did not disburse fairly to all zakat recipients, including al-riqab, ibn Sabil, algharimun and musafir [2]. It must be taken into notice that there are no strict guidelines on how to trace poor people who are entitled for zakat but do not want to present themselves to the commission or found to be contented with their lives. On the other hand, helping the poor people by directly giving them a sum of money to buy their necessities is indeed only a short term solution, which create a dependency on zakat recipient, thus, the strategy of disbursement should be based on capacity building approach to help zakat recipient gain certain skills, provide tools to work, send his/her children to school or give capital to start a business venture [25]. Hence, the zakat fund is now being used as an income generating initiative, a modern development approach to permanently release the poor people from poverty redefining and introducing the new ways of disbursement alongside with the economic perspective [4]. In addition, there are many methods of disbursements that might be problematic to monitor and audit such as by cash, cheque, credit, money transfer, medical assistance, supermarket voucher, livestock, house development or staple food [31].

Project has been done successfully in utilizing masjid as business network in Terengganu, Malaysia can be a good example on how well this solution can be to contribute to society by focusing certain aspects such as customer segments, customer relationship, channels, value propositions and key activities [32]. To support the increased production as the infrastructure development by government, the zakat disbursement should use proactive mechanism based on knowledge level of zakat recipients. It also supports the economy growth with real value compared to current mechanism that depends solely on debt and credit. The spirit for entrepreneurship should be encouraged to generate more demand for goods and services, more room for additional investments and finally, eliminating riba (interest in debt) [33] through the growth cycle based on balance consumption to improve the quality of life.

3 Research Methodology

Researcher used observation to examine the ZMS process in natural settings and through others' report in journals and article papers. During field work, the methods involved usage of field note to gather data through prolonged engagement in Medan and Bandung to investigate various aspects on design issues using PACT (people, activities, con-text and technology). In this study, the template used were based on five issues namely awareness, collection, organization, distribution and disbursement for verification and validation technique [34]. To achieve comprehensive process of observation based on strict criteria, researcher investigated various cases involving issues of ZMS in Indonesia and other countries, and then set several assumptions to generate requirements based on literature review. Theories and concept driven by the results in focused data collection and deflect attention from unnamed categories, unimagined and unanticipated activities that can be very important in order to understand a phenomenon and a setting.

4 Interaction Design

To design the interaction for the application development, this study used emotional design approach [35]. Collaborative and expansion system must be in the local officer or masjid in one place to improve the ZMS process, which requires receivers to be identified quickly and accurately. It is common issues in the registration process hindered by the reason of isolated area. Based on analysis, there are six groups of users in the system namely; administration staff, operational staff, financial staff, amil, asnaf and director who have access and privilege to access the application system. Meanwhile, there are five management activities to be handled involving monitoring, asset management, zakat fund management, amil info and asnaf info. In addition, there are four phases identified in developing application that allow connection or information sharing between zakat institution, masjid and zakat payers which are critical, essential, conditional and optional. The important attribute to be implemented is related to personal data protection of related user in the system [36]. The requirement analysis above does not necessary depict the finished product but merely to draft further classification through ontology process [37] to share domain of information by specification, conceptualization, formalization, implementation and maintenance. In this context, government's role includes, inter alia of making laws with the legislature and drafting technical regulations to optimize zakat management in party-related coordination [38]. In addition to the concept, the fundamental goals of this analysis are to produce efficient Zakat Management System. Researcher conducted requirement analysis and initial design to develop the system based on Moscow rules through any criteria and aspect from literature review (see Table 1).

Table 1. Moscow rules for functional and non-functional requirement

Heading level	Functional requirement	Non functional requirement
Must do (Critical – Extreme)	101 – User can see 'Home' domain with arrangement menu vertically based on manual search, monitoring activities, asset management, zakat fund management, amil info, asnaf info 102A – User can see the 'Account' menu in the right corner, which consist of 2 (two) form fill interface for user credentials (username & password), checkbox to 'remember me', link to 'forget password', sign up features and help button 102B – New user can be able to register through new layout after click 'sign up', in which they should provide minimum personal data (name, identity card, birthdate, etc.) 102C-1 – User shall be able to recover their password by clicking 'forget password' in the new pop up menu that asking to submit email address or phone number 102C-2 – The system will check the email that was input by user with the database, if matches, it will send the generated link to the respected email, if unknown the system will notify the user that the email do not exist 103 – Personalize quick serve as advanced search based on specific criteria type that customer can add, or based on historical log that will give the recommendation based on priorities, popularities and prices after typing certain word —	121. Security: Provide standard policy for password that will show to user when new user/old user input the specific value, which is combination of number and letter (preventing brute force or human error) 122. Platform constraint: the login functionality still behave the same in different browser (IE, safari, firefox, chrome) and operating system (MacOs, Windows, Linux) 123. Compliance: describing the legal requirement and constraints in term of legal agreement (checkbox and statement) between user and provider for using this application 124A. Create secure backups for users credential, personal information and operational data stores and the restoration of backups 124B. All processes can be made available after unplanned system downtime within 1 working day while backed-up daily 125. Sharing: There are different privilege sharing among user to access certain feature based on necessity 126. The middleware or web service that allow the integration with the financial technology from several provider to widen the coverage of service in the payment methods 127. The email and sms gateway that will sent the confirmation or receipt to inform the transaction has been done well or failure, so the user can response immediately —

(*continued*)

Table 1. (*continued*)

Heading level	Functional requirement	Non functional requirement
Should do (Essential – High)	201A – Create submenu of "Log" under "History" in the account feature that will list all activity (date, login & logout time, timeframe, browser, ip address, etc.) 201B-1 – Create submenu of "Transaction" under "History" in the account feature that will present all transaction have been done with detail information (asnaf, satisfaction, amount, date, time) 201B-2 – User can filter the list of transaction based on number of data to be shown or by specific keyword 202 – Create the statistic presentation from specific asnaf, amil and payers that user want to view/look by —	221. Response Time: Having clarity of indication in waiting time (loading process) to ensure the current response state of the system and avoiding confusion of user 222. The session will be expired under specific consideration, which browser/tab closes and idle within 30 min 223. Performance: Upon providing correct credential, user shall be redirected to 'Home' layout within 10 s (max) 224. Connection: web server load balancing in managing traffic in rush hour —
Could do (Conditional – Medium)	301 – Provide contextual guidance/explanation in each menu/category that user point or cover by his/her cursor in the navigation 302 – Create link to connect between related asnaf, director or staff with their history 303 – Categorize the notification messages as *read* and *unread* by highlighting them with red color in the user profile (right corner) to avoid user get distraction by pop up message after login 304 – Create inbox in the user profile that allow user to send and receive email from administrator or other user privately —	321. Resources: increase the capacity of RAM and storage space from web server to allow higher resolution photo or bigger size of document to be uploaded in the system 322. Fault tolerance: system maintain the auto format to ensure the data to be input to the system accurate and correct such as hand-phone number, weight, height, KTP, etc. 323. Provide different interface mode such as mobile to allow to reduce quota used by the user when accessing the application —
Want to do (Optional – Low)	401 – There are alternative languages besides Indonesian in the left corner under drop down menu that user can choose to customize the layout, such as English, Mandarin, Arabic, etc. 402 – User can set the notification message periodically (popup message) or to be sent to mobile number or email address 410 – User can look the asnaf population in geographical information system —	421. There are features tour that can be followed by the user if they want to know more about the application as well allowing them to give feedback to the developer 422. Provide different interface mode such as mobile to allow to reduce quota used by the user when accessing the application 423. Privacy: user can share, save and keep the relevant information easily and trustworthy based on certain circumstances —

As a result of different organizational governance, behavior and culture, unlike other types of institutions, director must adopt different method for leadership, strategies and change management, with respect to integrate and coordinate the relevant actors or parties [39]. To avoid errors in the design process of this application, the most important things is to follow specific needs and design standards that is specified in requirement analysis. The system will be tested through various scenario based on persona or fictional character to see the consequences and circumstances in each pro-cess. Theoretically, the number of interaction solution is endless, so an appropriate response should infer the identification of trends and influence factor on the current environment by working closely to other zakat institution to enhance the utilization of the external resources. Instead of analyzing how things are, the interaction design synthesizes and imagines things as they could be. It is important to note that the pro-posed system should also consider fatwa aspect to avoid misinterpretation or conflict of interest between zakat institutions, where the government find the solution by turning to the Majlis Ulama Indonesia (MUI) through drafting the recognition of its position and responsibility as the reliable institution in religious matters [40–42]. We designed main function of the system in accordance to the analysis that has been done before. The interface design of functional requirement is shown below (Figs. 1 and 2). Since the main purpose of ZMS is to create the efficient zakat distribution to the right eligible person, the main functionalities of the application are account page, list page, history, transaction and notification messages.

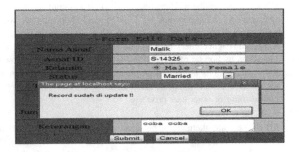

Fig. 1. User interface for edit data

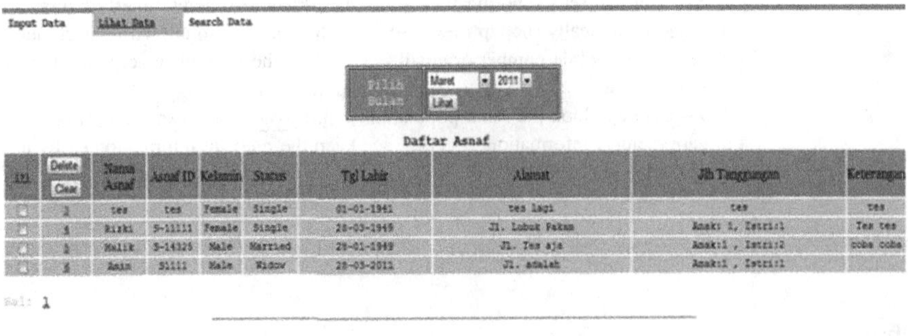

Fig. 2. User interface for view data

5 Conclusion

In conclusion, the result of the awakening of Islamic consciousness provides clearly of those who are bound and eligible to pay zakat. Thus, zakat institutions can improve the efficiency of ZMS by using integrated approach of application based on government supervision, which use various components and matches. The assumptions related to the zakat potential can replace the use of tax to provide affordability and sustainability at national level, where community must realize the benefits of zakat and relevant voluntary charities as the best approach to get reward from Allah ta'ala. To contribute to the society, the adoption of application in ZMS should consider functional and non-functional requirement, the relevant organization must eliminate the sectorial egoism to optimize the process and government must provide regulation to emphasize the importance of zakat as the medium for economic development. ZMS application can arrange zakat distribution exhaustively and prevalently through data management on an integrated system. Further research problem in this area is concerning the design optimization and location elaboration. In the end, the success of ZMS is expected to help buffer the effects of economic recession.

References

1. Al-Qurthubi: Al-Jami' Li Ahkam al-Quran, vol. 7–8. Dar al Kutub al Ilmiyah (1993)
2. Lubis, M., Yacoob, N.I.B., Omar, Y., Dahlan, A., Rahman, A.: Enhancement of zakat distribution management system. In: Proceeding of IMAC, Kuala Terengganu (2011)
3. Prayitno, B.: Optimalisasi Pengelolaan Zakat pada Badan Amil Zakat Daerah. Thesis, Universitas Diponegoro, June 2008
4. Johari, F., Ali, A.F.M., Abdul Aziz, M.R.: A review of literatures on current zakat issues: an analysis between 2003–2013. Int. Rev. Res. Emerg. Mark. Glob. Econ. (IRREM) 1(2), 336–363 (2015)
5. Dyarini, A., Jamilah, S.: Strategy of zakat and endowments productive management with the development of islamic microfinance institutions. In: 2nd International Proceedings on Multidisciplinary Conference, pp. 46–57. Univ. Muhammadiyah Jakarta (2016)
6. Suprayogi, N.: Sinergitas Pengelolaan Zakat. http://www.noven-suprayogi-feb.web.unair.ac.id. Accessed 17 Feb 2018
7. Widiastuti, T., Wahyuningsih, W., Indrawan, I.M.: Fund Management strategy in baznas zakat (Amil zakat national agency) East Java. Int. J. Islamic Bus. Ethics (IJIBE) 1(2), 161–170 (2016)
8. Armia, A.: Problematic of zakat management in medan. In: Islam Nusantara: Amal wa Tahdiyat, pp. 138–164. UIN Sumatera Utara (2016)
9. Syafei, Z.: The increasing of zakat management towards Muzakkis' trust at the office of religious affairs. Int. J. Soc. Sci. Hum. Invent. (IJSSHI) 3(12), 3158–3170 (2016)
10. Anwar: The law of productive zakat in islam and its impact towards economy. Int. J. Eng. Technol. Manag. Res. 4(2), 10–21 (2017)
11. Aedy, H.: Measuring the quality of zakat management of government-endorsed bodies (a case study on national zakat agency and zakat committee of mosque in the city of Kendari). Int. J. Sci. Res. (IJSR) 4(8), 2047–2051 (2015)
12. Sari, M.D.: Review on Indonesia zakah management and obstacles. Soc. Sci. 2(2), 76–89 (2013)

13. DJP. Laporan Kinerja (2016). http://www.pajak.go.id/. Accessed 17 Feb 2018
14. Al Farisi, S.: Overview of forecasting zakat collection in Indonesia using multiplicative decomposition. Int. J. Zakat 2(1), 45–59 (2017)
15. Syafei, Z.: Public trust of zakat management in the office of religious affairs, Cipocok Jaya, Serang Banten Indonesia. J. Manag. Sustain. 5(3), 155–164 (2015)
16. Chatib, A., Hidayat, H., Umar, H.M., Ali, H.: Management of zakat to support education: national agency in the Amil zakat of Jambi Province. J. Res. Method Educ. (IOSR-JRME) 6(6), 24–31 (2016)
17. Lubis, M., Kusumasari, T.F., Hakim, L.: The Indonesia public information disclosure act (UU-KIP): Its challenges and responses. IJECE 8(1), 94–103 (2018)
18. Ahlan, A.R., Lubis, M., Lubis, A.R.: Information security awareness at the knowledge-based institution: its antecedents and measures. Proc. Comput. Sci. 72, 361–373 (2015)
19. Ali, M.A.M., Khamar Tazilah, M.D.A.B., Shamsudin, A.I.B., Faisal Shukri, F.R.B., Nik Adelin, N.M.F.A.B., Zainol Zaman, W.M.S.B.: Factors that influence the zakat collection funds: a case in Kuantan. SEAJBEL 13(1), 30–37 (2017)
20. Abdullatif, L.: The Problems Faced by a State in the Collection of Zakat (Tax). University Nairobi, Thesis (2012)
21. Saad, R.J., Abdulaziz, N.M., Sawandi, N.: Islamic accountability framework in the zakat funds management. Proc. Soc. Behav. Sci. 164, 508–515 (2014)
22. Dewi, A.C.E., Dhewanto, W.: Key success factors of islamic family business. Proc. Soc. Behav. Sci. 57, 53–60 (2012)
23. Sukmana, H.T., Lestiani, D., Anggraeni, N., Soetarno, D.: The prototype of zakat management system in Indonesia by using the social society approach: a case study. In: Proceeding of CITSM, Denpasar (2017)
24. Maulana, H.O.: Application for determining mustahiq based on the priority using weight product method. In: Proceeding of CITSM, Denpasar (2017)
25. Rahman, A.A., Alias, M.H., Omar, S.M.N.S.: Zakat institution in Malaysia: problems and issues. GJAT 2(1), 35–41 (2012)
26. Sulaiman, H., Cob, C.Z., Ali, N.: Big data maturity model for Malaysian zakat institutions to embark on big data initiatives. In: Proceedings of ICSECS, Kuantan (2015)
27. Asnaini, A., Oktarina, A.: Improvement of social welfare through optimization of organization of zakat management in Indonesia. In: Batusangkar International Conference (2017)
28. Razimi, M.S.A., Romle, A.R., Erdris, M.F.M.: Zakat management in Malaysia: a review. Am.-Eurasian J. Sci. Res. 11(6), 453–457 (2016)
29. Lubis, A.R., Fachrizal, F., Lubis, M.: The effect of social media to cultural homecoming tradition of computer students in medan. Proc. Comp. Sci. 124, 423–428 (2017)
30. Hairunnizam, W., Radiah, A.K.: Localization of Malaysian zakat distribution: perception of Amil and zakat recipients. In: Proceedings of 7th International Conference – The Tawhidi Epistemology: Zakat and Waqf Economy (2010)
31. Ibrahim, S.M.: Towards improving the zakat distribution and management in the state of Kano. Nigeria. J. Stud. Manag. Plann. 1(7), 229–241 (2015)
32. Dahlan, A.R.A., Awang, S.N.B., Mahmood, A.B.: e-ZAKAT4U program: enhancing zakat distribution system by merging with network-of-mosque (NoM). Int. J. Manag. Commer. Innov. 3(1), 264–268 (2015)
33. Mohsin, M.I.A.: Potential of zakat in eliminating riba and eradicating poverty in muslim countries. Int. J. Islamic Manag. Bus. 1(1), 40–63 (2015)
34. Leedy, P.D., Ormrod, L.E.: Practical Research: Planning and Design, 8th edn. Pearson Education, Upper Saddle River (2010)
35. Norman, D.A.: The Design of Everyday Things. Basic Books, New York (2002)

36. Lubis, M., Kartiwi, M., Zulhuda, S.: Privacy and personal data protection in electronic voting: factors and measures. Telkomnika **15**(1), 512–521 (2017)
37. Harun, H., Nordin, N., Hussain, A.: Ontology of zakat management system. In: Proceeding of International Conference on KMICE (2008)
38. Duka, S.: The role of government in optimizing of zakat Mgmt at Mumuju District Province West Sulawesi. J. Econ. Sustain. Dev. **4**(18), 134–140 (2013)
39. Lubis, M.: Optimization of zakat management system in Indonesia using geographic information system (GIS). In: Kartiwi, M., Gunawan, S.T., Hashim, A.H.A. (eds.) Selected Readings in Computing and Telecommunications. IIUM Press, Gombak (2011)
40. Hassan, W.Z.W., Jamsari, E.A., Umar, A., Mohamad, Z., Alias, J., Muslim, N., Ahmad, M. Y.: The management of zakat distribution in the practice of fatwa in Terengganu, Malaysia. Int. J. Civil Eng. Technol. **8**(11), 834–851 (2017)
41. Lubis, M., Kartiwi, M.: Privacy and trust in the islamic perspective: implication of the digital age. In: IEEE ICTM (2013)
42. Rosmaini, E., Kusumasari, T.F., Lubis, M., Lubis, A.R.: Insights to develop privacy policy for organization in Indonesia. J. Phys.: Conf. Ser. **978**(1), 012042, 1–7 (2018)

An Investigation on a Suitable Information Structure of a Museum Environment for Large Display

Fasihah Mohammad Shuhaili[1(✉)], Suziah Sulaiman[1],
Saipunidzam Mahamad[1], Aliza Sarlan[1], and Ahsanullah Abro[2]

[1] Department of Computer and Information Sciences,
Universiti Teknologi PETRONAS, 32610 Seri Iskandar,
Perak Darul Ridzuan, Malaysia
{fasihah_g03599, suziah, saipunidzam_mahamad,
aliza_sarlan}@utp.edu.my
[2] Department of Computer Science, Sukkur IBA University,
Airport Road, Sukkur 65200, Sindh, Pakistan
ahsanullah.abro@iba-suk.edu.pk

Abstract. Understanding the structure or organization of an interface is important to make sense of the information presented. This is essential especially when involving information on a large display. The desired information architecture in terms of arranging the information becomes critical and pervasive. The huge interactional space conceives a challenge to the design process. This paper investigates a suitable information structure of a museum application on a large display in order to support navigation. A user study was conducted with ten participants interacting with a museum application interfaces, running on a Microsoft SUR40 tabletop. The study findings suggest that a suitable information structure for a large display depends on the purpose of the navigation. A scattered image concept is more appropriate for specific object finding while a structured tree concept is for information finding in a virtual environment. These findings could be useful for the development of museum interfaces on a huge display.

Keywords: Virtual museum · Information architecture · Information structure Multitouch tabletop display · Collaborative interaction

1 Introduction

An understanding on the information overview of a subject matter is required before one could interact meaningfully in an environment. In the aspect of human computer interaction, determining the structure of the environment involves a process of understanding the information architecture (IA) of the interface. IA is a design discipline that focuses on making information findable and understandable [1]. When displaying information on an interface for a shared workspace, such as a tabletop surface, IA needs to create a shared information environment for optimum findability and understandability. This involves organization on the structure design of the shared information, and significant cues for interface navigation.

© Springer Nature Singapore Pte Ltd. 2018
N. Abdullah et al. (Eds.): i-USEr 2018, CCIS 886, pp. 302–312, 2018.
https://doi.org/10.1007/978-981-13-1628-9_27

In this paper, the design principle that involves IA pertaining to designing a museum environment using a multi-touch tabletop platform will be discovered. Multi-touch tabletop is chosen as it supports collaborative learning [2]. People are able to discuss, understand and solve a particular task together while interacting with a multi-touch tabletop. By implementing a virtual environment, museum visitors can switch their roles from passive viewers and readers into active actors and players [3]. The nature of multi-touch tabletop that is able to support interaction and collaboration makes it easy to promote and disseminate cultural heritage to the public [4]. In order to make the collaborative interaction a success, the layout of the tabletop interface needs to be properly designed to allow communication between a user and the surface. A weak arrangement in terms of the information structure presented prevents users from interacting with the interface properly; thus, restricting a smooth interaction from happening [5]. Designing an appropriate information structure on a large display poses a more challenging task as the device involves a large interactional space.

This paper determines the information structure in designing a virtual museum interface on a multi-touch tabletop surface. The intention is to support a more "fluid" collaborative interaction [6]. The organisation of the paper is as follows; Sect. 2.1 presents the concept of information architecture (IA). This is followed by Sect. 2.2 that describes information structure as a subset of IA. Section 2.3 discusses on navigation on large display. Section 3 describes the procedure used in the study while Sect. 4 presents the findings and discusses the work in relation to interfaces for museum environments. Section 5 concludes the paper.

2 Background

2.1 Information Architecture

Information architecture (IA) is one of the most vital components in user experience design [7] and has come with various definition by many well-known people in this field. When discussing about IA, one cannot stop mentioning about Richard Saul Wurman who brought this term into wide attention in the 1970. His definition has highlighted the organization and presentation of information. He emphasized on the task carried out by an information architect as a person who is involved in (i) organizing the pattern innate in data from being complex to simpler, and (ii) building the structure or outline of information that enable others to find their personal paths to knowledge [8]. The definition given focuses on information architect in making complex organization and presentation of clearer or simpler information [7].

On the other hand, Rosenfield and Morville, two leading researchers in IA field, have together came out with a multi-perspective approach to describe IA. According to them, IA involved (i) a very wide view of information environment that focuses on structural design (ii) a lay out scope of information architecture in digital physical information space and (iii) a connection between IA, usability, findability and perceptive on information [1]. Meanwhile, through a recent book titled, "Information Architecture the Design and Integration of Information Spaces", IA has been defined as organizing and simplifying information to create usable interfaces to the expected users; thus, hold on top of information, and good for decision making [7].

Based on the definitions described, although there are many problems to be addressed in a particular context, priority should be given to information structure. In other words, the structure of the information rules the highest level in IA before other step could take place. This signals that the information structure needs to be properly organized to ease users' understanding.

2.2   Information Structure

Information structure is the most important component in information architecture. IA covers information environment which is ranked the highest priority, followed by its context. When we look at an interface, sometimes we will try to search for a noticeable sign to help us in the navigation. This may continue until in the end we will look for its content instead, as it leads to the next action to be taken. After having a glimpse on the interface for its information structure, we will then make an attempt to find any prominent signifier to guide us in the navigation.

There are various ways of how information has been structured (e.g. search system and labeling system) [1]. Among the most common examples are the scattered image concept, and tree concept. These concepts could enable information to appear in an organized manner. The design of graphical items involved assists in understanding of the users' assumption and perceivable as an output of their interaction [9]. Hence, a better information structure will affect the understanding of the users in gaining the knowledge and understanding. As cited by Kirk et al. [10], a scatter image concept has become a popular application where users like the randomness of physics in presenting the pictures [11, 12]. On the other hand, the structured tree concept is proven to ease the active learning among the users [13].

2.3   Navigation on Large Display

A large display, such as a multitouch tabletop surface, could facilitate many users to communicate with the content displayed on a table together. The device is created to afford multiple people standing or sitting around it and work together on tasks [14]. There are two types of screen orientation, in which tabletop surface is classified under the horizontal screen, while typical computer technologies are the vertical screen. This vertical screen orientation is relevant to desktop computer, laptops and projector screens as straight-up orientation always look similar for all viewers [15].

For tabletop surface, the viewer's perception is dependent on their position around the screen. Users shall gain benefit by having multiple viewpoints because it could increase proportionally the size of what will be displayed to each user [16]. Besides, horizontal orientation is able to enhance user performance in understanding the information structure. The ability of tabletop surface in supporting the nature of multi-touch interaction enables users to have a normal and natural communication [15]. As tabletop surface is meant for collaborative interaction through its control and visual representation on one screen [17], the horizontal screen allows interaction to take place using one or multiple fingers [15] thus, resulting in a natural and direct interaction with the users [18].

Tabletop surface has been highly utilized in social areas such as museums, art galleries and libraries to let the public engage with the collections. Past studies have shown that tabletop surface contributes a huge impact towards cultural heritage as users are allowed to communicate simultaneously [19]. This horizontal workspace is able to provide features that are not present in vertical displays such as privacy, face-to-face interaction with eye contact and support for placing physical objects on the display [20]. Besides, it equips chances for a group of users to stand in a face-to-face or side-by-side adjustment while communicating with the display [21]. It also allows users to navigate the virtual environment, and move freely around the display [22].

In the context of navigating in a museum environment, there are two major purposes for such an exploration i.e. (i) finding an artefact or collection, and (ii) finding information about the artefact. The former may involve specific or fewer objects to be identified in the environment while the latter deals with voluminous information pertaining to the objects. Regardless of which purpose is in question, navigation should enable users to understand the interface they explored through object identification [23] and modelling [24] where users will grasp and then interpret the cues present to interact with the information content. Getting lost while navigating a surface or an environment lead to anger, frustration and confusion. A good presentation of the cue or signifier, as well as having suitable information structure of the environment, are essential to the success of information navigation [25].

3   Methodology

The objective of the study is to identify a suitable information structure preferred by participants for museum environment on a large display.

(i) Participants
   Ten students (7 male, and 3 female) participated in the study. They were between 18 to 34 years old and from Computer and Information Sciences Department of Universiti Teknologi PETRONAS (UTP). All of the participants use computer on daily basis and have knowledge using touch-operated devices. Four participants had no prior experience with the interactive tabletop.

(ii) Questionnaire survey
   The participants were asked on the experiences in visiting the museum and using multi touch tabletop surface. They were given five minutes to fill in the survey form. The questions are divided into two parts. Part 1 consists of six questions while Part 2 has three. All of which are about participants' background on touch device.

(iii) Experimental setup
   The study involved two hardware to conduct the experiment. The tools used were a digital tabletop and a video camera. The multitouch digital tabletop used Samsung SUR 40 Model to support the system and Windows 7 professional for embedded systems 64-bit. It operated with processing unit of Athlon x2 dual-core 245e (2.9 GHz). The museum interface used for the study run on this large screen.

Fig. 1. The participant sat face-to-face around the screen

The whole study took about 40 min for each group to complete. Each group consisted of two participants. This is to allow the collaborative interaction. A video camera was used to record the activities of the participants while they interacted with the multitouch tabletop. All participants in each session sat face-to-face around the horizontal tabletop. Figure 1 shows an example of two participants facing one another interacting with the interface. The other person was the experimenter, being neutral to the study, and not involved in the interaction.

(iv) Research procedure

The study was conducted in virtual reality laboratory located at Block 2, UTP. A short briefing was given to the participants about Microsoft SUR40 tabletop surface and the objective of the study. The participants were then allowed to have a short practice for about 5 min with the multitouch tabletop. The intention was to have them acquainted and felt familiar while interacting with the device. Two categories of applications were used in the training. The first category involved a scattered type of information structure while the second involved a more structured type. Figure 2 shows the two types of information structure used in this study. Figure 2(a) shows the scattered type – puzzle game, photo manipulation game; Fig. 2(b) shows the structured type – medical/stroke rehabilitation application.

The study started with the participants in the group being introduced to four sections of Pasir Salak museum application which they had to interact during the study. The sections were; time tunnel, dagger gallery, J.W.W Birch murder, and buildings surrounding the museum. The application involved a scattered type of information as it was easy to implement, and common to other museum applications. Figure 3 shows a top view of museum interface used in the study.

(a)

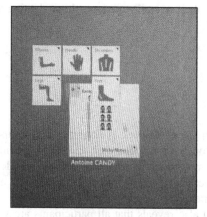
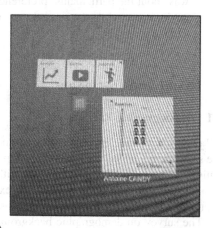

(b)

Fig. 2. (a) The scattered type of information structure. (b) The structured type of information structure

Fig. 3. Top view of interface design for museum environment for the study

The study started by inviting the participants to explore the four sections of Pasir Salak museum application. Two minutes were allocated per section. After going through one section, the participants were asked to answer two to three quiz questions together based on the explored section. This exercise was necessary to observe whether the information structure affect the users' navigation in the environment. After that, the participants were to continue with the next section. These steps were repeated for all four sections.

(v) Post-study

An interview was conducted after the study in order to collect their opinion towards the information structure used. There were two parts involved. The first was about the participants' preferences on the information structure for museum environment while the second was on their overall experience in navigating the surface.

4   Result and Discussion

4.1   Demographic Background

All participants have experience using touch screen devices. Among the devices used are smartphone, tablet, multitouch tabletop, touch screen computer, and ATM machine. Only 40% have experience interacting with multitouch tabletop surface. Nevertheless, through the study all participants have experienced interacting with the device, and been exposed to a virtual museum environment.

The survey on demographic background also reveals that all participants are very fond of art and history, particularly on those related to museums. The participants said that the reasons for visiting a museum are to gain information on its history, to know the sculptures available, to gain experience from the environment, to have fun, and to organize future field trips for school children. The participants revealed that museums have their own platform to advertise information. Eight out of ten participants said that they could find useful information through the museum websites but the other two disagreed with the opinion. The reason for such a disagreement is due to the information displayed being outdated and sometimes too brief to be understood. Nevertheless, majority of the participants preferred to visit and experience the physical museum environment themselves, if given an opportunity.

4.2   Information Structure Concept

The interview findings from the post study section were analyzed. The participants' preferences on the information structure for museum environment are presented in Fig. 4.

From Fig. 4, the number of participants who chose scattered image concept is higher with five people as compared to one who chose tree concept and four on either scattered image or tree concept. This shows that overall users preferred the scattered image concept for the museum application during their exploration with the sessions. This could be due to the scattered image concept being the default information structure

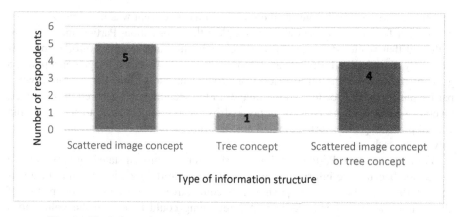

Fig. 4. The information representation concept preferred by the participants

for the museum application interfaces under study. Such a preference could also indicate that the participants enjoyed the experience interacting with the museum interfaces during the study. The fact that four participants preferred either a scattered image or a tree concept for the environment signals for the importance of both concepts. In other words, both concepts should be considered in the design process.

A further analysis was conducted to justify the choices made by the participants as presented in Fig. 4. This is to correlate participants' preferences on the information structure based on their collaborative interactions with the museum environment. A summary of findings is presented in Table 1.

Table 1. The information representation concept preferred by the participants

Scattered image concept	Tree concept
• Easy and entertaining (P2, P4, P8, P9, P10) • Good representation (P1) • Everyone can interact without any interruption (P2, P8) • Less information is suitable to use the concept (P2, P5, P8, P9, P10)	• More systematic (P7) • Huge information is preferable to use the concept (P1, P3, P5, P6)

Note: P1 = Participant 1, P2 = Participant 2, ..., P10 = Participant 10.

From Table 1, Participants 2, 4, 8, 9 and 10 preferred scattered image concept as they said that the concept is interesting and entertaining. During the study, there are some sections which require the participants to understand a chronological history of the museum. The images in the section were scattered but labeled with numbers to ease the participants in understanding the storyline. When the participants went to the section, they spontaneously organized the storyline together accordingly. This shows that the concept is able to connect multiple people to interact with the interface as they can help each other in arranging the storyline (Participant 8). For Participant 2, she felt triggered to arrange the images as the scattered image concept was like a puzzle where it made her feel motivated to find and complete the information. Participants 9 and 10 both said that scattered image concept was interesting and learning through pictures were easy to understand. Participant 1 commented that a scattered image concept had a good presentation as the information was brought in one screen. For example, when participants opened a section, all the images in the section were gathered in the center. Overall, scattered image concept is favored by the respondents due to its interesting way of presenting the information and able to bring people to communicate well when solving the task.

For a tree concept, Participant 7 who preferred the approach stated that it was more systematic because the information was displayed accordingly when the interface was opened. Based on the tree concept shown, he could have an overview or a big picture of all the information needed. Participant 7 reasoning could be due to the voluminous information from the museum environment despite him having no previous experience in using a tabletop surface. Participant 7 commented that scattered image concept could be messy; implying that the concept could restrict information finding. On the contrary, Participants 9 and 10, who preferred scattered image concept, commented otherwise. They felt that a tree structure approach could be chaotic and confusing.

As for Participants 1, 3, 5 and 6, they mentioned that the type of information structure used depends on the purpose of the navigation and type of knowledge being displayed. They were in favor to use a tree concept if the design was going to involve huge information to display and share. It will look more organized and orderly which is suitable for the information finding purpose since many information will be presented. On the other hand, it is preferable to have a scattered image concept for lesser information and suitable for specific object finding purpose (Participants 2, 5, 8, 9, 10). As the information is conveyed through images, the presentation might attract the users to have a general overview on the history presented.

From the study findings, Participants 7 and 8 have also suggested to have a mixture of both concepts in one application to benefit from the advantages that each concept offers. Both participants have no prior experience interacting with a tabletop surface but have interest in cultural heritage.

5 Conclusion

It is important for a user to understand the information of the environment they deal with. By understanding the information being displayed, it is able to help the users to navigate the surface. However, to ensure the users obtain the knowledge, the information structure of the interface need to be well organized. This is because, weak arrangement of the interface will affect the learning focus of the users, thus frustrate them to further navigate the interface.

This paper explores the information structure in designing a virtual museum interface on a multi-touch tabletop surface through users' behavior in interacting with the environment. The findings suggest that both approaches i.e. scattered image and tree structure concepts could be considered in the design process. A scattered image concept is more suitable for specific object finding while a structured tree concept is for presenting voluminous information in a virtual museum environment.

Upcoming work might include designing museum environments using both concepts and test the interfaces with potential museum visitors. The design process may not only involve information structure but also visual cues, another subset of IA, for better navigation in the environment.

Acknowledgement. We would like to thank all the participants who took part in the study. This research was financially supported by Universiti Teknologi PETRONAS.

References

1. Rosenfeld, L., Morville, P., Arango, J.: Information Architecture: For the Web and Beyond. O'Reilly Media, Sebastopol (2015)
2. Piper, A.M., Hollan, J.D.: Tabletop displays for small group study: affordances of paper and digital materials. In: Proceedings of the SIGCHI Conference on Human Factors in Computing Systems, pp. 1227–1236 (2009)
3. Wojciechowski, R., Walczak, K., White, M., Cellary, W.: Building virtual and augmented reality museum exhibitions. In: Proceedings of the Ninth International Conference on 3D Web Technology, pp. 135–144 (2004)
4. Neto, J.N., Neto, M.J.: Immersive cultural experience through innovative multimedia applications: the history of Monserrate Palace in Sintra (Portugal) presented by Virtual Agents. Int. J. Herit. Digit. Era **1**, 101–106 (2012)
5. Interface Design for Learning: Basic Principles A-Z—Accessibility—Peachpit (2018)
6. Johanson, B., Fox, A., Winograd, T.: The interactive workspaces project: experiences with ubiquitous computing rooms. IEEE Pervasive Comput. **1**, 67–74 (2002)
7. Ding, W., Lin, X., Zarro, M.: Information architecture: the design and integration of information spaces. Synth. Lect. Inf. Concepts Retr. Serv. **9**, i–152 (2017)
8. Bradford, P., Wurman, R.S., Corp, G.P.: Information Architects: Graphis (1997)
9. Instructor IC: Affordances and design. Interaction design foundation (2016). https://www.interaction-design.org/literature/article/affordances-and-design
10. Kirk, D., Izadi, S., Hilliges, O., Banks, R., Taylor, S., Sellen, A.: At home with surface computing? In: Proceedings of the SIGCHI Conference on Human Factors in Computing Systems, pp. 159–168 (2012)
11. Apted, T., Kay, J., Quigley, A.: Tabletop sharing of digital photographs for the elderly. In: Proceedings of the SIGCHI Conference on Human Factors in Computing Systems, pp. 781–790 (2006)
12. Shen, C., Ryall, K., Forlines, C., Esenther, A., Vernier, F.D., Everitt, K., et al.: Collaborative tabletop research and evaluation. In: Dillenbourg, P., Huang, J., Cherubini, M. (eds.) Interactive Artifacts and Furniture Supporting Collaborative Work and Learning, pp. 1–17. Springer, Boston (2009). https://doi.org/10.1007/978-0-387-77234-9_7
13. Block, F., Horn, M.S., Phillips, B.C., Diamond, J., Evans, E.M., Shen, C.: The deeptree exhibit: visualizing the tree of life to facilitate informal learning. IEEE Trans. Vis. Comput. Graph. **18**, 2789–2798 (2012)
14. Creed, C., Sivell, J., Sear, J.: Multi-touch tables for exploring heritage content in public spaces. In: Ch'ng, E., Gaffney, V., Chapman, H. (eds.) Visual Heritage in the Digital Age, pp. 67–90. Springer, London (2013). https://doi.org/10.1007/978-1-4471-5535-5_5

15. Madni, T.M., Nayan, Y., Sulaiman, S., Tahir, M., Abro, A.: Usability dimensions for content-orientation techniques in multi-touch tabletop displays: an overview. In: Proceedings of the 2nd International Conference in HCI and UX Indonesia 2016, pp. 93–101 (2016)

16. Dillenbourg, P., Evans, M.: Interactive tabletops in education. Int. J. Comput.-Supported Collab. Learn. **6**, 491–514 (2011)

17. Catala, A., Jaen, J., Martinez-Villaronga, A.A., Mocholi, J.A.: AGORAS: exploring creative learning on tangible user interfaces. In: 2011 IEEE 35th Annual Computer Software and Applications Conference (COMPSAC), pp. 326–335 (2011)

18. Schlatter, O., Migge, B., Kunz, A.: User-aware content orientation on interactive tabletop surfaces. In: 2012 International Conference on Cyberworlds (CW), pp. 246–250 (2012)

19. Isenberg, P., Hinrichs, U., Hancock, M., Carpendale, S.: Digital tables for collaborative information exploration. In: Müller-Tomfelde, C. (ed.) Tabletops-Horizontal Interactive Displays, pp. 387–405. Springer, London (2010). https://doi.org/10.1007/978-1-84996-113-4_16

20. Müller-Tomfelde, C., Wessels, A., Schremmer, C.: Tilted tabletops: in between horizontal and vertical workspaces. In: 3rd IEEE International Workshop on Horizontal Interactive Human Computer Systems, TABLETOP 2008, pp. 49–56 (2008)

21. Tang, A., Tory, M., Po, B., Neumann, P., Carpendale, S.: Collaborative coupling over tabletop displays. In: Proceedings of the SIGCHI Conference on Human Factors in Computing Systems, pp. 1181–1190 (2006)

22. Streitz, N.A., Geißler, J., Holmer, T., Konomi, S., Müller-Tomfelde, C., Reischl, W., et al.: i-LAND: an interactive landscape for creativity and innovation. In: Proceedings of the SIGCHI Conference on Human Factors in Computing Systems, pp. 120–127 (1999)

23. Benyon, D., Höök, K.: Navigation in information spaces: supporting the individual. In: Howard, S., Hammond, J., Lindgaard, G. (eds.) Human-Computer Interaction INTERACT 1997. ITIFIP, pp. 39–46. Springer, Boston, MA (1997). https://doi.org/10.1007/978-0-387-35175-9_7

24. Spence, R.: A framework for navigation. Int. J. Hum. Comput. Stud. **51**, 919–945 (1999)

25. Benyon, D.: The new HCI? Navigation of information space. Knowl.-Based Syst. **14**, 425–430 (2001)

Security Evaluation of Distortion Technique for Graphical Authentication

Mohd. Helmi Mat Lazim[1] and Nur Haryani Zakaria[2(✉)]

[1] Department of Information Technology and Communication,
Politeknik Tuanku Syed Sirajuddin, 02600 Arau, Perlis, Malaysia
[2] School of Computing, Universiti Utara Malaysia,
06010 Sintok, Kedah, Malaysia
haryani@uum.edu.my

Abstract. Extensive research has been done on graphical-based authentication schemes that focus on memorability issues. However, less consideration has been given to the new security threat imposed towards these schemes. The downside of this graphical authentication is that the images may expose more information than text, and this makes it more vulnerable to security threats such as shoulder surfing attack. This study evaluates the significance of using distorted images as a variable of countermeasure to shoulder surfing attack on graphical password systems. Filter strength was applied to indicate distortion level which may influence the resiliency of the graphical based password. An experiment was conducted on 45 participants to investigate whether image distortion may help to prevent or reduce shoulder surfing attack. The outcome showed that filter strength indeed plays a significant role to certain extends towards the distortion technique applied to combat shoulder surfing attack. The contributions of this study are valuable for improving the graphical based authentication system especially in providing better security as well as maintaining high usability.

Keywords: Distortion technique · Shoulder surfing attack
Graphical authentication

1 Introduction

In a computing system, most applications have acknowledged that human factors are considered as the weakest link. Researcher in [1] pointed out that most of the time the interaction between human and computer are divided into three major areas which are; authentication, security operations and development of secure systems. Token based, biometric based and knowledge based are the three types of authentication methods widely used.

In general, knowledge based techniques commonly include both text-based and picture-based passwords. Additionally, the picture-based techniques are divided into two categories; recognition-based and recall-based graphical techniques [2]. In recognition-based techniques, authentication process begins when a user has to identify the images he or she selects during the registration stage from a group of random pictures. On the other hand, recall-based techniques require a user to replicate

N. Abdullah et al. (Eds.): i-USEr 2018, CCIS 886, pp. 313–324, 2018.
https://doi.org/10.1007/978-981-13-1628-9_28

something that has been created or selected earlier during the registration stage. Studies showed that people possess better ability to memorize pictures rather than text [3, 4]. In fact, recognition based password allows user to select any image of their own or from a library and then perform several actions such as a tap on a single point, a line connecting two points, or a circle which begins and ends at the same point [5]. Microsoft, a leading operating system service provider applies this kind of authentication system in Windows 8 where the user is required to select an image and set exactly three actions.

However, recent studies showed that graphical password still has some flaw during its implementation [6]. For example, a password acquired in a public place for authentication, if not appropriately secured, is vulnerable to shoulder surfing attack [7]. Shoulder surfing can become a huge problem for graphical password authentication because the use of images may increase the vulnerability of the images to being peeped and memorized by the bystander [8]. To overcome these issues, an authentication method using blurred image was introduced in which that only genuine user knows the meaning by viewing the original image which corresponds to the blurred image [9].

The usage of blurred image demonstrates that distortion is possible to be used as a technique to conserve the usability and security of graphical password. Researcher in [9] also proved that distortion techniques can cope well against shoulder surfing attack as conducted via series of experimental work in his study. However, limited study has been done to discuss specifically what level of distortion is required to provide an adequate level of security while maintaining the usability. These two aspects are important as users should not suffer from the usability issues and at the same time can rely on the protection provided by the security level. Therefore, this paper intends to evaluate distortion techniques by focusing on several distortion levels in order to determine an adequate level which provides a balance of security and usability. This study involves control laboratory experiments as a method for data collection. The results are analysed statistically to evaluate the distortion levels used in the experiments from both security and usability aspects.

2 Related Work

2.1 Graphical Passwords and Should Surfing Attack

Generally, graphical password works like any other knowledge-based authentication mechanism [10]. The user has to validate undisclosed information that has been shared with the system. Comparing to textual password, graphical password depends more on visual memory. To authenticate, the user has to use the secret information which was in stored memory. There are three main approaches to access the memory; *recall, cued-recall and recognition based* [11].

Recall based graphical password extracted information from memory upon requirement. This is the approach embraced from traditional textual password authentication. Recall is basically a tough task. Hence, users tend to create alternative such as storing the password in some other places or notepad in case they forgot the password. Recall based password rely much on draw metric based and search metric schemes. Some examples of this approach are Draw-A-Secret (DAS) and Passdoodle [12].

Currently, graphical password mainly in the area of recognition based suffers from several problems; one of them is shoulder surfing attack [13] as illustrated in Fig. 1. According to researchers in [14], most of the attack was done remotely by using specific tools such as binoculars that can be used from distant. There are also attacks through cameras, which attacker randomly capture the picture of user's login during authentication. Tools such as keyboard acoustics and electromagnetic emanations are also widely used by the attacker during this kind of attack. The threat occurs when the attacker observes the user's password during authentication process with the intent of encrypting and bypassing any kind of protocols to the user's account. In some measure, human actions are identified as the weakest link of the authentication process [15].

Fig. 1. Example of a shoulder surfing attack [13].

2.2 Existing Studies on Distortion-Related as Shoulder Surfing

Countermeasures. Researcher in [9] examined the application of an oil-painting filter on graphical password images in order to make shoulder surfing and social engineering attacks more difficult (refer Fig. 2). They worked with personal photographs of the smartphone owner and argued that only is the owner was allowed to learn the combination of original and filtered photo so that the person could later able to recognize the filtered photo. The results showed that participants of the study performed well at recognizing the distorted images and even had fun with the task. In a subsequent publication, this authentication method was tested against educated guessing attacks. As the distortion prevents someone with no knowledge of the original image from recognizing its content, an attacker with knowledge about the victim is also prevented from guessing the right pass-images. Usually a dear person, a pet or certain things the user is fond of, are likely choices for a pass-image and thus can be guessed easily. But if the attacker does not recognize the dear person, the pet or the object, due to distortion this advantage is lost. Meanwhile researchers in [16] presented an authentication system based on the users implicit memory of images and the recognition of their incomplete counterparts (refer Fig. 3). Their main goal was to reduce the burden of memorizing complicated or difficult authentication patterns. Hence, they analyzed the viability of a priming effect. Although their results indicated that the priming effect for the tested images (line drawings of objects) was not very strong and that the authentication time was rather long, the authors were still confident that implicit memory based authentication is promising due to usability and security improvements compared to other solutions.

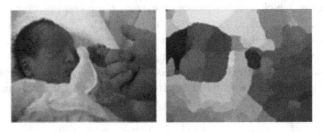

Fig. 2. Example of a original image and filtered counterpart [9].

Researchers in [17] improved the strength of a graphical authentication mechanism gradually over time by applying an edge detection filter to the pass-images and reducing the amount of visible edges over time (see Fig. 4). Due to repeated exposure to the filtered images, the legitimate user was still able to recognize them in a highly degraded state while the attacker's ability to understand the images decreased more and more. The study indicated that the authentication method provides protection from various attacks. The authors also made recommendations on the selection of good pass-images. For instance, if all pass-images are similar to each other, it might be easier for an attacker to detect a pattern.

Fig. 3. Example of a original images and degraded counterparts [16].

Fig. 4. Example of a original image and two stages of degraded counterparts [17].

3   The Proposed Technique

This study proposes a distortion technique known as twirl inspired by the work done by researchers in [9]. In fact, there are several researchers who applied twirl filter into their studies. For example, researchers in [18] implemented the approximate computation methods through twirl filter in demonstrating image transformation while researchers in [19] applied twirl filter into 3D areas which change the space and materials' view of the statue. Besides that, the twirl filter was also used by researchers in [20] in order to propose novel watermarking scheme for image authentication. In 2012, researchers in [21] used the same filter to test the robustness of watermarking scheme. Therefore, it shows that twirl filter has been widely used particularly in security and protection mechanism.

A distortion technique known as twirl was proposed. This technique is able to rotate any selected images in the center sharply rather than at its edges. There are two types of twirl; (1) twirl clockwise and (2) twirl anti-clockwise. On top of these two types, an additional twirl effect can be exposed onto it by having either positive or negative effect strength. In order to implement these options, a slider is placed on the interface for users to manipulate. The slider can be dragged to the right to twirl clockwise or drag to the left into negative values to twirl counterclockwise. Alternatively, user can also enter number between −999 (minimum) to 999 (maximum). With regards to this experiment, researcher only focused on twirl clockwise with both low and high strength but not the twirl anticlockwise. The reason for this is due to the objective of this experiment to determine the appropriate strength effect level but not on the type of twirl. In addition, we found that the difference between the twirl type is only on the rotation either to left or right and thus giving less significant impact on the technique itself. Figure 5 shows the example of interface for the prototype developed. The images have been applied with low and high positive value which rotates clockwise as shown in Fig. 5(a) and (b) respectively.

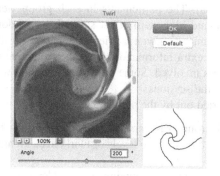
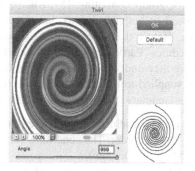

(a) Twirl with Low Effect Strength   (b) Twirl with High Effect Strength

Fig. 5. Example of interface of the prototype developed for the experiment.

4 Methodology

This study involves control-laboratory experiment which aims to explore the prospect of offering an alternative method to create distortion effects from the proposed technique. The focus is on examining the security perspective of the technique. The following sub-sections will describe in detail about the experiment conducted.

4.1 Experimental Design

The objective was to define the strongest distortion technique between the two under proposal. The between-subjects design was used to ensure that the exact same image was used in each technique so that the results were not biased even though this method required more participants. The main independent variable for this experiment is the distortion technique. In addition, this experiment also explores filter strength as a secondary independent variable. The dependent variable is the participant's response. The hypothesis is as follows:

H_1 – *Twirl technique* will be able to provide defence to certain extend and the defence strength will increase accordingly as twirl effect strength increases.

4.2 Procedures

Looking at the way humans understand images it becomes evident that finding the adequate strength to be applied on distortion technique for security enhancement is a challenge [22]. The proposed distortion technique is seen as a way of reducing information on image which is applicable to be applied in graphical authentication domain. Before the experiment started, each participant was required to provide their general background details such as age, educational background and gender. They also needed to sign the consent form to declare their acknowledgment to the experiment conducted.

The participants were distributed randomly to either the experimental group or control group consisting 15 participants each. The participants in each group were exposed to both conditions that were low and high twirl effect strength by random order. Before the experiment, each participant was given a brief explanation on the procedures. Participants were provided with extra information about the technique to ensure they understood the whole procedures involved. Some printed information was also supplied to the participants to support the sessions.

In summary, the experimental tasks carried out by the participants were as follows:

(1) Each participant in the experimental group was exposed to two conditions by random order. The conditions were based on the two levels of twirl effect strength (high versus low).
(2) The participants then acted as shoulder surfer attempting to shoulder surf the password from the victim.
(3) Once they completed their task as shoulder surfer, they were instructed to spend sometimes listening to one song chosen from the MP3 playlists.

(4) Next, the participant was asked to write down their answer that he/she had captured from the shoulder surf attempt for each of the session (high & low strength).

(5) The same procedure was repeated for control group whereby for the control group the participants will guess the password with neither distortion technique nor strength effect applied at all.

4.3   Apparatus

The experiment involved several apparatus such as mobile phone, graphical image, instruction sets and answer sheet folio. The model of the mobile phone used was Iphone 6 with 5.44 in. height and 2.64 in. width. Meanwhile the image chosen as the password is the image of red pepper (as shown in Fig. 6).

Fig. 6. Original sample and answer sheet folio used in the experiment. (Color figure online)

In order to maintain the validity of this experiment, the image chosen must be something that is categorize as general object that is not bias to any gender preference and is computer generated. This is to avoid bias condition that might occur, for example, an image of a car is more likely to be recognized by men while image of shoes or handbags are more synonym with women. All twirl effect strengths were applied on the images using Adobe Photoshop CS5. The strength levels high and low were achieved using a stroke of 20 and 5 respectively. Participants were also supplied with instruction set to support their understanding of the procedures involved. On top of the instruction set, participants were also given an answer sheet folio which contain the real image (i.e.: the password) plus three other decoy images (i.e.: the non-passwords) arranged in different orders for them to choose from after they had attempted to perform the shoulder surfing act (refer Fig. 6).

4.4   Measurements

As participants were instructed to act as shoulder surfers, they were required to produce the password (i.e.: distorted image) sometimes later after they completed the act. The process of memorizing the distorted image by shoulder surfing is considered *success* if the participants are able to select the correct answer from the answer sheet folio provided. As mentioned previously, the distortion technique was applied onto the password with additional twirl effect with the following scenario:

- Twirl low strength: 200
- Twirl high strength: 900

The scores obtained from each participant were calculated accordingly. The formula used to indicate the scores is as follows:

$$TSA = TP - TUSA \tag{1}$$

Whereby;

TSA – Total Successful Attempt
TP – Total Participants
TUSA – Total Unsuccessful Attempt.

5   Results and Findings

There were 45 participants which include 24 male and 21 female involved in this experiment. They were all between the ages of 18 and 45 where most of them are students undergoing first year degree in one of the public higher learning institution while the rest are employed. The participation was based on volunteer basis whereby participants need to complete the consent form provided to them prior to the experiment.

Table 1. Summary of shoulder surfing attack made by all participants arranged according to level of effect strengths

Distortion techniques/success rate	Successful	Unsuccessful	Total
Twirl distortion (low effect strength)	13	2	15
Twirl distortion (high effect strength)	2	13	15
Control group	15	0	15
Total	30	15	45

Table 1 summarizes shoulder surfing attack made by all participants according to the level effect strength applied on distortion technique towards the password. According to Table 1, twirl technique with high level effect strength performs extremely well in obfuscating image to prevent shoulder surfing attack. The test recorded a high value of 86.7% unsuccessful attempt in performing shoulder surfing attack on image with high twirl effect. This indicates that twirl distortion technique performed significantly better in obfuscating the images content when high effect strength is applied. Looking from another perspective, we also like to analyze the unsuccessful rate made from each shoulder surfing attempts. The red bars in Fig. 7 indicate the unsuccessful attempts made by the participants. It is clearly shown that as the effect increases from low to high, so does the number of unsuccessful attempts. This indicates that the effect strength does increase the defense of the password which makes the distortion technique better.

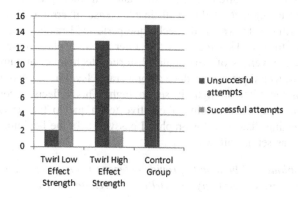

Fig. 7. Shoulder surfing attempts made by participants both using low and high effect strength (Color figure online)

The figure also gives reason to believe that the low strength effect performed rather poorly at obfuscating image content. For amounts of unsuccessful attempts made, a Kolmogorov-Smirnov test was conducted with the significant ($p < .05$) (refer Table 2).

Table 2. Kolmogorov-Smirnov test & Wilcoxon test for the number of unsuccessful attempts made by participants based on effect strength.

Effect strength	Kolmogorov-Smirnov	Wilcoxon test Asymp. sig. (2-tailed) pre-post
High	.000	.726
Low	.004	.480
None	.000	.480

The values of the dependent variable were not normally distributed. Consequently, non-parametric tests (Wilcoxon test and Friedman test) were used to analyze the data. Comparing the amount of unsuccessful attempts made with Wilcoxon test shows no significant differences in any of the effect strength levels. Thus, it appears that simulating the user perspective by showing the participants the original photographs prior to the experiment did not have a visible effect on their ability to recognize the distorted image. The experiment also collected several feedbacks from the participants after they have undergone the session. Based on the feedbacks given, all the participants agreed that authentication method such as graphical password in particular should have additional protection during authentication process to reduce the security threat such as shoulder surfing attack.

6 Discussion

In general, the results gathered from the experiment indicate that twirl technique can obfuscate the image to certain extent where the participants (attackers) fail to shoulder surfed the designated distorted image during authentication process. When the filter strength was set to high, it produced distinct increase of error (unsuccessful attack) during the experiment. However, the technique performed rather poor when the filter strength was set to low. This indicates that filter strength plays a significant role in increasing the effectiveness of a particular distortion technique. In summary, it gives the idea that twirl technique can produce a comparable level of protection for graphical password when the filter strength is set to high. This reflects accordingly to the objective of the study in providing alternative technique to the previously applied technique in creating distortion for graphical password. In the beginning of the study the hypothesis was set as follows:

H_1 – *Twirl technique will be able to provide defence to certain extend and the defence strength will increase accordingly as twirl effect strength increases.*

The results indicate that H_1 is partially supported in the sense that when twirl technique is set to high filter strength, it will perform better compared to when the filter strength is set to low. This can be seen through the success rate of shoulder surfing attack on the techniques with high filter setting that was proven to perform at their best in combating shoulder surfing attack.

7 Conclusion and Future Work

This study proposes an alternative method to create distortion effect on graphical password for user authentication that is secure and usable. The approach relies on the human ability to recognize a degraded version of a previously seen image. This study also illustrates how distorted images can improve the resiliency of graphical password from shoulder surfing attack. The technique was created using Adobe Photoshop CS5 and tested in a control laboratory experiment.

In conclusion, the filter selection and evaluation process successfully brought out a set of two suitable filters to use for further evaluation for graphical password security and usability enhancement. In the future, the filter strength could be made more precise in terms of percentage representation instead of high and low to test the exact filter strength that is suitable to be applied. Other possible extension on the research is also encouraged especially to investigate further on more alternatives to minimize shoulder surfing attack towards graphical password systems.

Acknowledgement. This research was supported by Fundamental Research Grant Scheme (FRGS – S/O Code: 13143) from the Ministry of Education (MoE) Malaysia.

References

1. Patrick, A.S., Long, A.C., Flinn, S.: HCI and security systems. In: Extended Abstracts on Human Factors in Computing Systems, CHI 2003 (2003). https://doi.org/10.1145/765891.766146

2. Hayashi, E., Hong, J., Christin, N.: Security through a different kind of obscurity. In: Proceedings of the 2011 Annual Conference on Human Factors in Computing Systems, CHI 2011 (2011). https://doi.org/10.1145/1978942.1979242

3. Everitt, K.M., Bragin, T., Fogarty, J., Kohno, T.: A comprehensive study of frequency, interference, and training of multiple graphical passwords. In: Proceedings of the 27th International Conference on Human Factors in Computing Systems, CHI 2009 (2009). https://doi.org/10.1145/1518701.1518837

4. Renaud, K., Mayer, P., Volkamer, M., Maguire, J.: Are graphical authentication mechanisms as strong as passwords? In: Federated Conference on Computer Science and Information Systems, pp. 837–844 (2013). Accessed ieeexplore.ieee.org/iel7/6628027/6643962/06644107.pdf

5. Mihajlov, M., Jerman-Blažič, B., Shuleska, A.C.: Why that picture? Discovering password properties in recognition-based graphical authentication. Int. J. Hum.-Comput. Interact. **32**(12), 975–988 (2016). https://doi.org/10.1080/10447318.2016.1220103

6. Alt, F., Schneegass, S., Shirazi, A.S., Hassib, M., Bulling, A.: Graphical passwords in the wild. In: Proceedings of the 17th International Conference on Human-Computer Interaction with Mobile Devices and Services, MobileHCI 2015 (2015). https://doi.org/10.1145/2785830.2785882

7. Suo, X., Zhu, Y., Owen, G.: Graphical passwords: a survey. In: 21st Annual Computer Security Applications Conference, ACSAC 2005 (2005). https://doi.org/10.1109/csac.2005.27

8. Sun, H.M., Chen, S.T., Yeh, J.H., Cheng, C.Y.: A shoulder surfing resistant graphical authentication system. IEEE Trans. Dependable Secur. Comput. **PP**(99), 1 (2015). https://doi.org/10.1109/TDSC.2016.2539942

9. Hayashi, E., Dhamija, R., Christin, N., Perrig, A.: Use your illusion. In: Proceedings of the 4th Symposium on Usable Privacy and Security, SOUPS 2008 (2008). https://doi.org/10.1145/1408664.1408670

10. Schaub, F., Walch, M., Könings, B., Weber, M.: Exploring the design space of graphical passwords on smartphones. In: Proceedings of the Ninth Symposium on Usable Privacy and Security, SOUPS 2013 (2013). https://doi.org/10.1145/2501604.2501615

11. Bulling, A., Alt, F., Schmidt, A.: Increasing the security of gaze-based cued-recall graphical passwords using saliency masks. In: Proceedings of the 2012 ACM Annual Conference on Human Factors in Computing Systems, CHI 2012 (2012). https://doi.org/10.1145/2207676.2208712

12. Zakaria, N.H., Griffiths, D., Brostoff, S., Yan, J.: Shoulder surfing defence for recall-based graphical passwords. In: Proceedings of the Seventh Symposium on Usable Privacy and Security, SOUPS 2011 (2011). https://doi.org/10.1145/2078827.2078835

13. Ho, P.F., Kam, Y.H., Wee, M.C., Chong, Y.N., Por, L.Y.: Preventing shoulder-surfing attack with the concept of concealing the password objects' information. Sci. World J. **2014**, 1–12 (2014). https://doi.org/10.1155/2014/838623

14. Zhuang, L., Zhou, F., Tygar, J.D.: Keyboard acoustic emanations revisited. In: Proceedings of the 12th ACM Conference on Computer and Communications Security, CCS 2005 (2005). https://doi.org/10.1145/1102120.1102169

15. Jenkins, R., Mclachlan, J.L., Renaud, K.: Facelock: familiarity-based graphical authentication. PeerJ **2**, e444 (2014). https://doi.org/10.7717/peerj.444

16. Denning, T., Bowers, K., Dijk, M.V., Juels, A.: Exploring implicit memory for painless password recovery. In: Proceedings of the 2011 Annual Conference on Human Factors in Computing Systems, CHI 2011 (2011). https://doi.org/10.1145/1978942.1979323
17. Wang, Z., Jing, J., Li, L.: Time evolving graphical password for securing mobile devices. In: Proceedings of the 8th ACM SIGSAC Symposium on Information, Computer and Communications Security, ASIA CCS 2013 (2013). https://doi.org/10.1145/2484313.2484358
18. Damasevicius, R., Ziberkas, G.: Energy consumption and quality of approximate image transformation. Electron. Electr. Eng. **120**(4), 79–82 (2012). https://doi.org/10.5755/j01.eee.120.4.1459
19. Halskov, K., Dalsgaard, P.: Using 3-D projection to bring a statue to life. Interactions **18**(3), 60 (2011). https://doi.org/10.1145/1962438.1962452
20. Wang, W., Men, A., Yang, B., Chen, X.: A novel robust zero watermarking scheme based on DWT and SVD. In: 4th International Congress on Image and Signal Processing, Shanghai, pp. 1012–1015 (2011). https://doi.org/10.1109/cisp.2011.6100320
21. Kale, S.A., Kulkarni, S.V.: Data leakage detection: a survey. IOSR J. Comput. Eng. **1**(6), 32–35 (2012). https://doi.org/10.9790/0661-0163235
22. Yu, X., Wang, Z., Li, Y., Li, L., Zhu, W.T., Song, L.: EvoPass: evolvable graphical password against shoulder-surfing attacks. Comput. Secur. **70**, 179–198 (2017). https://doi.org/10.1016/j.cose.2017.05.006

HCI and Analytics

A Study on Supporting Factors of Digital Workplace Diffusion in Public Sector

Mohamad Kamal Md Dahlan(✉), Natrah Abdullah,
and Ahmad Iqbal Hakim Suhaimi

Faculty of Mathematics and Computer Sciences, UiTM, Shah Alam, Malaysia
kamaldahlan@gmail.com,
{natrah, aiqbal}@tmsk.uitm.edu.my

Abstract. Digital workplace has become the working evolution in today's workplace. People nowadays tend to do job virtually compared to conventional. This is due to the fact that the people and the things around them can be linked, and shared information as well as helping in making a decision by using advanced technology tools. For organization, as the customers' expectations growing, workforce and work culture changes along with the growth, demographic shift, information overload as well as the usage of advanced technologies tools take place, employees will find a way to empower by ensuring that all the information and tools they need are at their fingertips, for them to share, collaborate and do jobs effectively and even to make decision in the workplace. This research focuses on literature in workplace, digital workplace and elements of digital workplace. We also performed a preliminary study on digital workplace, through interviewing selected respondents from different agencies in public sector and private sector, based on their job position, work experience and area of work. The result of the research identified that, supporting factors for digital workplace diffusion in public sector are advanced technologies tools, that consist of social technologies tools, contextual intelligence tools, mobility and communication infrastructure. Whereas other supporting factors are top management support and skilled/talented employees in the organization. These findings can be a basis of research for researchers and practitioners to further examine digital workplace in public sector.

Keywords: Digital workplace · Internet of Things (IoT)
Artificial Intelligence (AI) · Digital era · Collaboration
Advanced technology tools

1 Introduction

We are now in a digital era, in which innovation is driven by enabling technologies, such as Internet of Things (IoT), Artificial Intelligence (AI), and Big Data. These technologies are not only capable of becoming linked, searched, shared and analyzed information or data via Internet, but also will be able to balance economic development, as well as solving social issues. The Society 5.0 was introduced by Japan in the 5th Science and Technology Basic Plan, in which a definition as a human-centered society that balances economic advancement with the resolution of social problems by a system that is highly integrated to cyberspace and physical space [1]. Society 5.0

© Springer Nature Singapore Pte Ltd. 2018
N. Abdullah et al. (Eds.): i-USEr 2018, CCIS 886, pp. 327–335, 2018.
https://doi.org/10.1007/978-981-13-1628-9_29

create new value-added through innovation, that will eliminate regional, age, gender, and language gaps and that enables the provision of products and services properly tailored to diverse individual needs and latent needs with the use of technology advancement [1]. Human beings do no longer make decision based on information given, but AI helps in providing fed back to human being in physical space in many forms. In this way, it will be possible to achieve a society that can both promote economic development and find lasting solutions to social problems.

Malaysia has come out of an initiative of economic development, citizen well-being and innovation through introduction of 'Transformasi Nasional 2050' or TN50 plan. In this plan, technology AI, and IoT are being identified as the technology enabler to drive Malaysia into the digital future [1]. Through the use of advanced technologies, nature of work is changing, creating a world in which we work side-by-side with machine. For public sector, Information Technology and Communication (ICT) have been adopted in the workplace since Malaysia launched the Multimedia Super Corridor (MSC) in 1996, It was formed as a major strategy to improve delivery services in the government agencies. The use of technology in the workplace such as web-based applications, electronic forms, workflow management, and electronic document management has revolutionized the way Malaysian employee work. It has led to increase in transparency and play an important role in helping government to attain new levels of service effectiveness and efficiency.

This paper focuses on literature in workplace, digital workplace as well as elements of digital workplace. Besides that, we also identified the supporting factors of digital workplace diffusion in public service, through performing a preliminary study on a workplace through interviewing selected respondents from different agencies-public sector and private sector based on their job position, work experience and area of work.

2 Literature Review: Workplace and Digital Workplace

A workplace is a location, where an employee works for his or her employer or a place of employment where people perform their jobs. According to Serhan, the work environment or workplace is defined as a physical location where somebody works, such a place can be ranged from a home, office to a large office building or company [2]. Jackson and Suomi defined workplace as one of the most important space other than the home, establishing "a central concept for a number of things; the worker and his/her family, the employing organization, the customers of the organization, and the society as a whole" [3].

However, nowadays, workplace has become a bit complex, especially in today's knowledge economy. With the advancement of technologies, employers are no longer expected to always provide a workplace for the employees. Employers believed that, employees can work based on virtual workplace or digital workplace, a workplace that is not specifically located in a physical place. Through digital workplace, employees operate remotely from each other and this will become common in the future [4]. Digital workplace environment concept believed can improve employees' performances [5], agility [5], productivity [5] as well as work-life balance [6]. Digital work place is also not about where we work but how we work [7]. Recent transformations in the nature of employment, due to a series of demographic, organizational and technological factors have played a catalytic role [8]. The digital workplace is where people, technology, and the workplace converge to improve agility, productivity, and engagement [9]. This future workplace is largely expected to transform into a smart and connected network, that will facilitate remote work styles [10].

In that sense, office will no longer be considered as a place that you travel to, because digital workplace will not be confined to physical boundaries as one is seeing today. Deloitte has defined the digital workplace encompasses all the technologies people use to get work done in today's workplace, both the ones in operation and the ones that have not been implemented and it ranges from Human Resource applications and core business applications to e-mail, instant messaging and enterprise social media tools and virtual meeting tool [11]. This environment enables employees to find the same type of consumer-oriented experiences, they enjoy in their personal lives, with one-stop shopping for the technology tools to do their work more effectively and effortlessly. Digital workplace is built around employees with computer and Internet access [12]. According to Garner, the digital workplace enables new, more effective ways of working, raise employee engagement and agility; and exploits consumer-oriented styles and technologies [13]. Tubb, one of the members of Digital Workplace Group mentioned that, digital workplace as "The collection of all the digital tools provided by an organization to allow its employees to do their jobs" [14]. Another definition of the digital workplace is the virtual, digital equivalent of the physical workplace [15]. Actually, there is no precise definition because the term digital workplace is still evolving. Currently, the concept of digital workplace can be defined as an ecosystem of work, where advanced tools in technology and intelligent context help employees to work in a mobile/virtual workplace environment, in order to complete task with consistent experiences across different devices and locations.

According to previous research and preliminary interviews, a digital workplace concept consists of social technologies tools, contextual intelligence tools, communication infrastructure and mobility (see Fig. 1). Social technologies tools used in digital workplace are specific social purposes tools. The tool that can improve employees productivity, collaboration, and communication within the organization [16]. The tools also allow employees to find, process and share information when needed. Meanwhile, contextual intelligence tool refers to a practical application of knowledge and information to the real world situations. This advanced tool helps employees in searching, analyzing information as well as assisting in making decisions, based on information given within the time frame [17]. Social technologies tools and contextual intelligence tools are essential elements, as it related to each other in assisting employees to get the job done (see Table 1). According to previous research, the social and contextual components of the work environment that have been found to influence the occurrence of creativity [18]. With the creativity, employees would create a new way of innovation in the working environment. Besides that, digital workplace concept concerns on employees working in a different location, therefore, mobility is required as it allows employees to collaborate and share information, wherever they may be through the communication infrastructure. Mobility refers to enabling employees to access tools away from the physical office or workplace [11]. The last element of digital workplace is communication infrastructure. Communication infrastructure refers to the backbone of the communications system. In this case, a digital workplace concept uses network infrastructure as a medium to transmit data or information. Strong network connectivity remains a crucial requirement, in the digital workplace, both in the office and on the road, as to ensure that, the communications technologies, business and collaboration applications are functioning effectively [19].

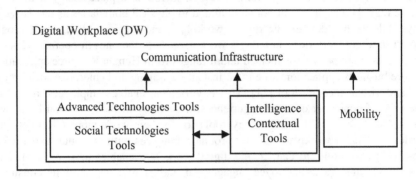

Fig. 1. Elements of digital workplace.

Table 1. List of advanced technologies tools for digital workplace.

Social technologies tools	Description	Intelligent contextual tools	Description
Microsoft Office 365 https://www.office.com/	Office applications plus other productivity services (OneNote, SharePoint, OneDrive and Microsoft Teams) that are enabled over the Internet. It can install them on multiple devices, including PCs, Macs, Android tablets, Android phones, iPad, and iPhone	Decision support tools https://www.gridspace.com/	A tool which combines new techniques in the fields of speech recognition, natural language processing, and artificial intelligence, turns conversational interactions into structured business data
Slack https://slack.com/	Slack is a cloud-based set of communication, tools, collaboration tools and workflow services	Data analytics tools https://analytics.google.com	A Google service that track, reports website traffic and analyze the customer data
Workplace Facebook https://www.facebook.com/workplace	Workplace is a collaborative platform run by Facebook, Inc. It used to communicate via groups, to chat with colleagues and offers the social networks features in a corporate environment	Search engines tools www.google.com www.yahoo.com www.bing.com	A tool designed to search for real-time information on the World Wide Web using algorithm

(continued)

Table 1. (*continued*)

Social technologies tools	Description	Intelligent contextual tools	Description
Google G-Suite https://gsuite.google.com/	A Google product where cloud computing, productivity and collaboration tools are used for business purpose		
WorkDo https://portal.workdo.co/	WorkDo is an application specifically designed to simplify team communication and enhance work efficiency suitable for small to medium size companies to accurately and effectively manage information		
Zoho https://www.zoho.com/	Zoho is online productivity tools and SaaS applications. Tools available are Customer Relation Management (CRM), workplace, finance, Information Technology management, collaboration, human resource		

3 Preliminary Study

A preliminary study has been done that involved respondents from the public sector and the private sector. Eight respondents have been selected for this study. From public sector - Human Resource Department, Intellectual Property Corporation of Malaysia (MyIPO), Information Technology Division, Department of Insolvency, Legal Affairs Division, Prime Minister's Department, ICT Consulting Division, MAMPU, Project Management Unit, Health Works Branch, Public Works Department, National Key Result Area (NKRA) Unit, Ministry of Women, Family and Community Development, while private sector respondents are from SEMNET Pte. Ltd, 10infinity Sdn. Bhd, Telekom Malaysia (TM) Berhad. The respondents were chosen based on their job positions, areas of work and work experiences. For this study, method of gathering information was through performing interviews (see Table 2). The aim of the interviews is to get ideas/views on what is digital workplace and to identify supporting factors towards digital workplace diffusion in public sector.

Table 2. List of questions.

	Questions
Q1	Do you know about digital workplace?
Q2	Do your organization practicing digital workplace?
Q3	What are the challenges in delivery service for the government?
Q4	What do you expect of a new way of working environment?
Q5	What are the other factors of digital workplace diffusion in public sector?

4   Research Methodology

Research methodology is a study about the methodology deployed in the research. For this study, method to gather information was through interviews. Interviews are a qualitative technique that involves a small number or respondents to explore their perspectives on a particular idea/view. In this research, the interview was done through unstructured means of interviews. Five questions had been asked during the interviews. The purpose of performing interviews was to get information on respondents experience, opinion and issues on digital workplace concept as well as to identify supporting factors towards digital workplace diffusion in public sector. The finding from the interviews can be a basis for further research for researchers and practitioners to further examine digital workplace in public sector.

5   Result and Discussion

5.1   Q1: Do You Know About the Digital Workplace?

From the interview, the researcher found that, since the term digital workplace was new, only a few respondents knew about the phenomena in public sector, compared to the private sector, they knew and had already implemented in the organization. They believed that through the practice of this working environment, digital workplace enables them to connect, communicate and collaborate in mobility and flexibility, without necessarily being together face to face. They believed that, by using digital workplace concept in an organization, it will allow them to response and work fast.

5.2   Q2: Do Your Organization Practicing Digital Workplace?

Based on the respondents, all private sectors are practicing the digital workplace concept, while for public sector, only MyIPO is practicing digital workplace in their organization, where employees are given the opportunity to work from home/telecommuting. The facility that organization provides is based on working culture, as well as working position. The reason for the organization implementing digital workplace is to allow flexibility for the employees that wanted the concept of work-life balance situation, as well as to avoid road congestion. Besides that, another key reason is for organization to control the increasing overhead cost of operation, organization to be able to cut off budget on renting a working space and office equipment. Meanwhile, other public sectors are still not practicing digital workplace as there is an issue of monitoring performance.

5.3   Q3: What Are Challenges in Delivery Service for the Government?

Furthermore, from the interview the researcher discovered that, challenges that public sector faced are that, as the expectation of customers is growing up, public service performance is very determined, by response of customers. In line with complex customers' expectations and personalization of services are essential for governments, to have a better understanding of the needs of citizens and communities, and to ensure that services are tailored towards the needs of people, who are using them. Besides that, due to geographical borderless, respondents claimed that, the demarcation between work and personal lives employees becomes less visible and gradually disappears. The distinction becomes increasingly intangible.

5.4   Q4: What Do You Expect of a New Way of Working Environment?

Respondents are expected that, the new way of working environment can leverage telecommunication infrastructure, digital technology, ICT info structure and infrastructure, data analytics and social media that enable employees to perform their jobs at anytime and anywhere. In this case, respondents agreed that, a digital workplace concept must consist of advanced technologies tools, communication infrastructure and mobility elements. The advanced technologies tools consist of social technologies tools and contextual intelligence. The tools must support each other, as it can enable employees to find, process, analyze, collaborate, share information and help them in making decision faster when needed. Meanwhile, mobility is where employees can work anywhere and stay connected. This can be done through the usage of mobile technologies such as smart phone, laptop and tablet. Finally, communication infrastructure is a very important element in the digital workplace, as it ensures that, the advanced technologies tools and mobility elements functioning effectively. Therefore, a strong and stable backbone of communication infrastructure is required to support the digital workplace environment.

5.5   Q5: What Are the Other Factors of Digital Workplace Diffusion in Public Sector?

Skilled/talented employees and support from the management are identified as tool that can help the success in implementing digital workplace concept in the organization. Skilled/talented employees refer to the capability of the employees to make use technology in their workplace. The technology does not only help them in their workplace, but also improve working engagement and performance. Whereas top management support is considered as one of the critical success factors of digital workplace diffusion. Top management refers to the highest rank of executive that responsible for the entire organization. Without top management support, respondents claimed that implementation is useless and a waste of time. It also affects budgetary allocation, because transforming the organization into a digital workplace concept requires money.

6 Future Works

For future works, this research can extend the study on supporting factors towards digital workplace in public sector. The researcher can investigate top management support and skilled employee's effectiveness towards digital workplace diffusion in public sector. Furthermore, the researcher can also propose a conceptual framework of the digital workplace for the public sector.

7 Conclusion

Digital workplace has become the alternative way of working concept. Through digital workplace, employees operate remotely from each other and it will become common in the future [4]. Digital workplace environment concept is capable of improving employees' performances [5], agility [5], productivity [5], collaboration [20], engagement [21] as well as work-life balance [6]. The implementation of digital workplace technology can enable the public sector to compete with the private sector for workers, improve the satisfaction of their current workforces, provide better tools for employee engagement, and improve their ability to manage and develop their workforces. In addition, the increasing and more complex needs and expectations of customers will showcase the full implementation of the digital workplace concept, which is aligned with the needs of the smart communities.

References

1. Razak, N.: Transformasi Nasional 2050, 1st edn. Yayasan Penyelidikan Transformasi, Selangor (2017)
2. Massoudi, D., Hamdi, D.: The effect of work environment on employees' productivity. Int. J. Sci. Res. 4(5), 387–403 (2015)
3. Jackson, J., Suomi, R.: e-Business and Workplace Redesign, 1st edn. Routledge Taylor and Francis Group, London (2004)
4. Cascio, F.: Managing a virtual workplace. Acad. Manag. Executive 14(3), 81–90 (2000)
5. Datacenterjournal Homepage. http://www.datacenterjournal.com/digital-workplace-vision-improving-productivity-anytime-anyplace-work/. Accessed 20 Apr 2018
6. Fedtechmagazine Homepage. https://fedtechmagazine.com/article/2014/05/work-life-balance-digital-workplace-0. Accessed 20 Apr 2018
7. Miller, P.: The Digital Workplace: How Technology Is Liberating Work. TECL Publishing New York, London (2012)
8. Alexopoulos, K.: The workplace as a factor of job satisfaction and productivity: a case study of administrative personnel at the University of Athens. J. Facil. Manag. 13, 332–349 (2015)
9. BMCsoftware Homepage. http://www.bmcsoftware.nl/it-solutions/building-digital-workplace.html. Accessed 22 Apr 2018
10. Frost Homepage. http://www.frost.com/c/481418/sublib/display-market-insight.do?searchQuery=digital+workplace&ctxixpLink=FcmCtx5&ctxixpLabel=FcmCtx6&id=295441714&bdata=aHR0cHM6Ly93d3cuZnJvc3QuY29tL3NyY2gvY2F0YWxvZy1zZWFyY2guZG8%2FcXVlcnlUZXh0PWRpZ2l0YWwrd29ya3BsYWNlYWNlUng9MC. Accessed 22 Apr 2018

11. Deloitte Homepage. https://www2.deloitte.com/content/dam/Deloitte/mx/Documents/human-capital/The_digital_workplace.pdf. Accessed 22 Apr 2018
12. Benson, A., Johnson, S., Kuchinke, K.: The use of technology in the digital workplace: a framework for human resource development. Adv. Dev. Hum. Resour. **4**(4), 392–404 (2002)
13. Gartner Homepage. http://www.gartner.com/it-glossary/digital-workplace. Accessed 8 Oct 2017
14. Digitalworkplacegroup Homepage. https://digitalworkplacegroup.com/2014/01/21/whats-employees-view-of-digital-workplace/. Accessed 8 Oct 2017
15. Digitalworkplacegroup Homepage. https://digitalworkplacegroup.com/2015/03/31/which-of-these-8-definitions-of-digital-workplace-works-best-for-you/. Accessed 26 Oct 2017
16. Intranetconnections Homepage. http://www.intranetconnections.com/blog/5-crucial-communication-tools-in-the-digital-workplace/. Accessed 27 Feb 2018
17. Avanade Homepage. https://www.avanade.com/en/blogs/avanade-insights/digital-business/sell-more-with-intelligent-context-in-the-digital-workplace. Accessed 27 Feb 2018
18. Shalley, C., Gilson, L.: What leaders need to know: a review of social and contextual factors that can foster or hinder creativity. Leadersh. Q. **15**(1), 33–53 (2004)
19. Strategy-business Homepage. https://www.strategy-business.com/blog/Five-Essential-Elements-of-the-Digital-Workplace?gko=eebed. Accessed 2 May 2018
20. Interact-intranet Homepage. https://www.interact-intranet.com/wp-content/uploads/2018/01/Employee-Collaboration-in-the-Digital-Workplace-Interact-Software-1.pdf. Accessed 22 Apr 2018
21. CIO Homepage. https://www.cio.co.nz/brand-post/content/630279/how-a-digital-workplace-can-help-boost-productivity-and-employee-engagement/. Accessed 22 Apr 2018

The PDCA Cycle of ISO/IEC 27005:2008 Maturity Assessment Framework

Rokhman Fauzi[1], Suhono H. Supangkat[2], and Muharman Lubis[1(✉)]

[1] Telkom University, Telekomunikasi 1, Bandung 40257, Indonesia
muharmanlubis@telkomuniversity.ac.id
[2] Institut Teknologi Bandung, Ganesha 10, Bandung 40132, Indonesia

Abstract. Most of the IT risk management framework/standard has not been given the tools to assess the maturity level. In fact, this information provides the basis for evaluation, repair and improvement of IT risk management of the Organization. This research objective is to design a framework that can be used to assess the maturity level of PDCA Cycle in ISO/IEC 27005. The PDCA Cycle is the managerial approach of this standard. Therefore, PDCA Cycle can represent the IT risk management based on ISO/IEC 27005. The assessment framework consists of a model, method and assessment worksheet. The model covers four assessment area (Plan, Do, Check, and Act), detail of the assessment area (8 domains, 35 subdomains and 82 elements), metric and assessment criteria which are supported by the method and worksheet assessment. The model represents the maturity of all processes (Plan, Do, Check, and Act) based on the clauses of ISO/IEC 27005. This Framework gives an enhancement of the existing model of; (1) all processes representation, (2) metric definition, (3) method for identifying evidences and (4) detail elements to repair and improve.

Keywords: Assessment framework · Maturity level · PDCA cycle
ISO/IEC 27005

1 Introduction

Information Technology Risk Management has become an important issue for the various user organizations' Information Technology/IT, particularly as it relates to compliance with the regulations and the efforts to minimize business risks of an organization [7, 14, 18, 37–39]. Principal risks of the IT implementation in an organization are the risks associated with information security aspects, namely; confidentiality, integrity, and availability [1]. In addition, aspect of information security is also a key implementation of IT Risk Management [33]. Therefore, Information Security Risk Management is terminology often used in research and industry to demonstrate the focus of an affirmation of IT Risk Management [3, 10]. When this has been or being developed, several standards and IT Risk Management framework focus on aspects of information security [4, 8, 11, 13, 29]. On the other hand, the implementation of IT Risk Management should be synergistic with efforts to achieve the objectives, implementation strategies, and organizational business processes [23]. In ISO/IEC 27005:2008, the PDCA Cycle is an approach that was taken in order to achieve

© Springer Nature Singapore Pte Ltd. 2018
N. Abdullah et al. (Eds.): i-USEr 2018, CCIS 886, pp. 336–348, 2018.
https://doi.org/10.1007/978-981-13-1628-9_30

optimal implementation of standards. In other words, the Cycle of PDCA is a representation of IT Risk Management based on ISO/IEC 27005 [19]. Cycle model also allows organizations to synergize with IT Risk Management, IT Governance and overall organizational management. Policy makers in the organization need information about the condition/actual achievement of its IT Risk Management. That information became the basis of evaluation and decision steps for optimizing IT Risk Management [6, 12, 22, 27, 34, 38]. A description of the PDCA Cycle Maturity Model in ISO/IEC 27005:2008 is expected to be a source of information.

PDCA cycle in IT Risk Management (ISO/IEC 27005) could not be separated from the company's overall risk management. Therefore, this study should also refer to the model and similar methods in the context of risk management at large. Researches that have been done related to this topic include: Business Risk Management Maturity Model [36], Enterprise Risk Management Maturity Assessment Tool-level [9], and Model to Assess the Maturity Level of the Risk Management Process in Information Security [28]. Here are some of the things that this study questions: (a) How to set a criterion of maturity PDCA Cycle? and (b) How to compile a maturity of each clause of ISO/IEC 27005 into the maturation process of PDCA? Meanwhile, objectives of this study are: (1) Develop Framework PDCA Cycle Assessment Maturity Model in ISO/IEC 27005:2008. Assessment Framework is intended, consisting of: (a) Model, (b) Method, and (c) Assessment Working Paper. (2) Provide examples of the application of this Assessment Framework. While limitations of this study are as follows: (1) PDCA cycle referred to in this research is the PDCA cycle in standard ISO/IEC 27005. (2) Maturity Model-Level which became the main reference is the Business Risk Management Maturity Model [36], 4.0/4.1 COBIT Maturity Model [21, 23] into the reference setting Metrics and Evaluation Criteria.

2 Literature Review

Information Technology Risk is the business risk associated with the use, ownership, operation, involvement, influence, and implementation of IT in a company [23, 24]. IT Risk is also defined as something that is wrong with IT and the negative impact on the business [25]. Symantec is grouping of IT risk into four categories; security, availability, performance, and compliance [35]. According to Abram, which became the general classification of the various threads of IT risk classification model were; confidentiality, integrity, and availability [1]. These three aspects are also the pillars of information security [15, 16]. In other words, IT risk has a very close correlation with information security. IT Risk Management is an integrated process that allows IT managers to balance operational and economic costs of protection against IT as well as benefit from such protection [2, 29, 30]. This definition is the classical definition of compromise between business and IT operational definition in the context of the organization. IT Risk Management is the foundation of the implementation of Information Security Management System (ISO/IEC 27001, 2005) [5]. ISO/IEC 27001 specifies that the control implemented within the scope, limitations, and context of the Information Security Management System (ISMS) should be based on risk [19]. PDCA (Plan-Do-Check-Act) Model is an approach that is widely used in ISO standards, including ISO 27001. This model was developed in the late 80s (Deming). PDCA model is assessed as the right choice in the development and maintenance of ISMS.

Stages of the PDCA Model can answer questions about how to establish policies, processes, and procedures relating to risk management (Phase 'Plan'), implement and run (Phase 'Do'), assess and measure the performance of the process (Phase 'Check'), and take action to repair and improve (Stage 'Act') [19]. Maturity Model aims to assess the suitability of the process of working towards a specific reference, e.g.: benefits, regulation, competition, etc. In addition, Maturity Model can also be used to determine the actual position of the organization to the particular reference and plan improvement steps in a structure [23, 32]. Risk Maturity Model is developed and documented at the end of the decade in the 90s [17]. This model describes four level of maturity, namely; naïve, novice, normalized, and natural. Each level reflects how risk management conditions are applied in an organization. RMM was later developed by The International Association for Contract & Commercial Management/IACCM - Business Risk Management Working Group with changes in; (a) Naming Model, becomes: Business Risk Management Maturity Model, (b) Level Naming, becomes: Novice, Competent, Proficient, Expert (c) Development of questionnaires to assess more accurately Maturity Model [36]. The advantage of both models is the description of the Maturity Model risk in a comprehensive organizational perspective. Perspectives are described in four attributes used in this model. On the other hand, the model is risk coverage in general, not specific to the risks associated with IT. Importantly, personal data of customer should be protected comprehensively to avoid worst case scenario [43–46].

3 Framework Design

This study was conducted using several phases namely literature review, framework design and case study (see Fig. 1).

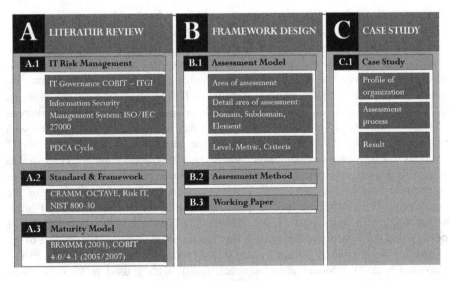

Fig. 1. Methodology.

Assessment Framework is comprised of a Model, Methods, and Assessment Working Paper with descriptive structure (see Fig. 2):

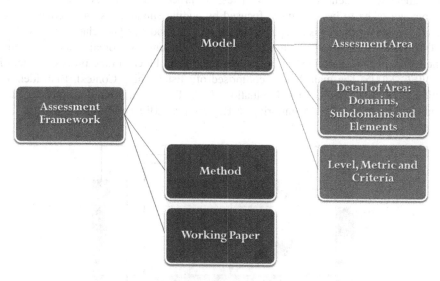

Fig. 2. Assessment framework.

The Assessment Model is a key component in this framework. The Model consists of four assessment area (PDCA), which detailed to 8 domains, 35 subdomains, and 82 elements. The Detail Area is a compilation of clauses of the ISO/IEC 27005 standard. The domains are taken from the main blocks in the standard process model. Subdomains and elements refer to clauses of the standard in each domain.

3.1   Assessment Area

The model in this assessment framework provides representation of the PDCA Cycle Maturity Model of ISO/IEC 27005. Maturity level in this model views the entire cycle of PDCA. The assessment results can also indicate the priority of repairs and improvement of each Element Area. Part of the PDCA cycle, namely; PLAN, DO, CHECK, and ACT hereinafter referred to as Area or Assessment Area. PLAN focuses on establishing the context, risk assessment, developing risk treatment plan and risk acceptance. Then DO is related to the implementation of risk treatment plan while CHECK concentrates to continual monitoring and reviewing of risk. For ACT, it is considered to maintain and improve the Information Security Risk Management Process. The scope of each area is determined by reference to the mapping processes in ISO/IEC 27005 for the processes in Information Security Management System (ISO/IEC 27001). The PLAN Area has the most extensive coverage for being the foundation of another Area (DO, CHECK, and ACT).

3.2   Detail of Assessment Area

This section describes the development of the Detail Areas. It is intended so that the assessment to be done per element. Thus the process of evaluation and corrective actions are taken to become more focused by adding subdomains and elements. The detail of assessment area is mapped from the process model and the clauses of ISO/IEC 27005. Here are the detail results which became; Domains, Subdomains, and Elements. The Domains are determined by reference to the main blocks in the process model of ISO/IEC 27005. The main blocks comprised of;: Establishing Context, Risk Identification, Risk Estimation, Risk Evaluation, Risk Treatment, Risk Acceptance, Risk Communication and Risk Monitoring & Review [19, 20] (see Fig. 3).

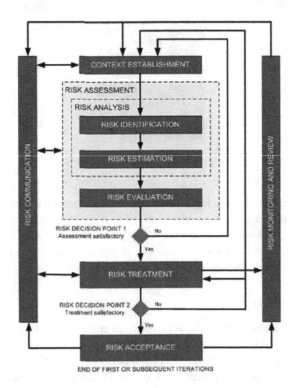

Fig. 3. Process model of ISO/IEC 27005.

Furthermore, with reference to clauses of the standard, each Domain is broken down into several Subdomain and Element. The results yielded 35 (thirty five) Subdomains and 82 (eighty two) Elements (Table 1). Entirety and then mapped into each Assessment Area.

Table 1. Subdomains and elements.

Domains	Subdomains	Elements
Context establishment	6	16
Risk communication	4	13
Risk identification	5	15
Risk estimation	4	6
Risk evaluation	3	4
Risk treatment	7	7
Risk acceptance	2	2
Risk monitoring & review	4	19
	35	82

3.3 Mapping of Elements to Assessment Area

Each element is mapped to the Assessment Area respectively (see Figs. 4, 5, 6 and 7):

AREA PLAN				CODE OF ELEMENTS			
1.1.1	1.3.1	1.4.2	1.4.4	1.4.6	1.4.8	1.4.10	1.5.1
1.2.1	1.4.1	1.4.3	1.4.5	1.4.7	1.4.9	1.4.11	1.6.1

2.1.1	2.3.1	2.3.3	2.3.8
2.2.2	2.3.2	2.3.7	2.3.9

3.1.1	3.1.3	3.2.1	3.2.3	3.3.2	3.4.2	3.5.1	3.5.3
3.1.2	3.1.4	3.2.2	3.3.1	3.4.1	3.4.3	3.5.2	

4.1.1	4.2.1	4.3.1
4.1.2	4.2.2	4.4.1

5.1.1	5.2.2
5.2.1	5.3.1

6.1.1	6.7.1
6.2.1	

7.1.1
7.1.2

Fig. 4. Area PLAN mapping.

AREA DO	CODE OF ELEMENTS
2.4.1	

6.3.1	6.5.1
6.4.1	

Fig. 5. Area DO mapping.

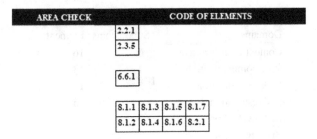

Fig. 6. Area CHECK mapping.

AREA ACT		CODE OF ELEMENTS				

Fig. 7. Area ACT mapping.

3.4 Level, Metric and Criteria

The main purpose of defining the level on this assessment model is to provide a structured description of the stages of process improvement of the PDCA Cycle. Table 2 defines the level using the Business Risk Management Maturity Model [36] and the Business Process Maturity Model [31].

Table 2. Level and criteria.

Level	Criteria
Level 5	Organizational focus is the ongoing improvement process. The whole process was in accordance with the reference standard
Level 4	Organizational focus is the evaluation and optimization of existing resources. Much of the process followed a reference standard
Level 3	Organizational focus is to build a standard managerial processes to achieve organizational goals. A small part of the process followed the reference standard
Level 2	Organizational focus is to build managerial foundation in every program or project. Some processes are standardized, without a reference standard
Level 1	No specific targets. Achievement of the organization depends on the competence and hard work of a handful of personnel. There is no standard process

Metric is a measure of the assessment process. In this model, the criterion is defined as a list of conditions refers to the determination of metrics and a requirement of an Element Score Level [5, 21, 23, 26]. Metrics and Evaluation Criteria are set for each Domain because it has a similar characteristic; input, process and output. In this case, it used governances, plans, procedures, goals and success measurements, roles and responsibilities, communications, skills and trainings, as well as tools.

3.5   Assessment Method

Generally, assessment process in the Framework consists of 4 (four) steps that begins with the Organization Profile Identification, Data Collection, Analysis, and lastly Presentation Maturity Profile. In the early stages to identify the profile of the Organization, profiles are useful for determining which data collection method is most appropriate to apply. The next step is data collection. Data collection methods that can be used are; (1) document analysis, (2) interviews, (3) questionnaires, and or (4) physical review [19]. Methods (1) and (2) are the main methods of collecting data because the methods will obtain evidence. Method (3) and or (4) are required if the Organization has a high complexity and is expected to have high IT risk. The data obtained were then processed in the working paper. The next step is data analysis and assessment. Assessment using the benchmark valuation method in the Business Risk Management Maturity Model [36, 40–47], which follows four steps; organization profiling, data collection, analysis and maturity profile. The initial steps of data analysis are to conduct assessments of each area. Area values obtained from Total of Actual Score divided by the Maximum Area Score. Formula to evaluate the maturity level normalized in Scale 5 to match the level used in this model is:

$$\text{Maturity Level} = \left(\sum \text{Area Score}\right) \times 1.25$$
$$\text{Area Score} = \left(\sum \text{Actual Score}\right) / (\text{Maximum Score})$$
$$\text{Maximum Score} = \left(\sum \text{Elements}\right) \times 5$$

Results at this stage are the PDCA Cycle Maturity. These values also indicate the position of Level (1–5) and their characteristics. In addition to PDCA Cycle Maturity Model, from the data processing is also the description of the condition of each element in each area. These results become the basis of evaluation of maturity per Element. The last step is the preparation of the PDCA Cycle Maturity Profile of the Organization. This profile consists of at least; (1) maturity model, (2) evaluation of maturity per element, (3) assessment of conclusions and recommendations.

4   Case Study

Brief profile of the organization is engaged in services that have branches in several cities, with more than 1000 staff members, IT was instrumental in supporting the core business, have IT Department (IT Department staff members between 30 to 60). The data was collected using interviews and document analysis. The data obtained were then stored and processed using the analytical methods have been described in earlier sections. Interviews were conducted with IT Risk Management Staff. Interview material used was material that was in the working paper as well as clarification of the assessment reference documents. Analysis carried out on the reference documents was directly related to IT Risk Management. Document analysis and interviews were complementary methods. List of documents included; MRTI/20xx Policy, Appendix MRTI/20xx Policy, Asset Register Software, Hardware Asset Registry, Personal Property Registry, the Registry of Asset Data/Information. The assessment result consisted of: (1) maturity of the PDCA cycle, (2) evaluation of maturity per element, and (3) conclusions and recommendations.

Table 3. Case study: maturity profile of the PDCA cycle.

Area	Area score
PLAN	0.65926
DO	0.45
CHECK	0.52727
ACT	0.6
Maturity of the PDCA cycle	2.79566

The recommendations of the assessment presented (see Table 3) in the following points: (1) IT Risk Management Maturity Model Organization (the PDCA Cycle) = 2.79566 or are in the range of Level 2 into the third. This condition indicates that the organization is building materials in the process of its IT Risk Management. Area "PLAN" is the current priority of the Organization. (2) Area "DO" and "CHECK" is a priority improvement in the future. (3) High Priority for Improvement = 20 Elements. Here are the maps of maturity per element in each Assessment Area (Figs. 8, 9, 10 and 11):

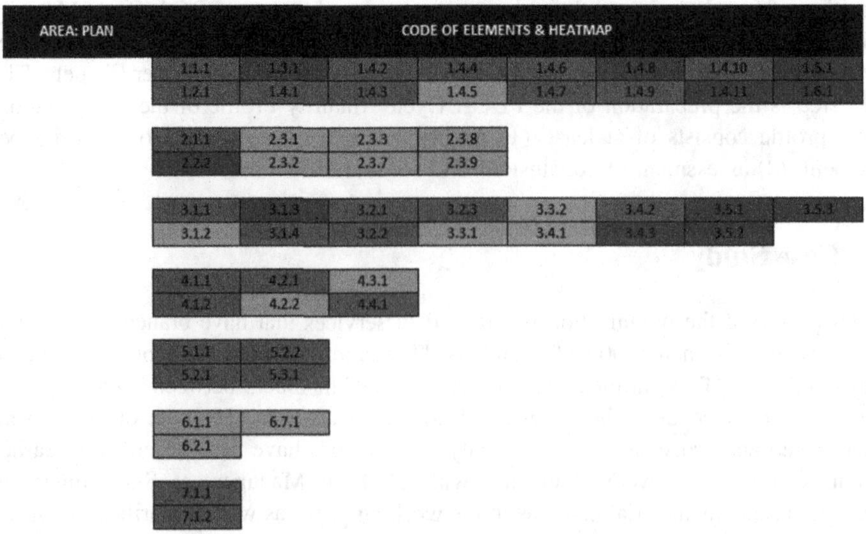

Fig. 8. Case study: area PLAN evaluation.

Fig. 9. Case study: area DO evaluation.

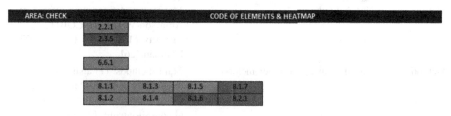

Fig. 10. Case study: area CHECK evaluation.

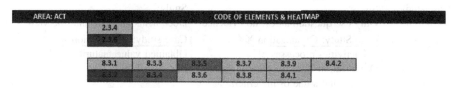

Fig. 11. Case study: area ACT evaluation.

5   Framework Model Comparison

This section shows the comparison between the proposed Assessment Framework with the existing model [28] (see Table 4). The fundamental difference lies in the approach to model development and assessment. Reference model of the existing model uses CMM/CMMI and focuses on the assessment of Maturity Rate per Activity/Process/Domain by using a reference model of the Business Risk Management Maturity Model and focuses on the PDCA cycle as a whole, or managerial processes.

Table 4. Framework model comparison.

Items	Existing model [28]	Proposed framework
Standard reference	ISO/IEC 27005	ISO/IEC 27005
Maturity model reference	CMM/CMMI	RMM/BRMMM
Model representation	*Continuous* representation (maturity rate per activity/process/domain)	Maturity PDCA cycle as a whole

(*continued*)

Table 4. (*continued*)

Items	Existing model [28]	Proposed framework
Model structure	Domains: 6	Domains: 8
	Subdomains: 43 (*control objective*)	Subdomains: 35
	Elements: Not defined	Elements: 82
	Levels: 5	Levels: 5
Metric	Not defined	Metrics are defined with reference: Arnasson-Willet [5], COBIT Maturity Model 4.0/4.1(2005/2007), Luftman [26]
Method	Questionnaires; no other method	Main methods: (1) analysis of documents and (2) interviews. Complementary methods: (1) questionnaire, (2) review the physical; Working Paper is used as a tool
Case study	Study: Only use questionnaires; no evidence	Study: Documents analysis and interview
	Case Study: Organization X All activities/processes of Organization X meets the criteria at Level 2 and some of the criteria at Level 3	Case study: organization X Obtained value maturity model cycle PDCA = 2.79
Additional	Accountability matrix and Risk Scorecard	Not defined

Basically these two FMs cannot be compared vis a vis due to differences in the maturity model as reference. However, it can be concluded that the Framework Proposed in this study has several aspects that can complement the missing aspect in the existing model [28], namely the representation, metric, method and presentation of assessment results.

6   Conclusion

The model represents the maturity of all processes (Plan, Do, Check, and Act) based on the clauses of ISO/IEC 27005. On the other hand, the existing models have defined the Accountability and Risk Matrix Scorecard that have not been defined in the Model/Framework proposed in this study. This Framework gives an enhancement of the existing model of; (a) all processes representation, (b) metric definition, (c) method for identifying evidences and (d) detail elements to repair and improve. The case study conducted showed that the organization X has actual score of maturity (the PDCA Cycle) = 2,79566. The organization X is developing a standard process of its Information Technology (security) risk management. The DO and CHECK Area and 20

Elements should be the priorities of repairment and improvement. Suggestions for further research include the actions below: (1) Enhancing of the metric, criteria and worksheet assessment. (2) Mapping of the PDCA Cycle of ISO/IEC 27005 to ISO 31000 and ISO 27000 series. (3) Increasing the number of case studies.

References

1. Abram, T.: The hidden values of IT risk management. ISACA J. **2**, 10–11 (2009)
2. AIRMIC - ALARM - IRM: Risk Management Standard (2002)
3. Al Aboodi, S.S.: A new approach for assessing the maturity of information security. ISACA J. Online **3**, 36–43 (2006)
4. Alberts, D.: Managing Information Security Risks: The OCTAVESM Approach. Addison Wesley, Boston (2002)
5. Arnasson, S.T., Willet, K.D.: How to Achieve 27001 Certification. Auerbach Pub., Boca Raton (2007)
6. AS/NZS: Risk Management Guidelines-Companion to AS/NZS 4360:2004 (2005). http://bch.cbd.int/database/attachment/?id=12285
7. Bank Indonesia: Pedoman Penerapan Manajemen Risiko Dalam Penggunaan TI oleh Bank Umum, Lampiran Surat Edaran Bank Indonesia Nomor: 9/30/DPNP Tgl, 12 December 2007
8. Bornmann, W.G., Labuschagne, L.: A comparative framework for evaluating information security risk management methods. RAU - Standard Bank Academy for Information Technology, Rand Afrikaans University, South Africa (2004)
9. Ciorciari, M., Blattner, P.: Enterprise risk management maturity-level assessment tool. In: ERM Symposium 14–16 April, Chicago (2008)
10. CISSP Forum: Top Information Security Risk for 2008 (2008)
11. CRAMM: How CRAMM Works. Siemens Enterprise Communication (2008)
12. De Bruin, T., et al.: Understanding the main phases of developing a maturity assessment model. In: 16th Australasian Conference on Information Systems 29 November–2 December, Sidney (2005)
13. ENISA: Risk management: implementation principles and inventories for risk management/risk assessment methods and tools. In: European Network and Security Agency (2006)
14. Ernst & Young: Strategic Business Risk - Top 10 Risks for Business (2008)
15. FIPS PUB 199. Federal Information Processing Standards Publication—Standard for Federal Information and Information Systems, February 2004. www.nist.gov
16. Senft, S., Gallegos, F.: Information Technology Control and Audit, 3rd edn. Auerbach Publications/Taylor & Francis Group, Auerbach (2008)
17. Hillson, D.A.: Towards a risk maturity model. Int. J. Proj. Bus. Risk Manag. **1**(1), 35–45 (1997)
18. ISACA: Top Business/Technology Issues Survey Results (2008)
19. ISO: ISO/IEC 27001:2005, ISO/IEC 27002:2005, ISO/IEC 27005:2008, Information technology—Security techniques—Information security risk management (2008)
20. ISO: ISO/IEC Guide 73:2009, Risk Management—Vocabulary—Guidelines for Use in Standards (2009)
21. ITGI: IG Measurement tools. Information Technology Governance Institute (2005)
22. ITGI: Information Risks: Whose Business Are They? Information Technology Governance Institute (2005)

23. ITGI: COBIT 4.0/COBIT 4.1. Information Technology Governance Institute (2007). https://www.isaca.org/Knowledge-Center/cobit/Documents/COBIT4.pdf
24. ITGI: Enterprise Risk: Identify, Govern and Manage IT Risk, The Risk IT Framework Exposure Draft (2009)
25. Jordan, E., Silcock, L.: Beating IT Risks. Wiley, England (2005)
26. Luftman, J.: Assesing business-IT alignment maturity. Commun. AIS **4**, 99 (2000). Article 14
27. Malette, D.: IT Performance Improvement with COBIT and the SEI CMM. ISACA J. **3**, 46–50 (2005)
28. Mayer, J., Fagundes, L.: A model to assess the maturity level of the risk management process in information security. IFIP/IEEE (2009)
29. NIST: Risk Management Guide for Information Technology Systems—Recommendations of the NIST, SP 800-30, USA, p. 4 (2002). http://csrc.nist.gov/publications/nistpubs/800-30/sp800-30.pdf
30. NIST: Directions in Security Metrics Research (2009)
31. Object Management Group: Business Process Maturity Model v1.0. Standard document (2007). http://www.omg.org/spec/BPMM/1.0/PDF
32. Persse, J.: The Capability Maturity Model. An Executive Overview of the Software Engineering Institute's Software Process Improvement Program (2001)
33. Pironti, J.P.: Key elements of an information risk management program. ISACA J. **2**, 42–47 (2008)
34. Singh, A.: Improving Information Security Risk Management. University of Minnesota (2009)
35. Symantec: IT Risk Management Report, vol. 2 (2008)
36. The IACCM Risk Management Working Group: Organizational Maturity in Business Risk Management (2003)
37. Tucci, L.: Governance, risk and compliance spending to grow in 2010. SearchCompliance.com (2009)
38. Vaish, A., Varma, S.: Proposed Next Generation Information Security Management Effectiveness Measurement Model (2009)
39. Lubis, M., Kartiwi, M., Zulhuda, S.: Privacy and personal data protection in electronic voting: factors and measures. Telkomnika **15**(1), 512–521 (2017)
40. Leedy, P.D., Ormrod, L.E.: Practical Research: Planning and Design, 8th edn. Pearson Education, Upper Saddle River (2010)
41. Lubis, M., Kusumasari, T.F., Hakim, L.: The Indonesia public information disclosure act (UU-KIP): its challenges and responses. IJECE **8**(1), 94–103 (2018)
42. Ahlan, A.R., Lubis, M., Lubis, A.R.: Information security awareness at the knowledge-based institution: its antecedennts and measures. Procedia Comput. Sci. **72**, 361–373 (2015)
43. Lubis, M., Kartiwi, M., Durachman, Y.: Assessing privacy and readiness of electronic voting system in Indonesia. In: Proceedings IEEE CITSM (2017)
44. Lubis, M., Kartiwi, M., Zulhuda, S.: Election fraud and privacy related issues: addressing electoral integrity. In: Proceedings IEEE ICIC, pp. 227–232 (2017)
45. Rosmaini, E., Kusumasari, T.F., Lubis, M., Lubis, A.R.: Insights to develop privacy policy for organization in Indonesia. J. Phys.: Conf. Ser. **978**(1), 012042 (2018)
46. Rosmaini, E., Kusumasari, T.F., Lubis, M., Lubis, A.R.: Study to the current protection of personal data in the educational sector in Indonesia. J. Phys.: Conf. Ser. **978**(1), 012037 (2018)
47. Ahlan, A.R., Lubis, M.: Information security awareness in university: maintaining learnability, performance and adaptability through roles of responsibility. In: IAS (2015)

Measuring User Experience of Mobile Augmented Reality Systems Through Non-instrumental Quality Attributes

Shafaq Irshad[✉], Dayang Rohaya Awang Rambli, Nur Intan Adhani Muhamad Nazri, Siti Rohkmah binti Mohd Shukri, and Yusoff Omar

Department of Computer and Information Sciences, Universiti Teknologi PETRONAS, Bandar Seri Iskandar, Malaysia
shafaqirshad223@gmail.com

Abstract. Augmented Reality is developing owing to the advancements in computer graphics and Human-Computer Interaction (HCI). Fast paced industrial development has permitted Augmented Reality experiences to be delivered on cell phones. Interaction and Design challenges are created due to the distinctive information presentation and interaction style of Mobile Augmented Reality systems (MAR). Latest research shows the need to comprehend the end User Experience (UX) in such systems to overcome these unique interaction and design challenges. This paper surveys the development and advancements in MAR from UX viewpoint. Furthermore, a systematic study on measuring user aesthetics as non-instrumental quality attributes to measure the UX for existing MAR applications is presented.

Keywords: Augmented Reality · User studies · Interaction design
Human Computer Interaction · Mobile augmented reality · User experience

1 Introduction

Augmented Reality (AR) is a prominent and valuable innovation which gives a carefully enhanced perspective of present reality, giving end users valuable and instructive feedback in various circumstances. Azuma et al. [1] states that the system is AR oriented when it combines existing and virtual conditions, interacts in real time and allows end client to experience the present reality in 3D. Even though Azuma's meaning of Augmented Reality is considered a benchmark by scientists and researchers, AR is additionally outlined as "a system that combines real and computer-generated information in a real environment, interactively and in real time, and aligns virtual objects with physical objects [2]."

Augmented Reality (AR) is a subdivision of Virtual Reality (VR) technology yet it differentiates from VR in such a way that it allows the user to experience feelings of practicality and authenticity [3]. When the real and computer-generated world is consolidated through AR, it turns out to be an instance of the blended reality introduced in an independent display as characterized in "Virtuality Continuum" [4] as shown in Fig. 1.

© Springer Nature Singapore Pte Ltd. 2018
N. Abdullah et al. (Eds.): i-USEr 2018, CCIS 886, pp. 349–357, 2018.
https://doi.org/10.1007/978-981-13-1628-9_31

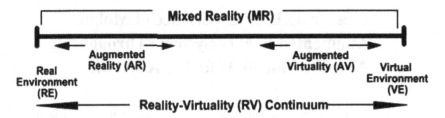

Fig. 1. Milgram's Virtual-reality continuum (a classification of mixed-reality graphic displays), reproduced from [4].

Quick paced improvement in the industry has allowed AR experiences to be delivered to cell phones. Scientists demonstrate how cell phones are utilized in computer-vision-based Augmented Reality tracing and recording [5, 6], simple video broadcast [7], context supported collaboration and interaction, browser-based interface [8] and other advance technologies.

Mobile Augmented Reality is a leading innovation that offers a carefully enhanced and upgraded three-dimensional perspective on the real world through various mobile devices, interfacing clients with a valuable virtual substance that can't be recognized with human faculties [26]. AR exhibits virtual data that enable the clients to perform troublesome undertakings, for example, offering headings to laborers through electrical cables in planes by means of computerized data via head mounted displays [27, 28].

The appropriation of MAR administrations is relied upon to increment of a Compound Annual Growth Rate (CAGR) at 135.35% from 2015 to 2019 [29]. In any case, when camera-fitted cell phone indicates towards digital information to get data, end user design challenges arises [30]. To prevail over these end user design challenges and deliver an effective MAR experience to the intended users, end user experience of MAR [31] needs to be inspected.

UX includes "an individual's attitude, behavior, and emotions towards a specific artifact, product or service". The International Organization for Standardization (ISO) characterizes UX by articulating that "A person's perceptions and responses resulting from the use and/or anticipated use of a product, system or service" [32]. Generally, UX is regarded as a comprehensive and context-dependent concept [33]. Moreover, it is primarily considered as subjective, as it happens just in users' mind and modifies based on his or her experience to the specific product in question with time. UX is generally described as an umbrella term for planning, assessing and examining the end user experience in a specific setting [34].

There is a research thrust for understanding and observing the end user experience for mobile AR systems to improve them further [30, 35]. Some noticeable MAR publications are presented in Table 1. It is observed from the literature that design, development and evaluation methods for mobile augmented reality systems are required [31, 36, 37]. This study measures the UX through non-instrumental quality attributes of MAR applications by measuring user aesthetics. The following section presents a thorough evaluation methodology for conducting the study.

Table 1. Salient MAR and UX research contributions highlighting end-user studies

Context of research	Authors	Research contribution
User interface of augmented reality	Hollerer et al. [9]	Interface study of indoor and outdoor AR systems
	Hollerer et al. [10]	User Interface managing tips and techniques for collaborative MAR
	Joslin et al. [11]	Mobile Augmented reality user interface
User centered design Studies of AR	Gabbard and Hix [12]	AR Design guidelines
	Dunser et al. [13]	Characteristics/features of Augmented Reality design
	Siltanen et al. [14]	AR interior design service through UCD
User experience studies of augmented reality	Olsson and Salo [15]	User study and Survey on MAR Applications
	Olsson et al. [16]	reported user Expectations and affordances of MAR
	Arol [17]	MAR supporting marketing
	Kamilakis et al. [18]	Mobile UX in AR vs Maps Interfaces
	Olsson et al. [19]	UX assessments on various MAR scenarios
	Olsson and Salo [20]	Categories of MAR practices
	Olsson et al. [16]	Impact of MAR elements on user experience
	Dhir and Al-kahtani [21]	UX evaluation through different scenarios
User experience frameworks for MAR	Jaasko and Mattelmaki [22]	Framework for measuring MAR product features
	Hassenzahl [23]	Model of User Experience for marketing
	Perritaz et al. [24]	Interaction framework for enhancing UX
	Olsson [25]	levels of user expectations for imminent technologies

2 Methodology

2.1 Measuring User Aesthetics as Non-instrumental Quality Attribute

There are several aspects that can be used to measure the aesthetics of any product. Non-Instrumental quality attributes measure user needs beyond usability and satisfaction i.e. aesthetics or product appeal [38]. This study uses a set of non-instrumental quality attributes [39] to investigate the aesthetic and emotional aspect of MAR applications.

This study measures excitement, captivity, exclusiveness, innovation, interest and impression of MAR applications under investigation [39]. Following is the detailed procedure for the study.

Participants: The study was conducted at university campus where 15 students participated. An aggregate of nine sittings were arranged with fifteen members, including thirteen men and two women. Members were shown the most proficient method to utilize MAR applications via tablet computer. Android tablet PC was used to examine the agreed applications. Members completed the study after going through the applications. Various mobile application used in the study are shown in Fig. 2.

Fig. 2. Various Mobile AR applications used in the UX study

In general, members were instructed to effortlessly use the application. A few members were under graduates and others were post-graduate students from different engineering departments. Examinations. All members possessed latest mobile phone aside from one. Most of the applicants were familiar with the applications as well. So, it required little to no training to conduct the study.

Applications Under Survey: Three mainstream and effectively accessible applications that develop applications particularly for cell phones e.g. Blippar, Layar and JUNAIO were utilized. Blippar [40] is a primary system for picture acknowledgment for cell phones and tablets. Layar platform is renowned for its printing arrangements and imaginative intelligent AR. Junaio cases to be the most exceptional program for enlarged reality. The client can peruse through many channels that offer computerized data and related substance on genuine items, spots, daily papers and boards everywhere throughout the world utilizing mobile or wearable with Junaio [41].

Study Design and Procedure: AR advertising campaigns were chosen to be shown with applications. A thorough demonstration on the use of MAR applications was given to the Applicants. An android powered device was used to discover the applications under study. A questionnaire was filled after the tasks given to the applicants were completed.

To measure the aesthetic aspects, dimensions identified by [39] were considered as dependent variables. The scale consisted of six items, and ratings ranged from 0 to 5 (low to high). The independent variable used in the experiment was "design factors" of MAR. Participants where shown the MAR applications and each participant used the applications for 7 to 10 min (mean = 8.5 min). Participants were give 3 tasks to complete before filling out the questionnaire. The overall results of measuring non- instrumental quality attributes are presented in next section.

2.2 Experimental Analysis

This section demonstrates the results and analysis on measuring the aesthetics. Figure 3 shows a graph demonstrating the results of each aspect in detail. 6.6% of the participants strongly agreed and 66% of the participants agreed that MAR is exciting to use. 20% of the participants neither agree nor disagree that MAR is exciting technology. For captivity of the MAR application 73.3% of the participants agreed or strongly agreed (6.6% strongly agree and 66.6% agree) that MAR is captivating to use.

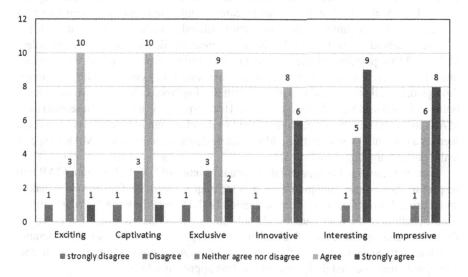

Fig. 3. Graphical representation shows the rate of responses for UX aesthetic properties

20% of the participants neither agree nor disagree that MAR is captivating. The experience was agreed to be exclusive (40% agree and 13.3% strongly agreed). But 20% of the participants in this category neither agree nor disagree that MAR is exclusive. 6.6% of the participants strongly disagree that MAR is exciting, captivating or exclusive. 40% of the members strongly agreed that MAR is an innovative technology. 53% of the members strongly agreed that MAR is an innovative technology. 60% of the members strongly agreed that MAR is an interesting technology. 33.3% of the members agreed that MAR is interesting. 53.3% of the members strongly agreed that MAR is an impressive to use. 40% of the members agreed that MAR is an impressive to use. 6.6% of the members neither agree nor disagree that MAR is interesting or impressive.

From the results it is evident that more that 70% of the participants in each category either agree or strongly agree that MAR is exciting, captivating, exclusive, innovative, interesting and impressive technology to be used in advertisement and marketing industry. However, there are users who neither agree nor disagree that MAR is aesthetically pleasing. From the study it was revealed that there were several shortcomings in the existing applications that affected the emotional experience of the users. For example, its dependability on the INTERNET, lack of previous knowledge about what AR is, lack of clear instructions on how to scan the applications and lack of flexibility to manipulate the 3D content.

3   Discussion

This research intends to investigate MAR from UX viewpoint. From the literature examined in the above section it is obvious that the dynamic and subjective nature of UX, its distinctive qualities (for example, emotional, aesthetics, pragmatic, hedonic), context and time are critical features to be considered in UX. Since it is a generally new idea, it is critical to lead observational research keeping in mind the end goal to additionally refine the techniques and instruments utilized as a part of UX research [30].

The potential utilization of MAR in different application spaces is boundless. Utilizing MAR permits end users to have more intuitive experiences. MAR stimulates unique cognitive and natural experiences when end users connect with 3D content through their cell phones and collaborate with the displayed content. As MAR is developing as an innovation, different methods and techniques (e.g. user based research) using MAR, are yet advancing. Regardless of the fast development in MAR, it is obvious that there is a need of UX studies that address the design and evaluation of MAR in specifically defined application areas [31].

From the research it is apparent that there is absence of UX studies about MAR with respect to the end user, unique interaction techniques, methods for browsing, making and sharing AR data and context of utilization [42]. Despite the boundless capability of MAR, challenges are confronted while out- lining a rich and emotionally fulfilled UX for mobile augmented reality. The difficulties emerge because of the novel cooperation with the enlarged data AR offers through cell phones. Augmented reality appears to need appropriate user focused design and evaluation approaches [37].

From the writing survey, a perceptible absence of UX framework that addresses the evaluation and designing aspect of MAR applications are also identified. Keeping in mind the end goal to enhance MAR, end UX should be comprehended in its particular application domains. After the literature review, we can argue that it is critical to design domain specific UX systems [31, 35] that address the issues in MAR and end user interaction conjured when utilizing MAR applications.

In this study User aesthetics were measured as part of the non-instrumental UX attributes. Methods used for UX investigation produced valuable results and can be used again in future for similar studies. From the preliminary study, various positive and negative aspects of MAR applications were identified. With the advent of new technology in the field of HCI, it is becoming obligatory to update the old practices. Despite the earlier research on usability issues in MAR, the community has been lacking in research results with focus on user experience. The experience people have when using these digital advertisement applications is very positive and can easily increase the sales of any product.

Furthermore, MAR also creates the joyful and engaging interactive environment which shows its potential. Several participants who have tested the prototype commented that it is exciting to use the system and it feels more interactive than online marketing websites. From the results of the preliminary study it is evident that MAR can be used as an effective medium to advertise and market products of almost all types.

4   Conclusion

Because of the growing importance of MAR in every domain it has become critical to evaluate the end users understanding and experience of mobile AR. This research papers aims at evaluating the existing MAR applications from UX perspective. The study measures UX through non-instrumental quality attributes. Results obtained from UX investigation using non- instrumental quality attributes are an important empirical contribution. Results highlight the design problems of existing Mobile Augmented Reality (MAR) marketing applications. From the results of the study it is evident that MAR can be used as an effective medium to advertise and market almost all types of products. Several weak aspects of MAR applications are also discovered and can be enhanced in future to improve the end user experience of MAR applications.

References

1. Azuma, R.T., et al.: A survey of augmented reality. Presence **6**(4), 355–385 (1997)
2. Hollerer, T., Feiner, S.: Mobile Augmented Reality. Telegeoinformatics: Location-Based Computing and Services. Taylor and Francis Books Ltd., London (2004)
3. Drascic, D., Milgram, P.: Perceptual issues in augmented reality. In: Electronic Imaging: Science and Technology, pp. 123–134. International Society for Optics and Photonics (1996)
4. Milgram, P., Takemura, H., Utsumi, A., Kishino, F.: Augmented reality: a class of displays on the reality-virtuality continuum. In: Photonics for Industrial Applications, pp. 282–292. International Society for Optics and Photonics (1995)
5. Reitmayr, G., Drummond, T.W.: Going out: robust model-based tracking for outdoor augmented reality. In: IEEE/ACM International Symposium on Mixed and Augmented Reality, ISMAR, pp. 109–118. IEEE (2006)
6. Zhou, F., Duh, H.B.L., Billinghurst, M.: Trends in augmented reality tracking, interaction and display: a review of ten years of ISMAR. In: Proceedings of the 7th IEEE/ACM International Symposium on Mixed and Augmented Reality, pp. 193–202. IEEE Computer Society (2008)
7. Dempski, K.L.: Arbitrary object tracking augmented reality applications. US Patent 7,050,078 J.Y, 23 May 2006
8. Lee, J.Y., Seo, D.W., Rhee, G.: Visualization and interaction of pervasive services using context-aware augmented reality. Expert Syst. Appl. **35**(4), 1873–1882 (2008)

9. Hollerer, T., Feiner, S., Terauchi, T., Rashid, G., Hallaway, D.: Exploring mars: developing indoor and outdoor user interfaces to a mobile augmented reality system. Comput. Graph. **23**(6), 779–785 (1999)

10. Hollerer, T., Feiner, S., Hallaway, D., Bell, B., Lanzagorta, M., Brown, D., Julier, S., Baillot, Y., Rosenblum, L.: User interface management techniques for collaborative mobile augmented reality. Comput. Graph. **25**(5), 799–810 (2001)

11. Joslin, P.: Augmented reality based user interface for mobile applications and services. Ph.D. thesis, P.O. Box 3000, FIN-90014 University of Oulu, Finland (2005)

12. Gabbard, J., Hix, D.: Researching usability design and evaluation guidelines for augmented reality (AR) systems. Laboratory for Scientific Visual Analysis, Virginia Tech, USA (2001)

13. Dunser, A., Grasset, R., Seichter, H., Billinghurst, M.: Applying HCI principles to AR systems design (2007)

14. Siltanen, S., Oksman, V., Ainasoja, M.: User-centered design of augmented reality interior design service. Int. J. Arts Sci. **6**(1), 547 (2013)

15. Olsson, T., Salo, M.: Online user survey on current mobile augmented reality applications. In: 2011 10th IEEE International Symposium on Mixed and Augmented Reality (ISMAR), pp. 75–84. IEEE (2011)

16. Olsson, T., Lagerstam, E., Karkkainen, T., Vaananen-Vainio-Mattila, K.: Expected user experience of mobile augmented reality services: a user study in the context of shopping centers. Pers. Ubiquitous Comput. **17**(2), 287–304 (2013)

17. Arol, K.P.: Mobile augmented reality supporting marketing, using mobile augmented reality based marketing applications to promote products or services to end customers. Ph.D. thesis, Lahti University of Applied Sciences (2014)

18. Kamilakis, M., Gavalas, D., Zaroliagis, C.: Mobile user experience in augmented reality vs. maps interfaces: a case study in public transportation. In: De Paolis, L.T., Mongelli, A. (eds.) AVR 2016. LNCS, vol. 9768, pp. 388–396. Springer, Cham (2016). https://doi.org/10.1007/978-3-319-40621-3_27

19. Olsson, T., Karkkainen, T., Lagerstam, E., Venta-Olkkonen, L.: User evaluation of mobile augmented reality scenarios. J. Ambient Intell. Smart Environ. **4**(1), 29–47 (2012)

20. Olsson, T., Salo, M.: Narratives of satisfying and unsatisfying experiences of current mobile augmented reality applications. In: Proceedings of the SIGCHI Conference on Human Factors in Computing Systems, pp. 2779–2788. ACM (2012)

21. Dhir, A., Al-kahtani, M.: A case study on user experience (UX) evaluation of mobile augmented reality prototypes. J. UCS **19**(8), 1175–1196 (2013)

22. Jaasko, V., Mattelmaki, T.: Observing and probing. In: Proceedings of the 2003 International Conference on Designing Pleasurable Products and Interfaces, pp. 126–131. ACM (2003)

23. Hassenzahl, M.: The thing and I: understanding the relationship between user and product. In: Blythe, M.A., Overbeeke, K., Monk, A.F., Wright, P.C. (eds.) Funology. Human-Computer Interaction Series, vol. 3, pp. 31–42. Springer, Dordrecht (2003). https://doi.org/10.1007/1-4020-2967-5_4

24. Perritaz, D., Salzmann, C., Gillet, D.: Quality of experience for adaptation in augmented reality. In: IEEE International Conference on Systems, Man and Cybernetics, SMC, pp. 888–893. IEEE (2009)

25. Olsson, T.: Layers of user expectations of future technologies: an early framework. In: CHI 2014 Extended Abstracts on Human Factors in Computing Systems, pp. 1957–1962. ACM (2014)

26. Barfield, W.: Fundamentals of Wearable Computers and Augmented Reality. CRC Press, Boca Raton (2015)

27. Carmigniani, J., Furht, B.: Augmented reality: an overview. In: Furht, B. (ed.) Handbook of Augmented Reality, pp. 3–46. Springer, New York (2011). https://doi.org/10.1007/978-1-4614-0064-6_1

28. Squire, K.D., Jan, M.: Mad city mystery: Developing scientific argumentation skills with a place-based augmented reality game on handheld computers. J. Sci. Educ. Technol. 16(1), 5–29 (2007)

29. TechNavio: Mobile augmented reality market for marketing and advertising in APAC 2015–2019 (2015)

30. Irshad, S., Rambli, D.R.B.A.: User experience of mobile augmented reality: a review of studies. In: 2014 3rd International Conference on User Science and Engineering (i-USEr), pp. 125–130, September 2014

31. Irshad, S., Rambli, D.R.A.: Preliminary user experience framework for designing mobile augmented reality technologies. In: 2015 4th International Conference on Interactive Digital Media (ICIDM), pp. 1–4, December 2015

32. Ergonomics of human system interaction - part 210: human-centered design for interactive systems. Technical report, Standard, International Organization for Standardization (2010)

33. Rambli, D.R.A., Irshad, S.: UX design evaluation of mobile augmented reality marketing products and services for Asia pacific region. In: Proceedings of the Asia Pacific HCI and UX Design Symposium, APCHIUX 2015, pp. 42–45. ACM, New York (2015)

34. Roto, V., Law, E., Vermeeren, A., Hoonhout, J.: User experience white paper. Bringing clarity to the concept of user experience (2011)

35. Irshad, S., Awang Rambli, D.R.: Multi-layered mobile augmented reality framework for positive user experience. In: Proceedings of the 2nd International Conference in HCI and UX Indonesia 2016, CHIuXiD 2016, pp. 21–26. ACM, New York (2016)

36. Irshad, S., Rambli, D.R.A.: Advances in mobile augmented reality from user experience perspective: a review of studies. In: Badioze Zaman, H., et al. (eds.) Advances in Visual Informatics, pp. 466–477. Springer International Publishing, Cham (2017). https://doi.org/10.1007/978-3-319-70010-6_43

37. Irshad, S., Rambli, D.R.A.: Design Implications for Quality User eXperience in Mobile Augmented Reality Applications. In: Sulaiman, H.A., Othman, M.A., Othman, M.F.I., Rahim, Y.A., Pee, N.C. (eds.) Advanced Computer and Communication Engineering Technology. LNEE, vol. 362, pp. 1283–1294. Springer, Cham (2016). https://doi.org/10.1007/978-3-319-24584-3_110

38. Mahlke, S.: User experience of interaction with technical systems (2008)

39. Hassenzahl, M., Platz, A., Burmester, M., Lehner, K.: Hedonic and ergonomic quality aspects determine a software's appeal. In: Proceedings of the SIGCHI Conference on Human Factors in Computing Systems, pp. 201–208. ACM (2000)

40. BlippAR: BlippAR (2011). https://blippar.com/en/. Accessed 7 Mar 2016

41. Junaio: The junaio 'AR' browser app. http://www.junaio.com. Accessed 7 Mar 2015

42. Irshad, S., Awang, D.R.B.: User perception on mobile augmented reality as a marketing tool. In: 2016 3rd International Conference on Computer and Information Sciences (ICCOINS), pp. 109–113, August 2016

Exploratory Study on Multimodal Information Presentation for Mobile AR Application

Nur Intan Adhani Muhamad Nazri,
Dayang Rohaya Awang Rambli$^{(\boxtimes)}$, and Shafaq Irshad$^{(\boxtimes)}$

Department of Computer and Information Sciences, Universiti Teknologi
PETRONAS, Bandar Seri Iskandar, Malaysia
{nur_9113,dayangrohaya.ar}@utp.edu.my,
shafaqirshad223@gmail.com

Abstract. This study is conducted in order to understand how does multimodal concept able to present a meaningful information in mobile AR and how multimodal information presentation able to support mobile AR application. Hence, to find suitable information modalities in mobile AR, questionnaire for User Interface Satisfaction (QUIS 5.5) was used to collect the data from this study. This tool is used to assess user subjective reaction on the specific human-computer interface. Throughout the study, the result shows that by combining visual together with sound and haptic feedback give a positive reaction towards the mobile AR application.

Keywords: Multimodal information presentation · Mobile augmented reality
User experience · Human-computer interaction

1 Introduction

The advancement of digital technology allows meaningful information to be gathered, stored, manipulated, and displayed in many techniques. One of it is through Augmented Reality (AR) technology. AR has a unique ways of presenting information. This is because it combines virtual environment and physical/real environment. There are various ways in experiencing AR such as via desktop, HMD and mobile. As years pass by, smartphone has become a necessity to people around the globe and people are using it as tools to find and retrieve information. Moreover, smartphone is more practical, affordable and has mobility features equipped with sensors, camera, gyroscope, AR lens and many more. However, despite its available functions, smartphone has a limitation which is small screen display. Due to this, meaningful and correct information is not presented well [1]. Sometimes, it is hard to view clearly and interact with the content due to the 'fat-finger' problem that occurs in many small mobile devices. Therefore, it is necessary to introduce additional sensory modalities to support mobile AR application which could help user to retrieve accurate and meaningful information in effective ways.

© Springer Nature Singapore Pte Ltd. 2018
N. Abdullah et al. (Eds.): i-USEr 2018, CCIS 886, pp. 358–369, 2018.
https://doi.org/10.1007/978-981-13-1628-9_32

1.1 Augmented Reality (AR)

The main purpose of AR is to enable the virtual content to be merged with the real world so that it gives the meaning to the object itself by giving the information to the user. Yet, AR still has its technology benefits and challenges that need to be considered.

By definition, AR is a combination of a real and virtual world, as well as it is interactive in real time and registered in 3D [2–4]. In short, it combines the virtual 3D object in the real environment where outdoor activities such as navigation using Google Earth are possible to be carried out using AR devices because the real environment (e.g. satellite map) can be embedded through AR.

1.2 Mobile Augmented Reality

The mobile or handheld devices have attracted attention as a tool that can benefit communication among user. The term 'mobile' can be used as long as the elements of portability occur and is not only limited to the mobile phone or smartphone but also to other devices. Due to that, advancement in mobile computing hardware is accelerating the development of mobile AR interfaces.

It holds the potential to manipulate the way information and data are presented to the people by using a system that is directly integrated with the real world environment. Hence, people can interact with it to display the related information to pose and resolve uncertainty as well as collaborating with other people. Thus, the world becomes user interface [5].

1.3 Information Presentation

AR has a unique ways to present information as it combines virtual object onto real environment. Hence, it generates a very interactive content. However, the increasing requirement to present meaningful and accurate information to the mobile AR has become a major challenge especially to the small mobile devices with limited capacity.

From previous research work that has been conducted, not many have addressed the problem from the perspective of the users especially on user experiences [6]. It is reported that the nature of the mobile device such as smartphones to have shaky viewpoint which can cause overlay image to deform, flickers or the disturbance of the task [7]. This happens when the user has to hold the device with one hand while the other hand is used for interacting with the content. Therefore, in that situation, some important information could be missing or hidden from user's point view.

1.4 Multimodal Information Presentation

Modality according to Azuma et al. [2] refers to the various communication canals used to express or acquire certain information that covers the way an idea is being expressed or perceived where an action is performed. Multimodal presentation refers to the used of more than 2 modalities (i.e. Audio, Auditory, Haptic, etc.) to perceive information.

Combining different modalities provides new possibilities for real-time interaction and engagement [8]. There are some works that combine 2 or more modalities, for example, EarPod [9] which enables eyes-free menu selection with the help of auditory feedback for the user and its performance is better in terms of both speed and accuracy than traditional visual technique. Luk et al. [10] created a handheld display platform to provide tactile feedback to users. Poupyrev et al. [11] applied tactile feedback not only to a desktop but also to mobile devices. Moreover, Liao et al. [12] developed a pen with multimodal pen-top feedback, which effectively helped user detects error early and provide support for interface discovery.

Another research was done where they conducted an experiment to examine feedback presented as visual, auditory and tactile modalities both individuality and combination [13]. The result showed that tactile feedback was most accurate. Their paper contributed the basic understanding of error feedback and how it impacts steering tasks.

However, Sarter [14] had done a research on the multimodal information presentation and his research was intended to explore possible uses and benefits of a rarely used sensory medium such as touching which is to ensure the robustness and effectiveness on multimodal interfaces. Based on this previous work, multimodal truly gives a lot of advantages once it has been implemented.

To date, the investigation on mobile AR application that adapts multimodal concept is very limited especially when focusing on user experience and presenting relevant information. Therefore, this research is aimed to fulfill the gap by examining the potential of multimodal concept in supporting mobile AR application. Specifically, investigating how multimodal concept affects and facilitates the information presentation in mobile AR application. Thus, this has become the main motivation for this research.

2 Method

For the purpose of this study, a set of information modalities and the type of information to be conveyed need to be defined. Five types of information modalities were selected which are text (visual, verbal), image/icon (visual, nonverbal), speech (auditory, verbal), sound (auditory, nonverbal), and vibration (haptic, nonverbal) [15–17].

Selected information presentation modalities were investigated and categorized into two conditions as shown in Table 1. The first condition was without sound and haptic feedback. The second condition was included with sound and haptic feedback.

Table 1. Information presentation modalities which has been investigated

Condition	Combination of information presentation modalities
Condition A	• Visual (text, image, graphic)
Condition B	• Visual (text, image, graphic) • Sound feedback (verbal or nonverbal) • Haptic feedback

The reason why these modalities were selected is because, visual and auditory modalities have been investigated in almost all application domains.

2.1 Experimental Procedures

Targeted Participants. A total of 40 participants (male = 20, female = 20) volunteered in this study. The age of participants ranged from 18 to 36, with the majority participants were between 20–28 years old.

Procedures of Experiment. There were 5 steps taken when conducting this study.

- Step 1: Before participants began the experiments, they were given an oral/written explanation of the nature of the study by the coordinator.
- Step 2: Participants were given 5 min to familiarize with the mobile AR prototype. They were then asked if they had any questions relating to the study.
- Step 3: Participants then tried the mobile AR prototype of the first condition. At this point, the coordinator started to observe the participants reaction and interaction with the prototype.
- Step 4: After completing the task, each participant were asked to answer a question relating the modalities involved. They were also given a chance to comment or give feedback on any aspect of the experience they had just gone through.
- Step 5: Repeated step 3 and step 4 for the second condition.

Data Collection. The Questionnaire for User Interaction Satisfaction (QUIS) is a measurement tool designed to assess a computer user's subjective satisfaction with the human-computer interface.

Mobile AR Prototype. A mobile AR Maze game was developed for the purpose of this study. The game allowed all different types of interaction modalities. AR marker was used (Fig. 1) to determine what content to overlay and where the game should be displayed. The camera would detect the image on the AR marker. Eventually, virtual object would appear on the mobile device screen where participants were able to view and interact with the information presented on the mobile screen.

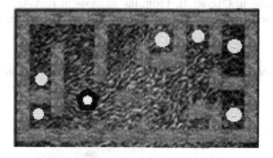

Fig. 1. AR marker

3 Results

Based from the survey conducted, it shows that all the participants own a smartphone. Half of them used audio interaction using their smartphone. Most of the participants never heard and tried any types of AR technology. Altogether, it can be concluded that participants were not familiar with AR technology.

There were 16 questions that was asked during this study. From Q1 until Q4, participants were asked about their overall reaction towards the application. From Q5 to Q7, participants were asked about their reaction on the display interface (screen). From Q8 until Q10 were about their reaction in learning experience gained when using the mobile AR application. From Q11 until Q13 were about participant's reaction towards system capabilities in mobile AR application. Lastly, for Q14 until 16 were about their reaction towards usability and UI in mobile AR application.

In order to determine whether the first condition, (A) and second condition, (B) have significance difference, a statistical test was used (in which same participants performed under every possible combination). Analysis was carried out in 5 categories which are; (a) overall reaction to the mobile AR application, (b) reaction to the screen, (c) reaction for learning, (d) system capabilities, and (e) usability and UI. Because the data did not meet with the criteria for parametric, a non-parametric test was used in this comparison analysis.

Therefore, a Shapiro-Wilk's test $(p > .05)$ [18, 19], an inspection of the skewness and kurtosis measures and standard errors [20, 21], and a visual inspection of their histograms, normal Q-Q plots and box plots showed that the data obtained were not approximately normally distributed for all conditions. A non-parametric Levene's test was used to verify the equality of variances in the samples (homogeneity of variance) $(p > .05)$.

3.1 Overall Reaction to the Mobile AR Application

With population of 40 participants, Table 2 shows the descriptive analysis for first and second condition (Overall_A and Overall_B). The mean for both conditions is 2.34 and 4.09 respectively. The standard deviation is from 0.728 to 0.748 respectively. Table 3 shows rank analysis for Overall_A and Overall_B. From Table 3, Overall_A shows lower rank compared to Overall_B. From the analysis of ranking, it was shown that participants have positive reaction towards second condition for overall reaction to the application.

Table 2. Descriptive analysis for first and second condition

Condition	N	Mean	SD	95% Confidence interval for mean	
				Lower	Upper
Overall_A	40	2.344	0.748	2.1044	2.5831
Overall_B	40	4.086	0.728	3.8545	4.3205

Table 3. Rank analysis for first and second condition

Condition		N	Mean rank	Sum of ranks
Overall_B − Overall_A	Negative ranks	0[a]	.00	.00
	Positive ranks	40[b]	20.50	820.00
	Ties	0[c]	–	–
	Total	40	–	–

[a]Overall_B < Overall_A; [b]Overall_B > Overall_A;
[c]Overall_B = Overall_A

Table 4. Wilcoxon signed ranks test

Condition	Overall_B − Overall_A
Z	−5.581[b]
Asymp. Sig. (2-tailed)	.000

[b]Based on negative ranks.

Within this comparison, a Wilcoxon signed rank test was used to determine if there was a significant difference between these two conditions. Tables 2 and 4 show comparison between Overall_A and Overall_B. The result suggests that there is a significant difference in median respond between first and second condition, with $Z = −5.581$; $p < .001$. Hence, it is concluded that Overall_B ($M = 4.09$, $SD = 0.73$) shows a significantly positive reaction compared to Overall_A ($M = 2.34$, $SD = 0.75$).

3.2   Screen Display

With population of 40 participants, Table 5 shows the descriptive analysis for first and second condition (Screen_A and Screen_B). The mean for both conditions is 3.05 and 4.4 respectively while the standard deviation is from 0.660 to 0.561 respectively.

Table 5. Descriptive analysis for first and second condition

Condition	N	Mean	SD	95% Confidence interval for mean	
				Lower	Upper
Screen_A	40	3.05	0.660	2.8388	3.2612
Screen_B	40	4.4	0.561	4.2206	4.5794

From Table 6, Screen_A shows lower rank compared to Screen_B. From the analysis of ranking, it was shown that participants have positive reaction on the screen for second condition (Screen_B).

Table 6. Rank analysis for first and second condition

Condition		N	Mean rank	Sum of ranks
Screen_B − Screen_A	Negative ranks	0[a]	.00	.00
	Positive ranks	40[b]	20.50	820.00
	Ties	0[c]		
	Total	40		

[a]Screen_B < Screen_A; [b]Screen_B > Screen_A; [c]Screen_B = Screen_A

Table 7. Wilcoxon signed ranks test

Condition	Screen_B − Screen_A
Z	−5.641[b]
Asymp. Sig. (2-tailed)	.000

[b]Based on negative ranks.

Within this comparison, a Wilcoxon signed rank test was used to determine if there was a significant difference between these two conditions for reaction to the screen in mobile AR application. Tables 5 and 7 show comparison between Screen_A and Screen_B. The result suggests that there is a significant difference in median respond between first and second condition, with $Z = -5.641$; $p < .001$. Hence, it was concluded that Screen_B (M = 4.4, SD = 0.561) shows a significantly positive reaction with the screen compared to Screen_A (M = 3.05, SD = 0.660).

3.3   Learning

Table 8 shows the descriptive analysis for first and second condition (Learning_A and Learning_B). The mean for both conditions is 3.48 and 4.33 respectively. The standard deviation is from 0.924 to 0.675 respectively. Table 9 shows rank analysis for Learning_A and Learning_B. Learning_A shows lower rank compared to Learning_B. From the analysis of ranking, it was shown that participants have positive reaction towards second condition for learning reaction with the application.

Table 8. Descriptive analysis for first and second condition

Condition	N	Mean	SD	95% Confidence interval for mean	
				Lower	Upper
Learning_A	40	3.48	0.924	3.1877	3.779
Learning_B	40	4.33	0.675	4.1174	4.5493

Table 9. Rank analysis for first and second condition

Condition		N	Mean rank	Sum of ranks
Learning_B − Learning_A	Negative ranks	0[a]	.00	.00
	Positive ranks	40[b]	20.50	820.00
	Ties	0[c]	–	–
	Total	40	–	–

[a]Learning_B < Learning_A; [b]Learning_B > Learning_A;
[c]Learning_B = Learning_A

Table 10. Wilcoxon signed ranks test

Condition	Learning_B − Learning_A
Z	−5.556[b]
Asymp. Sig. (2-tailed)	.000

[b]Based on negative ranks.

Within this comparison, a Wilcoxon signed rank test was used to determine if there was a significant difference between these two conditions. Tables 8 and 10 show comparison between Learning_A and Learning_B. The result suggests that there is a significant difference in median respond between first and second condition, with $Z = -5.556$; $p < .001$. Hence, it was concluded that Learning_B ($M = 4.33$, SD = 0.675) shows a significantly higher positive reaction compared to Learning_A ($M = 3.48$, SD = 0.924).

3.4 System Capabilities

Table 11 shows the descriptive analysis for first and second condition (SysCap_A and SysCap_B). The mean for both conditions is 3.58 to 4.39 respectively. The standard deviation is from 0.989 to 0.599 respectively. Table 12 shows rank analysis for SysCap_A and SysCap_B. SysCap_A shows lower rank compared to SysCap_B for system capabilities in mobile AR application. From the analysis of ranking, it was shown that participants have positive reaction towards second condition for system capabilities of the application.

Within this comparison, a Wilcoxon signed rank test was used to determine if there was a significant difference between these two conditions. Tables 11 and 13 show comparison between SysCap_A and SysCap_B. The result suggests that there is indeed a significant difference in median respond between first and second condition, with $Z = -5.120$; $p < .001$. Hence, it was concluded that SysCap_B ($M = 4.39$, SD = 0.599) shows a significantly higher positive reaction compared to SysCap_A ($M = 3.58$, SD = 0.989).

Table 11. Descriptive analysis for first and second condition

Condition	N	Mean	SD	95% Confidence interval for mean	
				Lower	Upper
SysCap_A	40	3.58	0.989	3.267	3.8997
SysCap_B	40	4.39	0.599	4.2002	4.5831

Table 12. Rank analysis for first and second condition

Condition		N	Mean rank	Sum of ranks
SysCap_B − SysCap_A	Negative ranks	0[a]	.00	.00
	Positive ranks	34[b]	17.50	595.00
	Ties	6[c]		
	Total	40		

[a]SysCap_B < SysCap_A; [b]SysCap_B > SysCap_A;
[c]SysCap_B = SysCap_A

Table 13. Wilcoxon signed ranks test

Condition	SysCap_B − SysCap_A
Z	−5.120[b]
Asymp. Sig. (2-tailed)	.000

[b]Based on negative ranks.

3.5 Usability and UI

Table 14 shows the descriptive analysis for first and second condition (Usability_A and Usability_B). The mean for both conditions is 2.05 and 3.77 respectively. The standard deviation is from 0.669 to 0.697 respectively. Table 15 shows rank analysis for Usability_A and Usability_B. Usability_A shows lower rank compared to Usability_B for usability and UI reaction in mobile AR application.

Within this comparison, a Wilcoxon signed rank test was used to determine if there was a significant difference between these two conditions. Tables 14 and 16 show comparison between Usability_A and Usability_B. The result suggests that there is indeed a significant difference in median respond between first and second condition, with $Z = -5.619$; $p < .001$. Hence, it was concluded that Usability_B (M = 3.77, SD = 0.697) shows a significantly higher reaction compared to Usability_A (M = 2.05, SD = 0.669), though participants gave a negative reaction response for Usability_B in system capabilities.

Table 14. Descriptive analysis for first and second condition

Condition	N	Mean	SD	95% Confidence interval for mean	
				Lower	Upper
Usability_A	40	2.05	0.669	1.836	2.264
Usability_B	40	3.77	0.697	3.5438	3.9895

Table 15. Rank analysis for first and second condition

Condition		N	Mean rank	Sum of ranks
Usability_B − Usability_A	Negative ranks	0[a]	.00	.00
	Positive ranks	40[b]	20.50	820.00
	Ties	0[c]		
	Total	40		

[a]Usability_B < Usability_A; [b]Usability_B > Usability_A;
[c]Usability_B = Usability_A

Table 16. Wilcoxon signed ranks test

Condition	Usability_B − Usability_A
Z	−5.619[b]
Asymp. Sig. (2-tailed)	.000

[b]Based on negative ranks.

4 Discussion

Based on the results shown above, Condition A, majority of the participants feel frustrated when using the application. They stated that the application was dull and it made them felt frustrated when using the application in the Condition A. This was due to no additional modalities were present except only visual modality in the first condition. Moreover, participants stated that they felt something was missing and lost when they were playing with the game. It turned out that there were no sound modality and haptic modality that were able to support or assist them in getting faster response time. Furthermore, participants mentioned that the color of the main object (avatar, 3D graphic) was almost the same as the image of AR marker. This has led them to confusion especially when the condition of participants' surrounding was too bright or too dark.

Most of the participants gave positive comments on the second condition, especially when sound modality (when participants getting each point or clicking a button) and haptic modality were included together. Participants commented that with these two modalities, they were aware of surrounding in the virtual scene. Moreover, participants found that it was stimulating when there was sound and vibration that came

368   N. I. A. Muhamad Nazri et al.

out when they clicked the button for the second condition. Participants' stated that sound and haptic modality did support them to play the game by instilling their awareness with the surrounding in the virtual environment.

5 Conclusion

From this study, it was found out that combination of sound and haptic feedbacks are able to support visual modality of information presentation in mobile AR. However, it needs to meet with certain conditions or requirements by simply answering these questions, which and when to use visual, auditory and haptic modalities? And what tasks are associated with modalities and type of information?

Result obtained could be used as evidence to show that multimodal approach is able to cater a large volume of information. Moreover, optimal combination of information modalities could be identified.

References

1. Hürst, W., van Wezel, C.: Multimodal interaction concepts for mobile augmented reality applications. In: Lee, K.-T., Tsai, W.-H., Liao, H.-Y.M., Chen, T., Hsieh, J.-W., Tseng, C.-C. (eds.) MMM 2011. LNCS, vol. 6524, pp. 157–167. Springer, Heidelberg (2011). https://doi.org/10.1007/978-3-642-17829-0_15
2. Azuma, R., Baillot, Y., Behringer, R., Feiner, S., Julier, S., MacIntyre, B.: Recent advances in augmented reality. IEEE Comput. Graph. Appl. 21(6), 34–47 (2001)
3. Azuma, R., Furmanski, C.: Evaluating label placement for augmented reality view management. In: Paper Presented at the Proceedings of the 2nd IEEE/ACM International Symposium on Mixed and Augmented Reality (2003)
4. Azuma, R.T.: A survey of augmented reality. Presence: Teleoper. Virtual Environ. 6(4), 355–385 (1997)
5. Papagiannakis, G., Singh, G., Magnenat-Thalmann, N.: A survey of mobile and wireless technologies for augmented reality systems. Comput. Anim. Virtual Worlds 19(1), 3–22 (2008)
6. Battarbee, K., Koskinen, I.: Co-experience: user experience as interaction. CoDesign 1(1), 5–18 (2005)
7. Lee, G.A., Yang, U., Kim, Y., Jo, D., Kim, K.-H., Kim, J.H., Choi, J.S.: Freeze-set-go interaction method for handheld mobile augmented reality environments. In: Paper Presented at the Proceedings of the 16th ACM Symposium on Virtual Reality Software and Technology (2009)
8. Scheible, J.: Empowering mobile art practice: a recontextualization of mobile and ubiquitous computing (2010)
9. Zhao, S., Dragicevic, P., Chignell, M., Balakrishnan, R., Baudisch, P.: Earpod: eyes-free menu selection using touch input and reactive audio feedback. In: Paper Presented at the Proceedings of the SIGCHI Conference on Human Factors in Computing Systems (2007)
10. Luk, J., Pasquero, J., Little, S., MacLean, K., Levesque, V., Hayward, V.: A role for haptics in mobile interaction: initial design using a handheld tactile display prototype. In: Paper Presented at the Proceedings of the SIGCHI Conference on Human Factors in Computing Systems (2006)

11. Poupyrev, I., Okabe, M., Maruyama, S.: Haptic feedback for pen computing: directions and strategies. In: Paper Presented at the CHI 2004 Extended Abstracts on Human Factors in Computing Systems (2004)
12. Liao, C., Guimbretière, F., Loeckenhoff, C.E.: Pen-top feedback for paper-based interfaces. In: Paper Presented at the Proceedings of the 19th Annual ACM Symposium on User Interface Software and Technology (2006)
13. Sun, M., Ren, X., Cao, X.: Effects of multimodal error feedback on human performance in steering tasks. Inf. Media Technol. **6**(1), 193–201 (2011)
14. Sarter, N.B.: Multimodal information presentation: design guidance and research challenges. Int. J. Ind. Ergon. **36**(5), 439–445 (2006)
15. Bensmaia, S.J., Killebrew, J.H., Craig, J.: Influence of visual motion on tactile motion perception. J. Neurophysiol. **96**(3), 1625–1637 (2006)
16. Bernsen, N.O.: Why are analogue graphics and natural language both needed in HCI? In: Paternó, F. (ed.) Interactive Systems: Design, Specification, and Verification. Focus on Computer Graphics, pp. 235–251. Springer, Berlin, Heidelberg (1995). https://doi.org/10.1007/978-3-642-87115-3_14
17. Bernsen, N.O.: Multimodality in language and speech systems—from theory to design support tool. In: Granström, B., House, D., Karlsson, I. (eds.) Multimodality in language and speech systems. Text, Speech and Language Technology, vol. 19, pp. 93–148. Springer, Dordrecht (2002). https://doi.org/10.1007/978-94-017-2367-1_6
18. Shapiro, S.S., Wilk, M.B.: An analysis of variance test for normality (complete samples). Biometrika **52**(3/4), 591–611 (1965)
19. Razali, N.M., Wah, Y.B.: Power comparisons of Shapiro-Wilk, Kolmogorov-Smirnov, Lilliefors and Anderson-Darling tests. J. Stat. Model. Anal. **2**(1), 21–33 (2011)
20. Cramer, D.: Fundamental Statistics for Social Research. Step-by-Step Calculations and Computer Techniques Using SPSS for Windows. Routledge, London and New York (1998)
21. Cramer, D., Howitt, D.L.: The Sage Dictionary of Statistics: A Practical Resource for Students in the Social Sciences. Sage, London (2004)

Author Index

Printed in the United States
By Bookmasters